CHOICES AND CHANCES

CHOICES AND CHANCES

Sociology for Everyday Life

SECOND EDITION

LORNE TEPPERMAN
University of Toronto

with the assistance of
Janaki Weerasinghe

HARCOURT BRACE CANADA

Harcourt Brace & Company, Canada

Toronto Montreal Orlando Fort Worth San Diego
Philadelphia London Sydney Tokyo

Canadian Cataloguing in Publication Data

Tepperman, Lorne, 1943–
Choices and chances : sociology for everyday life

2nd ed.
Includes bibliographical references and index.
ISBN 0-7747-3216-4

1. Life skills. 2. Quality of life–Canada.
3. Social indicators–Canada. I. Weerasinghe, Janaki. II. Title.

BJ1581.2.T46 1993 158 C93-094009-1

PUBLISHER: Heather McWhinney
EDITOR AND MARKETING MANAGER: Daniel Brooks
DEVELOPMENTAL EDITOR: Michael Bolton
EDITORIAL ASSISTANT: Susan Fisher
DIRECTOR OF PUBLISHING SERVICES: Jean Lancee
EDITORIAL MANAGER: Marcel Chiera
SUPERVISING EDITOR: Carol Tong
PRODUCTION MANAGER: Sue-Ann Becker
MANUFACTURING CO-ORDINATOR: Denise Wake
COPY EDITOR: Cy Strom
INTERIOR DESIGN: Steve Eby
COVER ILLUSTRATION: Erica Dornbusch
COVER DESIGN: Brett Miller
TYPESETTING AND ASSEMBLY: Louisa Schulz
PRINTING AND BINDING: Data Reproductions Corporation

∞ This book was printed in the United States on acid-free paper.
1 2 3 4 5 98 97 96 95 94

Our only guides are our interests, viewed in the largest possible sense; our interests made as self-aware as possible, since it is unlikely we can attain what we do not want, and impossible to want what is not conceived as attainable.

JACQUES BARZUN*

* *Darwin, Marx, Wagner: Critique of a Heritage* (2nd ed.). Garden City, NY: Doubleday Anchor Books, 1958.

PREFACE

This book urges you to examine your goals and opportunities, and then consider the chances that you will get what you want from your education, career, marriage, parenthood, and other parts of your life. It argues that we ought to live with our eyes open, gather evidence about the world, choose in our own best interests (broadly defined), and behave rationally.

People's lives are linked and limited by what sociologists call *social structure*. Our lives are shaped by the choices and actions of people around us: this is sociology's central insight. Popular belief teaches that people generally get what they want from life, if they want it badly enough and acquire the right skills and credentials. Supposedly, they alone are to blame if they fail to get what they want. Yet research shows that most people do *not* get what they want, but settle for what they can get. How can we explain this fact, and what does it teach us?

Sociology—the systematic study of social relations—emerged in the nineteenth century as an attempt to understand the enormous social changes caused by the Industrial Revolution and the French Revolution. Even today sociology remains, at its core, a debate about the human ability to improve social life through reason and organized action.

Sociology does not claim that people are entirely rational, or even that sociologists must be, or can be, entirely rational. But it does argue that we must all try to distinguish between beliefs and feelings on the one hand, and facts and reason on the other. That is what I am urging you to do when you read this book.

None of us thinks about life in a completely rational way. Often we find it hard, almost impossible, to change the way we live our lives. We may be imprisoned by our fears and passions, or by unexamined certainties. When faced with major decisions, we may prefer to consult our feelings, do what family and friends advise, go with hunches, or take a shot in the dark. Sometimes we even rely on luck to get us through. Yet deep down we all know that there must be a better way to make our important life choices.

I cannot claim that the advice this book offers is complete or foolproof. This analysis is only a first approximation, which I have found helpful in organizing my own thinking. Ideally, this book will make you wonder whether some of the things you feel sure about are really so, and it may get you thinking about the ways you make your own life choices. I assume, simply, that whatever your particular life goals may be, you are aiming to get as much satisfaction out of life—as much *life satisfaction* — as you possibly can. All the analyses that follow aim at that goal.

Research on life satisfaction has developed in interesting directions in the past decade or two. It now offers us rich information about who is most satisfied with life (and with various parts of life—work, marriage, and so on), under what conditions, and why.

You may choose to doubt or ignore the conclusions this book has drawn. After all, a sociologist's conclusion about a category of people to which you belong will not inevitably apply to you. No one knows which characteristics, alone or in combination, will guide or predict a given person's behaviour. But if I can get you to analyze the way you live your life, and the choices you are making, this book will have succeeded, whatever you decide to do.

This book shows how one sociologist goes about examining some major life concerns. Your own instructor may have a somewhat different approach. This is my personal version of what the American sociologist C. Wright Mills called "the sociological imagination," one that draws upon sociology's central goals, concepts, and insights.

Reader response to the first edition of this book was very satisfying, and I have looked forward to doing a second edition. But in revising the book I was faced with a difficult choice: to keep the book largely as it is and simply update the statistics, or to make major changes. I have tended toward the second path.

Though I have not made as many changes as I might have, the reader will find one important difference from the first edition: the inclusion of many more references to the recent literature on life satisfaction. The first edition aimed mainly at goading the reader to try out new ideas. This new edition also intends to introduce the reader to much of the actual research that has been published on life satisfaction. One thing has not changed, however: this is still a teaching book, for use in classrooms.

How This Book Relates to Your Textbook

This book was written to supplement the large multi-topic textbook you are probably using in your introductory course. How do the two books connect?

First, your textbook discusses sociological topics in an abstract, general way that you may have trouble relating to your own daily life. You may not see how the theories it discusses—especially those theories attributed to sociology's founders, Marx, Weber, and Durkheim—bear on life today. This problem has led some students to believe that theorizing is something that people used to do, but no longer do. As graduate students, my friends and I used to call the required course in sociological theory "Dead Guys 101."

Actually, all sociologists make and test theories. Even *you* make theories about society. This book uses theories that can be related back to the "dead guys" discussed in your textbook. But it does not draw an obvious connection with their theories; that is something your instructor may want to do in discussing this book with you. As you learn new things from this book, try connecting them to things you have heard in lectures or tutorials, or read in the textbook. Everything should connect.

Theorists do not always agree. Sociology thrives on theoretical debates fuelled by different assumptions about reality, findings that conflict with one another, and disagreements about the quality of evidence. Lively debates are the evidence of a living discipline, so do not be frustrated or annoyed if a point made in this book fails to match a point made somewhere else. Ask your instructor about the disagreement; talk about it; and think of ways to resolve it. That is how sociological research begins.

Another way that this book differs from your textbook is that it offers advice, while your textbook does not. You should not take the advice without thinking, but rather use it to sharpen your own investigation of personal goals, opportunities, and experiences. This book simply takes the sociological knowledge found in your textbook and asks, If this theory is true, what should follow? How does this affect *me?* Nothing will make you take a theory more seriously than if you consider risking your future on its being true. This book encourages you to think of sociological theories as predictions with important consequences for your own life.

The topics and data in this book are arranged around the concept of *life cycle*, the sequence of stages people typically pass through as they grow older. This specifically relates sociology to life in Canada in the 1990s, as some textbooks do not.

What you read in your textbook about education is augmented by what you read here about educational decisions you must make; what you read in your textbook about work, by what you read here about career choices; what you read about families in your textbook, by what you read here about marriage and parenthood; and so on. Thus, you will find a considerable overlap between this book and your textbook. Where this book differs is in its emphasis on life in Canada today; it is organized around the life cycle, and it turns sociological knowledge into advice.

This book will make your understanding of the course textbook richer and more personal. By showing how theories can apply to your own life, this book will show the ways sociology—a living, growing discipline—can shed light on issues of immense personal and social importance.

NOTE TO INSTRUCTORS

Using *Choices and Chances* in the Classroom

This book is intended to supplement the general textbook you are using in your introductory course. To that end, this book can be used in a number of different ways. Some of its suggested uses include the following:

1. *A brief introduction to sociology: two-semester course.*
   Assign this book as the first one students will read, to provide an overview of many of the concepts and concerns that they will later encounter in lectures and other readings.
2. *The basis of a book review or critical essay.*
   Ask students to write a critical review of the book. Such a review may compare this book with other books; compare one chapter's findings with another's; or reanalyze the data presented in this book from the standpoint of a given theoretical approach (for example, symbolic interactionism, conflict theory, or structural functionalism).
3. *A source of ideas for essay topics.*
   Suggest that students find their topics (and some references) for a major paper or essay among the issues and debates discussed in this book.
4. *A running supplement to your textbook.*
   Match individual chapters of this book with one or more chapters of the textbook you have assigned. Some of the possible matchups are suggested below:

Life Choices Chapter	Suggested Textbook Chapter
1. Patterns of Desire	Introduction to sociology
	Culture
	Socialization
	Aging/life cycle

Life Choices Chapter	Suggested Textbook Chapter
2. Patterns of Opportunity	Stratification/inequality Social roles/structure Ethnic/race relations Ideology
3. Education	Education
4. Career Choices	Work Industrial sociology Economic sociology Formal organizations
5. Single or Married	Marriage and family Gender relations
6. Childless or Parent	Marriage and family Population/demography
7. Locations and Lifestyles	Urban sociology Communities Lifestyles Mass media
8. What You Want and Get	Political sociology Social movements Deviance and control Social change

This book can also be used as the central text of a one-semester sociology course. As such, it will provide students with a brief introduction to sociology. Supplement it with readings in sociology (monographs, research papers, selected textbook chapters) and newspaper articles.

ACKNOWLEDGEMENTS

Many people have helped me revise this book, and I want to thank them.

Dan Brooks, Editor and Marketing Manager at Harcourt Brace, persuaded me to undertake the revision. I was encouraged to do so by people's response to the first edition—particularly by the many letters from students who had read the book in their courses. One instructor who has used the book in her teaching, Helen Douglas of Okanagan College, was particularly supportive. Even my father—always a tough critic—liked the book. So, I was ready to take the plunge again.

Janaki Weerasinghe, a graduating fourth-year student at the University of Toronto, has helped me bring the book up to date. I cannot praise her talent and good humour highly enough. I am also indebted to Lee Rubinoff, a student in my introductory sociology class last year, who volunteered his services to help us with the revisions. Among other things, he has generated some of the graphic displays of data in this edition.

Reviews were commissioned by the publisher at various stages of the project. I received comments and advice from Jim Curtis, Ed Thompson, Sue Wilson, Bill Hanna, Bonnie Erickson and Kevin McQuillan. I am grateful for their many useful suggestions; usually, I have taken their advice.

I have received some excellent help from the people at Harcourt Brace & Company. They include Michael Bolton and Susan Fisher, who were the Developmental Editors. Carol Tong was a most congenial and helpful Supervising Editor, and Cy Strom did a beautifully thorough copy edit. Thank you for making things so smooth for me.

Authors typically end their acknowledgements by saying that any faults that remain in the book are their own doing, and I shall not break this rule. My reviewers have done their best to inform and persuade me; I alone am responsible for mistakes in the pages that follow.

This second edition of the book is dedicated, with affection and admiration, to my parents. They gave me the best chances in life a person could have hoped for. As a parent myself, I know how hard it is to do that. So thanks, mom and dad. This is for you!

A Note from the Publisher

Thank you for selecting *Choices and Chances: Sociology for Everyday Life, 2nd edition*, by Lorne Tepperman. The author and publishers have devoted considerable time to the careful development of this book. We appreciate your recognition of this effort and accomplishment.

We want to hear what you think about *Choices and Chances: Sociology for Everyday Life, 2nd edition*. Please take a few minutes to fill in the stamped reply card that you will find at the back of the book. Your comments, suggestions, and criticisms will be valuable to us as we prepare new editions and other books.

Contents

Chapter One

◆

Patterns of Desire:
Why You Want What You Want

Introduction

Life in a modern society is full of choices. People seem to like having choices, but choosing well is difficult. The consequences of a wrong choice can be costly and painful. Taking responsibility for our choices is often unpleasant. We can close our eyes and try to pretend that there is only one way to live; but few of us these days can believe that for very long. Evidence of different kinds of lives surrounds us. The more we learn about the world, the more variety we can see, and the more things we learn to want. We find that we can choose for or against things in a great many situations.

Looked at in a different way, however, none of our choices is free. Every choice has a cost, if only the cost of giving up another choice we might have made. Moreover, every choice is limited by what we know, who we are, and what we have to trade for the thing we want. In those respects some people have more choice than others, a better choice of possible lives. But no one has unlimited choice, and no choice is cost-free. That is a condition of living.

Many major experiences in life are not chosen at all. These may include unwanted pregnancies, marriage breakdowns, forced unemployment, disabling accidents, abusive parents, betrayal by friends, the outbreak of war, and economic depression. They may also include passionate love, lucky winnings, devoted friends, inborn skills and aptitudes, peace, and prosperity. You are not to blame for the first category of experiences, nor to be praised for the second. These are simply the contexts within which you live your life.

Within this human condition, we all work out our life's desires. This fact never changes: only situations and desires change. So a book about life choices must look at the world as it exists today and ask, What do people want out of life? What satisfies them? What are people's main concerns? What kinds of people are most satisfied with their lives, and how do they get to be that way?

These are the kinds of questions that this book hopes to answer. Philosophers have been discussing these questions for thousands of years: the answers are important and hard to discover. I hope to answer these questions not as a philosopher, but as a sociologist, using evidence collected from the people around us.

Answering these questions will take the whole book. This chapter introduces the questions in their most general form, in relation to life satisfaction. It opens with a discussion of the kinds of people who are most satisfied with life, and concludes by examining two theories that try to explain why people want what they want and why they are satisfied with what they get.

People are complicated. Their mix of motives defies easy generalization. Moreover, people provide exceptions to every rule that social science can devise. It is this complexity of people—indeed, of everyday life—that makes social science challenging. Like natural scientists, historians, and novelists, sociologists seek the underlying order in apparent chaos: the laws that govern and predict tomorrow's universe. Let us begin by showing that this goal is at least approachable.

What You Want

Most of us are rather self-centred. By that I mean that we are wrapped up in our own ideas, plans, and values. We rarely take the time to think about other people's thinking. This lets us imagine that our own thoughts are unique. We believe that the things we want to get and do, the choices we plan to make in life, and even the ways we spend our time and money are uniquely our own. We may even believe that we have every opportunity to get what we want, and that with enough luck and planning, we will get it.

A national survey conducted in 1981 (referred to throughout this book as the Quality of Life survey), found that most Canadian adults thought they deserved a life close to the best one they could imagine. Fortunately, the best life they could imagine was also very close to the best life they could expect to have. As a result, the Canadians surveyed tended to be generally happy, and complacent.

Maybe Roos (1988) is right in claiming that happiness is ruled by social norms: people are expected to be happy and they want to be happy. So they devise strategies for being happy or, at least, for appearing happy. After all, unhappy people are losers, and no one wants to be a loser.

Does that make us all "contented cows," as some people fear? Not if happiness is really as useful and beneficial as research shows it is. For example, Veenhoven (1988) notes that data from around the world show that an enjoyment of life "broadens perception, encourages active involvement, and fosters political participation. It facilitates social contacts, in particular contacts with spouse and children, and buffers stress, thereby preserving health and lengthening life somewhat." He concludes that "society as a whole is more likely to flourish with happy citizens than with unhappy ones."

So it was a good thing that, by international standards, Canadians were fairly upbeat: they wanted and expected to be happy. According to the 1981 Quality of Life survey, most Canadians rated their lives—past and present—in the top half of the rating "ladder": closer to the best life than to the worst life that they could imagine. They did the same when they rated their (expected) future lives, believing that they would come close to the best lives they could imagine.

This level of happiness and optimism may have slipped in the last few years. A recent *Maclean's*/CTV poll (*Maclean's*, January 4, 1993, p. 42) shows that just over a quarter of Canadian adults are pessimistic or very pessimistic about their personal economic situation. As well, over half believe that the generation of Canadians being born now will be worse off than their parents; less than one respondent in five believes that it will be better off (p. 44). So it may be necessary to collect more recent data on Canadian happiness and optimism before we draw definitive conclusions.

Some people were even more optimistic than the Canadians surveyed in 1981. Gallup polls conducted in 30 countries during the 1980s (Michalos, 1988) asked people, "So far as you are concerned, do you think that [next year] will be better or worse than [the year just ending]?" By this measure, the world's greatest optimists turned out to live in Argentina, Greece, Korea, and the United States, where more than half the respondents expected the next year to be better than the current one. Along with Chileans and South African whites, Canadians ranked just above the world's average on optimism: 35 to 39 percent said that they expected next year to be better. On the other hand, Canadians were twice as likely to express optimism as Germans, Austrians, or Belgians.

Why are some people less optimistic or more satisfied with life than others? What makes people vary in this way?

We are tempted to respond, "Who knows why? People are just funny that way!" or, "Everybody's different." But we have already noted that people tend to judge their lives in similar ways. This uniformity suggests that social science may be able to explain optimism and satisfaction.

When people's desires and concerns differ, they do so in patterned, predictable ways. All social science—sociology, psychology, anthropology, and other related disciplines—rests on this fact of *patterned variation*.

Because the issue is so basic, this chapter will concentrate on showing that people's views about life vary in patterned, predictable ways. Later chapters follow the same theme through particular domains of life: education, career, marriage, child rearing, and so on. By the end of this book, we will have found that we really *can* understand people's lives better with the help of social science concepts and measurements.

Just as life satisfactions are patterned, so are life goals: the things that people hope to get out of life. What, then, are the most important life goals of average Canadians? What are they hoping to get out of life?

Two of the three life goals that Canadians identify as most important are classified as "social goals"—involving relationships with other people (Atkinson & Murray, 1982). Most important of all is "family security," defined as "providing love and care for family members." One in every two adult Canadians says that this is the first or second most important goal in life. Close in importance is "love"—"having the affection and romantic love of a man or woman." One in every three respondents cites that as the most or second most important goal in life.

The only other widely held goal is "economic stability," defined as "having a steady, secure income to provide for your basic needs and those of your family." About one respondent in three says that this is the most or second most important goal in life. This goal may be linked to the first two; it probably expresses a desire for family security through income security, not for income in its own right.

Few Canadians seem to want great wealth, outstanding achievement, social recognition, or excitement. The average Canadian adult comes across as a kind, loving, sociable person with limited life goals. That is why Canadians in 1981 were so convinced that, some time in the future, they would attain a life close to the best life they could imagine. The best life they could imagine was within their grasp. Canadians want what they can get.

Few Canadians attach much importance to spiritual understanding, salvation, and helping others. For example, fewer Canadians than Americans are religious fundamentalists. Rather, Canadians focus their attention on the world of everyday life and on the people they commonly see and care about. In this way, today's Canadians are quite different from Canadians a century ago and from Iranians today: for both these groups, religious and theological concerns would loom much larger.

Nor are most Canadians "rugged individualists" or "me-first" types. Few share in the "self-fulfilment ethic" that Yankelovich (1982) found to be so common in the United States. For many Americans, "creativity is a life-style." These Americans spend much of their time and money in a search for excitement, sensation, new experiences, self-discovery, and self-improvement. They focus their lives on themselves. About one American in six is strongly committed to this kind of self-fulfilment.

By contrast, Canadians are less committed to this ethic of self-fulfilment. Only one Canadian respondent in eight—typically younger, more educated, and drawing a higher income than average—cites self-development as a first or second most important goal; one in seven says that independence is most or second most important; and almost no Canadian surveyed reports excitement as a goal of main importance.

A poll conducted in November 1987 (*Maclean's*, January 4, 1988, p. 45) shows that Canadians contrast themselves with Americans on these very points. Respondents were six times as likely to consider Canadians more concerned than Americans about the environment and the poor; they were seven times as likely to consider Canadians more honest and fair. They also believed Canadians to be somewhat more hardworking, better informed, and sophisticated. On the other hand, respondents were more than twice as likely to consider Americans more competitive and eight times as likely to consider them more violent.

Summing up to this point, we might say that Canadians (at least until recently) have tended to hold similar views of their past, present, and future life. They have shown themselves to be generally satisfied and optimistic, and mainly concerned with loving and caring for their families. They are not strong individualists, nor much concerned about getting to heaven.

A Minor Digression

Now that you have some idea where this book is going, let me stop the flow for a moment. Books by professors are famous for their digressions and attempts to limit the generality of their conclusions. Following in this tradition, I want you to keep two warnings in mind throughout the book. That is because I am making certain assumptions about people in general—even about you, the reader—that may not be valid. I can't help it. There's no way to write this book without making some assumptions, since they simplify the book's argument. Otherwise, this book would be about 1000 pages long.

First, I am assuming that you, and everyone else, want to maximize your satisfaction with life. Satisfaction is related to, but different from, happiness—at least in the eyes of people who study this problem seriously. Satisfaction is a cognitive thing: your mind tells you if you are satisfied or not. Happiness is a visceral thing: your guts tell you if you are happy. (For discussions of the measurement of happiness and satisfaction, see Grichting, 1983; Kammann, Farry, & Herbison, 1984; and Stones & Kozma, 1985.)

You *know* whether you are happy or not, without a lot of deep soul-searching. When you're happy, you feel like smiling. Your heart races and you want to jump up and down, or shake hands with the person next to you. You feel *great!*

Happiness is a useful, as well as pleasant, state of being. According to a recent report (Glatzer & Bos, 1992), happiness increases a person's life expectancy, improves the quality of a marriage, increases the likelihood of finding and keeping a job, and raises a person's self-esteem and satisfaction with personal achievements.

Satisfaction is a good thing, too, but knowing whether you are satisfied isn't quite as easy as knowing whether you are happy. Often you have to think for a while. In part, that's because there's a complicated relationship between how satisfied we feel with life as a whole and with particular parts (or *domains*) of our lives.

Sometimes we are satisfied with life as a whole and with particular domains of life (for example, with our social activities). At other times, when we feel dissatisfied with a particular domain of life (for example, with marriage), we come to feel dissatisfied with life as a whole. That is, our feelings about one domain "spill over" into our views of life as a whole. We may even come to feel that everything is falling apart. (We'll discuss this spill-over effect later, in Chapter Four.)

Most of the time, the relationship between overall life satisfaction and satisfaction with particular domains is *reciprocal*—it runs both ways. An example is the relationship between life satisfaction and job satisfaction. So, when someone asks us how satisfied we are with life, we are forced to make a complex (if unconscious) assessment of a great many things all at once (Lance et al., 1989).

As well, studies have found varying degrees of correlation between happiness and satisfaction. Often, people who are happy with life are satisfied too, and vice versa. But this is not always the case. You can be satisfied without being happy and happy without being satisfied. This book focusses chiefly on *satisfaction*, not happiness. It assumes that people are trying to increase their satisfaction with life—not their happiness. And I believe that it is easier to increase your satisfaction than your happiness.

But bear in mind that this is an assumption, and I may be wrong. In any event, the book would be different if it assumed that people were attempting to increase their *happiness*. You may want to spend a few moments thinking about whether it is happiness or satisfaction that *you* are trying to increase. (After all, you may not want to read the book if you don't care about satisfaction.)

My second warning has to do with the assumption that people are trying to increase or even maximize their satisfaction. Real life tells us that many people—especially people who are poor, insecure, or unhealthy—are less concerned with maximizing satisfaction than they are with minimizing *dis*satisfaction. When people are very unhappy or unsafe, they are content if they can simply keep their lives from getting any worse. They have little hope of making life dramatically better.

As a result, their life strategies are more cautious than those of people who are trying to increase or maximize their satisfaction. They avoid taking risks. Instead of seeking a career that may bring them great rewards, they may seek a job that is secure and "good enough." They may carry this behaviour over into a large number of other domains, as well, and so miss out on a wide range of possible experiences.

I have no information about how many people are trying to maximize satisfaction and how many are trying to minimize risk and dissatisfaction. It seems certain that this book would have to offer somewhat different advice to each of these two groups of people. Therefore, I have tried to strike a compromise. I focus my attention on the first group of people: the satisfaction maximizers. From time to time, I also put in advice for people who want to minimize risk instead. But bear in mind that this book would be a different mixture of elements if I had taken the opposite course.

I cannot be certain that I have made the right decisions in focussing on satisfaction, not happiness, and maximization, not minimization. I simply urge readers to beware of my bias in these directions and to keep asking whether the advice I offer here *really* applies to them, given their own approach to life goals and life strategies.

With these warnings out of the way, we can now proceed with the main story.

PATTERNS OF VARIATION

The rest of this chapter will explore the ways in which desires and satisfactions vary, and look at theories about that variation. This exploration has two main purposes. The first is to understand why people want what they do out of life, and why some feel more satisfied than the average.

(Later chapters will answer similar questions about particular domains of life in greater detail.) A second and more important purpose is to demonstrate that people's desires and life concerns are patterned: they vary in predictable, understandable ways among different segments of the population.

Variations in Time

People's satisfaction with life, and their particular desires and concerns, vary over time. To understand what it was like to live in another historical period, we must understand the values people held, the goals they set for themselves, and the satisfaction they felt with social conditions that might not satisfy us today.

These variations are easiest to see when we compare large chunks of time—for example, the Middle Ages and today. An ambitious work of early American sociology studied how people's values have changed over thousands of years (Sorokin, 1941). Data collected from a variety of civilizations showed that major civilizations of the world have gone through cycles of value change.

One thing we note in making a broad comparison between today and, say, a thousand years ago is that people were much more religious in earlier times. What scholars have called the "secularization" of modern societies—a trend away from traditional patterns of religious belief—took place over a very long time, and was tied up with major changes such as the growth of science, democratic government, and a market economy.

Whatever the root cause of this secularization, we can be certain that it had powerful effects both on people's satisfaction and on their dominant concerns. We can say this with some confidence because, even today, some people are much more religious than other people; and religious people have a different set of concerns and satisfactions than nonreligious people.

In general, religiosity—strong religious sentiment and involvement—seems to make people feel better about life (Poloma & Pendleton, 1990; Chamberlain & Zika, 1988; Gee & Veevers, 1990). Cox and Hammonds (1988) show that people who attend church frequently experience more life satisfaction and are better adjusted than people who do not. They suggest that the church gives people a place for social integration and activity, and provides them—especially the elderly—with a sense of community and well-being.

However, Ellison, Gay, and Glass (1989) dispute that explanation, noting that even religious people who do *not* attend church seem to be more satisfied than average. Perhaps, as Koenig, Siegler, and George (1989) suggest, religion gives people (especially older people) a better way of coping with life's problems—for example, through prayer. More likely still, religion gives people a sense of purpose in life. University students with a strong belief in a personal God feel that they have more purpose in life, and get more excitement out of day-to-day living, than other people do (Molcart & Stuempfig, 1988).

So, it seems likely that religious people are more satisfied with life because religion invests their life with meaning. They may believe that they are doing what God wants them to do, and this gives them a sense of mission. But today, such people are rare. In the last century or two, science and secular thought have deprived most people of this sense of mission (which is, after all, what religious people most resented about Charles Darwin's theory of evolution).

The rise of religious fundamentalism around the world today reminds us that people's beliefs and values change slowly and repeatedly over long periods of time. Often, people return to earlier concerns and ways of thinking. So, historical context is all-important if we want to account for what people want out of life and how they feel about their lives in any given period.

However, we can also demonstrate that values and satisfactions vary over periods shorter than centuries. For example, the baby-boom generation, or *cohort*, has had to face more difficulties than other generations faced when they were the same age. People born at a time of high birthrates, as the baby-boom generation was, have to compete more intensely for spaces in colleges and universities, scholarships, entry-level jobs, higher career positions, housing, and other rewards throughout life (Easterlin, 1980). It was predictable that baby boomers would register comparatively low rates of satisfaction.

By contrast, people born between 1939 and 1948—who were teenagers in the 1950s and young adults in the 1960s—had it much easier. Since they were fewer in number, they enjoyed smaller school classes, expanding educational opportunities, and more job possibilities when they entered the work force.

Still, even this relatively small cohort grew less satisfied between 1968 and 1977, as they passed into their thirties. The reason was that an economic slowdown or recession started around 1974 and produced harsh effects in the early 1980s. During this period, employment and career opportunities worsened for everyone, and especially for younger people. Young adults' lower life satisfaction, as expressed in 1977 survey results, partly reflected their frustration and disappointment with the economic decline.

Whenever the economy improves, most people feel more satisfied with life; we have seen the economy improve (and worsen) several times in the last twenty years. Still, the baby boomers may continue to feel less satisfied than most throughout their entire lives. Their expectations about life—based on the experiences of older brothers and sisters who were enjoying prosperity while the baby boomers were growing up —may be too high.

People born after the baby boom—in the late 1960s and the years since—already show the change of desires that one would expect of people living in a period of economic difficulty. Research from many countries suggests that high-school and college students today have much more pragmatic goals than baby boomers did in the 1960s and early 1970s.

For example, an American study (*The Globe and Mail*, January 15, 1988) reported that three-quarters of first-year college students felt that being financially well off is an essential or very important goal. Most said that they were attending college primarily to achieve that goal. Fewer than two in every five first-year students attached the same importance to developing a meaningful philosophy of life. Moreover, data collected continuously since 1966 demonstrate that these views are part of a growing materialism and declining concern with a "meaningful philosophy." Indeed, in the last twenty years, these two concerns have completely reversed their degree of importance for first-year students.

Given their concern with financial well-being, young people's life satisfaction declined during the recessionary 1970s. By 1981, satisfaction was even lower than it had been in 1968 and 1977. Only 29 percent of all respondents (compared with 35 percent in 1977) said that they were very satisfied with life (Quality of Life survey, 1981).

Between 1981 and the peak of the economic boom of the 1980s, young people lowered their expectations and the baby boomers aged. For these two reasons, we would expect people polled during those years to be more satisfied with life, and the data bear this out. Statistics Canada (*The Globe and Mail*, February 27, 1988) reported that of Canadian adults "asked to describe themselves as very happy, somewhat happy, or unhappy, 48 percent ... said they were very happy, compared to only 21 percent when the same question was asked 10 years ago." In the wake of the recession of the 1990s, however, and another decline in employment and career opportunities, it is likely that surveys will once again reveal a mood of frustration and dissatisfaction.

So, life satisfaction changes for a variety of reasons. Basic conceptions of life may take generations and even centuries to change. In the course of a single lifetime, the average satisfaction in a society will be affected by the following:

- the relative numbers of old and young (since older people are more satisfied)
- the sizes of cohorts (since smaller than average cohorts are more satisfied)
- the economic conditions of the period (since periods of economic growth are more satisfying)
- the length of time people have had to lower their expectations (with more time to adjust, people become more satisfied)

However, other important influences on life satisfaction also emerge when we examine variations from one country to another.

Variations from Country to Country

At any given time, people living in different societies will differ in their life satisfaction.

For example, a 1979 study showed that, among nine nations surveyed, Canadians had the highest standard of living but only the fourth-highest proportion of people who said that they were very satisfied with life (Atkinson, 1979). Denmark, with a lower standard of living, ranked first in overall satisfaction. Ireland, with nearly the lowest standard of living among the countries studied, also had a higher proportion of people than Canada indicating great satisfaction with their lives.

So people can be poor but satisfied. We see this illustrated dramatically when we compare highly developed and less developed countries. The key article on this topic is by Easterlin (1974), who argues that happiness depends on *relative* wealth. It follows that if people compare themselves to others within the same country—not to people in other countries—we should find that (1) people in richer and poorer countries are about equally happy, on average, but (2) rich people are much happier than poor people within any given country.

An examination of the data convinces Easterlin that his theory is right. However, a reanalysis of the data convinces Veenhoven (1991) that Easterlin's theory is wrong—that Easterlin has misread his own data. Using Easterlin's and other data, Veenhoven concludes that (1) people in richer countries are (on average) happier than people in poorer countries, but (2) rich people are much happier than poor people *only* in poor countries, or in countries (such as the United States) where income inequality is very great.

Exhibit 1.1

Presentation of Cantril's data on average happiness in countries of different wealth in 1960

Figure a: Easterlin's presentation (Easterlin, 1974, p. 106)

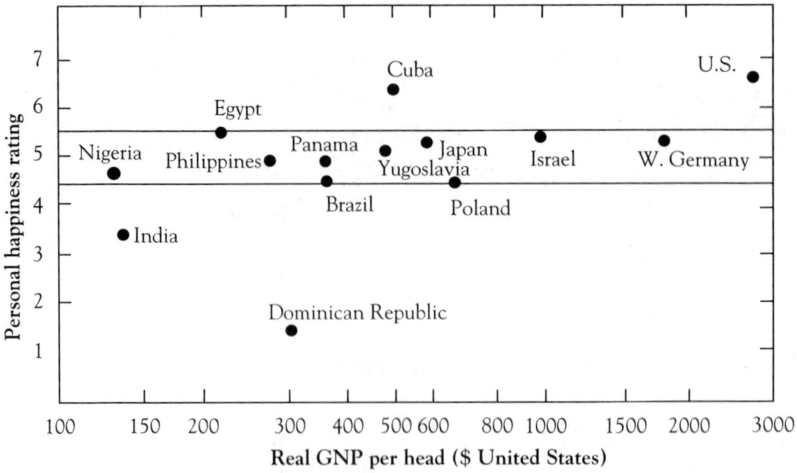

Figure b: Veenhoven's presentation (based on the same data)

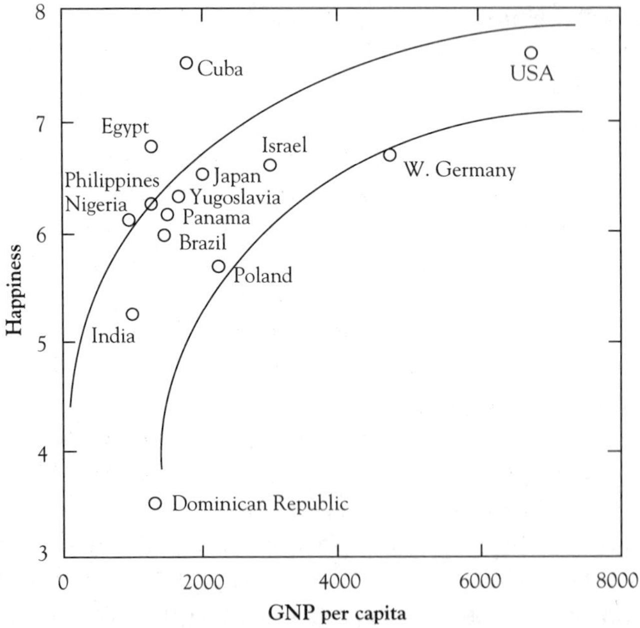

Source: Veenhoven, R. (1991). Is happiness relative? *Social Indicators Research*, 24, 1 (Feb.): 1–34. Reprinted by permission of Kluwer Academic Publishers.

My own sense is that the data are ambiguous, at least where satisfaction (not happiness) is concerned. Certainly, in Canada we continue to find little correlation between income and satisfaction. Even with Veenhoven's adjustments to Easterlin's data, we find a good deal of clustering: societies with very similar levels of wealth (measured as GNP—gross national product—per capita) show very different levels of happiness. It is far from certain, then, that economic development—growth in economic prosperity—leads to greater satisfaction or happiness.

For the time being, let us leave this question open. What is clear is that people have somewhat different life *concerns* in different societies. In an ambitious early study, Cantril (1965) asked the same questions of fourteen samples from around the world and found that the people living on Israeli kibbutzim were the most satisfied of all with their present lives. Next most satisfied were respondents in the United States and Cuba. Least satisfied with their lives were respondents in Poland, India, and the Dominican Republic. Using an index of socio-economic development, or *modernization*, that comprised eleven items (including GNP per capita; number of doctors per 10 000 people; percentage living in cities with populations over 100 000; and percentage of literate people) Cantril found that average life satisfaction is only weakly related to the level of development. Here, he was in full agreement with Easterlin.

Cantril also allowed people to speak freely about their hopes and fears, and then coded the answers they gave into categories including "personal economic situation," "family references," "health," "personal values and character," "job or work situation," and "social values." From this, he found that people had very different life concerns in different countries. Personal economic aspirations were the concern mentioned by more people than any other: they far outnumbered all other concerns in the poorest countries—such as the Dominican Republic, Brazil,and India—and even in some prosperous countries such as West Germany. Next in frequency of mention were family references: these were at least as common as personal economic concerns in the kibbutzim, and Israel generally, and in Nigeria, Yugoslavia, and the Philippines. References to personal values were extremely common in rapidly developing places (the kibbutzim, Nigeria, Cuba, and Egypt) and less common in countries where modernization had been stifled (India, the Dominican Republic, and the Philippines) or completed (the United States and West Germany).

People mentioned health concerns more often than social values, especially in the rapidly developing or developed countries. Jobs and work were the last category mentioned by large numbers of people.

About 5 to 15 percent of respondents in every country expressed hopes concerning this issue.

What, then, do we learn about people's desires from such an ambitious comparison of nations? Do people all share the same basic concerns and feel the same amount of satisfaction with life? In short, the answer is "No." Except at a very general level, people do *not* share the same life concerns around the world.

We learn the most about national differences by comparing countries that are similar in many ways. Such comparisons are most like controlled experiments, the preferred method of research in physical science. By comparing similar societies, we are in effect holding constant a great many factors, while allowing only one or two possible explanatory factors to vary. The few varying factors are, logically, the only possible cause of differences in the thing we are trying to explain.

Atkinson and Murray (1982) compared Canadian data on life satisfaction with similar American data collected by Campbell, Converse, and Rogers (1976). Despite the similarity of the two peoples, certain key differences in the kinds of satisfactions that may predict overall life satisfaction did emerge.

The most important difference was that Americans appeared to be "more diverse in their value orientations" than Canadians. Canadians showed themselves to be rather single-minded. They placed much more importance on romance and marriage than Americans. In fact, these relationships largely determined their satisfaction with life overall. When their intimate relationships were going well, Canadians felt, life as a whole was going well. Further, in Canada, "marital concerns would more often take precedence over material considerations" than in the United States. Conversely, work had much more influence on life satisfaction in the United States than in Canada.

The high value that the Canadians studied put on love and marriage supports the claim that Canadians are more "collectively oriented"—attached to groups—than Americans. On the other hand, the greater significance of work for Americans shows that Americans put a greater value on achievement. Atkinson and Murray (1982, p. 29) concluded that "the greater value of social relationships in Canada, and of achievement in the United States, reflect long-standing societal differences which will persist in the future."

To summarize, people's satisfaction and life concerns vary among societies in complex ways. Even such similar countries as Canada and the United States show different patterns, suggesting long-standing cultural differences that defy easy explanation.

Variations across Ages

People of different ages vary in their life satisfaction, with older people being generally more satisfied than younger ones (see, for example, Lance et al., 1989). People's life concerns also change as they get older. For example, a *Maclean's*/CTV poll (*Maclean's*, January 4, 1993, p. 31) reports that Canadians asked to name their top three wishes order their answers differently depending on their age. Respondents aged 18 to 24 answer first "financial security," followed by "youth and health" and "inner peace and happiness"; respondents aged 35 to 44 answer first "inner peace and happiness," followed by "youth and health" and "financial security"; while respondents aged 65 and older answer first "youth and health," followed by "inner peace and happiness" and, finally, "financial security."

What accounts for this difference in ordering? As they age, people pass through a life cycle—a sequence of typical, important stages. At each stage, certain concerns become paramount and others trivial. That is because as people age, they enter and leave social roles (Nicolson, 1980). Certain important life events are typically concentrated in certain periods of a person's life (Latten, 1989).

Early in life, we are most concerned about relations with our parents. Our childhood home is the culture and society we know best, and we measure everything else—including our wishes, hopes, and self-esteem—against what we have learned there. As we age, all this changes radically. We become acquainted with a much larger world at school; the peers whom we encounter there are much more varied than our parents and siblings. For the first time, we feel moral uncertainty. The question we face is not "Should I obey the rules?" but "What *are* the rules?" In adolescence, our needs for peer acceptance are increasing at the same time as we are searching for an identity and purpose of our very own. We often feel torn between the conflicting goals of finding our own true selves and gaining social acceptance as "one of the crowd."

Asked about their goals in life, or their *terminal values*, the vast majority (84 percent) of Canadian teenagers sampled answer that "freedom" is their main concern; 86 percent say that it is "very important" (Bibby & Posterski, 1992, p. 15). Next in importance are "friendship," which 84 percent rate as "very important," and "being loved," which 80 percent rate as "very important." In this respect, teenagers are very similar to Canadian adults asked the same questions. Where they differ is in respect to "success" and "a comfortable life," which teenagers rate more highly than adults. They differ even more markedly in respect to family life, which is the second most important goal of Canadian adults. For teenagers, family life is in ninth place. Only 60 percent rate it "very important."

Teenagers are busy rejecting family life and becoming individuals. Teenagers want to be loved and at the same time they want to be free: hence, they reject family life in favour of friends. As full-fledged adult individuals, they will eventually re-integrate themselves into family life, which so limits the freedom and privacy they value highly when they are young.

Is this a sign of some social pathology? Not at all. Our cultural norms invite this rejection of family life and re-integration into it as part of normal development and the passage from childhood to adulthood. A similar reason accounts for the finding that teenagers rate success and comfort more highly than adults do. To Canadian adults, material success and comfort are indicators of family well-being and security. To teenagers, they are means of freeing themselves from family constraints and proof that they have achieved full membership in adult society.

Differences between people of different ages do not end with the passage from adolescence into adulthood. People's values and goals continue to change as they get older. "Work and financial situation [occupy] more important positions ... for those under 30; marital and family concerns [dominate] the child-raising period between ages 30 and 44; while leisure and health considerations become more prevalent for those over age 65" (Atkinson & Murray, 1982, p. 29).

Exhibit 1.2

Self-reported happiness status of Canadians aged 55 and over, 1985 and 1990

	Men		Women	
	1985	1990	1985	1990
		%		
Very happy	46	56	45	49
Somewhat happy	48	39	49	43
Somewhat unhappy	4	2	5	5
Very unhappy	1	1	1	1
No opinion, not stated	1	3	1	2

Source: Statistics Canada, General Social Survey, Cycle 5, unpublished data. In Keith, J. and Landry, L., "Well-being of Older Canadians," *Canadian Social Trends*, Summer 1992, pp. 16, 17. Ottawa: Statistics Canada.

Not only life concerns change with age: so does overall life satisfaction. The proportion of older Canadians (aged 65 and over) who are very satisfied with life is about double the proportion of younger Canadians (aged 20 to 40) who are equally satisfied. People generally become more satisfied as they age. (For Japanese evidence on this, see Shimonaka & Nakazato, 1986.) The well-being of older people has become a growing preoccupation in our society, which is rapidly growing older. Quite a lot has been written about it recently. Fortunately, the evidence suggests that older people are now experiencing a healthier, more prosperous, and more satisfying old age than previously.

In many respects, older people crave and benefit from the same things as everyone else. The same factors that contribute to life satisfaction contribute to good health and longevity (Palmore, 1985; Lowry, 1984). These include the following:

- nutritious diet
- avoidance of obesity
- exercise and recreation (see also Russell, 1990)
- avoidance of tobacco
- moderate use of alcohol
- work satisfaction
- high socio-economic status, or good income (see also D'Amato, 1987; Doyle & Forehand, 1984)
- marriage (see also D'Amato, 1987; Yahya, 1988)
- satisfying sexual activity

Other research shows the importance of social and family support to the life satisfaction of the elderly (D'Amato, 1987; Levitt et al., 1985). Indeed, social integration is critical, whether in work or in leisure; what is important is not so much active involvement as affiliation (Salamon, 1985; Duff & Hong, 1982; Lowry, 1984) and the sense of being integrated into a community (Steinkamp & Kelly, 1985; also Steinkamp, 1987). Among the elderly, loneliness and boredom are particularly likely to be associated with low life satisfaction (Brown & Orlando, 1988; Doyle & Forehand, 1984). With fewer family and job concerns for them to think about, social and health concerns take on much greater importance.

The changes in satisfaction associated with aging are even more profound for women than for men: in fact, young women start out life more satisfied than men and end up in old age much less satisfied than men. Old age typically brings more loneliness and economic distress to women, who are more likely to have lost their spouse and to have an activity limitation, than it brings to men of the same age.

Of course, aging brings with it a host of physiological as well as social changes. George, Okun, and Landerman (1985) conclude that the physiological effects of aging interact with marital status, income, health, and social support to influence life satisfaction. It may be easier, for example, to deal with divorce or unemployment at the age of 30 than at the age of 60. Certainly, the relationship between age and satisfaction is a complicated one. We shall return to it throughout the book.

Variations across Status and Income Groups

Social position also influences people's life concerns. Common sense says that it is better to be rich than poor, famous than unknown, and powerful than powerless. But remember, Canadians place little importance on material wealth, compared to other sources of satisfaction such as love and family. Certain regions of Canada, such as the Maritimes, are particularly unlikely to value riches (Garreau, 1981). Similarly, a study of various regions within the state of Oklahoma reveals that people in that state's poorer regions tend to express average (or greater than average) levels of satisfaction in almost every aspect of their lives. This leads to the conclusion that people's standard of living determines not only *whether* people will be able to get what they want out of life, but *what* they want out of life, as well (Amos, Hitt, & Warner, 1982). Riches bring people satisfaction only if people value them, and not everyone does value them. Are rich people really more satisfied with life, then, as lay wisdom tells us?

The most common finding, exemplified in research by Ackerman and Paolucci (1983), is that increases in income lead to increased satisfaction with income and consumption level alone. They have little impact on people's overall life satisfaction. It is how people perceive the adequacy of their income—not how big their income really is—that affects their life satisfaction. Put another way, people are satisfied if they think that they are making a good income—whatever their income may be. There is little relationship between actual income and life satisfaction.

The research does not always turn out that way, especially if we focus on very rich people. Diener, Horowitz, and Emmons (1985) sampled people from *Forbes* business magazine's list of the wealthiest Americans, and compared them with people chosen randomly from the telephone book. People agreeing to participate completed a questionnaire about their life concerns. Wealthy respondents proved to be happy a higher percentage of the time, scored significantly higher than average on two different life satisfaction scales, and reported significantly lower than average levels of unhappiness.

Wealthy and ordinary people also reported differences in what satisfies them. Wealthy respondents more often mentioned self-esteem and self-actualization as sources of their satisfaction, while ordinary people more often mentioned physiological needs (food, shelter, and other basic human needs) and safety concerns.

Bear in mind that Diener, Horowitz, and Emmons were comparing ordinary people with some of the wealthiest people in the world. If we compare the poorer 99 percent of the population with one another, does income still make a difference? The answer is "No." Your income quintile (that is, the fifth of the income distribution in which you are located) makes little difference in your overall life satisfaction, at least in Canada.

Debates about the effects of income on happiness or satisfaction continue. Most recently, using national American samples at two points in time *and* samples of university students from 39 countries, Diener et al. (1993) show strong support for the hypothesis that increases in income increase happiness *significantly*, and this applies across the entire range of income levels.

However, though these increases in happiness are statistically "significant," meaning that they are unlikely to occur by chance, they are small. They fail to challenge Argyle's earlier conclusion that millionaires may be a little happier than other people but "the difference is less than might be produced by, for example, getting married" (1992, p. 287).

To repeat, more income increases people's satisfaction with their financial situation alone. But for Canadians, love and family are typically much more important than money. So, at least in Canada, a large income does not buy the average person life satisfaction (Atkinson, 1980).

Nor does socio-economic status (or SES—a combined measure of education, income, and job prestige) have much effect on life satisfaction, even in the United States. Consider a study (Willits, 1988) that followed up on the lives of a group of American high-school students after a period of 37 years (that is, 1947 graduates were surveyed again in 1984). As expected, the students who had earned good grades, enjoyed good relations with their parents, participated in student organizations, and held leadership roles ended up being successful adults as measured by high socio-economic status. However, none of these factors predicted life satisfaction.

We can restate this conclusion in another way: (1) richer, more "successful" people are not always more satisfied people; (2) therefore, strategies for gaining fame and fortune are not the same as strategies for gaining satisfaction.

In fact, people's social status—their "fame and fortune," if you like—has a stronger effect on life concerns than it does on their life satisfaction. People with high SES rate "social values" such as love, family security, and friendship significantly higher than people with low SES. Conversely, they rate "material values" such as prosperity and economic stability lower (Blishen & Atkinson, 1982). And, just as Diener, Horowitz, and Emmons (1985) discovered in comparing the very wealthy with ordinary people, high-status people in Canada place a much higher value on achievement, self-development, and excitement than low-status people do.

How can we explain the variations in life satisfaction and life concerns that we have observed so far? Two main theoretical approaches will help us: Maslow's theory of a need hierarchy and Michalos's multiple discrepancies theory.

TWO THEORIES OF SATISFACTION

Throughout this book, we shall see that there is a patterned variation in people's concerns and satisfactions. This means that different social and demographic characteristics—gender, age, class, and so on—are correlated with different concerns and degrees of satisfaction. However, finding a correlation between two variables is not the same as giving an explanation. We have to move beyond the correlation and explain *why* a particular gender, age group, or class (for example) is more or less satisfied, more or less concerned with one domain or another of life.

In the main, two kinds of explanation have been put forward by social scientists. One takes a more absolute approach: in effect, it argues that all people want more or less the same things out of life. Some kinds of people, however, have a better chance to get those things than other people have. The other kind of theory is comparative: it argues that people want different kinds of things. What they want is shaped by their past experiences and by comparisons they have learned to make between their own lives and other people's lives.

We shall consider two leading examples of these approaches: Maslow's theory of a need hierarchy and Michalos's multiple discrepancy theory (MDT).

Maslow's Need Hierarchy

Psychologist Abraham Maslow put forward a central theory in the study of life satisfactions. It holds that every person strives for self-actualization, the complete fulfilment of his or her unique potentiality. Attaining such fulfilment is the ultimate, basic human need. Such fulfilment will bring any person the greatest possible satisfaction.

The most distinctive feature of Maslow's theory is that it is a "stage theory." It proposes that people must pass through successive stages of fulfilment. People must successively meet needs for survival, security, belonging, and esteem before being able to reach, or even to want, total fulfilment in the form of "self-actualization." A failure to complete one stage prevents the person from successfully proceeding to the next stage.

Thus, for example, a person must gain physical security before gaining acceptance or belonging, and must attain belonging before gaining esteem. People must pass through the stages in order, and all lower-level needs must be satisfied before self-actualization is possible. Only those who have passed through all the lower stages of fulfilment can hope to reach self-actualization.

Often, we tend to think of those needed resources and attributes as an undifferentiated grouping. It is easy to see that people who lack many or all of them will be dissatisfied. This was the focus of a study of Vietnamese refugees in the United States who suffered from broken families, insufficient social support, inadequate family income, and anxiety about their interactions with the community around them (Van-Tran & Wright, 1986). In considering Maslow's theory, however, the question is, How do we separate out these various elements in order to know which need is more basic and more important than another?

One test of Maslow's stage theory uses representative survey data from Canada. Like Maslow, Atkinson and Murray (1982) distinguish between "sustenance values and needs"—needs for physical well-being and economic security—and higher-level values such as belonging, esteem, achievement, and actualization. They find that a failure to satisfy sustenance needs leads people to fixate on these needs, while satisfaction of sustenance needs reduces their importance. People with a low income or poor health are particularly likely to focus on improving their income or health, while other people are not. This is just what Maslow would have predicted.

There is certainly much evidence to support the conclusion that good health is an important determinant of life satisfaction, especially among the elderly (see, for example, Kennedy, King, & Muraco, 1983; McConnatha & McConnatha, 1988; and Bowling, 1990). In turn, good health often depends on the availability of social support (see, for example, Fusilier, Ganster, & Mayes, 1986), another of Maslow's basic needs.

Yet the evidence shows that, even for poor people and sick people, health and economic security are far from dominant concerns, and they have only a weak influence on overall life satisfaction. As for people who have fulfilled their basic health and economic needs, the survey evidence supports Maslow's theory even less. "Values of belonging, esteem, achievement and actualization ... do not appear to be stratified as Maslow suggests," say Atkinson and Murray (1982, p. 31). People failing to fulfil any of these secondary needs substitute other domains as sources of gratification. Thus, unmarried people with good jobs and high incomes place more than average value on their work, while unmarried people with lower incomes place more than average value on leisure. Doing so gives them the most satisfaction they can have, under the circumstances.

Stage-one and -two values seem to operate by different rules and have different potentials for influencing a person's life satisfaction. For example, poverty and poor health can reduce the quality of a person's life, but "high incomes and good physical condition seem to have limited potential for increasing well-being, at least directly." On the other hand, stage-two domains—for example, work, family, and leisure satisfactions —"carry the potential to make life genuinely enjoyable as well as miserable" (Atkinson & Murray, 1982, p. 33).

Atkinson and Murray conclude that "the substitutability of second-stage values offers some relief from frustrations encountered in particular domains," if other sources of reward are available.

We see, then, that survival and security needs must be satisfied before people can look to other domains for more satisfaction. For the majority in our society, who are able to meet their basic sustenance needs, higher-level needs can be satisfied in a variety of ways. In general, people make do with what they have at hand. They do not pine after the impossible. This means that the young, single person beginning his or her adult life can find satisfaction in a variety of ways. One will find it in a career, another in marriage, and a third in leisure activities or friendship.

However, there are important limits to what makes people satisfied, and these tend to support Maslow's ranking of satisfactions. The Quality of Life (1981) survey shows that, when we group people according to the goals they claim are most important, adult Canadians fall into four roughly equal-sized groups. I call these groups "money-centred," "family-centred," "heaven-centred," and "self-centred"—the labels are self-explanatory. These groupings are not so very different from those of Steinkamp and Kelly (1985), who did not, however, identify a "heaven-centred" group. Those researchers found three groups: "challenge-seeking" (my "self-centred"), "concerned with recognition and reward" (my "money-centred"), and "family-focussed" (my "family-centred").

The Quality of Life data lead to several important conclusions. First, people with different values tend to be different kinds of people. For example, the four groups vary widely in their age, sex, and educational composition; the "heaven-centreds" include a disproportionate number of middle-aged and older women, to take one particular illustration.

Second, the four groups have quite different levels of life satisfaction, with the heaven-centred and family-centred people most satisfied. (This agrees with Grichting's [1983] finding that the typical satisfied individual is female, married, middle-aged, and conservative.)

Third, and perhaps most important of all, the factors that influence people's life satisfaction are pretty similar for everyone, despite their different life goals. Three variables seem to characterize the Canadian adults who are most satisfied with life: (1) control over their own lives —for example, they have autonomy at work, good health, free time, and a secure income; (2) social integration—for example, they live in a family, have intimate relations, and have friends; and (3) a commitment to something larger than themselves—for example, to religion or family, *not* career or personal development. In short, we could say that the three ingredients of satisfaction are work, love, and hope.

The data also suggest that people who are striving for self-actualization—people who value achievement, independence, and excitement—are dissatisfied because they have to give up some or all of the three satisfaction-producing factors in order to "achieve." Perhaps they do not even value satisfaction and see it as irrelevant to "self-actualization," and *that* is why they are not happy. In any event, high levels of education, money, and achievement do not produce satisfaction unless they are funnelled into autonomy, social integration, and commitment. (They rarely are, by this group.)

To reiterate, Maslow argues that everyone wants the same things in life—essential or universal wants. He believes that people must attain them in the same sequence in order to maximize life satisfaction. We have seen that data support this theory in part, but also that it suffers from serious weaknesses. First, it is simply not true that everyone wants the same things. Rather, people's wants (their concerns, hopes, and desires) vary by age, period, country, and social class. They vary in other ways too, which we shall consider later. Second, people can deal with frustrated desires by substituting one satisfaction for another. Once people have satisfied their most basic needs for food and shelter, they can increase their life satisfaction with a wide variety of material, social, and cultural "goods." There is no need for people to attain these goods in stages.

On the other hand, our examination of the four groups into which Canadians may be classified has shown that these "goods" do not bring people equal satisfaction. Clearly, some satisfy people more than others.

So Maslow's theory does give us an important insight into the causes of human satisfaction; however, it also leaves us with important unanswered questions. In particular, Why are human wants so varied? Why are the sources of satisfaction so substitutable? For help with these questions, we need to turn to Michalos's multiple discrepancies theory.

Multiple Discrepancies Theory

We have already noted that people's needs and desires vary. That is largely because people's backgrounds and personal histories present them with different images of the "good life." We grow up hoping for a certain kind of future. Often our hoped-for futures are strikingly similar to the adult lives we witnessed as children. Sometimes they are strikingly different. What is remarkable is the strength of the relationship—whether positive or negative—between what we see as children and what we become as adults.

Our hopes—what we want and expect—are not only shaped by parents and siblings. They are also influenced by other significant people we encounter in growing up: role models, mentors, idols, good friends, enemies, and so on. Indeed, we are a product of all the groups we belong to and of all the outlooks, norms, and behaviours they teach us. Finally, there are a number of secondary institutions and groups in our society that influence our wants. They include the media, advertising agencies, politicians, interest groups, and churches. Other influences at work or school—agents of "adult socialization"—continue to mould us throughout life. These groups and institutions all shape what we expect out of life: what we think life will be or should be.

Michalos's (1985, 1986) multiple discrepancies theory (MDT) argues that our satisfaction with life is determined by the gap (or discrepancy) between life as it is and life as we once thought it should and would be. The more our real life departs from the ideal life that we have imagined for ourselves, the more dissatisfied we will be.

To state the theory more formally, life satisfaction is determined by the size of the discrepancy between what people have attained and what they want. Unlike Maslow, however, Michalos does not argue that everyone wants the same things. Rather, his theory holds that what you want is determined by (1) what "relevant others" appear to have (see also Emmons & Diener, 1985); (2) the best you had in the past; (3) what you expected three years ago that you would have today; (4) what you expect to have five years from now; (5) what you think you deserve; and (6) what you think you need. According to this theory, people are driven by a personal picture of the future, an image of what life "should" be for them. They are also driven by the desire to close the gap between what they expect, what they want, and what they actually get.

This is not only a matter of discrepancies that we imagine in our minds. Objective reality has some influence on this process. The gaps we perceive all have a basis in reality. "All discrepancies, satisfactions and actions are directly and indirectly affected by age, sex, education, ethnicity, income, self-esteem, and social support" (Michalos, 1985, p. 348). These social characteristics, which influence our perceptions and our sense of whether we have succeeded in getting what we want out of life, also influence our opportunities for getting what we want.

We could even state this case more strongly. Many factors—especially gender, race, and class—limit a person's life chances. (We will discuss this further in the next chapter.) These social characteristics are "risk factors": you risk having a lower income and less power and status if you are a woman rather than a man, a non-white rather than a white person, and a working-class person rather than a middle-class person, for example. What's more, these risk factors can combine to create "double" and even "triple jeopardy." By this reasoning, a working-class Native (or black) woman will have the most limited life chances of all.

Multiple discrepancies theory helps us understand why people tend to be cautious, conservative, and politically naïve. According to this theory, people become dissatisfied with their own lives only when they perceive a gap between what they have and what other people have. From this fact, Michalos concludes that it may be possible to "manage" satisfaction and happiness (Michalos, 1985, p. 393)—a very frightening thought. For example, people's satisfaction can be increased by having them compare themselves with less fortunate people, or by making them want less, misremember the past, and expect little from the future. The dangerous potential that this has for engineering contentment is a topic that we shall consider toward the end of the book.

Political engineering aside, people have a built-in tendency toward moderation and caution, if this theory is correct. Because the same factors that influence our opportunities to get what we want—age, gender, education, ethnicity, income, self-esteem, and social support, for example—also influence what we want, there comes to be a kind of balance between what we want and what we can get. So we get what we want because we learn to want what we get. This attitude of resignation is the perfect tranquillizer.

Consider the problem that women have faced for many centuries. Women have long been denied the same rights and opportunities as men. At the same time, women have been taught to want different things from men. The result has been, very often, what Mann (1970) called a "pragmatic acceptance" of inequality. Training people to expect little out of life lowers their dissatisfaction when they end up getting little.

Or consider why there is so little protest by the poor, the jobless, and other disadvantaged people in our society. Multiple discrepancies theory tells us that the disadvantaged form their visions of the future in a backward-looking, conformist, and moderate way; therefore, disadvantage seems normal and acceptable. I do not compare my bank account with Conrad Black's and then strive to narrow the discrepancy between what I want and what I have, any more than I compare my face with Tom Cruise's and then try to close that gap. My actual, everyday experience forms the basis for what I come to believe is possible. This is simply a specific instance of the general argument that people lower their expectations and aspirations as they confront limited opportunities; they substitute attainable desires for unattainable ones. A second explanation suggested by this theory may apply, as well. It holds that the images of the future that pull us forward are often remembrances of an even more limiting past.

Usually, what people want is what they can get and what they are used to getting. The result is social conservatism, especially among adults. People tend to know most about people much like themselves; therefore, they set low standards for their own futures. It is no wonder that most people in our society are moderately satisfied with life.

How, then, are we to explain the occasional outbreak of violent protest? The theory would argue that people protest only when opportunities can no longer keep up with expectations. In fact, people may become dissatisfied even if opportunities are actually increasing, as long as their expectations are rising more rapidly than the opportunities for satisfying them.

The key here is the relationship between rates of change in opportunities and desires. When opportunities grow more slowly than desires, the gap between them increases and satisfaction decreases. Vermunt, Spaans, and Zorge (1989) argue that it is the presence or absence of such a gap between one's actual and desired situation that explains people's satisfaction with life. When a decline in opportunity threatens people's ability to satisfy needs whose satisfaction they have come to expect, they will not adjust their desires downward. Rather, they are apt to protest. The result can be civil violence (Park & Mason, 1986).

Protest, however, may be no more useful to the disadvantaged than passivity. Directed, realistic action is needed. People need more and better information about possible futures and possible lives—in particular, about other people with whom they might reasonably compare themselves—if they are to strive for a better life. Accurate information about the present and the commitment to a better future are necessary conditions for self-improvement and social change (Michalos, 1987, pp. 44–46).

How do we judge what we can really achieve? Consider this analogy. An excellent runner has just run a four-minute mile and wants to decide whether to shoot for a three-minute mile. Is that truly possible—a worthwhile goal—or truly impossible—a ridiculous and possibly dangerous goal? The runner needs more information in order to make a sensible decision. Available information confirms that no one has ever run a three-minute mile. On the other hand, evidence shows that people have been running ever faster miles. Therefore, a three-minute mile may be possible for some runner, some day. The question has now changed form. It is now, Can *this* runner hope to run a three-minute mile in his or her lifetime?

Most people never get to that stage of the inquiry. They never ask, What can human beings achieve? What can I, in particular, achieve? The result is modesty, moderation, and social conservatism. Society and its individual members fail to reach their potential because of a common failure to investigate the limits of the possible, as a result of limited information, misinformation, and the backward- rather than forward-looking images of the future that people hold.

In what Michalos calls a "Real Paradise," well-informed people travel to the limits of the truly possible and then accept the result. (This contrasts with a "Fool's Paradise," in which satisfaction is based on poorly founded information.) "People's satisfaction and happiness can be more or less cognitively well-founded, and reasonable people will want to be sure that they are essentially well-founded" (Michalos, 1987). Knowing what is truly possible is no easy matter, nor is accepting a less than ideal result. But if multiple discrepancies theory is valid, this is the only sensible and satisfying life strategy.

In a nutshell, "cognitive well-foundedness" is the goal of this book. It tries to explore patterns of desire and opportunity in real life, so that we know what we are pursuing in life, as well as how and why we are doing so. Good information can help us all live more reasonable and thus more satisfying lives. Sociology has an important role to play in providing that information.

Criticisms of the Two Approaches

It would be gratifying to think that the two approaches that we have examined—Maslow's stage theory and Michalos's multiple discrepancies theory—give us all the answers to happiness and satisfaction. Nothing could be further from the truth, however.

Take, for example, the critique by Davis (1984), who tested five hypotheses about happiness with data from nine national surveys. Neither Maslow's nor Michalos's theory fits his data: happiness is not strongly correlated with income or rank; nor is it strongly predicted by social comparison or adaptation. The only good predictors of happiness that Davis can find are race (Afro-Americans are less happy than average), marital status (all categories of unmarried people are less happy than average) and financial change (people whose finances are improving are happier than average).

Wright (1985) argues that MDT fails to predict health satisfaction in a sample that he has studied. Papadakis and Taylor-Goody (1986) find that people's ideas about their own relative positions are not strong influences on their satisfaction with welfare-state services. Gubrium and Lynott (1983) call for a move away from measures (such as those used by MDT) that dwell on the past. They argue that present-day life has a stronger influence on people's satisfaction, and especially on elderly people's satisfaction.

Perhaps the strongest attack on the comparative approach exemplified by MDT has been made by Veenhoven. He notes that "the theory that happiness is relative is based on three postulates: (1) happiness results from comparison, (2) standards of comparison adjust, [and] (3) standards of comparison are arbitrary. On the basis of these postulates the theory predicts: (a) happiness does not depend on real quality of life, (b) changes in living conditions ... have only a shortlived effect on happiness, (c) people are happier after hard times, [and] people are typically neutral about their life" (Veenhoven, 1991, p.1). Veenhoven examines these claims with data from studies of rich and poor countries, lucky and unlucky people, and stable and unstable living conditions, and finds that they are unjustified. Instead, he says "(a) people tend to be unhappy under adverse conditions such as poverty, war and isolation, (b) improvement or deterioration of at least some conditions does affect happiness lastingly, (c) earlier hardship does not favour later happiness, [and] people are typically positive about their life rather than neutral" (1991, p. 1).

Notice that Veenhoven is speaking here of "happiness." "To the extent that happiness depends on need-gratification, it is not relative," he concludes (1991, p. 32). And yet MDT aims primarily at accounting for satisfaction, which, according to Veenhoven, may or may not be relative. (Veenhoven uses the term "contentment.") You can see how important it is to keep the distinction between happiness and satisfaction (or contentment) clearly in mind.

The debate about the two theories, or models, of satisfaction is far from over. You will no doubt see me sliding from one approach to another, sometimes arguing for universal or basic human needs, and at other times for a more relative or comparative approach. That is because there is support for both approaches. In my view, people judge their lives against both absolute and relative standards of well-being.

CONCLUSION

Within our culture today, people share similar life goals and life satisfactions. However, their goals and satisfactions are far from identical. Nor are they universal. People's goals and satisfactions vary over time and place. They vary over millenia, and they vary less dramatically over decades. They vary from one civilization to another, one country to another, and even one region of Canada to another. They also vary by age, gender, and class. That is why it is important to know the social and cultural context if we are to understand people's view of their own lives.

In a very abstract sense, everyone wants the same things: family, security, peace, a job, and good health. This gives support to Maslow's theory of a need hierarchy. Yet countries and individuals order their concerns in different ways. So it may not always be useful to talk about "essential" or "universal" needs beyond food, shelter, and physical safety.

Age is a major variable shaping life concerns and satisfactions, and we shall return to it time and again. People of different ages see life differently and have different concerns. As well, aging increases satisfaction significantly (though, apparently, not happiness). The reasons for greater satisfaction through aging are many. Multiple discrepancies theory helps identify them. Aging seems to produce low and diminishing expectations, narrower bases for comparison, less (and often worse) information about what is truly possible, an increasing tendency to look backward rather than forward, and an increasing aversion to risk. But older people may also possess a better sense of the truly possible than younger people. They may have learned from life.

People in different income groups also see life differently. Wealthier people have different concerns from poorer people: more concerns about self-actualization, for example, and fewer concerns about food and shelter. But they are not necessarily more satisfied. Rich people—who have a great deal of information, high expectations, and great opportunities for high achievement—run the greatest risk of disappointment. Paradoxically, the poor—who expect less, know less about what they do not have, and know that they have little chance of getting it anyway—sometimes find it easier to achieve satisfaction than rich people.

Above the level of bare subsistence, people's needs, concerns, and satisfactions are culture-specific and even subculture-specific. Comparisons with people around us shape our satisfaction. A further measure of our adaptability is that we are able and willing to substitute attainable for unattainable goals to increase our potential for satisfaction. When all else fails, we scale down our aspirations to increase our satisfaction. We teach ourselves to want what we can get.

The next chapter discusses patterns of opportunity—why you get what you get.

CHAPTER TWO

◆

PATTERNS OF OPPORTUNITY: WHY YOU GET WHAT YOU GET

INTRODUCTION

Some of the things that happen to you in life have little to do with social inequality. A good friend dies, your partner falls out of love with you, you lose interest in your work: these things happen to people of every social class. They have happened in every society throughout history.

However, many important things that happen to you in life *are* a direct result of social inequality. Poor people are more likely to lose their jobs, get sick, and be victimized by crime. Meanwhile, rich people live in relative comfort, security, and good health. Poverty and wealth make up only one kind of social inequality. In the course of this chapter, we will discuss inequalities based on class, sex, age, ethnicity, and level of education—among others—that determine why some people and not others are able to get what they want out of life.

Two main categories of social inequality are inequalities of condition and inequalities of opportunity. Inequalities of *condition* refer to differences in physical and material well-being: food, shelter, physical security, good health, and so on. Indirectly, these inequalities lead to differences in mental health and happiness. Inequalities of *opportunity* are differences in chances of gaining power, respect, and well-being. Research shows that some people are more "socially mobile" than others; this means that they have a higher-than-average chance of improving their social position. This is another way of saying that some people have a greater chance to get what they want out of life than others.

These two kinds of inequality are different but related. People who start out with more wealth, power, and respect—that is, people favoured in condition—always find it easier to get even more wealth, power, and respect. They have the opportunity to exchange their wealth, power, and prestige or to "invest" them for further gains. So, if people are to have equal opportunity, they have to start out under equal conditions. Unequal conditions and opportunities may be *analytically* different; in everyday life, however, they are closely connected.

This fact has two important consequences. First, getting the most out of your own life may mean joining others to protest the range of inequality in our society. You can achieve only so much by yourself. Your own life chances are tied up with those of other Canadians in the same situation as you.

Second, getting the most out of your life will mean thinking clearly about what you want and how you personally might go about getting it. In the long run, everyone may be much better off than they are today. (If so, it will probably be the result of collective action.) But as the British economist John Maynard Keynes said, in the long run, we are all dead. So we must pay attention to the short run as well. Getting as much as you can out of life will mean making sensible use of what you've got to work with, personally.

PEOPLE'S BELIEFS ABOUT INEQUALITY

Why are some people very rich and others very poor? On this topic, people's beliefs vary widely. Consider a study of adult Texans by Smith and Stone (1989). I have included short versions of their questionnaires here, in Exhibits 2.1 and 2.2, and want you to try answering the same questions that they put to their respondents.

When Smith and Stone (1989) analyzed the answers of 200 adults, randomly selected from a metropolitan area in southeast Texas, they found that people's thinking showed a patterning into what the researchers came to refer to as "meta-theories" about poverty and wealth. That is, responses to the questions fell into three main groupings, or clusters, which Smith and Stone called "individualism," "structuralism," and "fatalism." Of these, individualism and structuralism proved to be the most common meta-theories.

A respondent who holds individualistic views about poverty thinks that poor people are poor because they are not trying hard to succeed: they are able to receive welfare without any effort on their own part, they lack drive and perseverance, have loose morals, abuse drugs and alcohol, are not thrifty, and are lazy. A respondent with individualistic views about wealth, usually the same person, thinks that people get rich because they try harder than anyone else: they possess drive and perseverance, are willing to take risks, and are hard-working and thrifty.

These views are "individualistic" because they attribute all success and failure to the personal characteristics of the individual. Only the individual is to blame, or to praise, for failure or success.

A person who holds structuralist views sees things in a different way and focusses not on the individual, but on the situation in which an

Exhibit 2.1
Causes of poverty questionnaire

From the list below, select the 3 most important causes of poverty, in order to complete the following sentence:
POOR PEOPLE (the poorest 20 percent) exist in America today because they ...

A. are not motivated because of welfare
B. lack drive and perseverance
C. have loose morals; abuse drugs and alcohol
D. have too many children
E. are not thrifty
F. are unwilling to take risks
G. are lazy
H. are not greedy
I. live in weak, often broken homes
J. do not have contacts or "pull"
K. are victims of discrimination in hiring
L. are victims of discrimination in promotions and wages
M. are taken advantage of by rich people
N. are victims of the federal government, which is insensitive to their plight
O. are forced to attend bad schools
P. lack the talent and ability to succeed
Q. are born with low intelligence
R. are victims of bad luck
S. are born inferior

Source: Adapted from Smith, K.B. and Stone, L.H. (1989). "Rags, riches and bootstraps: Beliefs about the causes of wealth and poverty," *Sociological Quarterly*, *30*(1), pp. 103–107

individual finds himself or herself. A structuralist explains poverty by saying that poor people lack contacts or pull, are victims of discrimination in hiring, promotions, and wages, are taken advantage of by the rich, are forced to attend bad schools, and are ignored by an insensitive government. Similarly, a structuralist explains wealth by noting that rich people exploit their pull or contacts, attend good schools, inherit a great deal of money, are favoured in hiring, wages, and promotions, receive special treatment from the government, sacrifice their families for their careers, and take advantage of the poor.

A third and much less popular view (or meta-theory) is "fatalism," which Smith and Stone describe as "a simplistic view that attributes the causes of wealth and poverty to luck, quirks of birth, human nature,

Exhibit 2.2
Causes of wealth questionnaire

From the list below, select the 3 most important causes of wealth, in order to complete the following sentence:
WEALTHY PEOPLE (the wealthiest 20 percent) exist in America today because they ...

A. possess drive and perseverance
B. are willing to take risks
C. are hard-working
D. are thrifty
E. live in strong, intact families
F. have high moral standards
G. are greedy
H. have contacts and "pull"
I. attend good schools
J. receive large inheritances
K. receive favouritism in hiring
L. receive special treatment from the federal government
M. are shown favouritism in promotions and wages
N. sacrifice their families for their careers
O. take advantage of the poor
P. have the talent and ability to succeed
Q. are lucky and get breaks
R. are born with high intelligence
S. are born superior

Source: Adapted from Smith, K.B. and Stone, L.H. (1989). "Rags, riches and bootstraps: Belief about the causes of wealth and poverty," *Sociological Quarterly*, *30*(1), pp. 103–107.

chance and related forces over which people and social structures have no control" (1989, p. 95).

The research showed that, in Texas, the most common outlook is individualism, especially as the explanation for poverty. This should not surprise us; after all, Texas embodies individualism, in myth and reality.

Perhaps most interesting of all, the researchers found no connection between the respondent's own sex, race, age, income, or educational attainment and his or her explanation of wealth and poverty. What this means is that poor people are just as likely as rich people to attribute poverty to personal failure, and wealth to personal virtue. This state of mind—self-blame and even self-hatred on the part of the poor, self-congratulation on the part of the rich—creates a powerful force against reforms intended to bring about more equality. I shall have more to say about this when we discuss disability later in this chapter.

As you will find, Texans and sociologists tend to view things differently. Sociologists lean toward a structuralist view of social inequality. This is the view that our data seem to support best. So let's consider four structural limits on people's opportunity to become wealthy, or even financially secure.

Four Limits on Opportunity

Getting as much as you can out of life means knowing the limits on your own opportunities as well as knowing some ways of getting past these limits. Four things seem to limit people's opportunity to get what they want out of life: exclusion, disability, decoupling, and scarcity.

Exclusion

Exclusion is the first way of controlling access to rewards and opportunities. It prevents people from entering contests they might win, and rewards people unequally for equal performances. Organizations practise exclusion against other organizations, ethnic groups practise it against other ethnic groups, classes practise it against other classes, and individuals practise it against other individuals. Exclusion is a very widespread way of limiting opportunities.

Disability

A *disability* is a label attached to certain categories of people that discourages them from competing for the rewards everyone desires. Some people simply think of themselves as unable to compete. Women, the poor, the old, the physically disabled, and young people have all been taught that certain kinds of behaviour are inappropriate, undignified, and hopeless. Socially disabled people "choose" not to compete for what they want out of life.

Decoupling

Decoupling disconnects certain groups from rewards by keeping them uninformed about good opportunities and ways of taking advantage of them. It also keeps people from knowing others who could help them gain rewards. People who are decoupled simply do not "know the ropes" or "have the contacts."

Scarcity

Scarcity refers to a shortage of opportunities to be shared out. True scarcity (as opposed to unequal distribution of goods) can be reduced by producing more of the desired goods. Most often, we become aware of scarcity when we get a poor return on an investment we have made. One example is the "underemployment" of recent college and university graduates, who have invested much time and effort in their education. We shall discuss this problem at length in the next chapter.

EXCLUSION

At least three kinds of exclusion are worth examining at length. Exclusion due to the class structure, exclusion due to professionalization, and exclusion due to ethnic organization. We shall consider each of these in turn.

Exclusion and Class Structure

If power is nothing else, it is certainly the ability to make rules about who will get the biggest share of social "goods": wealth, authority, and prestige (Murphy, 1982). Research by Porter (1965), Clement (1975), and Newman (1979) confirms that power in Canadian society is exercised by people in elite positions. An *elite* is a small group that holds power or influence over others. Every group has an elite: the top few percent in a society, business, university, or political party is that group's elite. In his study of American society, C. Wright Mills (1959) argued that a *power elite* dominates all other members of society. This elite makes decisions that affect the entire society and sets the trends that everyone else tries to follow.

The most interesting thing about the North American elite is its internal consistency: for the most part, it is made up of white Anglo-Saxon men. When we speak of Canada's elite, then, we are talking about the top white Anglo-Saxon men in business, politics, and government.

Societies vary in the extent to which their political, intellectual, economic, and other elites form a cohesive ruling group. In Canada, the dominant elite is the *corporate elite:* the top executives of the largest Canadian businesses. Through their executive positions, these people hold more economic power than anyone else. Their decisions affect the economic conditions in the country (which determine, among other things, the availability of jobs) and in this way, affect the lives of all Canadians.

The corporate elite includes both the owners and controlling stockholders of Canada's major companies, and also the senior executives, who often own smaller blocks of company stock. The group exercises its economic power through its directorships of the major corporations.

It also exercises political power by influencing the government. It contributes to political campaigns, lobbies elected officials, and influences the media—which it owns. The elite can also embarrass politicians by publicly questioning their competence or honesty. Sometimes it will use privately funded research by sympathetic scholars, pollsters, or think tanks for this purpose. This gives the one-sided views of the elite the appearance of scholarship and impartiality. Many politicians are indebted to the corporate elite. They may have served corporate interests as lawyers or executives before taking political office; equally important, they may intend to return to the corporate world after leaving office. So it is easy for the economic elite to exert great influence over the people who make government policy.

How do you become one of these powerful people? The answer is self-recruitment: people born into the wealthy social classes are more likely to enter elite positions than people born into poorer social classes. People appoint you to the elite because you are just like them—born into wealth or power. Almost all the members of Canada's elite come from a middle- or upper-class background, and the upper class has traditionally closed its ranks to outsiders. In most societies, the children of elite people have the best chance of entering the elite themselves.

Ruling elites differ in the extent to which they are open to entry from outside, by children of non-elite parents. Certain peculiarities of Canadian history tend to make entry into the elite here easier than it is in many other societies, such as Britain. For example, there has never been a landed aristocracy in Canada. Much of the Canadian economy is controlled by foreign-owned (especially American-owned) multinational corporations; strange to say, this seems to make entry into the elite easier. As well, the state, which recruits administrative personnel more widely than the traditonal elites, has always played a particularly vigorous part in Canada's social and economic development. Finally, Canada has always had a very high rate of immigration. Peter Newman (1981) presents evidence in his book *The New Acquisitors* that some kinds of people who had always been excluded, including ethnic minorities, have entered the elite in the last 30 years. This number is likely to keep growing if the economy grows.

Still, rags-to-riches mobility remains rare in Canada, as elsewhere. After analyzing changes in Canadian social mobility between 1973 and 1986, Wanner (1993) writes: "Although we have seen that Canadian society has become more open and the availability of opportunities less driven by shifts in the occupational structure ... Canada is still a stratified society characterized by a considerable amount of inheritance of privilege" (p. 178).

The key to gaining elite status is still financial capital, cultural capital, the accident of birth, and a lot of luck. So long as there is inequality in human societies, there will always be elites. This is just another way of stating Robert Michels's "iron law of oligarchy." In the early years of the twentieth century, Michels (1962) studied the German socialist party, which was ideologically committed to democracy and equality. He found that in practice, it was run as an oligarchy: it was not particularly egalitarian or democratic in its leadership and structures.

Ruling groups want to hold on to their power, no matter how committed they are to democracy and equality in principle. The twentieth century has given us repeated examples of the same tendency in socialist and communist countries, as well as capitalist and fascist ones. It seems that elites are with us to stay, by virtue of their power to exclude others from positions of advantage. We would find the same thing if we were to study union elites rather than corporate elites!

Exclusion and Professionalization

We also find exclusion in the job market. Increasingly, access to high-paying jobs has required a credential, often in the form of an educational degree, that proves that its possessor has qualified for selection. Degrees from medical schools are particularly valuable in this way, since almost no doctors are unemployed or poorly paid. Who decides how these scarce degrees will be handed out—who will get them, and in return for what investments?

To practise medicine, a person needs a medical degree and a licence. In the end, this requirement protects doctors as much as it protects their patients: it is a mechanism of exclusion. We see exclusion at work in the continuing battles over health care—the debates about who shall pay and who is entitled to receive how much; and the exclusion of such competitors as chiropractors, homeopaths, and midwives from public recognition and coverage under public health plans. The medical monopoly on health activities that generate high incomes prevents competent nurses, paramedics, and other health professionals from enjoying similar rewards.

Doctors acquired this power to exclude others in the field of health care by "professionalizing" the business of medicine. In North America, professionalization has been part of the general rise of the middle class through its own efforts—and especially, through the creation of "careers." The notion of "career" is a relatively new idea tied to the growth of a new middle class, the expansion of higher education, and the spread of a new demand for more credentials for more people (Bledstein, 1976).

In other countries—France, Germany, Russia, and Italy among them—it was the state that brought professions into being. For example, Napoleon instituded national schools of engineering as breeding grounds for higher-level civil servants (Larson, 1977). In these countries, the state took the lead in modernizing the society. It shaped the professions—their training, credentials, and career paths—from the top down. Professionalization was part of national economic and political planning.

In the United States, professionalization was largely a matter of self-initiated upward mobility. It was a process that satisfied the American hunger for stable sources of authority in a rootless democratic society. This difference may help to explain why, in the United States, the professions are neither part of an overall social plan, nor easily ruled by any state authority. American professionals largely set their own income and social status, and are free from many state-imposed controls. In contrast, Canada had followed the state-regulated European model somewhat more closely. This largely explains why many Canadian medical graduates settle in the United States.

The organization of the American health industry on these lines has had two notable results. The first is that American doctors are richer, on average, than Canadian doctors. The second is that an estimated 37 million Americans have no guaranteed access to health care: they can't afford to carry private health insurance. (*U.S. News and World Report*, May 10, 1993, p. 81). Many simply cannot afford to get treated, if sick.

Professional interests are protected by professional associations. In many respects, these associations are little different from trade unions. Both aim to protect and promote the economic interests of their members. They differ in two important respects, however. First, professional associations help middle-class people protect middle-class incomes, and unions help working-class people protect working-class incomes. Second, professional associations use special means to protect their members. Unions typically strike, or threaten to strike, to increase workers' incomes; they employ collective means to pursue collective guarantees for their members. Professional associations tend to rely on political lobbying and the manipulation of public sentiment through the mass media.

In this way, professional associations help their members earn whatever the market will bear, while maintaining an image of moral concern. Because of the higher social origins of professionals, people are more willing to believe that professional associations and their members really act in the public interest. The evidence does not support this belief.

In North America and elsewhere, the reduction of illness and mortality has owed more to public works (sewage and garbage management, clean water, and so on) than to the work of practising physicians. Even today, medical associations show little interest in workplace safety, environmental pollution, and many other campaigns against major causes of illness and death. Instead, medicine—especially American medicine—increasingly addresses itself to high-tech, high-cost remedies that benefit only a very few: for example, the recipients of organ transplants.

The example of medicine shows clearly that successful professionalization gives restricted groups the power to exclude others and to control public and private spending on specialized services.

Exclusion and Ethnic Organization

Another kind of exclusion is based on ethnic or racial origin. All ethnic groups practise exclusion to some degree, but they vary widely in this respect. That is because minority ethnic communities differ as much from one another as they do from the dominant Anglo-Saxon community.

Ethnic community organization—the term that we shall use to refer to the "institutional completeness" studied by Breton (1964)—is what makes this kind of exclusion possible. An ethnic community that is highly organized has created enough social, cultural, and economic organizations to insulate its members from the rest of society. These organizations include schools, summer camps, churches, business associations, social clubs, and credit unions. They all provide a context within which community members can meet and do business with other community members. These organizations make people more conscious of their common ethnic origins. Like professional associations and unions, these organizations press for group interests.

In Canada, the degree of a community's ethnic organization is largely determined by the number of problems immigrants face on arrival, as well as by certain characteristics of the immigrants themselves. Some groups face serious discrimination on their arrival in Canada. (When we speak of "discrimination," we are usually referring to exclusion practised by the majority against a minority group.) Living in a highly organized community can protect immigrants from a hostile social environment. The Jews and Chinese, both victims of serious discrimination, have practised this strategy as a means of protecting themselves in Canada.

Other groups that have suffered discrimination have little opportunity to practise exclusion in their own interest. For example, Canadian blacks are in a worse position than the Jews and the Chinese. They suffer severe discrimination, yet lack the ethnic organization that would help them prosper. One important reason for this is that blacks come from different continents and a variety of cultural backgrounds.

A recent study of ethnic groups in Toronto (Breton et al., 1990) suggests that various ethnic minorities have adjusted to inequality and discrimination in different ways. Some have remained outside the mainstream of society. Members of most, however, have "to a considerable degree ... become full participants in the social fabric of Canadian society: ... they become incorporated in its social and institutional life." This involvement in the larger society does not rule out the retention of an ethnic identity or collective goals. "It is not necessarily true that if members of a group are fully incorporated in Canadian society they have abandoned all elements of their ethnic identity and background" (Breton et al., 1990, p. 263). In principle, then, a person can be very much involved in both an ethnic group and the larger society.

The same study finds that, contrary to what Porter (1965) had suggested, "cultural retention does not necessarily retard or impede incorporation [in the broader society]; it may facilitate it" (Breton et al., 1990, p. 263). If an ethnic group makes a wide variety of resources and contacts available to its members, these may be used to enter the wider society more successfully.

How do ethnic minority groups retain their identity in Canadian society? According to Breton et al., different groups exhibit different patterns of group survival. For some groups, residential or occupational segregation may be most important. Generally, however, retention and use of the ethnic language plays a key part in keeping the community together.

Writing in 1965, Porter predicted that acquiring a Canadian education and assimilating into the Canadian culture would allow members of ethnic minorities to attain economic equality with the majority group. However, Agocs and Boyd (1993) have found that this has not been the case.

> The expectation that ethnic occupational inequality would diminish or disappear, as ethnic groups acquired educational credentials and became culturally assimilated into Canadian society, has proved illusory. The strategy of investment in human capital has not led to equality for racial minorities and women, and the First Nations, who have been the targets of aggressive policies intended to result in their assimilation, have resisted and survived as distinct peoples (p. 346).

Most ethnic minorities are still not represented among the Canadian economic elite. This is not to deny that some ethnic communities and some individuals within those communities have prospered. The strategy that the most successful among them have employed, both to insulate their members and to promote their interests in the wider community, is the practice of exclusion.

DISABILITY

As we grow up, we learn to play our social roles reasonably well. Socialization teaches us how and why to conform to cultural values and social norms. But socialization also teaches us how *not* to function in our social roles. This crippling socialization, which we all receive, is *social disability* (or *disability*, for short). For many people, disability means learning ways of thinking about ourselves that make us less than what we might otherwise be. Disability is any kind of socialization that induces low self-esteem, a low sense of mastery and control, alienation, and distrust. It arises from training or experience that makes people believe that they cannot and should not try to do what they want to do. This kind of socialization leads to lower aspirations, a lack of assertiveness, and even withdrawal from competition.

Consider a widespread but somewhat unexplored example of disability: the "relative age effect." Researchers studying people's performance in baseball (Thompson, Barnsley, & Stebelsky, 1991), hockey (Barnsley & Thompson, 1988), and even grade school (Barnsley & Thompson, 1985) have concluded that, wherever age cut-offs bring together children of somewhat different ages, the older children will benefit. By competing against children who are typically smaller, weaker, and less developed, they will succeed more often than fail: "The overall result is greater skill development and, just as important, a greatly enhanced level of self-confidence and perceived self-efficacy ... [But also,] children with a relative age disadvantage may become discouraged and quit the sport" (Thompson, Barnsey, & Stebelsky, 1991, p. 147).

We are all more or less disabled from the time we are born. Youngsters are routinely taught that there are a great many things they cannot understand because they lack the necessary experience, wisdom, and insight. They are told to wait until they are older; then, presumably, they will understand, and see that their elders were right. Youngsters have their age held against them; their ability goes untested.

Often, old people are also treated like children, as if they lacked common sense and insight. From the moment people are forced to retire from the work force, we pamper and ignore them, and no longer treat them as adults. Age is held against older people as well; their ability also goes untested.

Women make up the largest number of socially disabled people in our society. They are denied the chance to try a great many things; they are taught that they cannot do them and should not want to. For example, until a recent Supreme Court decision, Canadian females were kept from trying out for male hockey teams. Even today, women continue to play a more limited role than men in the Canadian Armed Forces. Traditional notions of "femininity" are as limiting to women as the bustles and other encumbering clothes women used to wear a century ago.

Often, we take notice of problems such as ageism and sexism one at a time, as though they were unrelated. This is known as "exceptionalism," and it is an error that we must avoid. Problems of disability are common to young people, old people, women, the poor (see, for example, Lewis, 1966; Sennett & Cobb, 1973), the unemployed (Grayson, 1986; Schlozman & Verba, 1979), and the stigmatized (Goffman, 1963; Lemert, 1972), among others. As Mills (1943) pointed out, the problems of all these groups have a great deal in common. The common element is our society's dominant ideology—specifically, the ideas that our culture promotes about success and failure.

The dominant ideology teaches all of us, including those of us who are victimized by the class structure, to blame ourselves (Ryan, 1976). That is why over two-thirds of Canadians surveyed in the Quality of Life (1981) survey said that what you get out of life is your own doing. Accordingly, eight in every ten respondents felt that people should try to improve their position, rather than accept it, and that people's problems are never too big to keep them from running their lives the way they want to. Nearly half of all Canadians expressed the belief that people should set goals that are hard to achieve. A committed person can overcome all odds, according to this way of thinking.

This shows that many Canadians hold "individualistic" views about wealth and poverty—just like the adult Texans discussed at the start of this chapter.

But Canadians are also taught to expect failure. That is why nearly two Canadians in three questioned in the Quality of Life survey said that people should lower their hopes to avoid disappointment in life. Almost as many felt that people should be content with what they have, since you never know the future. People are largely resigned to the limits on their opportunity. This shows that a great many Canadians hold what we earlier called "fatalist" or "structuralist" views about the causes of wealth and poverty.

The wide acceptance of *both* kinds of views, structuralist and individualistic—often by the very same people—suggests that a great many Canadians are ambivalent about their chances for life satisfaction. In a sense, everyone knows about things like exclusion, disability, decoupling, and scarcity. But people rarely confront such knowledge consciously and rationally, then take the appropriate action. Our thinking is largely "ideological," based on acquired beliefs that we keep insulated from reality and everyday experience.

Moreover, these beliefs are very old—about 350 years old, to be precise. Political theorist C.B. Macpherson (1962) has called the entire package of beliefs "possessive individualism." This "possessive individualism" is at the root of our culture. Others have called these same beliefs the principles of "laissez-faire capitalism," "liberal democracy," and the "liberal ideology."

Whatever we call it, this set of beliefs emphasizes the rights of individuals against government interference, and protects people's rights to carry out economic exchange however they want, as long as they do not break any laws.

Liberal democracy rests on (supposedly) free choice, free competition, and a free market in labour, goods, and ideas (Macpherson, 1965). These freedoms apply to all citizens alike. As Anatole France said, the law treats people equally, equally forbidding rich and poor to sleep under bridges. We usually find freedom of this kind in societies with a capitalist economy, universal suffrage, and two or more political parties.

But given that there is social inequality, so that people set out from unequal starting points, freedom *from* interference is not the same as freedom *to* live a full and equal life. Under liberal democracy, freedom comes into conflict with fairness. That is because liberal democracy holds people responsible for protecting their own interests. It denies that any collective interests—for example, interests in environmental protection and world peace—may be more important than individual interests. It also forgets that some people are less able to protect their own interests than other people.

Nevertheless, our "institutions of information"—the mass media, churches, and even schools—continue to spread the belief that people are free to make their lives whatever they want to. Hard work and merit are rewarded. Sloth and crime are punished. Government and other collective bodies—especially trade unions—actively interfere with people's right to choose. These kinds of ideas, trumpeted by leaders of business through the mass media they control, are appealing enough to survive year after year.

Yet our own experiences tell us that these ideas are false (see, for example, Marchak, 1987). People we know are often *not* rewarded for hard work and merit. At the same time, the upper classes inherit enormous wealth, generation after generation. These facts tell us that hard work and merit have little to do with rewards. Moreover, corporate crime, government patronage, and tax laws that favour the rich over the poor all prove that the cards are stacked against ordinary people, however hardworking they may be.

What keeps our society together in the face of this systematic inequality and demonstrated untruth? Surveying studies of public opinion from several capitalist countries, Mann (1970) finds little evidence that people generally agree with the central tenets of liberal democracy. To a large degree, it is people's ambivalence that keeps the system working. "Cohesion in liberal democracy depends on the lack of consistent commitment to general values of any sort and on the 'pragmatic acceptance' by subordinate classes of their limited roles in society" (Mann, 1970, p. 423).

Mann also finds evidence that *false consciousness* has a role in maintaining order and social cohesion. False consciousness is a view of society that incorrectly describes everyday reality to disadvantaged people. For example, it holds disadvantaged people responsible for circumstances beyond their control, and in that way, it disables them.

This is why a person who is unable to find work is likely to blame personal failings rather than the high unemployment rate, discrimination, business mismanagement, or poor handling of the economy by the government. It explains why a two-earner family that is struggling unsuccessfully to meet all its obligations may turn its aggression inward: spouse against spouse, parent against child, child against parent. In this way family members end up destroying their family, rather than blame exploitive employers or bad government—not easy targets to attack.

Mann (1970) argues that false consciousness disables voters. The main political parties lead voters to believe in vague political philosophies that contradict their everyday experience and support the status quo; the politicians appeal to patriotism, tradition, harmony, and national unity, to mask their economic failings. In this way, voters are disabled by their own optimism and gullibility.

People are also disabled by failed attempts to change their circumstances. Consider the case of workers who lost their jobs when two Canadian factories closed down. Grayson (1986) shows that former employees and their spouses were not radicalized by the experience: they did not reject the traditonal ways of influencing government that had failed to save their jobs. They simply felt more powerless than ever. Grayson (1986, p. 347) writes, "Because of the sense of inefficacy that afflicts the victims of plant exclusions, unions and politicians will have to fight even harder" to prevent and remedy shutdowns.

Below these types of false consciousness—a willingness to blame oneself, a readiness to re-invest in the status quo, a tendency to see public issues as personal problems—we find a more general set of illusory beliefs about social inequality. In our society, people have been taught to believe that social inequality—even extreme inequality—is necessary and useful. Further, they have been taught that people at the top of the heap deserve to be there. This belief shows up even among children. Baldus and Tribe (1978) studied the social perceptions of schoolchildren. By Grade 6, a high proportion have learned to group social class indicators together: they know that fancy clothes, a nice house, a new car, and so on "go together." They have also come to believe that people with good clothes, houses, and cars care more about their appearance and are trying harder than anyone else. Finally, they believe that richer people are "nicer" and "better" than anyone else: more honest, better behaved, and harder working.

Children from poor families are just as likely as children from rich families to make these judgements. (In this respect, they resemble our sample of Texan adults.) Moreover, these beliefs grow stronger and more consistent with age. The result is what Sennett and Cobb (1973) have called "hidden injuries of class." People who are neither rich, nor powerful, nor famous cannot easily live with such a negative image of themselves. Rather than working for social change, they pour their energy into making themselves feel better.

One way to cope is by humiliating other people who are even less powerful: poor whites discriminating against poor blacks; poor men dominating their wives and children; children tormenting other children or pets. Another way is by using "dreams and defences" to soothe hidden injuries (Sennett & Cobb, 1973). If people feel worthless, they dream of becoming "worthwhile" through promotion at work, winning a lottery, or some other stroke of good fortune. Women's romance books and magazines dwell on this dream. A third way of coping is through the use of humour. Simon (1990) reports that although humour doesn't increase life satisfaction, it does help people keep their spirits up in the face of adversity.

People also try to defend themselves against their feelings of worthlessness by splitting the "real person" from the "performing person." That is, they try not to feel that they belong to the despised and menial role they play. They think: "In reality, I am someone else: not Clark Kent, but Superman. I possess incredible hidden powers that I will reveal at just the right moment. Then people will admire me." This theme of the dual or hidden personality runs throughout mass entertainment.

This "split personality" defence gives many people temporary relief from the effects of a cruel social order. "It stills pain in the short run, [even though it] does not remove the conditions that made a defence necessary in the first place" (Sennett & Cobb, 1973, p. 219). Defences that they erect against feelings of worthlessness and powerlessness allow life to go on; however, they also keep people from fighting the system of inequality that is at the root of their troubles.

Does religion function in the same way? Marx characterized religion as an "opiate" of the people, in that it deadened them to the pain of inequality and injustice. Yet this appears to be more true of some religions than others. Also, similar religious beliefs may not have uniform effects in this regard. For example, Fazel and Young (1988) find that Tibetan refugees in India display more life satisfaction than local Indian Hindus, despite language problems and fewer financial resources. Though both the Hindus and Tibetans subscribe to a fatalistic attitude of *karma*, the Tibetans adopt a "proactive" posture, compared with the "reactive fatalism" of the Hindus.

In the end, minimizing the pain of a disability can take a person only so far toward satisfaction. A much more effective (if self-deluding) strategy is illustrated by Australians. Headey and Wearing (1988) write that, as a group, Australians report a high level of satisfaction, or "subjective well-being." They attribute this to the tendency of Australians to experience a sense of relative superiority in every area of their lives. For example, about 86 percent of Australians report that they perform above average in their main job; only 1 percent report performing below average. They achieve this feat of self-congratulation by giving particular weight (in their own minds) to things that really are going smoothly, and comparing themselves with reference groups that are, as the authors say, "restricted." This attitude deters them from perceiving actual problems with their own performance and taking corrective action.

In the end we are left with what satisfaction researchers have called the "satisfaction-paradox": namely, reports of positive life satisfaction from people who are living in poverty (or are objectively disadvantaged in another way). Olson and Schober (1993) provide an inventory of explanations often encountered in the literature dealing with this question. Finally, they opt for the explanation of "learned helplessness"—the equivalent to what I am calling "disability."

According to this "learned helplessness" theory, poor people may be happy because they feel they cannot control their own lives. They also feel that they are right to develop long-term dependence on the assistance others provide, even if that assistance was originally intended only for emergencies.

In this sense, people who have learned helplessness, or have learned to be "disabled," have come to expect little of themselves. They are like people who admit to an addiction (such as alcoholism), a compulsion (such as gambling) or a deep character flaw (such as an inability to tell the truth), and are happy they have faced the problem, though they feel they cannot hope to cure it.

DECOUPLING

A third limit on opportunity is *decoupling*. Often without knowing it, people are disconnected from the main sources of opportunity and power in society, and they suffer as a result.

The word "decoupling" makes us think of a disconnected railway car that has been shunted on to a side track. Like train cars, people are connected to one another and often pull one another forward and back. Contrary to the dominant ideology that holds each of us personally responsible for his or her own fate, much of what happens in life results from the actions of others, many unknown and distantly connected to us.

Consider how the careers of ministers are shaped by very distant events. The job vacancy created by a minister's death or retirement may set off a chain reaction and lead to the upward movement of dozens of other ministers (White, 1970). For this reason, social mobility is as much the result of "vacancy chains" as of the accomplishment of the individuals promoted. Depending on economic conditions, an initial change (such as retirement or death) may produce a longer or shorter chain of reactions. Sometimes the organization eliminates the departed person's job, makes it into a part-time job, or fills the job with a newcomer brought in from outside. In that case, no one inside the organization benefits. These kinds of reactions are probably most common in organizations "downsizing" in the face of economic difficulty.

Even when a vacancy chain fails to operate, however, your opportunities still rely on your contacts with other people. This fact is brought out clearly in studies of the Canadian upper class (for example, Clement, 1975; Newman, 1979; Porter, 1965). Upper-class people are tied to one another by a variety of activities and experiences: marriage; kinship; attendance at the same private schools, summer camps, and universities; membership in the same social clubs; and service on the same boards of directors. The small size of the Canadian upper class—perhaps a few thousand families—makes it easy to know most other members. Its communal organization produces collegiality through sharing of experiences. Upper-class institutions and activities are just as exclusive as the ethnic institutions discussed earlier, and for many of the same reasons. Upper-class people have property interests to protect against demands by the government and the lower classes. Wide contacts among upper-class people form the basis for recruitment into elite positions.

Social contacts are important in every social class. A survey of managers showed that people typically find the best white-collar jobs through personal contacts (Granovetter, 1974). That is because employers know that hiring through networks of personal contact is the simplest, most trustworthy way of hiring. Many people have suitable qualifications. If a job opening is advertised, the employer will have to screen and interview many applicants. Investigating every applicant to find the best would be very expensive. So employers often ask their personal contacts—people they know and trust—to recommend someone for the job. In this way, the employer can find someone with the right qualifications at relatively little cost. That person may not be the best candidate, but will be good enough to do the job. Employers want a satisfactory candidate, not a perfect one.

This method of hiring also gives the employer information that is unlikely to surface in a candidate's résumé. It often provides information about the candidate's personal habits and attitudes. The candidate who is recommended by a trusted acquaintance probably has the right attitude as well as credentials.

This strategy is not limited to employers. People find jobs in the same way as employers find job candidates. For their part, job-seekers want to know if the job is a good one, the boss a good boss, the prospects for advancement bright, and so on. They are bound to find out more by talking to an acquaintance with first-hand knowledge of the organization, the job, and the boss than in any other way. Impersonal sources of information such as organizational brochures and formal interviews are less likely to reveal much.

So on both sides of the job market—among people who are hiring and people who want to be hired—networks of personal contact provide the best information. As a result, many jobs find people, and people find jobs, through networks of personal contact.

Granovetter found that the most valuable job information is passed on by acquaintances. "Acquaintances" are people you call by their first name, but who are not close friends. Because we have a great many more acquaintances than close friends, we are more likely to get useful information from an acquaintance. As well, close friends tend to have the same information about jobs. They are likely to know the same people and the same things. By contrast, acquaintances are more likely to know many other people and, therefore, more useful information.

Acquaintance networks can become very large indeed, numbering hundreds and even thousands of people. In theory, therefore, job referral chains could be enormously long. In practice, though, they are not. People do not trust information that comes from someone at five removes any more than they trust information from a stranger. That is because we live in a "small world," as psychologist Stanley Milgram showed in his studies of social networks (Travers & Milgram, 1969). People are likely to have thousands, even tens of thousands, of acquaintances at five removes. At ten or fifteen removes, every pair of people in the country probably has someone in common. Therefore, in practice, only acquaintances and acquaintances of acquaintances are likely to pass on valuable job information.

Each acquaintance provides you with information and connections that other acquaintances are unlikely to duplicate. That explains why acquaintances are so valuable in helping you find a job. Your chances of hearing about a job or having an employer hear about you are best if you have many acquaintances.

Granovetter found that people who have changed organizations often have many such acquaintances. In fact, a person changing jobs three or four times over fifteen years might end up knowing people in 30 or 40 different companies. (Remember, that person's acquaintances have also been changing companies.) People who stay in any given job for an average of three to five years seem to do best.

Further, people who begin moving between organizations early in their careers seem to benefit most. This process creates a "snowballing" of career opportunities over time. By contrast, people who stay with the same organization for much of their working life have trouble finding a new job when forced to do so.

In higher-status jobs, making many contacts and then moving on to another organization seems the career strategy that best avoids decoupling. However, this strategy will work better for some people than for others. First, some organizations value stability and loyalty; they might distrust workers who have moved every three to five years. Second, people seeking careers within ethnic communities might do better by maintaining contact with old friends and kin, not by seeking new acquaintances.

The value of acquaintanceships for finding good jobs within ethnic communities will vary according to the kinds of jobs the ethnic community controls. For example, acquaintanceship will be much more likely to uncover a good job in the prosperous and economically diverse

Jewish or Italian communities than in the Portuguese or West Indian communities.

The process Granovetter describes may favour rich or highly educated people. Such people usually have much larger and more varied networks of contact than poorer, less educated people. They also have more time and money to travel, meet people, and interact socially. All these activities help richer people form acquaintanceships. Also, because they have higher status and more access to scarce resources, higher-status people are likely to receive more attention from other people. Lower-status people seek out higher-status people for advice, encouragement, and help. This gives higher-status people a great many contacts at very little effort. Finally, as we noted earlier, elite and upper-class institutions bring higher-status people together on a regular basis.

Yet working-class people make use of personal contacts, too. They are likely to find their first job through friends and relatives in a similar line of work. Later in life, they start finding jobs by answering advertisements and other formal means. Middle-class people do the opposite: they use their educational credentials to find a first job, then they find later jobs through acquaintances they have met at work.

The networking process works *against* groups who are underrepresented in the better jobs and socially decoupled from the dominant group. For example, whites usually make the acquaintance of other whites, and men the acquaintance of other men. When asked to recommend people for jobs, white men will tend to recommend other white men. Even without intending to discriminate, the process has a discriminatory outcome in that the organization remains racially or sexually unbalanced.

A final point is that decoupling affects not only your chances of getting what you want, it also affects your life satisfaction directly. Burt (1987) has shown that people with larger networks of acquaintances are happier than people with smaller networks, even after taking into account differences in socio-economic status, age, sex, race, and marital status. It is *acquaintances* who are key here, not friends or relatives. Burt finds that the presence of close relations has no positive effect on people's happiness, while the presence of strangers has a negative effect.

SCARCITY

A fourth reason for limited opportunity is that, often, there is too little to go around: what people want is in short supply. *Scarcity* varies with the ratio of competitors to desired goods. Thus, it can be reduced by eliminating competitors through the practice of exclusion, disability, and decoupling. It can also be reduced by increasing the supply of goods to be shared out.

We see scarcity all around us. The poor may be its greatest victims, but most of us suffer from scarcity some of the time. Increasingly, the middle classes are being subjected to scarcity, as witnessed by the falling opportunity of young adults to own homes as their parents had done (Berljawsky, 1986). The gap that separates the rich from everyone else has been widening. As the rich get even richer, the rest get poorer and the traditional middle class disappears.

Beyond this material deprivation, we find "social limits to growth" (Hirsch, 1978) expressed in a growing *sense* of scarcity. Increasingly, people value scarce items—the unique vacation, the unusual home, designer clothing, and so on—*because* they are scarce. People want something that is all their own in a society of increasing uniformity. The sheer growth in our numbers makes this goal more and more attractive and yet harder to attain.

Often we adapt by giving up something that we have long valued and even loved. We give up going to a beach that was once secluded, a perfect refuge, and is now packed with noisy portable stereo players. We give up going back to our home town, where everyone once knew everyone else; now it is a bedroom suburb full of strangers. We give up going to a restaurant that used to be wonderful; today, it is full of plastic, junk food, and Walt Disney decor. Can we replace these lost pleasures?

It is becoming ever more difficult to enjoy the truly scarce qualities of quiet, good craftsmanship, privacy, and politeness. We cannot bring the old things back, and only if we have a great deal of money can we replace them. So, like employers searching for job candidates, we seek satisfactory, though imperfect, solutions. This may mean looking at our choices in a new way and giving value to things we had not valued before. Consider the problem in scarcity that demographers have called the "marriage squeeze."

Between 1945 and 1957, more babies were born each year than in the year before. Of these, roughly half were male and half were female. But women tend to marry men who are a few years older. A woman about 30 years old in 1987 would find a shortage, or scarcity, of men between 33 and 35 years old. Men of this age would have been born between 1952 and 1954, and fewer men were born in each of these years than were born in each of the years 1955 through 1957, when the woman in question was born. This is the "marriage squeeze" from the standpoint of a single woman about 30 years old in 1987.

As you might imagine, the situation eventually reverses. A woman about 30 years old in 1992 would find no shortage of men several years older, since more males were still being born in each of the years 1959 through 1961 than females in 1962 through 1964. So there is a shortage of brides, a marriage squeeze, for single men under 25 years old in 1992.

People use creative strategies to deal with scarcity. In response to these marriage squeezes, many traditional constraints on mate selection are disappearing. First, people are marrying mates who, in the past, might have been considered too old or too young. Others are marrying outside their own racial and ethnic groups. More often than before, people are marrying previously married people and people from other social classes.

Many others choose unmarried motherhood or sequential cohabitation. Still others find fulfilment in a single life by putting their energies into work, leisure, and friendship. Singles today are not stigmatized as they were in the past. So, we see that adjustments to the marriage squeeze are both personal and cultural; they include new conceptions of adult life, family, and marriage. Making adjustments always helps in the face of scarcity.

Scarcity is a normal state of affairs, but it is not inevitable. Often, it is due to exclusion—the monopolization of desired goods by people powerful enough to control access to them. The powerful can always get far more than their share of what everyone wants: money, good housing, respect, and so on. Marx and Engels (Meek, 1954) argued that capitalism itself tends to produce scarcity. Capitalists want a large "reserve army of the unemployed" to keep down wages, and they want shortages to keep up prices. Moreover, with the technical improvements in capitalist production, certain jobs are bound to disappear. The investment in technology rises continually and the capital invested in workers' wages falls. According to this theory, capitalism creates too few, indeed ever fewer, jobs; prices rise; and inequality increases steadily.

The nineteenth-century English Luddites tried to solve this problem by breaking the new machinery introduced into the factories where they worked. But the best long-term answer to this problem is to break the monopolies on production and prices. Marx believed that a political revolution was needed. Most North Americans however, reject this solution. They prefer higher productivity as a solution to the problem of scarcity. Typically, high rates of economic growth give most people more of the goods they want without breaking the existing monopolies. Such growth makes inequality less visible and less painful.

It is becoming harder and harder to ignore the effect of our own society's prosperity on other parts of the world. Canada's prosperity has been achieved partly by making less developed countries our source of cheap resources and labour power. We have solved the problem of local

Exhibit 2.3
The indebtedness of developing nations

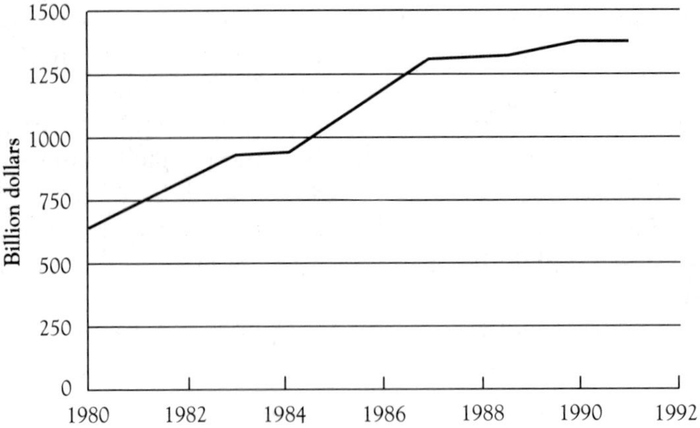

Figure a: External Debt of Developing Countries, 1980–91

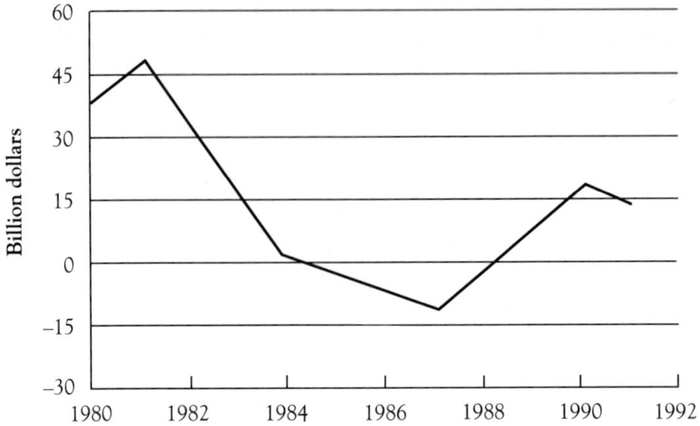

Figure b: Net Movement of Public and Private Capital from Industrial to Developing Countries, 1980–91

Source: Brown, L.R., et al. (1992). *Vital signs* (p. 69). Worldwatch Institute. New York: W.W. Norton. Reprinted with permission.

scarcity by exporting it, worsening the economic situation of others in order to improve our own. The primary needs for food, shelter, and physical security are simply not being met for many people today in many parts of the world. More economic growth is only part of the solution. Parts of the Third World remain locked out of the benefits of economic growth and locked into huge amounts of debt (see Exhibit 2.3).

In our own society, professional associations, workers' unions, ethnic groups, and others use monopolization to their own advantage. In the long run, this strategy cannot succeed. If every collectivity in the world mobilizes to gain a greater advantage over every other, inequality will take more aggressive forms. Compare the situation to a crowd of people who have gathered to watch a parade. At first, a few people stand on their toes to see the parade better; then a few more; and so on. When everyone is standing on tiptoe, the spectators' ability to see the parade is as unequal as it was before, and everyone has sore toes.

Long-run solutions to the problem of unequal opportunity must be worldwide and co-operative. Anything less will result in economic and political conflict, and even warfare.

Working against the human race are greed, extreme and widening inequality, and rapid population growth. Working in its favour is a proven ability to use knowledge and science creatively, adapt to new circumstances, and (occasionally) to co-operate for mutual benefit. The European Community provides an example of an attempt at this kind of co-operation.

A BRIEF DISCUSSION OF THE POOR

Knowing the four limits on opportunity should help us understand the problem of poverty, and the powerlessness and low status that are associated with it.

Sociologists distinguish between relative and absolute poverty. *Absolute poverty* refers to the lack of the basic necessities—including food, shelter, and medicine—for physical survival. *Relative poverty* is defined by the general living standards of the society or social group, and refers to the gap between the incomes of its better-off and worse-off members. What is considered "poor" varies from one society to another and, within a given society, from one group to another. In Canada, we consider people with much less than the average income to be "poor."

According to the data in Exhibit 2.4, the countries having the widest gap between rich and poor are developing nations such as Turkey, Mexico, and Brazil. Yet Canada's distribution of wealth is far from egalitarian: it lies somewhere between that of the United Kingdom and the United States.

What does it mean to be "poor"—to have much less income than other people? That question may be answered in a great many ways.

Exhibit 2.4

Approximate income distribution of most populous nations, and of world, most recent available year[a]

		Share of National Income		
Country	**Year**	**Poorest 20 percent of households**	**Richest 20 percent of households**	**Ratio of richest share to poorest**
China (cities)	1984	12	31	3
Soviet Union	1980	9	36	4
Japan	1979	9	37	4
West Germany	1978	8	40	5
United Kingdom	1982	7	40	6
Italy	1977	6	44	7
Indonesia	1976	7	49	8
Egypt	1974	6	48	8
India	1976	5	50	10
Philippines	1985	5	53	10
United States	1986	4	46	12
France	1975	4	50	13
Turkey	1973	4	57	16
Mexico	1977	3	54	18
Brazil	1982	2	64	28
World[b]	1985	4	58	15

[a] Equity ratios are based on unrounded income share figures and therefore may appear inconsistent with income shares listed.
[b] Estimated from average national incomes; income distribution based on individual incomes is much less equitable.

Source: Brown, L.R., et al. (1992). *Vital signs* (p. 111). Worldwatch Institute. New York: W.W. Norton. Reprinted with permission.

Here, we shall consider just one effect of poverty. Data presented in Exhibit 2.5 show the relationship between income and life expectancy. Men who live in the richest neighbourhoods of Canadian cities—presumably, rich men—live nearly six years longer, on average, than men who live in the poorest neighbourhoods. (The difference is smaller for rich and poor women.)

Income inequality appears to be increasing in Canada, and so is poverty. In 1989, Health and Welfare Canada (1989, p. 35) reported that "the incidence of low income among Canadians [had] fallen from

Exhibit 2.5
Life expectancy of males by neighbourhood income, 1986

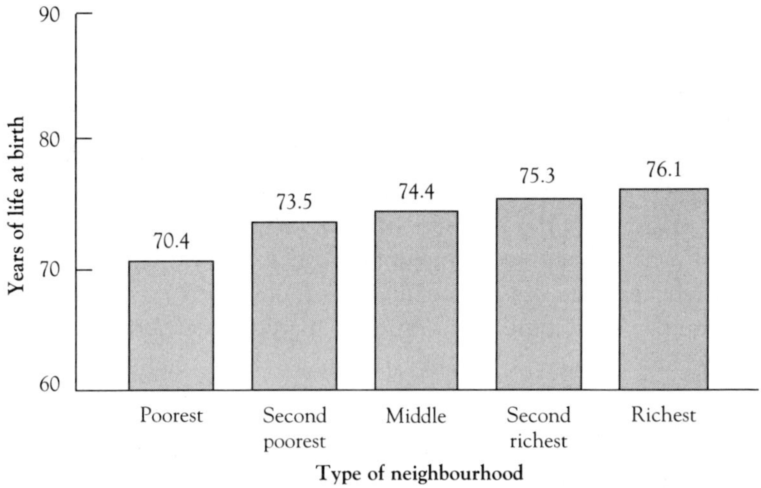

Source: Health Reports Vol. 1, No. 2. Reproduced with the permission of the Minister of Supply and Services Canada, 1993.

26 to 15 percent." It attributed this decline to improvements in coverage and benefits in the social security system. Recent reports, however, suggest a reversal of this trend. The percentage of Canadian children in poor, or "low-income," families fell from 17.3 percent in 1987 to 15 percent in 1989, but climbed again to 17.4 percent in 1990 (*The Globe and Mail*, December 28, 1991, p. A9).

The government measures poverty by establishing "low-income cut-off points," which vary with family size and the size of the community. Larger families who live in larger communities require more income to maintain the same standard of living as smaller families in smaller communities. The guiding principle is that 58.5 percent or more of a low-income person's or family's income is spent on food, shelter, and clothing. Each year, statisticians account for changes in the cost of living by updating the specific monetary cut-off lines, using the Consumer Price Index.

Methot (1987) reports that low incomes are more common than average among families whose head has completed little formal education; is not in the labour force at all; did not work full-time all year long; or has experienced some unemployment during the year. The incidence of low income is greatest in families with three or more children, and in families headed by mothers (most of which are single-parent families). Nearly half of all single-parent families headed by women have low incomes, a percentage that has increased since 1981. Indeed, families headed by lone female parents make up about one-third of all low-income families (Methot, 1987, p. 2). This growing problem has been called the *feminization of poverty*.

Among unattached individuals, the incidence of low income is highest among the young (those under age 25), the old (those 65 and over), and women. The explanation for this is largely that these groups are least likely to be in the paid labour force or to hold a well-paying job.

Finally, a higher than average proportion of families in Quebec and the Atlantic provinces (especially Newfoundland) have a low income. In general, low incomes are common in regions where unemployment and low education are common: namely, in the Canadian hinterlands.

> In Canada's many rural and remote communities ... economies are largely based on primary industries such as fishing, forestry, mining and farming. Residents must often contend with weather extremes, physical isolation and limited access to affordable housing, food, clothing, and health and social services. They also tend to be unemployed more frequently and for longer periods of time. (Health and Welfare Canada, 1989, pp. 35, 36)

Examination of provincial welfare legislation leads to the conclusion that the amount of assistance provided to poor people depends on the perceived causes of their poverty. Old people and the physically disabled typically receive the most help: our society tends to consider them the "deserving poor," who are not to be blamed for their condition. Single mothers and the chronically unemployed are more likely to be seen as the "undeserving poor." As a result, they receive less generous and less secure assistance. Social assistance payments to this latter group fail to meet their actual living expenses. This is especially true for people living in large cities where rents and other costs are high.

Many Canadians believe that if social assistance payments were higher than the minimum wage, unemployed people would be reluctant to get off welfare and take a job. Yet many of the unemployed cannot find a job. Many other Canadians resent what they perceive as the luxurious life of the idle welfare recipient. But a report by Statistics Canada (*The Globe and Mail*, December 28, 1991, p. A9) shows that welfare payments to a couple with two children are 30 percent below the poverty line in Ontario and Prince Edward Island—the most generous provinces—and as much as 56 percent below the poverty line in New Brunswick, the least generous.

Exhibit 2.6
People living below Statistics Canada's Low Income Cutoffs (1986 base), 1980–1990

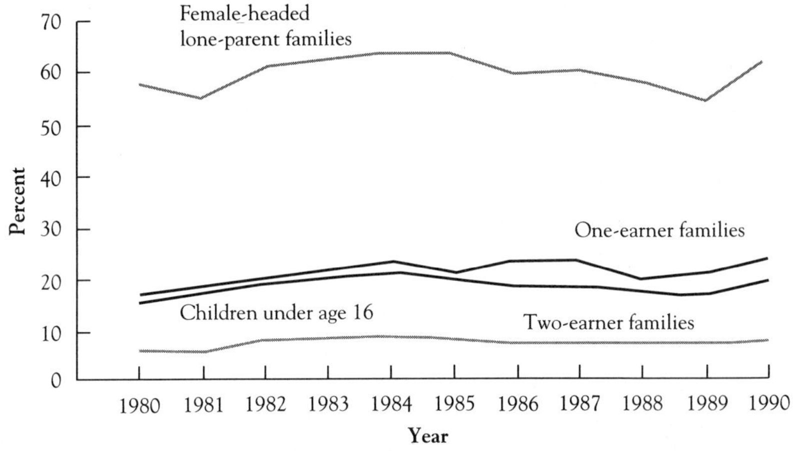

Source: Statistics Canada, Catalogue No. 13–207 and unpublished data. In Spector, A., "Measuring Low Incomes in Canada," *Canadian Social Trends*, Summer 1992, pp. 8–10. Ottawa: Statistics Canada.

Ben-Sira (1986) argues that although welfare assistance may provide for basic living needs, it creates dependence in recipients, who experience a sense of deprivation and feel hostility toward the welfare system itself. In the end, welfare is a source of frustration, not satisfaction. To a great degree, welfare keeps the poor in an inferior position and protects the interests of those who are not poor—including welfare workers.

Much of the poverty problem is caused by unemployment. Since the 1980s, the Canadian unemployment rate has hovered around 10 to 11 percent. In some regions and for some groups the rate has been very much higher. Of the groups most affected, lone female parents of small children often cannot afford to pay the day-care costs that would allow them to take a job. Many of the physically disabled cannot find suitable jobs.

By 1990, over one child in six was living in a low-income family (*The Globe and Mail*, December 28, 1991, p. A9), a proportion that had increased since the early 1980s. (At the same time, the proportion of elderly with low incomes was decreasing.) Of all groups, children are the most numerous victims of poverty. Childhood poverty demonstrates the error in thinking that a poor person has only himself or herself to blame, for it is due to forces beyond children's control: especially, the inability of their parents to find work and the insufficiency of social supports (such as free day care) that would permit the parents to keep a job they had found. Further, since 1981, the greatest increase in numbers of poor children has come among children with two parents (aged 25 to 44) at home. Their poverty problem is not the result of marital breakdown. It stems from economic and social structures in which their parents cannot find work, or can find only poorly paid work.

The poverty problem is not going to be solved without decisive action. This will have to include (1) job creation; (2) job retraining for people whose skills are inappropriate; and (3) social supports, such as cheap, high-quality day care for mothers who need to go out and earn an income. Poverty exists because people are excluded, disabled, and decoupled, and because we live in a system that is committed *not* to eliminating scarcity, but to providing luxury for those who can afford it.

Perhaps better than any other group, the poor illustrate a major point about the four mechanisms of inequality that we have discussed in this chapter: namely, that these mechanisms do not exist independently. More often than not, they work together, so that a group of people who are excluded are also disabled and decoupled. During times of prosperity, these people are usually the last to prosper and those who prosper least; during times of scarcity, they are the most likely to suffer extremes of privation.

CONCLUSION

We started by asking why you will not get everything you want out of life, and why some people will get more of what they want than you will. The answer to both questions is the same: social inequality. A few will enjoy enormous benefits and privileges, and the majority will not. So in one sense, your situation is not only unlike other people's, it is opposed to other people's. As they grow richer, you grow poorer, and vice versa. Yet this view is partly an illusion.

Your opportunities are actually tied up with everyone else's. You share common problems with other people of the same social class, gender, and racial or ethnic group. We have discussed personal, individual remedies in this chapter, and they are important. But in what Canadian social philosopher Marshall McLuhan called the "global village"—the planet Earth—personal remedies have limited long-term value. The structure of social inequality must be changed for you, and most other people, to achieve maximum satisfaction out of life.

We shall discuss other solutions to unequal opportunity in the final chapter. They fall into two main categories: individual and group remedies. The group remedies, as we shall see, take longer but do a better job.

Why you get what you get is the result of an extremely complex set of arrangements that sociologists call *social structure*. The processes of exclusion, disability, decoupling, and scarcity maintain that social structure by limiting what you get, and also by limiting what you want. When a gap develops between what you want and what you can get, the inequalities built into the social structure limit your ability to close that gap.

A great many people today feel that their lives and their acccomplishments are less than they should be. A great many blame themselves, when forces beyond their control and understanding are really to blame. Other people who solve their problems in an ideologically "wrong" way—for example, the "unladylike" woman, or the person who finds a job through acquaintances—think that they are deviant and wonder if they deserve the rewards they get.

Social inequality structures the way we think about our problems. It teaches us to believe that our common problems are actually individual problems, for which we alone are to blame. For this reason, people try to find individual, not collective, solutions to their problems; hold themselves responsible for what they get out of life; and try to close the gap between what they want and what they get by wanting less.

In the rest of this book we shall examine the ways in which social structure affects your aspirations and rewards in a variety of everyday domains.

CHAPTER THREE

◆

EDUCATION:

WHAT YOU WANT AND WHAT YOU GET

INTRODUCTION

This chapter and others that follow examine specific areas of everyday life. In later chapters we shall discuss careers, marriage, child-raising, and other areas in which you will have to make choices as your life progresses. This chapter discusses an area in which you are already involved: the educational choices that you are making, and their likely outcome.

We shall pay particularly attention to two issues that many students wonder about: Why do people make the educational choices they do? and Which choices pay off best, in terms of getting a job, earning a good income, and finding enjoyable work?

You may think you already know everything you need to know about education: after all, you have been sitting in one school or another for ten or fifteen years now. So I'd like to test your knowledge about education by having you answer these true-false questions:

1. People with more education lead more satisfying lives.
   True ___ False ___
2. More education means a more secure job and less chance of unemployment.
   True ___ False ___
3. The more you learn, the more you earn.
   True ___ False ___
4. The more education you have, the more likely you are to find a job doing what you were trained to do.
   True ___ False ___
5. With so many university graduates around, a community college degree is worth more than a BA today.
   True ___ False ___

We'll find out the answers to all of these questions by the end of this chapter. We shall start with a general look at the role education plays in a modern society. Then we shall consider how educational choices determine employability, job satisfaction, income, and social status.

THE PROMISE OF EDUCATION

We've all heard claims about the benefits of education. These claims are centuries old. British philosopher James Mill wrote in the nineteenth century that "if education cannot do everything, there is hardly anything it cannot do" (quoted in Michalos, 1981, p. 94). School reformer Egerton Ryerson promoted free schooling for all children in Upper Canada, arguing that sending rich and poor children to the same schools would bring people closer together and create more harmony (Prentice, 1977, p. 126). Today, many continue to believe in the promise of education. Many believe that education can help solve major social problems such as crime and poverty. Others feel that combating ignorance through schooling will lead to social progress. Still others associate education with personal success.

A 1979 survey conducted by the Ontario Institute for Studies in Education found that 34 percent of the respondents believed that a university or college education was "very important today." By 1986, the proportion had increased to 61 percent (Livingston & Hart, 1991). This reflects the common opinion that education promises personal success: people think of it as a ticket to better-paid, more interesting work and a more enjoyable lifestyle than their parents had (Michalos, 1981, pp. 95–96).

This kind of thinking is consistent with the way our society is organized. Every modern, bureaucratic society needs schools to train its young people and help identify the best candidates for society's most important roles (Hunter, 1988). To accomplish these tasks, schools have to work effectively. That means the educational system has to be open to everyone, maintain high standards, reward good work, apply rules fairly, and teach things that are relevant to the society of which it is a part. But how far has our society moved toward an "effective" school system?

It is clear that higher education changed radically in Canada after World War II. One reason for this radical change was the role played by education promoters like the sociologist John Porter (1979). Another was the launching of Sputnik by the USSR in 1957. This technical coup alarmed the West and alerted educators and policy-makers to the need for more scientific research and training, if the capitalist countries were to compete effectively for world power. A third factor was the baby boom, which brought huge numbers of children to the doors of primary and secondary schools in the 1950s and 1960s, and then to post-secondary schools in the 1960s and 1970s. These three factors largely account for the dramatic changes in Canadian education between 1960 and 1980.

One sign of these changes was the growth in scientific and technical education after 1957. A new kind of postsecondary institution, the community college, was created to offer more students technical and semiprofessional training. Technical and scientific programs expanded in the universities, thanks to more funding from the government.

The result was seen in the graduation of larger numbers of students from bachelor-degree programs in physical science, mathematics, and engineering. The number of students awarded engineering degrees tripled between 1960 and 1980; the number awarded bachelor's degrees in mathematics and physical science increased by one-third between 1970 and 1980. Undergraduate enrollments increased threefold in engineering courses and fivefold in mathematics and science courses between 1960 and 1980 (Statistics Canada, 1985a).

Even the types of students studying mathematics and sciences changed. An increase in the availability of part-time studies opened up higher education to older students and working students. As a result, the proportion of students studying science part-time swelled from 11 percent to 24 percent of all science students between 1970 and 1984. And finally, women broke the traditional male monopoly on mathematics and sciences. Between 1970 and 1984, the proportion of women enrolled grew from 25 percent to 39 percent in mathematics and physical science, and from 2 percent to 11 percent in engineering.

Gradually, enrollments expanded and programs and students became more varied throughout the higher educational system. At the same time, students were given more freedom to choose the courses they wanted. The traditional program of studies in arts and sciences was overhauled.

Not everyone was pleased by these changes. Many continue to argue that postsecondary education has been watered down. Some say that "Canadian universities no longer take only the best students and no longer give their students the best education" (Bercuson, Bothwell, & Granatstein, 1984; for an American critique, see Bloom, 1987). Critics complain that recruitment and grading standards have fallen, and that new kinds of disciplines and programs (for example, Women's Studies, Canadian Studies, and other interdisciplinary courses) have low standards and no scholarly reason for existing.

Recent years have seen a slow return to more highly structured programs and stiffer grading. Nonetheless, the interdisciplinary programs continue to enjoy a wide popularity. Part-time and remedial programs have continued to expand, reaching out to larger and larger numbers of students who would have been excluded in the past. The schools have started to widen their course content to include material from non-European cultural traditions. Increasingly, women enter and graduate from programs that train them for traditionally male-dominated professions (Marshall, 1987). This institutional change has provided a wider variety of students with greater educational choice. Women, older students, and members of previously excluded ethnic and racial minorities have been particular beneficiaries of these changes.

Traditionalists are not the only critics to assail the postsecondary system. During the late 1960s and early 1970s, radical students protested against the "system" and held demonstrations denouncing research in science and technology, which they saw as collaboration in the North American "military-industrial complex." Even during that turbulent period, enrollments in science and engineering continued to grow; since then, enrollments in these programs have skyrocketed.

It is unlikely that colleges and universities will return to limited course offerings, limited program choice, and limited student recruitment. Educational change has occurred, but has it given people what they had hoped for? Does postsecondary education provide the prosperity and high economic returns that reformers thought it would? Has higher education in Canada today delivered on its promise of more opportunity for the traditionally disadvantaged?

WHO GETS A POSTSECONDARY EDUCATION?

Every year, when I begin my Introduction to Sociology course, I ask the huge group of strangers in front of me the following questions: How many of you have parents who were born in another country? (a forest of hands goes up: the vast majority); How many of you belong to the first generation of your family to attend university? (again, a forest of hands goes up: again, the vast majority). I look around the room and see people of every age, colour, size, and shape. I tell them that the University of Toronto is a working-class university for upwardly mobile immigrants. Welcome to the University of Toronto!

Yet if we take Canadian higher education as a whole, white middle-class people continue to be overrepresented. They are overrepresented because they are more likely than other people to fill out the application. This "self-selection" begins long before the end of high school. It is based on gender, place of residence, social class and SES, and ethnicity much more than on ability. Let us examine each of these influences in turn.

Gender

More females than males enter secondary school academic programs. However, women who complete these programs are more likely to go on to a terminal (that is, non-transfer) community college program than men, by a margin of 42 percent to 28 percent. Men, on the other hand, are more likely than women to go on to university, by a margin of 32 percent (Looker & McNutt, 1989). No wonder there have been, until now, so many more male university graduates.

There are signs that gender differences in education are starting to disappear. Since the mid-1970s, males and females have been about equally likely to obtain a higher education. While in 1961 only one-quarter of Canadian university undergraduates were female, today half are female. Gender-related differences in enrollment levels among graduate (MA and PhD) students have also diminished (Pike, 1988, p. 269), though they have not disappeared.

Many traditional barriers to female postsecondary education have fallen in recent years, but men and women continue to enter different fields of study in what Anisef, Paasche, and Turrittin (1980, p. xxiv)

Exhibit 3.1

Bachelor's and first professional degrees granted by sex, Canada, 1975–1990

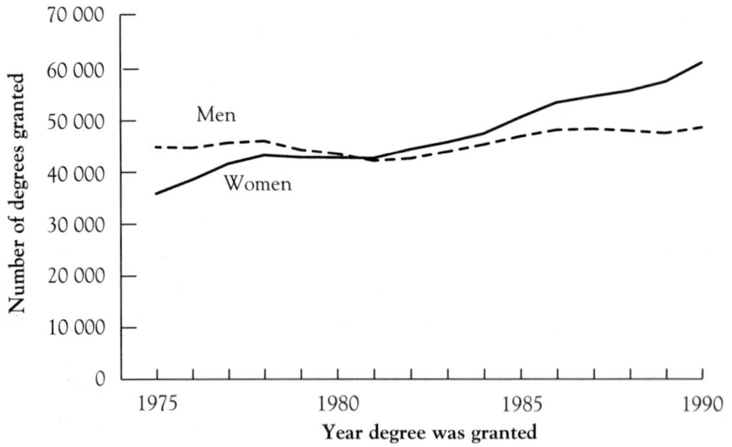

Source: Data from "A Statistical Review for 1990–1991," *Education in Canada*, October 1992, p. 174. (Catalogue No. 81–229). Ottawa: Statistics Canada.

Exhibit 3.2
Master's degrees granted by sex, Canada, 1975–1990

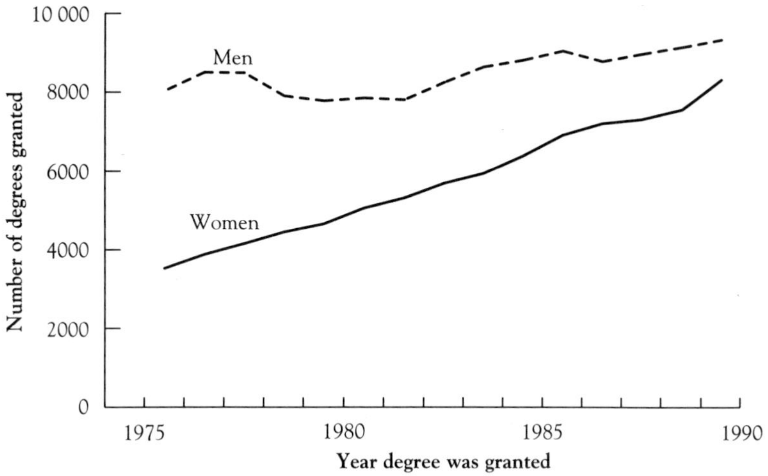

Source: Data from "A Statistical Review for 1990–1991," *Education in Canada*, October 1992, p. 185. (Catalogue No. 81–229). Ottawa: Statistics Canada.

have described as "internal tracking based on sex." In Canadian community colleges, far more men than women study architecture, engineering, natural resources, electronics, and transportation. For their part, women predominate in secretarial, community and social services, nursing, and medical treatment technology programs. In universities, women undergraduates outnumber men in education, biology, nursing, social work, pharmacy, and household science programs, while more men than women specialize in commerce and business administration, dentistry, medicine, engineering, science, and applied science (Statistics Canada, 1992).

This pattern of self-selection has been attributed to family preferences as well as personal attitudes regarding traditional gender roles (Gaskell, 1985). Gaskell points to a link between the gendered division of labour—the existence of "men's jobs" and "women's jobs"—and the educational tracking of females. "One of the major barriers to women entering non-traditional programs has been that neither they nor their teachers and advisors are convinced that they will be employed at the end of [the programs]" (Gaskell, 1985, p. 52).

Exhibit 3.3

Doctoral degrees granted by sex, Canada, 1975–1990

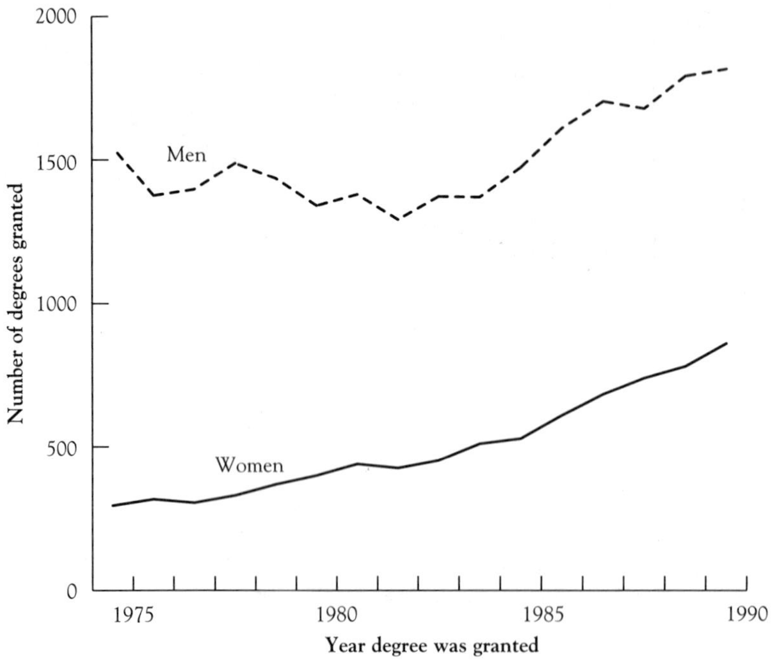

Source: Data from "A Statistical Review from 1990–1991," *Education in Canada*, October 1992, p. 189. (Catalogue No. 81–229). Ottawa: Statistics Canada.

Other factors play a part as well. Stereotypically male occupations are generally better paid, so it is to be expected that men continue to flock to them. Women's disproportionate representation in part-time education provides another possible explanation. It has been suggested that part-time study, especially in university, allows women from families with lower education levels a "port of entry" to postsecondary education (Guppy & Pendakur, 1989). On the other hand, not all professional faculties are open to part-time students.

In recent years, female enrollments have been increasing in traditionally male-dominated fields such as veterinary medicine, agriculture, commerce, and law. Women from higher socio-economic backgrounds have been particularly active in making these inroads (Guppy, 1984). Still, gender imbalances persist in many disciplines (Marshall, 1987).

Location and Residence

Like gender, location influences students' plans for postsecondary education. Some provinces produce a higher proportion of high-school drop-outs—who usually do not go on to postsecondary education—than others. And just as high-school completion rates vary by province, so do enrollments in postsecondary institutions: the two go together. Even the balance between community college and university enrollments varies among provinces. In theory, young people from provinces with low rates of educational attainment could continue their studies elsewhere, but the trouble and cost discourage many.

Students in the Atlantic provinces have to pay higher tuition fees and take out larger loans than other Canadian students. High-school graduates there may calculate that the returns from postsecondary education do not justify the costs involved (Canada, 1976, p. 90).

Just as residence in some provinces makes higher education less likely, so does residence in rural instead of urban areas. Anisef, Paasche, and Turrittin (1980, Table 4.2) found that postsecondary enrollment rates for Ontario high-school graduates vary sharply by size of community. Nearly 75 percent of the young people sampled in Toronto, and 67 percent in other cities, but only 52 percent living in Ontario towns and rural areas, continue their education after finishing high school.

The larger the community, the more likely a high-school graduate will attend a university. Students from smaller communities are more likely to stop studying altogether or enrol in a terminal community college program. They also depend more on government assistance to help pay for their education. Fewer can rely on summer employment earnings or parental support (Anisef, Paasche, & Turrittin, 1980, Table 4.24).

Small-town and rural students are discouraged from studying past high school by the prospect of large debts and the scarcity of good summer jobs in their community. Further, young people from smaller communities have to leave home to get a higher education. The added cost and trouble of leaving home discourages small-town and rural youths all the more from continuing their education.

Social Class and SES

Social class and socio-economic status—a combination of parental income, occupational status, and education—also affect students' decisions about postsecondary education (Pain, 1986; Guppy, 1984, Tables 2, 3; Zur-Muehlen, 1978, p. 42).

In particular, parents influence the educational plans their children make. Of course, many students do not carry through their original plans (Porter, Porter, & Blishen, 1982, p. 314). Students who have prepared to go to university sometimes decide not to go after all. These students can change their plans about education without any difficulty. However, students who have not prepared to go to university will find that the decision to continue is a difficult one. Because of the educational and financial preparation that attendance at university entails, early decisions *not* to go to university are more likely to stick than early decisions to go.

The early decision to go to university is related to both social class and gender, assuming the same level of ability. "Of the Grade 12 students with high mental ability, 75 percent of upper-middle-class boys but only 42 percent of lower-class boys wanted to graduate from university. The equivalent percentages for girls were 61 and 36 percent (Porter, Porter, & Blishen, 1982, p. 312).

Students with higher-status fathers (especially if they are boys) are the most likely of all to receive encouragement at home and feel able to handle university. As a result, middle-class children are more likely than working-class children to enter high-school programs for students who are university-bound. According to Porter, Porter, and Blishen (1982), mental ability (measured as IQ) has no direct influence on these plans, and only a small influence on school grades—an interesting fact to consider.

By the time they enter high school, students usually have a sense of their own ability, inclination to study, and desire (or reluctance) to take courses that can lead to higher education. "Parents who do not understand the consequences of courses that their children take in the early years of high school will very likely acquiesce when their children decide to take undemanding courses" (Porter, Porter, & Blishen, 1982, p. 317).

When parents fail to encourage their children, teachers and guidance counsellors must step in and try to create aspirations for higher education.

> They must see their task as providing a bridge between the family environment and the educational and occupational world. Social workers employed by school boards could also increase awareness of opportunities by going into lower-income homes, especially those whose children [have] high mental ability, and explaining to parents the opportunities that exist. Other possibilities are enrichment programs for lower-class children at an early age, introducing children while they are still in elementary school to the university and explaining its role and its value both for the individual and the society. (Porter, Porter, & Blishen, 1982, p. 317)

Social and economic barriers to higher education still remain, then. Capable young people from less privileged backgrounds are more likely than other students to drop out of school. Over the course of this century it has been found that students from families of higher socioeconomic backgrounds are more likely to get a higher education, especially a university education, than their less privileged peers (Guppy & Pendakur, 1989, p. 50). Students from lower socio-economic backgrounds are also more likely to enrol in terminal community college programs than in universities (Guppy, 1984, p. 88). Such differences in access to postsecondary education have long-term effects. They mean that a great many young people will end up with the same jobs, incomes, and statuses as their parents. Postsecondary education still transmits social status from one generation to the next. Unequal access to education maintains social inequality.

Race and Ethnicity

Canadian society includes many ethnic (or ancestral) groups: the Native peoples (Inuit, Indian, and Métis), the English, the French, and a variety of comparatively recent immigrants and their descendants. Access to higher education in Canada varies almost as much by ethnic and racial group as it does by gender, residence, and socio-economic status. Although some minority groups have benefited considerably from the greater educational opportunities they have found in Canada, others, especially Native peoples and French Canadians, have benefited far less (Baril & Mori, 1991; Hull, 1990).

Few Native people come close to getting the high-school diploma they need to qualify for postsecondary education. Nearly 80 percent have less than a secondary education, and only 5 percent ever enter college or university (Anderson & Frideres, 1981, p. 181; Statistics Canada, 1980, Table 10.7).

When religious missions ran Native schools before World War II, academic subjects formed only a small part of the instruction given. Later, as the federal government increased its involvement in Native education, the academic content was improved and enrollments rose. However, large numbers of Native students fell behind and dropped out.

There are a great many reasons for their difficulties in the education system. Children were often removed from home and community to attend school; they were taught in a foreign language (English or French); and they were taught things they had never cared about and could not relate to. Those who attended residential schools ran a high risk of being sexually abused. Some researchers (for example, Bouvier, 1991, p. 294) blame the failure of white education systems to teach traditional Native history, culture, language, experience, and aspirations for Native students' poor experience with formal education.

Added to this are the disabilities resulting from low socio-economic status. Today, the average income of Native people is about half the national average; Native communities have unemployment rates ranging from 35 to 90 percent; and five times as many aboriginal children as the national average are in the care of the state (Sigurdjonsson, 1989, p. 8, cited in Bouvier, 1991, pp. 294–95).

Happily, the past 25 years have seen a strong increase in the number of years of schooling attained by Native Indians between 18 and 24 years of age. The retention rate for Native students from Grade 2 to Grade 12 increased from 18 percent in 1975–76 to 31 percent in 1984–85. In 1971, less than 3 percent of the Native out-of-school population had obtained at least some postsecondary education; by 1981, that figure had risen to almost 19 percent.

Yet the proportion of Native people with a higher education is still only half that of the total Canadian population (Siggner, 1986, pp. 8–9). Moreover, a widening gap has developed within the Indian community itself. Among registered Indians, children of parents with high socio-economic status are more than twice as likely to have completed high school than children of parents with low socio-economic status—70 percent compared to only 30 percent (Hull, 1990, p. 3). Therefore, while high-school completion seems to be the norm for non-Native students, it is a rarity for most Native students.

Blacks were among Canada's earliest immigrant groups. For many years, like Native children, black children attended racially segregated schools, if any at all. The result was dramatic and long-lasting. Only 6 percent of the 319 blacks in a 1973 Nova Scotia study had achieved a Grade 12 education, and only one person held a university degree. Many had quit high school for jobs to help support their families. Others had quit because their parents could not afford to keep them in school (Henry, 1973, cited in Martin & Macdonell, 1982, p. 242). More recent statistics will be needed to determine whether greater educational opportunity has benefited this group.

French Canadians are another ethnic group with traditionally low rates of educational attainment. In schools outside Quebec, francophones have often been forced to speak English, the language of the majority. As well, French-Canadian cultural values have tended to work against higher education. Instead, they have promoted family "togetherness and belongingness ... at the expense of personal ambition and competitiveness" (Rocher, 1975, p. 151).

The gap between French Canadians and other groups has narrowed slightly in recent years. But as recently as 1983, only 11 percent of Quebec youths aged 18 to 24 were enrolled in university full-time, compared with a rate of 15.6 percent in Ontario and 13.5 percent for the entire country (Anisef, 1985, Table 5.3). Admittedly, the proportion increases when students enrolled in part-time education are included.

Full-time university attendance, however, remains low in the province of Quebec (Anisef, 1985, p. 35).

When we compare educational attainments by linguistic group in Canada, we find that francophones lag behind the anglophones but not the allophones (those who use a language other than English or French at home). In 1986, only 11 percent of anglophones had less than a Grade 9 education, compared to 24 percent of francophones and 32 percent of allophones (Baril & Mori, 1991). On the other hand, allophones contain the highest proportion of people with university degrees.

Some ethnic groups show a higher than average level of educational attainment. People from Jewish, Chinese, and Japanese backgrounds are much more likely than average to attend school full-time between the ages of 18 and 24, and to attend university.

Educational data collected in Metropolitan Toronto show that the proportion of people with at least some university education increased considerably between 1971 and 1982 in every ethnic category. (The increase is far greater for females than for males of the same generation and ethnic origin.) The most dramatic increase in university attendance has been made by British- or American-born women, and Canadian-born women with Canadian-born parents (see Kalbach, et al., 1984, Tables 1, 2, 4, 5).

At least in Toronto, with its many immigrants of varied ethnic origins, and its many postsecondary educational institutions, people who have traditionally been excluded are getting more education as educational institutions expand.

Is Education Becoming More Accessible?

The expansion of the educational system has slowly made access to postsecondary education more democratic (Guppy, 1984). Ancestry, socio-economic origin, and gender matter less today than they did in the past. Much of the expansion of the educational system came about through the establishment of community colleges which made room for more students in higher education. Community colleges are "a major postsecondary alternative for lower social and economic strata" (Guppy, 1984, p. 89).

However, access to universities has not increased at the same rate as massive government spending on higher education (Pike, 1988, p. 271). To a large degree, universities are still the preserve of middle-class students, and not only because of cost. This was demonstrated by the failure of lower-class university attendance to increase significantly in Australia when tuition fees were abolished in 1974.

Guppy and Arai (1993) conclude that "no consensus exists in the sociological literature as to which among many explanations best accounts for the social class effects we observe, whether among women or men. There is growing agreement that while money does matter, explanations of a more cultural nature are key" (p. 233). Generally, research shows that students with higher-status, better-educated parents and those from ethnic groups that strongly value education end up with more of the motivation and skills necessary to achieve educational success. "The offspring of the 'cultured classes' know better than the children of working-class background how to deal with the social and academic demands of the educational system, and are more aware of the long-term consequences which their programme and course choices entail" (Pike, 1988, pp. 271–72).

Children from the higher classes seem to have something extra, which Bourdieu (1977) calls "cultural capital." This includes a knowledge of music and literature; frequent attendance at cultural events such as concerts, museums, and plays; interest in reading books and listening to music; and, equally important, the tendency to think of themselves as educated, artistic, and "cultured." Students with the most "cultural capital" are the most likely to complete postsecondary education and gain a high-status job, regardless of parental social status and education (DiMaggio & Mohr, 1985).

Recent research in Toronto (Erickson, 1990) has suggested that a different kind of cultural capital operates in Canada. Erickson finds some evidence that higher-status Torontonians have more knowledge of good restaurants, books, movies, and artists than lower-status people do. Yet although this kind of knowledge enters into business conversation and implies social and economic success in Europe, it appears not to do so in Canada.

Instead, the business culture has much more importance here. The cultural capital of the business culture is less a set of facts than a way of behaving, thinking, and speaking.

> As respondents talked at length about their past, present and future work, they showed dramatic differences in expression. Some sounded articulate, informed, dramatic, convincing; some sounded voiceless and adrift.
>
> "Concreteness" is not just a matter of specific bits of knowledge, such as vocabulary, but of the overall relationship between the speaker and the business world.... People who could speak well [about their career] also spoke impressively about other aspects of work and business life. Their expert command of business language is itself a form of cultural capital, and a form directly useful as a resource in careers. (Erickson, 1991, pp. 265–66)

This kind of cultural capital demonstrates career commitment. Israeli research (Koslowsky, 1987) shows that career commitment, unlike some other forms of cultural capital, is not strongly correlated with gender and social class. Career commitment has important consequences for students. Those students who are most committed to their careers meet with their instructors more often and spend more time on their written work than other students. This leads to success in their studies, and eventually in their careers.

Generally, acquiring this kind of cultural capital requires a wide variety of personal experiences, as well as devoted teachers, adult mentors, and a great deal of spare time and money. Most important of all, it seems to depend on having educated parents who themselves maintain a network of key contacts.

Few schools give their students this kind of cultural capital. Those that do tend to be the private schools and those secondary schools that draw their students disproportionately from the upper and upper-middle classes. Such cultural capital plays a large part in students' later plans and achievements, marking them out from the rest of the field and streaming them toward higher education.

Financial costs may play little direct role in students' decisions about higher education, but they do play an important indirect role. Despite their eligibility for student aid and reduced tuition, lower-income students continue to feel pressure to give up studying and contribute financially to support their families or themselves. Lower-income students are more reluctant than others to take out student loans, which they fear they will have difficulty repaying. "In order to increase participation [by children from lower-income families], programs would have to be targeted to helping them much earlier in their educational careers" (Standing Senate Committee, 1987, p. 49).

As we have seen, gender, region, community size, social class, ethnicity, and cultural capital all play a role in streaming young Canadians into (or away from) postsecondary education. But these patterns are not rigid and unchanging. Government policies have made postsecondary education more accessible to women and certain ethnic minority groups. Some change has occurred. "These changes would not have occurred unless accompanied by specific value changes and institutions' willingness to make accommodations" (Anisef, 1985, p. 11).

Even the ideology underlying education has changed. In the 1960s, providing postsecondary education for the largest possible number was seen as a societal responsibility that would bring the society benefits. Now, postsecondary education tends to be viewed as benefiting individual graduates, not society as a whole. This new view justifies passing a larger part of the cost of education back to the student. Unfortunately, this practice will make it harder for low-income students to continue in school unless more and better scholarships are available.

An awareness of the factors that influence other people's educational plans may lead you to a clearer examination of your own educational choices. You may discover that your upbringing has led you to limit your educational horizons. Other educational choices might have been, and may still be, more fulfilling. We now turn to the question of fulfilment.

THE RETURNS ON A POSTSECONDARY EDUCATION

When asked what concerns them most about their education, college and university students usually mention job opportunities first. This section will look at how your postsecondary education will affect employability, income, and job satisfaction. However, you should balance the emphasis here on job-related returns by also considering how higher education will influence the overall quality of your life.

Non-monetary Returns

Anyone who has received a good education will tell you that education can bring many benefits that cannot be measured in dollars. Like strenuous physical exercise, strenuous mental exercise—a regular diet of learning, debate, and new ideas—can be exhilarating and fulfilling. It can be exciting and even inspirational to learn what earlier thinkers have accomplished.

Of course, not everyone likes school. Okun, Braver, and Weir (1990) have found that, at least in the first twelve grades, girls like school better than boys do, and all students prefer some grades to others. There is evidence that alternative schools—including alternative public schools — can satisfy students more than mainstream schools, while maintaining high academic standards. They can even improve interracial attitudes (Trickett et al., 1985). Graduates of part-time programs—many of whom work full-time while attending school—also prove to be more satisfied with their overall educational experience than students who take a traditional, full-time program of studies (Rosenthal, Wedel, & Wilson, 1989). This seems to argue in favour of continuing to develop flexible education programs that serve the needs of non-traditional students.

Postsecondary students enjoy their studies if they have a strong intellectual drive, if their school presents a congenial environment for study (Burbach, Cnaan, & Babbitt, 1986), and if they perceive that their education is leading to positive job outcomes (Geyer, Brannon, & Shearon, 1987). Students who adapt well to their educational experience report less than average depression, loneliness, and interpersonal helplessness (van Rooijen, 1986).

However, education, and higher education in particular, can be the source of a great deal of distress for students who dislike the experience. Jobes (1987) raises the doubt that curriculum counselling can solve this problem. Women students who cannot adapt are likely to report psychosomatic stress symptoms, while men often resort to problem drinking.

People who find that they are prepared for the challenge of postsecondary education, however, feel a sense of greater mastery: they become more able to understand complicated arguments and create their own. By increasing their knowledge, education increases people's sense of control over their own lives. This is satisfying and reassuring, though it is often daunting as well, for education teaches us how much we do not know and cannot control.

Education in the sciences gives people more insight into the logic of the universe and the technological revolution that is sweeping everyone's lives. Education in the humanities puts people in touch with the vast variety of human cultures and ideas. It gives us a sense of the continuity of the human race, and lets us admire how much people have achieved that is good and beautiful. Education in the social sciences helps us understand why we live the way we do and how we can change ourselves—individually and collectively—before we suffer disastrous consequences.

Higher education is more than a ticket to a good job. In the space of three or four years, students gain in critical ability, aesthetic sense, and tolerance for divergent values (Bowen, 1977). College graduates are better informed and more politically active citizens. They even make better parents. Along these lines, Bowen (1977, p. 201) writes:

> The effects of college education on the family are numerous and strong—so much so that these effects may be among the most significant outcomes of higher education.... Among the familial impacts are the following:
>
> 1. Narrowing the traditional differences in attitudes and behavior between the two sexes.
> 2. Selection of college-educated persons as marriage partners.
> 3. Delay in age of marriage.
> 4. Slight reduction in the divorce rate.
> 5. Reduction in the birth rate.
> 6. More thought, time, energy and money devoted to the rearing of children.
> 7. Influences on parents, spouses and siblings of the college educated.

In a comparative study of six developing nations, Inkeles (1973) shows that the amount of education a person has received is the single best predictor of how "modern" he or she is likely to be. By "modern," Inkeles means all the characteristics that Bowen has mentioned; he also means "capable of living in a modern world." More highly educated people even lead longer, healthier lives. So the more education you get, the better off you will be.

But what does all this have to say about our concern over finding a good career? Is today's general arts degree a ticket to a good job? Do non-transfer community college programs really give more marketable, job-oriented training? Do recent graduates feel that their postsecondary education was a waste of time?

Job Status Returns

Education is an important "intervening variable" between the social characteristics you start out with in life and the rewards you end up with as an adult. You can break free from your past by using higher education as a lever. By seizing the opportunity for higher education, you can get on a somewhat more equal footing with people who started life with more advantages.

Consider the effects of postsecondary education on social mobility. Education has an important impact on your social status and upward social mobility; a postsecondary degree is the single most important factor in getting beyond your inherited class position. This is because the best paying, most prestigious and secure jobs increasingly require the most educational training and credentials.

People with the same amount of education are likely to find jobs of equal prestige, whatever their class of origin. Using data from a national sample of Canadians, Creese, Guppy, and Meissner (1991) report the following findings:

1. A person's first job in the labour market is principally influenced by that person's level of education;
2. Controlling for his or her education, parental education and occupation have little direct influence on the first job a person gets; and,
3. Peoples' current jobs are influenced most by their starting positions in the labour force.

Postsecondary education—a very effective form of human capital—provides the skills and credentials you need to find a good job and also to advance your career. But, as we have seen, the class structure limits the ability of education to promote social mobility, by determining how much and what kind of education people get. People born into the lower classes are less likely than average to get a higher education and to enjoy the career opportunities it provides (see also Anisef, Ashbury, & Turrittin, 1992).

Unfortunately, factors other than education also influence occupational attainment. Discrimination in employment still limits the opportunities of highly trained women and members of ethnic minorities. Human rights and affirmative action laws may have diminished the problem somewhat but visible minorities of either sex do much worse in the job market than white males with an equal amount of postsecondary education.

Increasingly, immigrants to Canada are coming from non-European countries. In Canada, they are identified as visible minorities—and they are easy targets for discrimination. Thus, recent immigration patterns have forced many Canadians to confront the reality of racial prejudice for the first time.

Immigrants to Canada are typically chosen for their economic value; thus they are required to meet Canada's needs for a highly educated work force. The system of selecting immigrants on the basis of age, education, and occupational demand *should* give immigrants an advantage over the Canadian-born population in the labour market; to some degree, it does. Data collected by Beaujot, Basavarajappa, and Verma (1988) show that higher than average proportions of immigrants are (1) in the labour force; (2) working full-time; (3) in the prime working ages of 25–54 years; (4) in managerial and professional occupations (except for immigrant women); (5) living in urban areas; and (6) the holders of a university degree. As a result, we find that "in 1980, immigrant men earned ... 4.9 percent more than the average ... earned by Canadian-born men." Yet "when the effects of differences in age-composition and educational attainment were removed, immigrant men and women earned 3.1 and 4.5 percent *less* than did Canadian-born men and women, respectively" [emphasis added]. This difference in incomes suggests that immigrants are experiencing discrimination in employment. Further, evidence appears to show that the worst victims of discrimination in employment are non-white immigrants from the Third World.

"Immigrant groups from traditional sources, particularly the United Kingdom, United States and Northern and Western Europe, earned [as much as] or more than ... their Canadian-born counterparts, [but] the new immigrant groups from Asia, South and Central America and Africa earned from 5 to 22 percent less."(Beaujot, Basavarajappa, & Verma, 1988, Highlights, n.p.) Part of the explanation for this is that immigrants improve their economic position the longer they live in

Canada. Still, comparatively recent immigrants from African, Latin American, and Caribbean countries take much longer to catch up to or exceed the incomes of native-born Canadians—as much as twenty years, for some—than immigrants from northern European countries.

Of all Canada's immigrants, those who come from the Caribbean are the worst off in occupational attainment, although many of them come with good educational credentials. Richmond (1989, p. 5) quotes from a Statistics Canada report:

> Altogether 17% of males and 10% of females had some university education ... [and] labour force participation rates for men and women were high. [However] unemployment among Caribbean immigrants at the time of the 1981 Census was measurably higher than that among comparable Canadian-born persons.... Among males, the average total income for those born in the Caribbean was below that for men born in Canada and substantially below that of other immigrants. Francophone males showed the largest income differential, earning only 60% as much as did corresponding Canadian-born men.

Male immigrants from the Caribbean who had been in Canada for more than ten years still earned less than Canadian-born males with the same socio-economic characteristics.

Discrimination also persists against highly educated women. Creese, Guppy, and Meissner (1991) show that Canadian men and women with similar educations continue to have very different chances of social mobility. They write:

1. Women in the labour force ... have a higher average number of years of schooling than do men; and because of this,
2. Women typically enter the labour force in higher status jobs than men do. However,
3. Men experience more upward mobility than women, even though they have fewer years of schooling;
4. For this reason, there is a stronger link between the first job and current job for women than for men; further,
5. Of all women, young foreign-born women experience the least upward mobility; and
6. Francophone women experience less upward, intra-generational mobility than Anglophone women do.

What this means is that higher education has a different "value" for women than it has for men. Further, foreign-born or francophone women suffer the disabilities of both gender and birthplace (or ancestry).

The gender difference in incomes is partly the result of labour market segmentation. Men and women typically do different kinds of work.

Women tend to work at a small number of poorly paid low-to-medium prestige jobs: in sales, clerical work, service jobs, light manufacturing, and the semi-professions such as nursing and schoolteaching. Although these jobs may mean upward mobility to women from working-class backgrounds, they mean the opposite to women from middle- or upper-middle-class backgrounds. A great many women have not benefited from their education as their husbands and brothers have.

Employability Returns

Over the past fifteen or twenty years, the more education a person has attained, the lower his or her likelihood of unemployment. As national unemployment rates have fluctuated, people with higher education have been in the best position to ride out the storm. They have always been the most likely to hold a job, all other things (such as gender and place of residence) being equal. This pattern holds true for people of all ages, including youths (aged 15 to 24), who typically have the highest unemployment rates, and this is true throughout the industrial world, as evidence on unemployment in Exhibit 3.4 suggests.

Not even a rapid growth in the number of graduates has hurt their employability. However, many graduates have been forced to settle for work that had not traditionally called for a postsecondary education (Zsigmond et al., 1978, p. 170), and it is this that has kept the unemployment rate for graduates low. Today, more and more highly educated people work in jobs that are below their level of skill and ability (Livingston, 1987, p. 12; Berg, 1970; see Hunter, 1988, for an opposing argument). In a sense, employers have encouraged this trend. As more postsecondary graduates enter the labour market, employers demand higher qualifications.

This hiring strategy is not without problems. Putting a highly educated person into an undemanding job risks employee boredom, loss of motivation, and rebelliousness. (We shall discuss the problem of "underemployment" further in the next chapter.) But for several reasons many employers are willing to take this chance. University graduates lend the organization an air of professionalism and credibility. Employers assume that graduates in general, and university graduates in particular, learn new things faster, have better interpersonal skills, and come from a higher class of family. This makes them more desirable employees.

Beyond this, higher education teaches people to be ambitious and career oriented (Bowles & Gintis, 1976). Colleges and universities teach their students that merit will be rewarded and that continuous hard work is a worthwhile investment in the future. Employers know

Exhibit 3.4
The effect of education level on unemployment

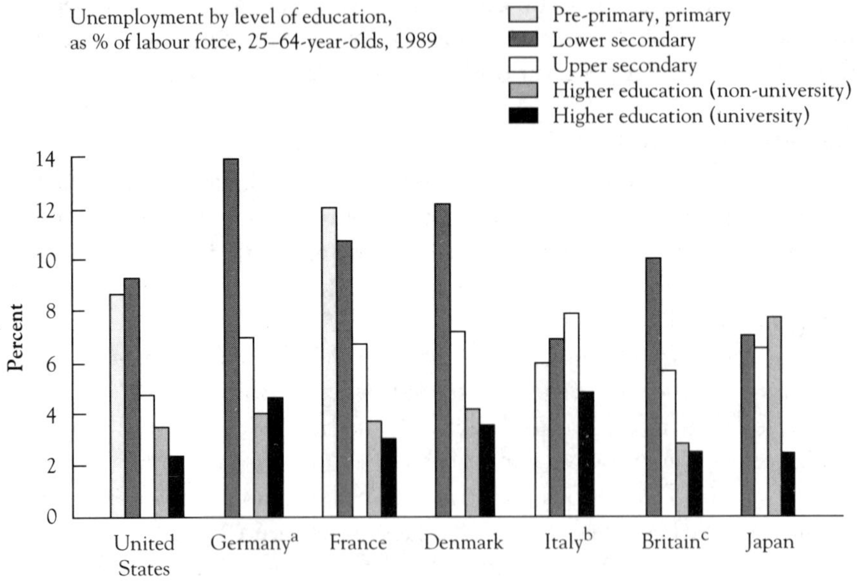

a People in apprenticeships not considered part of the active population
b Nonuniversity and university
c Women 60–64 years excluded from relevant population

Source: A survey of education. (November 21, 1992.) *The Economist*, p. 5. Reprinted with permission.

that graduates carry these ideas into the work world. They also know that colleges and universities select for a middle-class background, higher than average cultural capital, and high motivation. The evidence that an educational degree or diploma provides saves the employer a lot of trouble in identifying good candidates for independent work. This is why graduates are so rarely unemployed, though often "underemployed."

Higher education not only increases employability; for women, it also increases participation in the labour force. Nearly all adult men, whatever their level of education, work full-time. The situation is quite different for adult women, many of whom have tradionally stayed home or taken part-time work. Today, higher-educated women are the most likely of all women to take full-time paid work (Boyd, 1985, Table 7.5).

Income Returns

Throughout the 1960s, university graduates earned well above the industrial average in their first job. Since then, they have earned relatively less, at first. However, workers with more education catch up soon, and in the long run their earnings surpass those of others (Zsigmond et al., 1978, Chart 31, Table V-15). Further, the salary of a university graduate (BA or BSc) two years after leaving school averages $5000 higher than that of a community college graduate. The effort is worth it, if higher income is your goal.

The financial benefits of an education are, with some exceptions, *discontinuous:* the year spent completing a degree is much more important than any other single year leading up to that degree. A person who completes all but the last year of a medical degree is not "nearly a doctor" in the work world, entitled to *nearly* the same rewards as a doctor. That person will have to compete for jobs with high-school and community college graduates and other university drop-outs. Such jobs will not be found in the highly protected market for medical services, but in the more competitive market for technical or personal services—for example, travelling as a sales representative for a drug company, or working in a chemical laboratory.

Along the same lines, *which* degree you complete is also important. Different degrees not only make you eligible for different jobs, they also make you competitive in different job markets.

Still, incomes increase more or less steadily with the amount of education you complete. Jencks et al. (1977) tried to isolate the effect of education on earnings from that of other factors such as work experience, family background, and IQ. In the job market that prevailed until 1970, completing four years of high school raised average earnings by at most 15 to 25 percent. Completing four years of university added as much as 40 percent, because a bachelor's degree provided entry to higher-status occupations—that is, better job markets. The economic recessions since then, and the continued supply of new university graduates, have probably reduced this income advantage; but graduates are still ahead of the rest.

The income value of postsecondary education varies from one country to another, as data in Exhibit 3.5 indicate.

The income value of a higher education also varies by gender. On average, men earn more than women in every line of work. In large part, women earn less than men because they enter relatively poorly paid traditionally female occupations (Clark & Zsigmond, 1981, p. 141; Fox, 1989, cited in Anisef, Ashbury, & Turrittin, 1992, p. 77). But even if we

Exhibit 3.5
The effect of education level on earnings

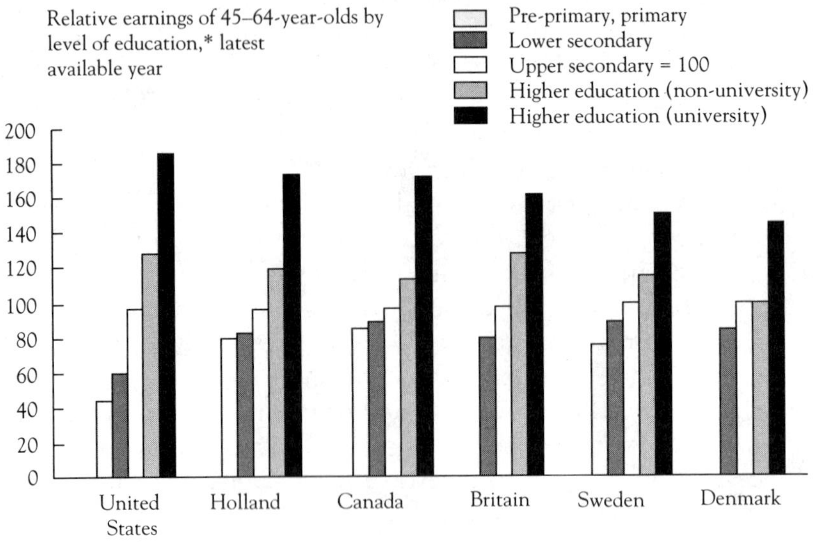

* Comparison of (a) average earnings for people 45–64 years of age with highest level of education completed with (b) those who have an upper secondary education at their highest level

Source: A survey of education. (November 21, 1992.) *The Economist*, p. 5. Reprinted with permission.

compare men and women of the same ages in well-paid, traditionally male-dominated professions such as engineering, the physical sciences, medicine, and dentistry, "women [in 1981] ... had average employment incomes that were only 77% those of comparable men" (Marshall, 1987, p. 11). Age, marital status, and parental status might account for some of the male–female differences in income. But these data lead sociologists to suspect there is some sex discrimination in the labour market. Higher education might not eliminate the effects of discrimination on incomes, but it does improve the situation of groups such as women who are subject to discrimination.

Predicting future income returns on education is difficult. The growing number of young BAs seeking jobs increases the competition and drives down the price that employers must pay to hire a BA. This, in turn, diminishes the value of a high-school diploma on the job market. The spillover of postsecondary graduates into lower-status jobs will continue to block the advancement of high-school graduates. In the long run, postsecondary graduates will still push ahead of the competition, though probably not by as much as in the past (Olneck, cited in Jencks et al., 1977, pp. 183–84, 188–89).

The most recent evidence supporting this view is provided by a *Maclean's*/CTV poll (*Maclean's*, January 4, 1993, p. 35), which shows that only 26 percent of university graduates are "dissatisfied" or "very dissatisfied" with their economic situation right now. The comparable figure for vocational/technical college graduates is 32 percent; for high-school graduates it is 37 percent; and for people with public-school or some high-school education it is 40 percent.

Education versus Work Experience

How does work experience compare with formal education in ensuring employability and a good income? When graduates are asked why they were hired for their current full-time job, they say that "personality" was the single most important reason (Anisef, 1985, Tables 6, 17, 19). "Educational qualifications" is the second most common answer, and "qualifications obtained elsewhere" (that is, work experience) is third.

For a great many applicants, hiring *is* based on personal characteristics, supported by educational qualifications. People with high-school or some postsecondary education tend to believe that work experience matters most, and they may be right, when it comes to the jobs that are open to them. In a world with ever more college and university graduates available to employers, high-school or some (uncompleted) postsecondary training is worth little: it is like having no educational qualification whatever. No surprise, then, that for these young people, educational qualifications counted for little!

The earnings for people with a postsecondary degree increase more rapidly with age than the earnings of those with less education (Featherman & Hauser, 1978, Table 5.27). Attending college or university initially lowers a person's income; a year's work experience yields more income than a year's education for people under age 30. After age 30 the situation changes: the relative advantage of work experience declines, and the growth in earnings of those without a degree slows considerably. Work experience yields immediate and impressive dividends for people without postsecondary education. But the benefit is short-lived. In the long run, higher education is the better investment of youthful energy (Featherman & Hauser, 1978, pp. 306–308).

However, this is not to deny the value of work experience. The combination of education and experience is unbeatable. For every type of higher education, having prior work experience increases a graduate's income (Clark, Laing, & Rechnitzer, 1986, Chart 13).

Payoffs to Different Kinds of Education

Between 1976 and 1982, the chance of full-time employment worsened slightly for college graduates and BAs. The proportion of all post-secondary graduates working full-time two years after graduation dropped during those years, but the drop was least for people with the most education—MAs and PhDs (Clark, Laing, & Rechnitzer, 1986, Table 4).

Even with their ostensibly more practical and job-oriented education, community college trade/vocational graduates had more trouble finding a job than any other group. Not only were they the most likely to suffer unemployment, but their periods of unemployment were on average much longer: 10 months out of the 24 elapsing since graduation, compared with only 7 months for other graduates of higher educational institutions (Clark, Laing, & Rechnitzer, 1986, Table 8).

Less often unemployed than community college graduates, BAs are more likely to become underemployed. The 1978 economy apparently failed to generate nearly enough jobs for newly graduated BAs. Subsequently, the underemployment of BAs declined slightly and rose for community college graduates. But on the whole, underemployment remains quite high for both groups. Instead of becoming unemployed, recent graduates are increasingly taking jobs for which they are overqualified.

Between the late 1950s and early 1970s, the average status of postsecondary graduates' first jobs also declined. University degrees however, consistently led to more prestigious first jobs (Anisef, Paaschen, & Turrittin, 1980, 1992). In terms of job status attained, an incomplete university education was worth about the same as a community college diploma. The job status that a bachelor's degree could earn broadened gradually from the mid-1960s through the mid-1970s; that is to say, a BA could lead to a wider variety of outcomes in 1975—good and bad—than it did a decade earlier (Goyder, 1980, Table 4; Harvey, 1984, Table 1).

Eight out of ten graduates with jobs related to their education would take the same educational program again; but only four out of ten with unrelated jobs would repeat. Among people who would change their program, nine out of ten university graduates would enrol in university again. Only four out of ten community college graduates would return; most say they would attend university instead.

Surprisingly, in many fields, job satisfaction is greater for those who took three-year instead of four-year degrees. Many four-year graduates may have discovered that an extra year of university at the BA level yields no advantage in the job market, and no higher income (University of Toronto Career Centre, n.d., Table 8).

We should not underestimate the credentialling function of a university education. "Although a job may not require particular skills or knowledge gained in university, the possession of a BA is evidence of an applicant's maturity, motivation and aptitude for further learning, and thus provides the employer with a means of selecting suitable candidates who will then acquire additional training on the job" (Selleck, 1980, pp. 36–37).

Satisfaction Returns

Does education make people more satisfied with their lives overall, or with particular domains of life, such as their job? That is a complicated question to answer. The evidence seems to argue for both sides.

Most published research points to the conclusion that education makes people less satisfied with their job. Glenn and Weaver (1982), however, examined American survey data from 1974 to 1980 and found no negative effect of education on job satisfaction, even when the people studied were doing work below their level of skill and training. Likewise, a survey of employed workers (Martin & Shehan, 1989) found that education has no significant effect on job satisfaction, when the researchers controlled for job conditions and rewards. Nor did King and Hautaluoma (1987) report any difference in the life satisfaction of overeducated workers and other (matched) workers. These three studies are in the minority. The preponderance of American as well as Canadian evidence argues for the contrary position.

Among Canadians, the proportion claiming to be "very satisfied" with their job has been found to drop as level of education increases. Moreover, this same pattern has been found within every job category (Statistics Canada, 1980, Charts 14.7, 14.8).

The Quality of Life (1981) data do not suggest that higher education makes people more satisfied with life overall, or with their jobs in particular. Among people over the age of 25, life satisfaction is usually greatest for those with a high-school diploma or less. Postsecondary education is slightly more likely to increase job satisfaction, but even here the evidence is very mixed. One cannot conclude from these data that job satisfaction or life satisfaction will increase if you get more education.

This accords with the results of an American follow-up study of 3333 former college students conducted by Phelan and Phelan (1983). The researchers found that higher education has the expected positive impact on earnings attained, but not on job satisfaction or life satisfaction. Another study (Mottaz, 1984) found that more education produced higher work satisfaction, when it led to better jobs (that is, jobs with more autonomy, significance, and involvement), but much lower work satisfaction when it did not lead to better jobs.

This, the most common finding, is illustrated by the results of an Arizona study. Following an era of riots and judicial intervention in the prison system, the state decided to professionalize prison security staff by requiring higher education for guards and other officials. Research by Jurik et al. (1987) in a medium security correctional institution found that higher education had the effect of reducing job satisfaction among prison guards, when other factors were held constant.

More education, then, may be a bad thing—that is, it may have a negative impact on satisfaction—if people get jobs that are below their level of training. Highly educated people in this position may be dissatisfied because their expectations have been violated. Their education has given them broader horizons, a richer sense of alternatives, and a wider basis for comparison.

But there are other possible explanations as well. An American study of happiness concluded that people with higher education and income levels may be more sensitive and psychologically responsive to their environment. This would help to explain why "better-educated and higher-income groups, although happier, [have] greater feelings of social inadequacy and more problems" (Bradburn & Caplovitz, 1965, p. 24).

Well-educated people may also express a lack of satisfaction because they are not *interested* in seeking satisfaction. They may place little value on satisfaction and happiness, and instead be seeking new challenges, personal growth, and what Maslow calls "self-actualization" (see Chapter One). If higher education does not produce satisfaction, it may be because (1) higher education teaches people to raise their aspirations, or (2) the kind of people who are ready to settle for satisfaction are unlikely to get a higher education.

But the most likely reason for a lack of satisfaction among the highly educated is underemployment and the underpayment that is often associated with it. Highly educated people become dissatisfied with their jobs (and lives) when they are paid to do work that makes only partial use of their training and skills. Eight out of ten university graduates and nine out of ten community college graduates believe that it is important that their job be related to their field of study (Clark & Zsigmond, 1981, Tables 6 & 7). Since job satisfaction varies little among different types of graduates working at what they were trained to do, underemployment and its effect on income appear to make a big difference.

Underemployed and underpaid people are likely to suffer from social strain and uncertainty (Johnson, 1989). It is possible that the strategies they use to respond to these problems will vary by race and gender. Black workers, whose underemployment may be a result of racial discrimination, appear to rely on social supports that address that specific problem. There may also be differences in the ways men and women respond to underemployment, according to research by Martin and Shehan (1989). However, it is wage-earning responsibility and not gender that appears to account for these variations. Presumably, the greater a worker's responsibility for earning the family's wage, the worse the effect of underemployment (or underpayment) is on that worker's satisfaction.

Underemployment may even radicalize people in a political sense. Lambert and Curtis (1979) show that highly educated adults who are dissatisfied with their economic status are more likely than anyone else to express a lack of confidence in major Canadian institutions such as schools, Parliament, the Supreme Court, and newspapers. In contrast, highly educated people who are economically satisfied are no more likely to do this than less-educated people.

Low earnings alone are rarely sufficient to affect the satisfaction level of postsecondary graduates. Differences in earnings hardly affect the job satisfaction of people who are doing the job they were trained to do. But when a job is not related to education, differences in earnings affect job satisfaction to a much greater degree.

From the standpoint of satisfaction, higher education is a high-risk, potentially high-yield undertaking. Risks include income lost while in school, large debts, and the chance of having to accept work unrelated to one's education. After unemployment, the worst possible scenario is low-paying work outside one's area of training. The best possible scenario is full-time, high-paying work in one's chosen field. Between these extremes the range of employment outcomes, and satisfaction, is immense.

CONCLUSION

Different people value their investments in higher education differently. Some people place a low value on the non-monetary benefits of education. Others find ways of achieving employment security and social status without a higher education; for example, by entering the family business. Higher education is not for everyone, then.

Higher education is not certain to increase life satisfaction or work satisfaction. On the one hand, it gives people the many benefits— financial and non-financial—that Bowen (1977) described. On the other hand, it gives people too much information about the rewards available in life that other people may be getting. Education raises your standards of comparison. Although it increases your chances of achieving job and income rewards, it may not do so as much or as quickly as you would like.

There is a real risk that education will raise your expectations beyond your reach and more quickly than you are able to satisfy them.

Today, postsecondary education is still a worthwhile investment of time and money. In terms of employability, earnings, socio-economic status, and potential job satisfaction, a university degree brings the greatest rewards. Even terminal community college graduates are better off than people with a high-school education or less. And from the standpoint of non-monetary benefits, the more education you get, the better off you are.

Where education is concerned, do people get what they want or learn to want what they can get? On the one hand, people get what they want: the amount of higher education people complete is primarily shaped by how much they want (their aspirations), not by tuition costs or other economic concerns. Likewise, the kind of higher education people get is also the kind they want, in most cases. Choices between university and terminal community college programs, and between one course of study and another, are "free," subject only to limits on the total number of students who will be admitted to any given program.

On the other hand the amount and kinds of education people want are patterned by gender, place of residence, and socio-economic status, and to some degree by other factors such as ethnicity and race. As children, we have been programmed to want what we (or our parents) expect we can get. For this reason, educational "choice" is an illusion: our choices and their outcomes are largely predetermined. That is why social position is, so very often, passed from one generation to the next.

Do people learn to want what they get in education? Not entirely. If they did, people would not change their choices, as increasing numbers of older students do when they return for additional education or new kinds of training. Further, large numbers of graduates are dissatisfied with their past educational decisions. They are particularly dissatisfied when these decisions do not result in the expected job and pay level, or when their training does not prove useful on the job.

The educational decision process starts early. People who have received little encouragement for their educational goals at home would do well to find mentors who could advise them about their goals and help them increase their cultural capital. In many ways, your educational choices will become clearer once you have made some career choices.

The next chapter takes us a little further through the life cycle. It discusses some likely changes in the world of work and factors that influence the rewards—the pay, security, status, intrinsic interest, and job satisfaction—that people actually get out of their jobs.

Chapter Four

◆

Career Choices:
What You Want and What You Get

Introduction

This chapter answers two questions about jobs and careers: specifically, What are the long-term employment prospects for different occupations? and What makes a job satisfying? To answer the first question, we shall consider some of the forecasts that social scientists have made about the future job market: which kinds of job opportunities are increasing, and which are shrinking? To answer the second question, we shall examine data on job and career satisfaction. These data tell us which kinds of jobs satisfy people most, and which kinds of people are hardest to please.

A great many factors influence the kind of job a person gets: they include personal contacts and community resources (both discussed in Chapter Two), and educational attainment. The kind and amount of education a person gets are largely determined by factors discussed in Chapter Three: these include gender, place of residence, SES, race, and ethnicity. Taken together, these factors have a powerful effect on the first job you get; that first job, in turn, influences your later work life (Blau & Duncan, 1967; Boyd et al., 1985; Creese, Guppy, & Meissner, 1991).

Your work life is also influenced by other forces, far larger and beyond your immediate control. They include changes in technology and in the overall health of the economy. Not only are these enormously powerful influences, but they are also quite unpredictable.

You may be one of many students who has already gained a good deal of first-hand experience about the world of work. An increasing number of students today attend classes part-time, while holding down job and family responsibilities the rest of the time. Some mature students have returned to school in hopes of entering another, more rewarding line of work. For these readers, what this book has to say about careers may be old hat.

Before we begin, perhaps we should find out what you already know about the topic. Here are a few true-false questions to test your knowledge:

1. Good pay is mainly what makes people happy with their work.
   True ___ False ___
2. Good jobs make everyone feel satisfied—even people who are usually quite miserable.
   True ___ False ___
3. Jobs today are more satisfying than they were a generation ago.
   True ___ False ___
4. People who like the work they are doing don't care about the working conditions.
   True ___ False ___
5. In the next century, work will be much more creative than it is today.
   True ___ False ___

By the time you reach the end of the chapter, you should know if your answers were right.

THE FUTURE JOB MARKET

Many working people found the past decade uncertain, frustrating, and even chaotic. It was a decade of too many surprises. Yet most of the recent changes in people's work lives have their origins in a gradual process that began well before the 1990s. These changes grew out of the development of a global economy and advances in technology—especially, those that transformed the movement of people and information.

Our ability to follow such trends over time allows us to plan ahead to meet the challenges of the future. Common sense says that you are better off knowing the employment prospects for an occupation before preparing to enter it. Choosing systematically will help you make better choices, but it cannot guarantee you the results you desire. Even though a great deal of social change is slow and gradual, revolutionary changes do occur. Back in 1940, who was predicting the hydrogen bomb, personal computers, or the baby boom?

Changes that disrupt old trends and set new ones in motion take us by surprise. We would be wrong to consider history an infallible guide to the future. But we would be even more wrong to ignore the signs of change that can affect our lives.

Social scientists have devised three ways of "reading" these signs; we shall discuss each one in turn.

THREE WAYS OF GUESSING THE FUTURE

Linear Extrapolation

The first method, *linear extrapolation*, uses recent history as a guide to the future. It assumes that recent trends will continue without significant change for some time to come—that the patterns we have witnessed up to now will continue to hold.

When *Maclean's* magazine (January 4, 1993, p. 22) asked a sample of Canadian adults which job they would be most likely to recommend to a child as a career, the most popular answers (in decreasing order) were doctor (28 percent), business executive (19 percent), scientist (16 percent), university professor (11 percent), and lawyer (9 percent). Few considered farming, blue-collar occupations, small business, or semi-skilled white-collar work to be good options. This "lay wisdom" is quite close to the mark: highly paid occupations requiring a large amount of education *are* a good bet for the future. It is fairly certain that respondents were extrapolating from their present-day experience, even if they were doing so in a rather naïve way.

Linear extrapolation is by no means perfectly reliable, even when performed by "experts." Consider another example of this method. A newspaper article headlined "Headhunters big winners as job market picks up speed" (*The Globe and Mail,* August 27, 1987) claimed that "it's a good time to be an accountant or finance expert but a lousy time to be in medicine, dentistry or most kinds of engineering." Allegedly, the demand was "hot" for marketing specialists, health-care administrators, and finance executives, but cooler for "many middle-management corporate jobs and in-house public relations positions."

Predictions like these, often carried in the daily paper's business pages usually suffer from their short time horizon. The authors of these predictions often admit that many of their ideas are speculative. General theories of social and economic change are rarely taken into account, and longer-range predictions are seldom attempted. The writers rarely return to their earlier predictions in order to learn from them.

Such journalistic accounts make interesting reading over breakfast and usually contain some insight. But you are likely to find that these predictions change quickly and unexpectedly. Avoid basing your future plans on what you read in the newspaper.

A better option is to consult forecasts based on more systematic methods. In recent years, governments have developed sophisticated ways of predicting the future of labour markets. Predictions based on the Canadian Occupation Projection System (COPS) are published in a series known as *Job Futures* (Employment and Immigration Canada, 1986, 1988, 1990). This method predicted rapid growth by 1992 in the demand for service managers, dentists, denturists and dental technicians, photographers and camera operators, producers and directors in the performing and audio-visual arts, coaches and trainers in sport and recreation, chefs and cooks, food and beverage preparation supervisors, and sound and video recording equipment operators. On the other hand, it predicted little or no growth in the demand for teachers in universities, community colleges and secondary schools, and for farmers (Employment and Immigration Canada, 1986).

Since 1992 has come and gone, you can judge the accuracy of these predictions for yourself. Some were correct; most were not. The result: a new set of predictions was published (see Exhibit 4.1 below).

In 1988, COPS was predicting that the following ten occupations would need the most new recruits by 1995 (numbers in parentheses represent job openings expected between 1989 and 1995): retail salespeople (557 300); bookkeepers (318 700); secretaries and stenographers (300 000); cashiers and tellers (300 000); waiters (220 000); janitors (195 000); chefs and cooks (194 000); sales and advertising management occupations (167 000); electronic data processing equipment operators (158 000); general office clerks (126 000).

Yet even these more recent predictions are of doubtful validity. When we compare old COPS projections published in 1986, 1988, and 1990 with the actual job situation, we find the reality has rarely played itself out the way the projections suggested. No wonder the projections keep changing!

Some inaccuracy is introduced when job-seekers follow the COPS predictions—a process known as the "self-fulfilling prophecy." After reading the 1990 COPS forecast, for example, many people may decide to train for jobs that look promising. Others reading the same COPS forecast a year later will make similar plans without knowing what the 1990 readers had decided. By 1995, huge numbers of recruits are training for positions that have already been filled many times over.

Other inaccuracies appear to be the result of faulty methods of calculation. In two short years—from 1988 to 1990—the predicted number of waiters needed by 1995 grew from 89 000 to 220 000, and the predicted number of chefs from 51 000 to 194 000. In 1986, the projected openings for waiters and chefs were only 28 700 and 18 000 respectively. It took only four years for COPS to revise its estimate for waiters by 800 percent and for chefs by 1000 percent.

Exhibit 4.1
Occupations contributing most to employment growth, 1990–2000

	1990	1990–2000	
Occupations	**Employment**	**Average annual growth rate**	**Share of total employment growth**
Nurses	250 734	3.3%	6.7%
Systems Analysts	132 506	4.5%	5.2%
Office Managers	161 166	3.6%	4.8%
Sales Management Occs.	264 159	2.3%	4.8%
Cashiers and Tellers	312 677	1.9%	4.6%
Electronic data processing Equipment Operators	135 820	4.0%	4.6%
Child Care Workers	107 181	4.3%	4.0%
Secretaries and Stenographers	455 353	1.1%	3.8%
Salespersons	667 138	0.7%	3.4%
General Managers	189 891	2.1%	3.0%
Chefs and Cooks	191 894	2.0%	2.9%
Receptionists	121 322	2.5%	2.4%
Financial Officers	213 092	1.3%	2.1%
Bookkeepers	403 863	0.6%	1.8%
Food/Beverage Prep. Assist.	55 323	3.6%	1.7%
Elementary/Kind. Teachers	198 938	1.1%	1.6%
Hairdressers	103 596	1.9%	1.5%
Occs. Welfare/Commu. Serv.	68 717	2.6%	1.4%
Social Workers	53 873	2.9%	1.3%
Nursing Attendants	81 636	2.0%	1.3%
Financial Managers	80 735	1.9%	1.2%
Finance Clerks	56 654	2.4%	1.1%
Dental Hygienists	25 443	4.4%	1.0%
Services Management Occs.	69 202	1.8%	1.0%
Personnel Management Occs.	37 021	3.1%	0.9%

Source: Employment and Immigration Canada, COPS (1992). Ottawa: Supply and Services Canada. Reprinted with permission.

Obviously, there must be more accurate ways of making long-term predictions. One such way is demographic projection.

Demographic Projection

The method known as *demographic projection* focusses on the changing size and composition of the nation's population. Job opportunities are influenced by the ratio of jobs to people seeking jobs. Opportunities grow with *either* increases in the total number of jobs *or* decreases in the total number of workers. Demographers, who study population scientifically, take an interest in the factors that increase or decrease the rate of labour force participation and the numbers of working-age people in the population.

Canada has always depended on immigration to provide settlers, skills and, most recently, capital. Immigration rates have been relatively low in the last few decades, compared with earlier in the century. If the rate of immigration increases, will your opportunities for a high-paying job diminish significantly? Not necessarily, so long as patterns of discrimination against visible minorities continue. In recent years, a growing percentage of immigrants has come from Africa, Asia, and the Caribbean. Although many of these visible minorities have attained a higher education and are eligible for good jobs, they often have trouble laying claim to these jobs.

Since the publication of John Porter's *The Vertical Mosaic* in 1965, many researchers have studied the ethno-racial stratification of Canadian society (for example, Breton et al., 1990; Herberg, 1990; for a review of the studies, see Brym & Fox, 1989). It appears that most minorities have improved their socio-economic status and educational levels since Porter wrote his classic work. But the systemic discrimination against visible minorities in employment has not disappeared. The best-paying jobs are still predominantly given to highly educated white people.

Canada's population is aging. If the Canadian birthrate remains low, the proportion of children in the population will continue to fall throughout your lifetime. The result will be a shortage of young workers and an oversupply of middle-aged and older workers. Demographers say that, by the year 2031, half the population will be over age 42 (Foot, 1982, Tables 3–9 & pp. 107–108).

How will changes in the age composition of Canada's population affect your employment opportunities? First, consider that many occupations aim their services and products at particular age groups. Teachers, for example, serve mainly young people. When children born during the 1950s and early 1960s were at school, teaching was a secure and growing occupation. But as the baby boomers graduated from school, enrollments dropped and fewer new teachers were hired. The demographic shift affected the need for teachers at the primary, then secondary, and then postsecondary levels of education. During the late 1970s, teachers seeking employment experienced great frustration and disappointment. The "baby boom of the '80s" revived teaching opportunities only temporarily. The same pattern will apply to other industries catering to baby boomers' young children.

Industries catering to the aging baby boomers themselves, however, can be expected to become increasingly large employers of labour. As the numbers of middle-aged people grow, more service workers in health, leisure, recreation, and travel will be needed. When the boomers reach old age, the demand for nursing-home workers, gerontologists, and funeral directors will swell.

Both population aging and immigration affect the supply of workers who are the "right" age. Today, there are too few young workers compared to middle-aged workers. Because they are so numerous, middle-aged workers are suffering from a "promotion squeeze." Aging baby boomers have a smaller chance than earlier generations of getting into upper-management positions (Kettle, 1980, pp. 192–93).

Attrition—the movement of workers out of particular occupations—increases younger workers' chances of moving up the employment ladder. There is a high rate of attrition in occupations that put a premium on physical strength and agility (for example, professional sports) and youthful good looks (for example, rock music and entertainment).

In occupations with large numbers of older workers, attrition due to retirements is likely to be high in the near future, therefore creating new opportunities for younger workers. Occupations with especially high proportions of workers over 54 years old include medicine, dentistry, pharmacy, optometry, chiropractic, health-care administration, and tool-and-die making (Employment and Immigration Canada, 1986). These are good occupations to consider.

It is not easy to predict whether the job opportunities created by attrition will be shared equally between men and women. Nor can we predict how fairly they will be shared among young people from different class, racial, religious, and regional backgrounds. What *is* clear, given the restructuring of Canada's industries, is that many jobs will simply be eliminated.

In periods of economic stability, demographic methods predict the future reasonably well. However, the economy is not very stable these days. A broader theory of change is needed: one that takes account of social, economic, political, technological, and demographic realities. That is precisely what futures researchers try to provide.

Futures Research

The method that predicts changes in employment trends as part of a general pattern of social change is known as *futures research*. Sociologist Daniel Bell's (1973) thesis of "post-industrial society" holds that, in today's most advanced societies, the economic base is shifting from industrial manufacturing to the production and processing of information. Others have called this the "information society."

According to this thesis, the economic emphasis will change from producing goods to providing services. Therefore, manual work will decline as a greater portion of the work force engages in cleaner, more interesting white-collar work. Automation will improve the factory jobs that remain. Office jobs, too, will require more training and allow workers greater scope for autonomy and creativity.

Looking ahead to the distant future, some see a massive transformation of agriculture and manufacturing and the kinds of jobs they offer. Increasingly, it is predicted, food will be produced on the ocean floor, in space, and in factories and laboratories. Workers employed in manufacturing will build, program, repair, and supervise robots. Employment patterns will be conditioned by innovative applications of scientific knowledge and a new attitude toward the environment.

Changes in white-collar work that can already be seen are the replacement of clerical personnel in banks and offices by computerized equipment, and the increasing importance of new technical specialties and services in sales and in information supply, a field that includes education, guidance, consulting, and lobbying. Some futures researchers predict that

> five of the ten fastest-growing jobs over the next few years will be computer-related, with programmers and systems analysts growing by 70 percent in the next ten years ... services will account for 92 percent of the jobs and 85 percent of the gross national product by the year 2000, compared with 70 percent of U.S. jobs and 60 percent of GNP today ... [and] 25 to 35 percent of all paid work in the United States will be done from people's homes by the turn of the century (*Outlook '87*, 1986, p. 5).

Many advanced societies (such as Canada) have already entered the post-industrial stage. Just as Bell would predict, the proportion of workers employed in the service sector is steadily increasing. Between 1951 and 1981, the proportion of Canadians employed in the service sector grew from 47 percent to 66 percent of the total labour force (Picot, 1987, p. 8). Canada has also seen a significant increase in the proportion of the labour force performing white-collar work. From

15.2 percent at the beginning of this century, the proportion of white-collar workers rose to 52.2 percent by 1981.

However, large increases in the service sector and white-collar work have not been accompanied by large decreases in industrial jobs. Agricultural, not industrial, work has declined throughout this century: the percentage of Canadian workers employed in agriculture fell from 40 in 1901 to less than 4 in 1991. It is still unclear whether the massive job losses in Ontario's manufacturing sector during the 1990s are due to post-industrial economic restructuring, free trade with the United States, a combination of the two, or other factors such as competition in a globalized economy.

The post-industrial thesis holds that future jobs will offer more challenge and creativity by drawing on more of people's skills. To some degree, this has already started to happen. Workers are likely to say that electronic technology has made their work more interesting, less hazardous to their health, less stressful, and better paid (Harvey, 1988, Table 8). Yet few of the rapid-growth occupations identified by COPS (see Exhibit 4.1), call for a higher education, and none is outstandingly creative or stimulating. "Many of the growth occupations have little impact on training volumes. For many of them, there are numbers of unemployed people who can take the jobs without major training. Others involve low skill levels" (Canada, 1984, p. 4).

Interestingly, 20 to 30 percent of respondents deny that new technology has had any impact on their workplace (Harvey, 1988). And a Gallup poll (reported in *The Toronto Star,* November 19, 1990) shows 56 percent of Canadian workers saying that new technology has not significantly changed their job in the last five years. This agrees with the results of a study of social service agencies in Ontario (Gandy & Tepperman, 1990), which showed that computerization had done little, if anything, to change the way in which the agencies were working. In general, the type of technology used has little effect on job satisfaction in a social service agency (Dubey & Meller, 1988).

It is because the new technology has *not* revolutionized work that most workplaces have been able to integrate the new technology without much difficulty. Nearly two in every three cases of reported technological innovation involve simple technologies such as word processing, personal computers, and office networks (Betcherman & McMullen, 1986). Many new jobs require the same amount of skill as the jobs they replaced.

Typically, new skill requirements mean retraining the affected employees on the job. But skills that workers learn quickly on the job do little to increase the complexity and challenge of their work. Currently, about half the retraining is intended to prepare women for routine computerized clerical work. In turn, this raises the issue of job de-skilling: many kinds of jobs are actually becoming more narrow and boring, not more creative.

Another of the promises of post-industrialism is economic improvement. It seems obvious, however, that many jobs simply disappear when new technology is introduced. Between 1980 and 1986, a period when many offices introduced microtechnology, Canadian banks cut 9000 employees (Rinehart, 1987, p. 85). While each older-generation robot in West Germany eliminated 2.5 manufacturing jobs, newer ones eliminate 5 to 10 jobs (Words Associated, 1986, p. 20). The Japanese Ministry of Labour found that 40 percent of companies introducing microelectronics later reduced their numbers of employees, and French job losses in banking and insurance due to information technology have been estimated at 30 percent (Schneider, 1984, p. 164).

The post-industrial thesis leaves us with a great many questions. Along with demographic projection and linear extrapolation, futures research helps us understand changes in the world of work and careers. Yet the evidence supporting all these models is confused and contradictory. What should we conclude from the forecasts that we have examined?

What Does the Future (Appear to) Hold?

Different forecasting techniques yield somewhat different forecasts. But as those we have discussed tend, for the most part, to point in the same direction, we should consider taking that direction.

Cetron (1984), a futures researcher, has been bold enough to predict the 500 best jobs of the future—"where they'll be and how to get them." Cetron's forecast and the COPS forecast agree that large numbers of additional waiters and waitresses, retail sales clerks, secretaries and stenographers, bookkeepers, chefs and cooks, truck drivers, accountants, and elementary school teachers will be needed in the near future.

Both approaches—futures research and linear extrapolation— show that many older jobs are becoming obsolete. Cetron's list includes factory assembler (assembly-line worker), bank cashier, farm worker, and farm manager.

Another thing that almost everyone agrees on is that more and better education will be important from now on. To avoid being replaced by a machine, you have to be more complex and more flexible than a machine. Basic education for a post-industrial world includes learning to read and write effectively, communicate simply, manage information, and operate a computer. Moreover, Cetron advises you to "learn to learn

... learn to think ... and learn how to do it for the rest of your life" (Cetron, 1984, p. 129).

This conclusion is supported by a Conference Board of Canada report called *The Employability Skills Profile: What Are Employers Looking For?* (1992; reported in *The Toronto Star*, May 30, 1992, p. F1). Employers claim to be looking for people who

- understand the need for lifelong learning;
- communicate well, listen carefully, and understand, speak, and write effectively in the languages used in business;
- think clearly, assess critically, act logically, and are able to make decisions;
- have mathematical skills that can be used to solve problems;
- can "use technology, instruments, tools and information systems ... and can access and apply specialized knowledge" from a variety of sources;
- demonstrate self-confidence and know how to manage their lives well and with integrity;
- take responsibility, set goals and priorities, and manage their own time well;
- think creatively; and
- work successfully in a team, showing respect for the opinions and concerns of co-workers.

In spite of the confidence of these forecasts and the consensus on the kind of education and attitudes that will be most valuable, there are many reasons for doubt and uncertainty. Per capita growth in the world economy has become less predictable since the early 1970s (see Exhibit 4.2, Figure b). It may even be slowing down. An unstable or shrinking economy is not a safe haven for either forecasters or job-seekers.

What career should you enter? In the face of uncertainty, you should do what seems most certain: get a good general education and examine your own heart. Learn how to learn, and keep on learning throughout your life. Pay attention to your preferences and your strengths. If you love, and are good at, a lot of things, use forecasts to choose a career from among your "loves."

JOB SATISFACTION

Job satisfaction is important. Most Canadians consider job satisfaction only slightly less important than marital, familial, and romantic satisfaction. People can learn to compensate for a dissatisfaction in one life

Exhibit 4.2
World economic production

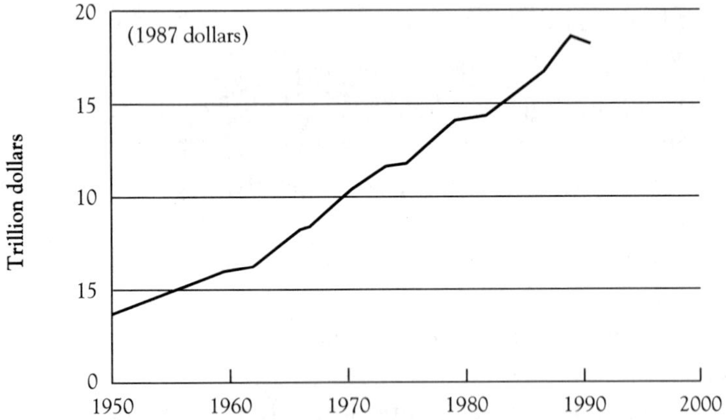

Figure a: Gross World Product, 1950–91

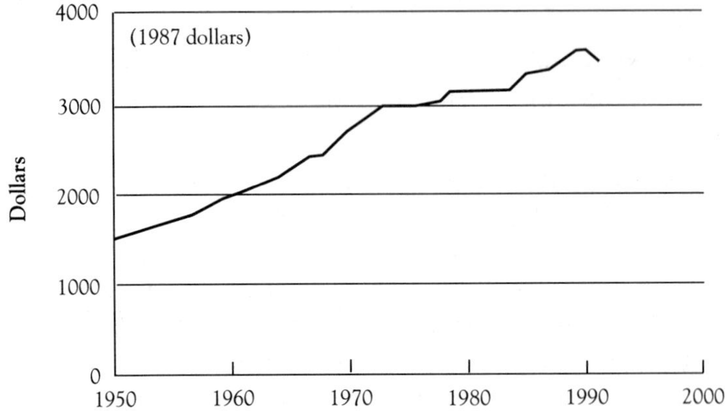

Figure b: Gross World Product Per Person, 1950–91

Source: Brown, L.R., et al. (1992). *Vital signs* (p. 67). Worldwatch Institute. New York: W.W. Norton. Reprinted with permission.

domain by finding satisfaction in another, as we saw in Chapter One. But any full-time job will be an important part of a person's life. For a satisfying life, you will need to know more about job satisfaction: what it is, who has it, and how you can get it.

Nationality is the single best predictor of job satisfaction. A Louis Harris poll (reported in *The Toronto Star,* November 1, 1991) shows that 39 percent of Canadian office workers say that they are "very satisfied" with their job, compared with 43 percent of American workers and only 17 percent of Japanese and 28 percent of European Community workers. Canadian office workers explain that top executives in their firms are in touch with their attitudes and that continuous improvement (that is, promotion) programs are more common in Canada than in other countries.

Most Canadians say that they are "fairly satisfied" or "very satisfied" with their job (Atkinson, 1983a, Table 1; Environics, 1987). This is consistent with results from across the industrialized world. Data from the Meaning of Work Project (England & Harpaz, 1990) were used to examine differences in job satisfaction in Belgium, the Federal Republic of Germany, Israel, Japan, the Netherlands, and the United States. The vast majority of respondents reported a positive attitude to their jobs: only 4 percent defined their work as unpleasant, and more than 85 percent said that they would continue working even if they had enough income to retire immediately.

Job satisfaction is closely tied to life satisfaction. Although exceptions have been found to this rule (see for example, Whiteside, 1985), most researchers agree that the two forms of satisfaction interact and build on one another (Liou, Sylvia, & Brunk, 1990).

It may be that the same factors determine both independently (see Keon & McDonald, 1982); or perhaps non-work satisfactions themselves (such as satisfaction with family life, standard of living, and quality of leisure time) affect the level of work satisfaction (Hawkes et al., 1984). Other researchers think that both work activities and non-work activities can allow people to gain recognition and use valued skills, so that both give rise to the same kinds of satisfactions (Brook & Brook, 1989). Job satisfaction does *not* predict life satisfaction in the absence of certain key variables such as adequate income, recognition, and health (Near, 1984). This suggests that job satisfaction works through these kinds of "intervening" variables (see also Tahlin, 1989). Cultural conditions and work attitudes may be another key variable: the relationship between job satisfaction and life satisfaction is stronger among Japanese workers than it is among American workers (Near, 1987).

By the late 1970s, at least 3350 articles and doctoral dissertations had been written on the topic of job satisfaction (Locke, 1976). The number must have doubled by now. Researchers have looked in three main directions to explain what causes people to be satisfied or dissatisfied with their jobs: *objective job characteristics*, such as working conditions, salary schemes, work schedules, union membership, and supervision patterns; *biographic* (or *demographic*) *characteristics*, such as age, gender, marital status, education, and religion; and *personality characteristics*, such as self-esteem, feelings of trust toward others, sense of mastery, and control over one's life (Burstein et al., 1975, p. 26; Khaleque & Rahman, 1987).

Objective Job Characteristics

Most research into the causes of job satisfaction has focussed on objective job characteristics. Researchers studying both blue-collar workers and office workers have found a fairly consistent pattern:

> Work satisfaction is engendered by work which is varied, allows autonomy, is not physically fatiguing,... is mentally challenging and yet allows the individual to experience success, and ... is personally interesting. Satisfaction with rewards such as pay, promotions, and recognition depends on the fairness or equity with which they are administered and the degree to which they are congruent with the individual's personal aspirations.... The employee will be satisfied with agents in the work situation (supervisors, subordinates, co-workers, management) to the degree that they are seen as facilitating the attainment of his work goals and work rewards, and to the degree that these agents are perceived as having important values in common with him. (Locke, 1976, p. 1342)

More recent research (Conway, Williams, & Green, 1987; King, Murray, & Atkinson, 1982) reaches very similar conclusions. If you want a really satisfying job, find one that has high prestige, pays well, has regular hours, is safe, does not wear you out, and allows you to set your own hours and pace of work. If you are unable to be your own boss, make sure that you belong to a union (on this, see also Schwochau, 1987; Childs, 1985; Pfeffer & Davis-Blake, 1990).

What does this mean in more specific terms? Las Vegas casino card dealers are a good example of a group of dissatisfied workers. Frey and Carns (1988) report that dealers know that they can be hired and fired at will, since there is a large pool of replacements near at hand. As a result, they become sensitive to problems with the security, income, supervision, and routine associated with their work. Almost none wanted to move up to management, and few saw themselves dealing cards in five years time.

This contrasts sharply with the work satisfaction expressed by the employees of the Scottish restaurant studied by Marshall (1986) over a two-year period. He reports that although the staff earned low wages and worked many hours of unpaid overtime, they enjoyed their work and rarely looked for other jobs. Considerable job autonomy and an informal, leisurely environment led the employees to enjoy being at the restaurant for its own sake.

The list of objective variables that influence job satisfaction is as long as the list of possible jobs and work situations. Other things being equal, people seem to prefer working in small, local organizations rather than large, national ones (Hodson & Sullivan, 1985; Hodson, 1984). Many people—including farmers (Coughenour & Swanson, 1988), fishers (Gatewood & McCay, 1990), and gravediggers (Petrillo, 1989)—seem to find that working outdoors adds a great deal to their job satisfaction. The presence of a mentor—an older and more experienced adviser on the job—seems to increase job satisfaction and also success (Fagenson, 1989). And contrary to what many people believe, shift work and night work do *not* have a negative effect on job satisfaction or life satisfaction (Cunningham, 1989; Weiss & Liss, 1988; Redmond, 1988).

The objective satisfactions of jobs can be classified as either intrinsic or extrinsic. Work offers *intrinsic* satisfaction when it is interesting and fulfilling. Where intrinsic satisfaction is lacking, workers pay much more attention to *extrinsic* satisfactions such as pay level, working hours, and working conditions (Gruenberg, 1980, p. 268; also, Mottaz, 1985). Postal workers whose work environment has recently been mechanized and automated can expect to see the intrinsic satisfaction of their jobs further reduced; their job satisfaction is best predicted by such extrinsic rewards as opportunity for promotion and good relations with their supervisor (Baxter, 1990). Because different workers value extrinsic and intrinsic job rewards differently, "research must be careful to distinguish between the categories of employees when discussing the contribution of various job factors to employee job satisfaction" (Ronen & Sadan, 1984, pp. 92, 94).

Highly educated workers tend—at least when they begin their careers —to be motivated by intrinsic job factors. They bring a particularly high degree of commitment (and high educational credentials) to their work. When that work turns out to be limiting and frustrating, as is often the case, they become dissatisfied. The work has violated their expectations. Often, the result is a condition people have come to call "burnout."

Job Dissatisfaction and Burnout

Burnout, the ultimate sign of job dissatisfaction, is a problem that many professional and managerial workers are faced with. Meier (1983) defines burnout as a state in which people expect little reward (and even much punishment) from their work because of a lack of valued reinforcement, controllable outcomes, or personal competence. Burnout shows up in such symptoms as depression, anxiety, irritability—and even reduced marital satisfaction (Jayaratne, Chess, & Kunkel, 1986). According to Freudenberger and Richelson (1981), those who run a particularly high risk of burnout tend to be highly motivated people who work in settings that impose strong external controls or give unpredictable rewards for performance.

Many professions that are devoted to helping or changing people—for example, social work, nursing, teaching, and medicine—place a great deal of responsibility on the job-holder. For a variety of reasons that may include a lack of resources, time, autonomy, or co-operation, these jobs are almost impossible to do as well or as completely as one would hope. The result is often low work satisfaction (Penn, Romano & Foat, 1988.) Unlike other workers who face frustration, workers in these professions seldom deal with their dissatisfaction by walking away: absenteeism among them remains low (Tziner & Vardi, 1984). On the other hand, the rate of turnover is quite high in some of these jobs (Herrick et al., 1983); workers feel "burnt out" and abandon their profession to look for another kind of work.

Burnout and job satisfaction have somewhat different causes and consequences in different occupations (Jayaratne & Chess, 1984). Meller and Macarov (1986) report that the most important conditions affecting the job satisfaction of social workers are an ability to achieve results, the quality of relations with clients and members of multidisciplinary staffs, and the availability of time and money needed to do the job. Because these conditions are often unmet, social workers are likely to feel alienated at work, despite their good pay and chances for career advancement (Davies, 1990). One social worker in three reports dissatisfaction with his or her work, although satisfaction varies according to type of service and whether the employing agency is a private or public one (Vinokur-Kaplan, 1991). Social workers with a master's degree in social work (MSW) are more satisfied with their profession than those with only a bachelor's (BSW) degree (McCullagh, 1985; Jerrell & Knight, 1985). According to Dhooper and Byars (1989), younger workers with BSW degrees—especially those in direct-service positions—report much higher levels of stress and less life satisfaction than older social workers who have more education, income, and autonomy.

"Human services" (or "social services") personnel may range from graduates of specialized university programs to high-school graduates; their work may be highly skilled or mainly clerical. What they all have in common is the size of the organizations where they work alongside many other human services personnel, and a body of clients who are trying to deal with a personal problem—poverty, family conflict, drug addiction, law-breaking, and so on. Human services workers experience problems of dissatisfaction, stress, and burnout as serious as those that affect social workers (Zedeck et al., 1988; Hagen, 1989; Brookings et al., 1985). The objective characteristics of the organizations in which they work appear to be at the root of their problems.

Nursing, like social work, is a "heteronomous profession," where workers take on many different roles. Some nurses are independent professionals; others work directly for doctors. Most nurses, however, are members of a hospital staff, where they have little autonomy (Alexander, 1984). Only half of the nurses interviewed by Caston and Braito (1985a) ranked the pursuit of job satisfaction high among their employment goals. Yet nurses working in hospitals, present ample evidence of burnout and job dissatisfaction; their complaints have been well documented (see, for example, Turner, 1986; McDowell & Forsyth, 1990). Nurses working in psychiatric settings report even less work satisfaction and more problems of health and stress than nurses in general hospital settings (Landeweerd & Boumans, 1988).

Along with others in the helping professions, nurses tend to value intrinsic work satisfactions such as task interest more highly than extrinsic satisfactions such as adequate pay and good working conditions (Caston & Braito, 1985b). In the context of frequent job dissatisfaction, however, they do tend to complain about working conditions and levels of reward. Both personal and objective factors appear to affect nurses' job satisfaction: seniority, rank, sex, and types of basic training (Gray, 1984).

Teachers also run the risk of stress and burnout. Those who leave the profession list among their complaints an unexpectedly heavy workload, lack of support from administrators, and difficulties in dealing with students from varied cultural backgrounds (Haberman & Rickards, 1990). They tend to express disillusion with teaching as a career.

Neither personal characteristics nor teaching background influence satisfaction among teachers (DeFrank & Stroup, 1989). Organizational factors seem to carry most weight. Webb and Ashton (1986) state that seven conditions threaten teachers' sense of competence and job satisfaction: excessive role demands, low salaries and social status, isolation from peers and administrators, uncertainty, powerlessness, alienation, and declining morale (see Mykletun, 1985, for a similar finding in Norway).

In general, academics teaching in colleges and universities have a high level of job satisfaction; their work is a major source of life satisfaction (Schell & Loeb, 1986; but, for a contrary view, see Carnegie Foundation, 1985, 1986). Academics expect their career to allow them the opportunity for intellectual growth and the chance to influence people (Resnick & Mason, 1988). As a result, anything that diminishes the perfect autonomy they had expected when they went into higher education is a source of dissatisfaction (Copur, 1990). Thus, academics tend to complain about university administrators (French, Gross, & Resnick, 1986) and bureaucratic organization (Bonjean et al., 1982). They voice concerns about the effects of budget cuts on their institutions, and about the integrity of their profession and the institution in which they are working (Carnegie Foundation, 1985). The conflicting demands of teaching and research are responsible for a great deal of dissatisfaction among academics.

As least as important is the stress that competition brings: competition both with colleagues for recognition and the personal striving to meet some absolute standard of achievement. Gmelch, Wilke, and Lovrich (1986) find that questions of reward and recognition are the most common and important sources of stress among academics.

Faculty in professional schools are the most satisfied academics on almost all dimensions (Pearson & Seiler, 1983). Perhaps this stems from their comparatively high salaries and practice-based requirements for tenure and promotion. Yet salary and academic rank have less impact on academics' satisfaction with work than tenure, teaching load, age, and sex. Those who lack tenure are least secure; they report lower levels of satisfaction than all others (Davis, 1985).

Is burnout inevitable in these profession and others like them? Not at all. They provide satisfying and fulfilling careers for many who enter them. The likelihood of burnout is especially reduced when the employing organizations are alert to the problem (Finn, 1990).

Certain factors consistently increase or decrease work satisfaction in *all* the helping professions. A review of the literature produces the following list of characteristics making for satisfying professional work:

1. good organizational conditions, including ample organizational resources and a clear policy mandate
2. participation in decision making, including democratic leadership, decentralization, and informality
3. open communication in the workplace, especially with supervisors and top management
4. social support on the job, including good relationships with supervisors and co-workers
5. job challenge, including skill variety and the opportunity to work with varied types of people
6. possibility of advancement

7. good income and status, and fair allocation of rewards at the workplace
8. autonomy and control over the work process
9. co-operation between client (or patient, or student) and agency (or hospital, or school)
10. limited work pressure, including manageable caseloads
11. use of strategies for coping with stress

In many ways, this list conforms to Locke's general set of objective characteristics governing job satisfaction. Workers in the helping occupations are special in one important respect, however: they start out with higher expectations and are subject to deeper disappointment.

Biographic and Personality Characteristics

Specific objective job conditions are more important to some people than to others. This suggests that objective job conditions interact with personality and biographic (or demographic) factors to influence job satisfaction.

Less is known about the effects of personality and biographic characteristics on job satisfaction than the effects of objective job conditions. Few studies have compared the relative influence of these three factors. Two studies of job satisfaction—one a study of Canadians by King, Murray, and Atkinson (1982), and another a study of Americans by Rice, Near, and Hunt (1979)—make the attempt.

The two studies reach quite different conclusions about the importance of biographic characteristics in predicting job satisfaction. Of the two, the study by King, Murray and Atkinson—more believable because it collects more detailed data—reports that biographic characteristics add little to our understanding of job satisfaction once objective job and personality characteristics are taken into account. This conclusion finds some support in the work of Brush, Moch, and Pooyan (1987), who observe that of all biographic variables, only age and length of service in a job have a significant bearing on job satisfaction. In view of these findings, it might prove more fruitful to turn our attention to a discussion of personality characteristics.

Most people are able to change their behaviours, attitudes, expectations, desires, and even their values (for examples, see Haas & Shaffir, 1978). Rarely can they change their basic personality. As if to illustrate this, Staw, Bell, and Clausen (1986) have studied the same individuals over time and shown that measures of temperament (or disposition) gathered in adolescence predict adult job satisfaction over a 50-year period. Both King, Murray, and Atkinson (1982) and Rice, Near, and Hunt (1979) find that personality characteristics are highly correlated with work satisfaction. For this reason, it is important to choose a career that is suited to your individual personality.

Self-esteem appears to influence job satisfaction, perhaps because it is related to a task-related "sense of competence" (Sekaran, 1986). Locke reports that "high self-esteem individuals will experience more pleasure in their work, other things being equal, than individuals with low self-esteem" (1976, p. 1344).

Alienation and *perceived locus of control* are two related psychological characteristics that influence job satisfaction. People who feel alienated and who feel that they have little control over their own lives are less satisfied with their jobs than other people. It seems likely that alienation is a general personality trait that develops prior to workplace experience—one that interacts with experiences at work, but is not caused by them. Nevertheless, certain kinds of work can be alienating. People tend to feel alienated and to hate their job when their work is routine and tightly controlled, and they believe that the firm's method of control is illegitimate—that is, unnecessary and unjust (Fuller & Dornbusch, 1988). People who feel that they have little control over their lives and who are dissatisfied with their jobs participate in politics less, trust government less, and are more politically alienated than other people (Delli-Carpini, Sigel, & Snyder, 1983).

King, Murray, and Atkinson (1982) and Rice, Near, and Hunt (1979) agree that these personality variables predict job satisfaction about as well as objective characteristics of the job itself. People's "individual expectations and traits" interact with "objective characteristics of their experience" to shape their feelings about their job (King, Murray, and Atkinson, 1982, p. 129). Whatever the job, feelings of alienation, distrust, and external control reduce job satisfaction. They may also combine with objective job characteristics such as danger, unpredictability, long hours, excessive supervision, and low occupational prestige to magnify job satisfaction.

A mismatch between job and personality can cause job burnout, or worse: chronic sickness and absenteeism (see, for example, Martin & Miller, 1986), depression, frequent job turnover (Roborgh & Stacey, 1987), and alcohol and drug use on the job (Hollinger, 1988; but, arguing the other side, see Mensch & Kandel, 1988).

People need to know enough about their own personalities and the jobs they are considering to be able to anticipate whether they will find a particular job satisfying. You should not become a police officer if you hate rules and routines, or a novelist if you need imposed order, or a door-to-door sales representative if you need continuous approval.

Unfortunately, social class may set limits on people's choice of work and so influence what they get out of their work life, just as it affects the rest of their lives. People in the working class and lower-middle class are particularly likely to hold jobs with objectively dissatisfying features: low pay, high risk of unemployment, unpleasant working conditions, and so on.

Moreover, these jobs typically combine low prestige and a high degree of external control. Ornstein (1988, Table 5) shows that 45 percent of manual workers report being supervised frequently on their job, 34 percent are required to produce a quota at work, and only 30 percent are able to leave work to do an errand at any time. Further, 31 percent had suffered some unemployment and 25 percent had been laid off in the preceding two years. All of these conditions and experiences produce feelings of alienation, external control, and distrust.

By contrast, only 8 percent of managers and technocrats report being supervised frequently and only 15 percent are required to meet a quota. More than 80 percent are able to leave work to do an errand at any time. Only 15 percent of the managers and technocrats had experienced unemployment in the preceding two years, and a mere 4 percent had experienced a layoff in the same period. (The numbers are probably higher today, but no comparable statistics are available.) Managers' objective job conditions are better and more satisfying than those of manual workers. They are much less likely to give rise to feelings of alienation, external control, and distrust.

Aging and Job Satisfaction

One of the few biographic characteristics that predicts job satisfaction quite reliably is age. People tend to become more satisfied with their job as well as with life as they get older (Kalleberg & Loscocco, 1983; Janson & Martin, 1982; Lee & Wilbur, 1985; Mottaz, 1987; Zeitz, 1990; but for exceptions to this rule, see Anand & Sohal, 1983; Karp, 1987).

Lee and Wilbur (1985) believe that the rise in job satisfaction among older workers may be due to lower expectations, high rewards gained through long employment, and a greater emphasis on the work itself (intrinsic satisfactions) than on money (an extrinsic satisfaction). But the explanation is probably more complicated than that, since the relationship between age and job satisfaction does not develop at a steady rate (Zeitz, 1990; De Vries et al., 1984).

Moreover, the (positive) aging effect on satisfaction may be offset by a (negative) cohort—or generation—effect. Glenn and Weaver (1985) note that each cohort to reach adulthood in recent years has been less satisfied with work than the preceding cohort. Likewise, a Gallup poll (*Society*, 1989) suggests that the overall level of job satisfaction is tied to generation (and not to income). Earlier cohorts are more work-oriented —more likely to value work for itself—than later ones have been. As well, recent "period effects" have included a decline in the job market since the early 1970s and an excess of middle-aged people which has made career advancement difficult for everyone.

Aging, therefore, may increase work satisfaction for only certain generations of people. If Canada's economy remains unsettled, we may see an aging and dissatisfied work force exhibiting declining performance on the job.

Retirement: Life Satisfaction after Work

Paid work does not go on forever. Most people retire. The twentieth century has seen a steady decline in the average age of retirement, and that is partly why the question of retirement—whether it should be mandatory, and if so, at what age—is so hotly debated throughout the industrial world. The German gerontologist Tokarski (1988) writes:

> Prior to the 19th century, there was no official retirement age. Retirement was usually linked to illness or death. Only when pension systems were introduced in particular countries was a retirement age specified. In recent years the retirement age has become fluid. Today, in many countries, women and men retire at different ages. Certain occupations have earlier retirement ages than others, e.g., soldiers, police, civil servants, miners, etc. Conversely, for employers, self-employed professionals, university professors and politicians, a later retirement age is often acceptable. (p. 3)

Tokarski goes on to observe that the increasing interest in early retirement we find in many countries is "more often the result of labor market policy rather than concern for the quality of life of older persons."

Given that fewer workers have been waiting until age 65 to retire and that the average life span has been increasing, people are spending a longer portion of their lives in retirement. Most workers today retire at or near the minimum age for retirement, motivated either by a strong desire to retire or by poor health. Workers retiring voluntarily have little or no difficulty adjusting to the transition to retired life. A positive attitude usually means that the process will be quite benign (Atchley, 1982). Those forced out by mandatory retirement policies tend to be dissatisfied at first, but eventually they too adjust.

Atchley finds that although retirement reduces a person's activity level, it has no negative effect on physical health, self-esteem, or life satisfaction. The key to satisfaction in the retirement years is a combination of meaningful activities, a high level of marital satisfaction, and especially, a secure income and good health.

People who take early retirement usually adapt well to their new status. Morse and Gray (1980) surveyed managerial, professional, and technical personnel working in three large corporations who retired early. Three out of four respondents were satisfied that they had retired at the right time. One in five regretted having left work as soon as they did; they found that inflation was eroding their income, they missed the challenge of work and the contact with people, and they did not have enough to do. More than half the respondents found retirement to be very much what they expected. The major dissatisfactions reported relate to lessened income and poor health. "For many, postretirement employment experience has been the source of large, often extraordinary, financial and psychic rewards. And for an even larger proportion, postretirement employment has permitted the development of entirely new careers and interests" (Morse & Gray, 1980, pp. 109–10).

Financial assets and attractive pension packages are key elements in the early retirement decision, and later satisfaction, of retirees. Such findings are supported by studies of a cross-section of public and private industries in North America and abroad. Two-thirds of survey respondents in a study by McGoldrick and Cooper (1988, p. 95) report that one influence on their decision to retire early was their belief that early retirement is a good thing.

The buying patterns of people aged 50 to 64 reflect a radical shift toward early retirement and preparation for an enjoyable life away from their job. Married, affluent "empty-nesters" in this age bracket are good prospects for retirement travel, second homes, and investments (Townsend & Riche, 1987, p. 28). Ostroff (1989) calls the same group "prime-lifers." These "young-old" people increasingly seek goods and services that can help them manage time more effectively, provide a comfortable living environment, and increase leisure time. The receational activities they look for are invigorating as well as entertaining. They create a huge market for restaurants, hotels, airlines, cruise lines, tours, resorts, theme parks, recreational vehicles, and luxury vans.

This age group is increasingly demanding personal and developmental services. Such services include individual counselling on how to deal with divorce, the death of a parent or spouse, career plateauing, job burnout, and the stress caused by a chronically ill parent; instruction in spiritual self-help as well as practical tasks; information on aging; health and fitness products, including athletic equipment, and exercise, fitness, and weight-reduction centres; cosmetic surgery; rehabilitation services; anti-aging products; healthful foods; drugs or devices that combat or mask a decline in health; and expert advice in planning for a retirement that could well last over 30 years (Ostroff, 1989, pp. 28, 33, 58). These and other recent findings of market research show a widespread perception that life after the age of 50 can be a time of child-free pleasure and career-changing or recreation. (For more on this theme, see Dychtwald & Flower, 1987.)

People today seem to know what satisfactions they can expect from their retirement years, especially if they retire when they are young enough to enjoy them. Walker and Lazar (1978) write, "retirement is now widely viewed as a desirable objective, opening up new forms of activity and productivity. A major factor in the changed attitude has been the increasingly adequate financial protection available to retirees" (p. 61).

Your own retirement may seem quite remote. However, it is never too early to start thinking about the challenges that it will bring. Sooner or later, you will have to find satisfaction *outside* your paid work.

TRENDS IN JOB SATISFACTION

The key to job satisfaction—and all satisfaction—is matching expectations to possibilities. Given enough time, people can change their expectations and learn to take satisfaction from "substitute" rewards, once they come to expect them. Trends in job satisfaction will come to reflect changes in the match-up between what people are getting and what they have learned to expect. What, then, are these trends?

In a review of the research on changes in job satisfaction in the United States, Mortimer reports that "workers in all occupations are expressing greater discontent with their jobs." He finds evidence of "declines in satisfaction in virtually all segments of the working population ... [despite] a continuing high involvement with work as a central focus of life" (1979, p. 16).

Likewise, between 1977 and 1981 the percentage of Canadian workers saying that they were "very satisfied" with their jobs dropped substantially (Atkinson, 1983b, p. 48). Workers aged 30 to 44 showed the biggest drop in satisfaction of all. One important reason for this was the belief they shared with women, professionals, managers, and skilled labourers that opportunities for promotion had declined. These workers were beginning to feel the onset of the baby boom's "promotion squeeze."

The recession of the 1980s forced employers to reduce the number and cost of their employees. They singled out employees with high salaries—managers, professionals, and skilled labourers—and encouraged them to take early retirement. Some industries removed senior employees and did not replace them with others in line for promotion.

Canadian women, who reported even greater losses of influence and opportunity than men, became dissatisfied even more rapidly. In 1977, women had reported greater job satisfaction than men, but by 1981 the situation was reversed. As the economy continued to worsen, issues of concern to women—such as pay equity, job security, and job flexibility —were moved to the back burner. By the early 1990s, only a small minority of organizations planned to make major policy changes that would be of particular benefit to women (see the results of a survey of 1500 organizations in *The Financial Post*, September 2, 1991, p. 30).

Many of these trends are continuing. Job satisfaction continues to fall, particularly among middle-aged and highly educated workers who have seen a diminution in their opportunities for advancement, benefits, and the chance to participate in decision making. Among professional workers, women remain less satisfied with their opportunities for advancement than men (Environics, 1987).

Responses to the frustration over limited opportunity take various forms. Some people are working longer hours than ever before. On the other hand, increasing numbers say that they expect to make major changes: 16 percent of workers hope to be in another line of work within one year; another 25 percent plan to be in another line of work (or retirement) within five years (taken from a Gallup survey reported in *The Toronto Star*, November 19, 1990).

As the baby boom generation ages, people's orientations to work are changing. Many are substituting family and leisure activities for job and career concerns. In a national poll (Environics, 1987), 42 percent of people surveyed indicate that they are unwilling to give up leisure time, and 51 percent are unwilling to accept a transfer, even if it would advance their career. Women are particularly unwilling to give up leisure and family time for the sake of their careers.

CONCLUSION

Do people get what they want out of their work and careers, or learn to want what they can get? In general, people learn to want what they can get. But doing so is harder for some people than others, and harder under some conditions than others.

What people get out of work often results from earlier choices, especially educational ones. For women, marital and childbearing choices also influence work and career, as we shall see in the chapters that follow. Yet most people are just as unaware of the long-term consequences of their educational, marital, and childbearing choices as they are of long-term trends in the job market. They need better information about the likely consequences of their decisions.

Many people do not choose jobs or careers so much as fall into them. They respond to the first opportunity that is offered, or are forced to take the first thing that comes their way. This may be particularly true of people who suffer from the limits on opportunity discussed in Chapter Two: single parents, the poor, physically disabled people, members of visible minorities, and others.

Others who do choose careers often do so without considering their own aptitudes and interests. They fail to get what they wanted because they did not know what they were choosing when they made their choice. As well, people are likely to change their minds about what they want as they get older. What they want at one age or stage in the life cycle is not necessarily what they will want later. So the process of choosing a career is no longer a one-time-only experience. It pays to periodically re-think your plans and re-evaluate them, however far along the career path you may be.

Do people learn to want what they get? To a large degree they do. As people age, they become more satisfied with their work and career. And people who grow up in difficult economic conditions, as have the post-baby boomers, tend to start out with moderate, practical goals. They will always be more satisfied than people whose goals are unrealistically high.

How can you relate this information to your own life? Some people believe that no forecasts—indeed, no statistics—can be useful in planning their own lives (Selleck, 1982, pp. 41–42). Others (for example, Stager, 1983) argue that forecasts are essential to any effective career strategy. This book shares their view.

Our economy is increasingly becoming a service economy, in which work depends on flexibility and general cognitive and interpersonal skills (Hunter, 1988). It follows that you should get as much education and as many appropriate credentials as you can. Most of all, learn how to learn, think, and communicate.

Choosing the job that is right for you—the job that will satisfy you—demands much more than knowing which fields will be doing most of the hiring in the near future. Pay attention to your own interests and aptitudes: they are a surer guide than career forecasts in an unpredictable economy. If you can, choose a career that interests you, for that is the career that it is most likely to satisfy you. Some of you may even find that a job that makes use of your training in sociology is what will give you the most satisfaction. For information on the result of this choice, see Exhibit 4.3.

Look for work that provides you with autonomy—an important source of job satisfaction. Find out whether the job or career that you are considering offers you enough independence and responsibility as well as a secure career ladder. And get to know your strengths and weaknesses well enough to choose a job that plays to your strengths.

The self-examination that goes into making educational and career choices will prove equally important in considering the next life stage we shall discuss—marriage and family life.

Exhibit 4.3
Satisfaction in Sociology

Sociology
Undergraduate
University (3 years)

Graduates Who Entered the Labour Force
Sociology graduates find jobs in a wide variety of occupations, ranging from social workers to elementary and secondary school teachers, sales and advertising managers, secretaries and stenographers. Employment is found in the health and social services sector, the educational sector, federal and provincial governments, and in business service industries. For teaching positions, these graduates must first obtain an education degree and then compete with university graduates in all fields. For social work positions, they must compete with university graduates at all levels in psychology and social work, and for management jobs they compete primarily with community college and university graduates in commerce.

Regardless of occupation, 1986 graduates earned virtually the same average income two years after graduating as all other graduates at this level. The earnings of 1982 graduates, however, grew at a somewhat slower rate than the average between 1984 and 1987. Many changed jobs between the third and fifth years of their careers, moving from the clerical occupations into elementary school teaching, government administration or various sales occupations.

The Course in Retrospect
Graduates in sociology were somewhat unhappy with their educational experience, as a significantly smaller-than-average proportion reported that they would make the same educational choices again. Moreover, the proportion who found jobs matching their undergraduate training was also sharply below the average, while the proportion who believed themselves to be overqualified for

their jobs was substantially above average. With their earnings matching the average, only about 75% of sociology graduates reported that they were satisfied with their jobs, significantly below the average. Overall working conditions for these graduates improved significantly, however, in terms of employment, job satisfaction and earnings between the third and fifth years of their careers.

Sociology
Master's
University (3 years)

Graduates Who Entered the Labour Force
The majority of these graduates find work as university teachers, whereas a smaller number work as sociologists, social workers, community college teachers and writers and editors. Regardless of occupation, 1986 graduates earned 15% less in 1988 than the average for all master's graduates. Graduates from this field of study generally face competition from people with an undergraduate degree or a doctorate in sociology.

About 50% of 1982 graduates from this field changed jobs between 1984 and 1987, mostly moving out of social work into occupations related to management and administration. Their average salary increased somewhat faster over the 1984-to-1987 period than that of other master's graduates.

The Course in Retrospect
An approximately average proportion of sociology graduates would select the same educational program if they had to make the choice again. This may reflect their somewhat greater-than-average likelihood of finding work which matched their educational training and their relatively high level of job satisfaction, as well as the fact that a slightly lower-than-average proportion felt overqualified for their job. This situation changed little over the 1984-to-1987 period, with the exceptions that the proportion who expressed satisfaction with their job and the proportion who found work related to their educational training increased greatly.

Sociology
Doctorate
University (5 years)

Graduates Who Entered the Labour Force
Sociology doctorates generally obtain employment as university professors, community college and vocational teachers, and financial managers and service managers in provincial and local government. They face virtually no direct competition from doctorates in other fields for university teaching positions, but they must compete with university graduates from other fields (especially law and history) for government positions. Two years after graduation, 1986 doctorates were earning somewhat more than all others on average. Earnings for 1982 doctorates, however, rose at a somewhat slower rate over the 1984-to-1987 period than the average. Virtually none changed occupations between the third and fifth years of their careers.

The Course in Retrospect

Sociology doctorates appeared to be fairly dissatisfied with their education experience, as the proportion who reported that they would make the same educational choices again was sharply below the average. The proportion who found jobs that matched their training was also below average, and the proportion who believed that they were overqualified for their jobs was sharply higher than average. Ninety percent reported that they were satisfied with their jobs, however. Overall working conditions for these doctorates improved somewhat in terms of employment and earnings but deteriorated in terms of job satisfaction between the third and fifth years of their careers.

Source: Employment and Immigration Canada (1990). *Job futures: An occupational outlook to 1995* (Catalogue No. MP43-181/1990E). Ottawa: Supply and Services Canada. Reprinted with permission.

CHAPTER FIVE

◆

SINGLE OR MARRIED:

WHAT YOU WANT AND WHAT YOU GET

INTRODUCTION

Chapter One showed that Canadians put a high value on romance and family life. It follows that average Canadians should attach great importance to getting married, being married, and staying married. If so, married Canadians should be more satisfied with their lives than unmarried Canadians.

On the other hand, evidence of dramatic change in family life surrounds us. Change is the rule in social life. Diversity is found in every large society. Yet change today may be more rapid and diversity more marked than in the past. It may be impossible today to talk about the *typical* family or the *typical* marriage. Major trends include smaller families, more single-parent families, more families created by remarriage, more dual-earner families, and more people living alone. Exhibit 5.1 shows a few of the pertinent statistics for Canada in the mid-1980s and allows us to make the comparison with the United States—where these changes were even more dramatic.

Three questions about marriage and relationships seem to interest most students: (1) What should I look for in a partner? (2) Should I become involved in cohabiting relationships? and (3) Should I marry or remain single? Let's restate these questions so that they can be addressed with data:

1. *What qualities in a mate satisfy people the most?* To answer this, we will need to find out whether people get more satisfaction by marrying people like themselves or quite different from themselves.
2. *Do cohabiting relationships satisfy people as much as marriage does?* To answer this, we will need to know something about the prevalence and duration of cohabitation, and the satisfaction that people get out of that kind of relationship.
3. *Are married people more satisfied with life than single, separated, or divorced people?* Answering this question forces us to examine evidence that marriage brings the benefits people hope it will.

Exhibit 5.1

Statistical indicators of marriage, divorce, and remarriage: Canada and United States, mid-1980s

	Canada	United States
Men		
% never marrying	17	16
% marrying	83	84
Mean age at first marriage	28.3	26.8
No. of marriages per person marrying	1.3	1.7
% of marriages ending in divorce	28	44
Mean duration of marriage until divorce	8.3	6.0
% of widowed persons remarrying	14	19
% of divorced persons remarrying	76	85
Women		
% never marrying	14	12
% marrying	86	88
Mean age at first marriage	25.7	24.5
No. of marriages person person marrying	1.3	1.6
% of marriages ending in divorce	28	44
Mean duration of marriage until divorce	15.8	11.8
% of widowed persons remarrying	5	7
% of divorced persons remarrying	64	76

Canadian Data
Source: Statistics Canada (1988). Adams, O.B., and Nagnur, D.N., *Marriage, Divorce, and Mortality: A Life Table Analysis for Canada and Regions*. Ottawa: Statistics Canada. Reproduced with the permission of the Minister of Industry, Science and Technology, 1993.

American Data
Source: Schoen, R. The Continuing Retreat from Marriage: Figures from U.S. Marital Status Life Tables. *Sociology and Social Research* 71, no. 2. Los Angeles: University of Southern California.

Readers who are already married may find that this chapter helps them understand the choices they have already made: when and why they got married, and to whom. Moreover, they may find that it helps them understand and evaluate the experiences they are having in marriage. All readers, married or unmarried, may find that this discussion puts the notions of marital choices and satisfactions in a new light.

Before we start, perhaps you'd care to find out what you know about this topic. Here are a few true-false questions to answer:

1. People get much more enjoyment out of marriage than they do out of single life.

   True ___ False ___

2. Marital happiness depends mainly on finding the perfect mate.
   True ___ False ___

3. Cohabiting with a partner largely rules out the chance of marrying that person.

   True___ False ___

4. High divorce rates prove that marriage is almost dead as a social institution.

   True ___ False ___

5. You can tell a great deal about the quality of a marriage from the spouses' willingness to hug and kiss.

   True ___ False ___

CHOOSING A MATE

Sooner or later, most people end up in a serious, intimate relationship. Research suggests that the key to a happy marriage is not—I repeat, *not* —a matter of finding the perfect mate. No method of selecting a marriage partner, however sound, will guarantee the survival of your marriage. This is because, throughout your lives, you and your mate will continue to change, and so will the world around you. But some choices may produce more marital satisfaction than others, and some are riskier than others. That makes it worth our while examining what social science knows about mate selection and about the results of better and worse choices.

I will soon argue that the very idea of "mate selection" is misguided, in the same way that "job selection" wrongly describes how people find work. For the time being, however, let's go ahead with the metaphor of mate selection, since most people think of mating as a selection process.

People bring their various attributes and skills to the "mating game" and offer them in hopes of an exchange. Failure to make a fair or balanced exchange causes disappointment and resentment. In any relationship, the partner with the greater "resources" has more to offer and, therefore, more power (Blood & Wolfe, 1960; Scanzoni, 1972).

For this reason, we should expect to find that people mate with others of similar social "value," since both stand to gain equally from the relationship. That may explain why most mating takes place between people of approximately equal physical attractiveness (Hatfield &

Sprecher, 1986). When mates are not equally attractive, the less attractive person usually brings another valued attribute—wealth, power, or social position—to the relationship.

This process of balancing attributes is not the same for men and women, however. Townsend and Levy (1990) interviewed hundreds of American college students and found that female students tend to consider men who are less physically attractive equally acceptable as a mate, providing they have high social status. On the other hand, male students are less likely to find less attractive women acceptable, in spite of high social status. So men and women bring somewhat different requirements to the mating game; but in all cases, the exchange has to balance. If a balance is not achieved, satisfaction soon declines and the relationship deteriorates (Hatfield & Sprecher, 1986).

Our tendency to trade off one attribute for another helps explain the so-called mating gradient—the mating of attractive young women with older, more prosperous men. The most common marriages between people of different occupational levels, educational levels, and other status characteristics are those between men and attractive younger women of a lower social status. This means that marriage is a more common means of upward social mobility for women than it is for men.

In our own society, the age gap between brides and grooms is particularly wide—nearly ten years, on average—when grooms are marrying for the second time. To such a union, the younger woman brings youthful good looks and an ability to bear children; the older man usually brings a higher social position. The opposite match (that is, a bride much older than the groom) is less common. Perhaps that is because older women are less often able to bring a high social position to the relationship. And, as we have seen, men may not find high social position alluring in a woman, given our culture's patriarchal acceptance of male domination over females (see Ambert, 1988, for a discussion on age differences in remarriage).

So, often mating is a bargain struck between people of unequal wealth and power. Yet in most cases the mates are similar in a great many ways. Homogamy, the tendency for like people to marry, "has been verified for age, marital status, social status, race, religion, and ethnic background" (Leslie & Korman, 1985, pp. 396–97). It is partly because of the need for balance that, in the past, people have raised doubts about "mixed marriages"—marriages between very different *kinds* of people, as determined by race, ethnicity, and religion.

Findings on intermarriage (or outmarriage) show that communal pressure to marry within the group is particularly intense in small ethnic and religious communities. Attitudinal barriers to marriage outside one's ethnic, racial, or religious group have dropped somewhat in the last two decades (Lambert & Curtis, 1985). Anglo-Saxon and francophone groups apparently have grown more tolerant of marriages between whites and non-whites, Jews and non-Jews, and Protestants and Catholics. But intolerance remains great among many ethnic and religious minorities.

Recent research by Larson and Munro (1990) shows that the proportion of interfaith marriages has doubled since 1972 and accounted for 54 percent of all marriages in 1982. These authors agree with Lambert and Curtis that tolerance is greatest in groups that allow their members the most contact with members of other groups and are least threatened with group disappearance through outmarriage.

Marriages between people of the same religion tend to be more satisfying than other marriages *if* one or both mates are seriously involved in their religion (Heaton, 1984), but not otherwise. Ortega, Whitt, and Williams (1988) show that the degree of difference between the spouses' religions is correlated with unhappiness in marriage. Couples of the same denomination who attend church with similar frequency have the most successful, stable marriages (Heaton & Pratt, 1990; Dudley & Kosinski, 1990). However, spouses need not hold similar beliefs about the Bible to achieve marital satisfaction (Heaton & Pratt, 1990).

It appears that religious homogamy increases marital satisfaction not because spouses hold identical spiritual beliefs, but because social and familial integration are strengthened through church attendance. People who identify themselves as having no religion are less socially integrated than other people. According to Bock and Radelet (1988), they are less likely than others to get married, and if they do marry, more likely to divorce, separate, or remarry. What this means is that marrying a person of the same religion increases your social integration—which in turn increases your marital satisfaction.

Comparative divorce rates reveal that the difficulties supposed to beset interracial or interreligious marriages are rarely as great as people believe. In fact, differences in age and status may pose a greater problem (Leslie & Korman, 1985, p. 397), as well as differences in education. Israeli research (Weller & Rofe, 1988) has found no difference in the marital happiness of homogeneous marriages and "mixed" marriages between Asian or African and European Jews. Rather, these researchers find education to be the most important factor affecting marital happiness. Similarly, Tynes (1990) notes that when a husband has more education than his wife, both partners report a less satisfying marriage and more frequent disagreement. The same problems do not arise when the wife has more education than her husband, however.

Age differences affect marital satisfaction in many countries. In North America, younger women married to (usually divorced) much older men are relatively unhappy with their marriages, and such marriages run a higher than average risk of divorce (Ambert, 1988).

What are the most satisfying qualities in a mate? We have no certain answer to this question. Some "mixes" may have better results than others. Differences in age, education, and (under some circumstances) religion may cause problems. However, I am not advising you to avoid certain kinds of mates, or seek out others, because you will not follow my advice anyway. That's not how people mate. Let's consider the reasons why.

Why People Do Not Optimize

The metaphor of a mating or marriage "market" in which people rationally seek "perfect mates" is wholly fictional. In fact, finding a mate is much like finding a job—it is socially structured but largely unplanned and unconscious.

We learned in Chapter Two that people find the best jobs through personal contacts, not by shopping around as you might shop for a television set. Similarly, people usually find mates through personal contacts. We do not shop for a mate because we do not really know what we want, and will not know until we find it. More important still, we could never live long enough to marry if we treated mating as a shopping problem.

Rational people shop carefully for cars, television sets, and apartments; but they do not shop for mates. That is because rational people do not seek the ideal or "optimal" solution to their most important *personal* concerns. They do not try to optimize; rather, they "satisfice": they seek a "good enough" solution, within the constraints life has handed them (March & Simon, 1958). For most purposes, whatever satisfies us is ideal.

According to March and Simon, most human decision making aims at discovering and selecting satisfactory alternatives. "Only in exceptional cases is it concerned with the discovery of optimal alternatives. To optimize requires processes several orders of magnitude more complex than those required to satisfice" (1958, p. 141). The difference between optimizing and satisficing is the difference between searching a haystack for the sharpest needle and merely searching for a needle that is sharp enough to sew with.

Think of it another way: the human race could not reproduce itself and survive if people were romantic optimizers. We would have died out as a species millions of years ago. Consider the arithmetic of the problem.

Suppose that, as an idealistic teenager, you had listed ten qualities you felt you absolutely must have in a mate. Your mate must be attractive—at least in the top fifth of all possible mates, by your own standards of attractiveness. Your mate must be fun—again, at least in the top fifth of all possible mates. He or she must be interesting to talk to—again, at least in the top fifth of all possible mates. Imagine making up a "shopping list" in this way. Now, what is the probability that your ideal mate actually exists?

If the various qualities you are looking for in a mate are uncorrelated, only one person in five to the tenth power—one in 9.8 million—will meet all your requirements. That's about *one* adult person of the right sex, aged 20 to 60, in *all of Canada*. Equally, there is only one chance in 9.8 million your "perfect mate" will consider *you* the perfect mate. So by this scenario, the chances in favour of meeting and marrying the perfect mate are one in 9.8 million squared (or nearly zero).

Even more modest goals will not find you a mate if you try to optimize. Suppose that, instead of requiring your perfect mate to be among the top fifth in attractiveness, you only require him or her to be in the top half. You similarly lower your standards for each of your other requirements. This makes your mating problem more manageable: now, you only need to look for that one "perfect" person in a thousand (that is, two to the tenth power). The probability of meeting and mating with an ideal mate who is making similar calculations has improved: now it is only one in a thousand squared, or one in a million. (There are likely to be nine or ten of these in all of Canada.)

At most, you know only a few thousand people by their first name. The chance of meeting and mating this way is quite unlikely.

With this in mind, you may try to solve the shopping problem by reducing the number of qualities you require in a mate. Suppose your potential mate has to excel in only one respect and satisfy you in four others. Now you and your perfect mate are each looking for someone who is in the top fifth in one quality and in the top half in just four other qualities. The probability of finding a person with the qualities you seek is one in 1250. The probability that you will satisfy his or her requirements is also one in 1250. Even so, the chance of meeting and mating is still well below one in a million (that is, one in 1250 squared).

If you try to optimize, then, you will fail to solve your mating problem, even by lowering your original standards. Some people adopt the strategy of trying to meet more potential partners. After all, if you knew six thousand people instead of two thousand, your chances would triple. But getting on a first-name basis with six thousand people is very difficult and time-consuming, and the odds are still stacked against you.

Carefully expanding your network of acquaintances seems to be one way around this. By joining certain kinds of groups, placing or answering personal advertisements, or hiring a matchmaker, you will more quickly meet new people with the qualities you require. These mating techniques have become much more popular in the last few decades, especially among middle-aged people, whose opportunity to meet a large number of new people is seriously restricted. (Take note: you will meet more potential mates at college or university than you will ever meet again.)

Still, many people hesitate to look for mates in this way. They find it demeaning, fear the unpleasantness of blind dates that do not work out, or worry about getting sexually transmitted diseases from a new sexual partner.

However you revise the shopping list and extend your range and number of contacts, the chance of finding the perfect mate this way is nearly zero. Most people cannot and do not find a mate in this way. Rather, people fall in love with those who are close at hand—often, people they know through others. As in so many areas of life, we come to value what we know best and have available: people like ourselves. We become satisfied with the possible, not the ideal; then come to love the person who satisfies us.

Whether we choose homogamy or heterogamy (intermarriage) depends on what kinds of people are close at hand. That explains why our chances of mating with people of other religious, ethnic, and racial groups increase when we have more contact with them. To illustrate this, a study of Canada's major language groups concludes that "endogamy [that is, within-group marriage] varies positively with the number of available potential mates belonging to the same group; negatively with the average distance to them; negatively with the number of available potential mates belonging to different groups; and positively with the average distance to the latter" (De Vries & Vallee, 1980, p. 168). Said more simply, people usually marry others who are socially and geographically near at hand, even if slightly "better" (meaning, more similar) mates can be found much farther away.

This process of "satisficing," of marrying the close at hand, may sound very cold-blooded and unromantic, but in practice, the feelings of love are genuine. People in love believe that they have discovered the one perfect mate. In a sense, they have. But they have not done it, and could not have done it, by following a shopping list of the "right" characteristics. The chances against that are a million to one. Instead, they have decided, after the fact, that their mate is perfect—and *that* is what's so amazing about falling in love.

LIVING WITH SOMEONE

Early Marriage

So now you have fallen in love with that perfect someone. You're in a state of delightful enchantment and cannot imagine how you can go on living without the person you love. What should you do? Three solutions suggest themselves: marry your beloved, cohabit but do not marry, or delay making a decision until you have more evidence about the relationship. What choice makes the most sense?

The sociological evidence argues forcefully against early marriage. "The divorce rate among [people who marry young] is estimated at from two to four times that among persons who marry after 20 years of age. The divorce rate is related to low educational levels, low economic levels, premarital pregnancies, and possibly to personality difficulties" (Leslie & Korman, 1985, p. 396; see also Scanzoni, 1972, pp. 6–28). A longitudinal study of Ohio families (Kurdek, 1991) found that separated and divorced couples had less education, earned less, had more children or stepchildren, and—most pertinent to our point—had known each other for a shorter time before marriage than couples that remained together.

As we shall see later in this chapter, the cost of a marriage breakdown falls most heavily on women. By far, most single parents are separated and divorced women; and a great many single-parent families live below the poverty line.

The message is clear: do not marry too early. But when is a marriage "too early?" There are several answers to this question. First, marrying "too early" means marrying someone you don't really know. Grover et al. (1985) found a strong correlation between the length of time people had spent dating their current spouses and their current marital satisfaction. A longer period of dating was associated with a higher probability of a happy marriage.

Second, it means getting married before you are emotionally ready to settle down—that is, ready to give up going on dates, drinking to all hours of the night, doing things the way you want to. Beaujot (1991b, p. 8) reports on the attitudes of the people he sampled in and around London, Ontario:

> The ideal age for a man to get married [is] in the mid to late 20s, after having achieved a certain maturity and stability in life, having had the freedom to do things as a single person first, and achieved a certain "state of mind" appropriate for marriage. They should have ... a sense of direction in life. Many said that a man should have lived on his own first, be independent, learn to take care of himself, had his opportunity to ride

> motorcycles or whatever he needed to do as a single person, find himself, had time "between families." The ages stated were largely minimum ages, with marriage at older ages being considered acceptable ...
>
> For women, the responses were similar, possibly a year or two younger. They also need a level of maturity, be able to handle the responsibilities of marriage, have the education necessary to get a job. Many said that women mature faster and are ready for marriage sooner, they can handle the responsibilities sooner, men take longer to settle down.

Third, marrying "too early" means marrying before you get established. Often, parents tell their children not to marry before they can support themselves, which means finishing their education and getting started in a career. Hogan (1981) calls this the "normative pattern."

Yet many factors conspire against this normative pattern. Wars tend to interrupt young men's formal education and take them away from their loved ones. This separation puts powerful pressure on people to marry before they have completed their education or started building a career. More commonly, economic recessions disrupt traditional patterns: they make it harder for young people to find work and achieve economic security. Under these conditions, getting married seems no more foolish than not getting married.

Wars and depressions aside, Hogan detects a continuing movement away from the normative pattern: a trend toward marriage before the completion of education and career building. Reasons for this change include the progressive lengthening of formal education, the growing availability of student loans and married-student housing, the rising availability of full- and part-time work for students and/or their spouses, the growth of part-time education, and, of course, the increased protection from unwanted pregnancy that modern birth control provides.

What happens to the increasing numbers of young people who marry before their education is complete and their career has been set in motion? "Initially, married men who seek employment tend to find better-paying and somewhat higher-status jobs than single men.... But the man who is single has greater freedom to seek a better job. Unrestricted by family responsibilities, single men tend to enjoy quicker career advancement" (Hogan, 1981, pp. 200–201). Men who (for reasons of marriage) leave school and enter the work force relatively early tend to rely more on family connections to find a first job. This tends to land them in jobs with poorer prospects for career advancement. (Remember Granovetter's finding, discussed in Chapter Two, that the best jobs travel through networks of acquaintanceship, not kinship.) Men who marry early and rely on family connections for work are more likely to start out in organizations that are small and limiting. Marriage restricts their geographic mobility: they are less able to risk moves and changes that would increase their opportunity for advancement in the long run.

For these and other reasons, early marriage increases the chance of divorce. Like others who have studied early marriage, Hogan finds that early marriers

> have rates of marital instability more than 50% higher than men marrying on time or relatively late.... It seems likely that men who marry early are relatively immature at the time of marriage. Their choice of a marriage partner might be ill-considered because of this immaturity, or problems associated with the sudden entry of an immature man into a marital union may produce strains that result in marital discord. (1981, pp. 204–206)

These risks appear to have lessened somewhat in recent decades. But despite improved chances, the data still argue against early marriage. By implication, they argue in favour of finishing school and getting started in a career first—just as your parents advised you to do.

Cohabitation

Does this argue that the love-sick couple should live together unmarried—that is, cohabit? Probably so; cohabition has a better record than early marriage.

There are few impediments to cohabitation today. Premarital relations are now more varied and sexually active than ever before. Data from the *Maclean's*/CTV national survey show that 86 percent of Canadians aged 18 to 24 had sex in the previous year, some of them (more than 30 percent of the men and just under 20 percent of the women) with two or more different partners. Perhaps a more telling statistic for our present purposes, since it shows the weakening of the connection between sex and marriage, is that fully 17 percent of widowed, divorced, and separated Canadians, 22 percent of single Canadians, and 30 percent of married Canadians say they have sex eleven or more times a month (*Maclean's*, January 4, 1993, pp. 39–40). The moral objections that once inhibited couples from cohabiting, then, seem to to have little force today. Some practical difficulties have diminished, too. New housing patterns make it easier than ever to live with someone to whom you are not married. For these and other reasons cohabitation, also known as common-law marriage, is on the increase. In 1981, 6.4 percent of all people living as couples were in cohabiting relationships; by 1986, this proportion had risen to 8.3 percent (Turcotte, 1990). By Census Day, 1991, 10 percent of couples were in a cohabiting relationship (reported in *The Globe and Mail*, July 8, 1992, p. A1).

Exhibit 5.2
Common-law partners as a percentage of all people in couple unions, by age, 1981 and 1990[a]

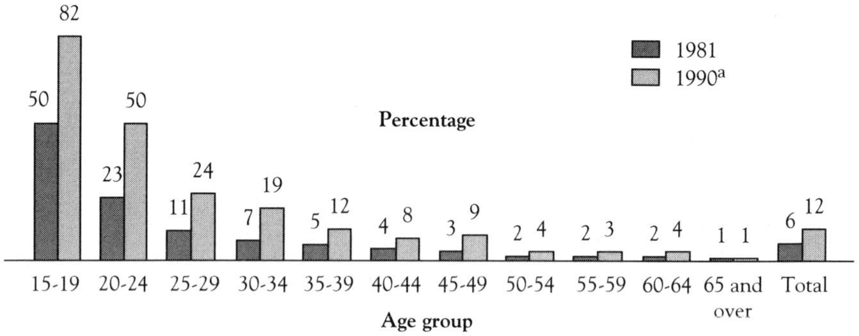

[a] Excludes Northwest and Yukon Territories

Source: Turcotte, P. "Common-law Unions: Nearly Half a Million in 1986," *Canadian Social Trends*, Autumn 1988 and General Social Survey, 1990. In Stout, C., "Common-law: a Growing Alternative," *Canadian Social Trends*, Winter 1991, pp. 18–20. Ottawa: Statistics Canada.

What do people experience in these intimate relationships? How does cohabitation compare in satisfaction to marriage? Research on the experience of cohabitation gives mixed answers. For reasons that are not entirely clear, cohabitation *before* marriage appears to be associated with significantly lower satisfaction *after* marriage. De Maris and Leslie (1984) note that neither differential commitment to marital permanence nor the greater length of their intimate involvement explains why former cohabitors have a lower level of marital satisfaction.

There seems to be no difference in the verbal and sexual communication practices and marital satisfaction of older couples, whether married or cohabiting. However, younger couples are both more communicative and more satisfied if they are married than if they are cohabiting (Yelsma, 1986). So age seems to make a difference to the success of such relationships. Apparently, so does race. Crohan and Veroff (1989) find that cohabitation before marriage is not at all related to marital satisfaction for whites who eventually married, but is negatively related to marital satisfaction for blacks.

Booth and Johnson (1988) note that cohabitation is positively related to marital disagreement and proneness to divorce (see also Halli

Exhibit 5.3

Percentage of people ever in a common-law union, by age and sex, 1984 and 1990[a]

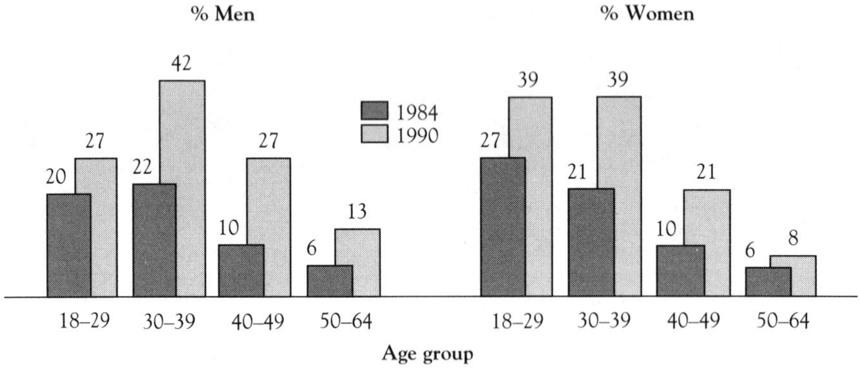

[a] Excludes Northwest and Yukon Territories.

Source: Statistics Canada, Catalogue No. 99–955 and General Social Survey, 1990. In Stout, C., "Common-law: A Growing Alternative," *Canadian Social Trends*, Winter 1991, pp. 18–20. Ottawa: Statistics Canada.

& Zimmer, 1991; Balakrishnan et al., 1987). Cohabitation does not, apparently, improve mate selection or "training" for marriage. On the other hand, these researchers find no evidence that previous cohabitation is itself the cause of the marital dissatisfaction. They observe; rather, people who cohabit may be "poor marriage risks" *before* they marry.

This "divorce-proneness" of former cohabitors may only be temporary and subject to change as people become more accustomed to cohabitation and the wise use of their freedom. Or it may be that people who are inclined to cohabit before marriage are the least reluctant to divorce after marrying. They have less than average fear of social stigma, public criticism, and changing their lives.

Data from the Quality of Life (1981) study showed that cohabiting couples were nearly twice as likely as married couples to feel that their freedom was limited by the relationship. They were more than five times as likely to report having considered ending the relationship during the previous year. In fact, about half of these cohabiting relationships do break up, according to the 1984 Family History Survey. Most of the rest end in marriage (Burch, 1985, Table 5). On the other hand, the high likelihood of marrying a cohabiting partner suggests that many people think of common-law unions as trial marriages. No wonder, then, that the vast majority of people who have ever been in a cohabiting relationship have been in only one (Burch, 1985, Table 4A).

There is, however, an important difference between married and cohabiting relationships: typically, marriage is based on a firm commitment and cohabitation is not. People who are married are more likely to have committed themselves to a spouse mentally, as well as legally. Then, they typically follow up with actions that rest on that commitment: having children and taking on major expenses such as buying a home. Even this is changing, though: according to the 1991 census, 42 percent of cohabiting relationships include children, whether born to the partners or brought into the family from an earlier union (reported in *The Globe and Mail*, July 8, 1992).

Are non-marital romantic relationships as satisfying as marriage? Marriage and cohabitation are becoming increasingly similar. Of two risky choices, early marriage remains the riskier. There is no practical reason not to go through with it if the couple is comfortable with the idea of a serious non-marital relationship and feels that they cannot delay living together. Cohabitation gives the partners more knowledge about each other and the quality of their relationship; half the time, it ends in marriage. By leaving open the door for a decision to *not* marry, it allows for further maturation and personal change. But, as we have seen, cohabitation does not reduce the risks of later marital breakup.

There is no reason to fear that cohabitation will become so popular that it will replace marriage. On average, cohabitation is no more enchanting than marriage, other factors (such as childbearing) being equal. So far, there is no place on earth where people have stopped marrying just because cohabitation is an accepted alternative.

Should you live with your partner before marriage? To answer that question, you should consider that commitment to a marriage is usually more serious than commitment to a non-marital relationship. So, if you have doubts about your prospective mate or your willingness to make a commitment, you are advised to cohabit.

TO MARRY OR NOT TO MARRY

Is marriage really satisfying? Surveys show that marriages range from the peak of satisfaction to the trough of despair. Yet we know that most Canadians report being very satisfied with their marriage. Moreover, married Canadians—both male and female—are twice as likely to be very satisfied with their lives than separated Canadians, and 60 percent

Exhibit 5.4
You have to work at marriage

In Chapter Four, the following factors proved to be particularly important in shaping people's job satisfaction:

- good organizational conditions
- participation in decision making
- open communication
- social support
- job challenge
- chance for advancement
- good income and status
- autonomy and control
- co-operation

Do you think that the same factors influence people's satisfaction with marriage? Which ones do you think are *not* important in marriage, and why?

On the other hand, if both job satisfaction and marital satisfaction *are* influenced by the same kinds of factors, does that mean that marriage is a job? Or that a job is somehow like a marriage?

---

more likely to be very satisfied than divorced Canadians (Quality of Life survey, 1981). On average, never-married people are less satisfied than married people—not surprising in view of the importance Canadians attach to being married—but much more satisfied than divorced and separated people.

The spill-over effect that marital satisfaction has into many domains of life has been frequently confirmed (for example, by Zollar & Williams, 1987; Shichman & Cooper, 1984; Broman, 1988b; Rosen, Ickovics, & Moghadam, 1990; Gove, Style, & Hughes, 1990).

Of all single and separated people, women are particularly likely to prove much less satisfied with life than their married counterparts (see, for example, Ball, 1983). Yet women find lifelong singlehood more satisfying than divorce or widowhood, since it is continuous and less disruptive (see, for example, Fengler, Danigelis, & Grams, 1982; see also Rice, 1989, for data on widows and divorced women).

Veenhoven (1983) uses evidence from Europe to argue that—contrary to what many people believe—marriage is gaining in importance. Married people continue to be happier (especially in the most modernized European countries), less disturbed, healthier, and longer-living than unmarried people. Since 1950, these benefits of marriage have increased, Veenhoven finds. Between 1950 and 1980, Dutch suicide rates rose far faster among unmarried than among married people. Likewise, overall life satisfaction is more strongly correlated with marital satisfaction today than it was several decades ago.

Other researchers have reached different conclusions. Glenn and Weaver (1988) note a steady decline from 1972 through 1986 in the likelihood that married Americans will report being happy. Farrell and Markides (1985) find no consistent relationship between marital status and physical well-being among Mexican Americans. Finally, Keith, Braito and Breci (1990) conclude that (relative) social isolation may not pose problems for unmarried people. Singlehood represents a problem only when people have less social interaction than they want.

Given the satisfaction that marriage appears to bring, we must confront the fact that, by 1985, rates of first marriage had fallen to an all-time low in Canada. This falling marriage rate has been led by large declines in Quebec, which "has not only the lowest rate of all the provinces but one of the lowest rates in the world" (Statistics Canada, 1987a, p. 19; also, Statistics Canada, 1991). The reason for this, in part, is that people—particularly young people—are opting for cohabiting relationships over marriage. Many others are merely delaying marriage, so that the average age at first marriage is increasing. In 1986, the average age of women at first marriage was 26 years, surpassing the highest figure since registration began in 1921 (namely, 24.9 years, recorded in 1942 during World War II). For men, the average age at first marriage was 28 years, an increase of 3 years over the early 1970s figures (Adams & Nagnur, 1989).

Late marriage, whenever it has been noted, has been associated with high proportions never marrying (Hajnal, 1965). People who delay marriage beyond a certain age often lose interest in marrying at all. They become accustomed to the single life. For women who delay marriage, childbearing becomes risky or impossible.

The Changing Qualities of a Relationship

Most research on marital satisfaction shows that it varies in a U-shaped pattern over the duration of a marriage. That is, satisfaction starts out very high, falls quickly for nearly twenty years, and then improves again (see, for example, Lupri & Frideres, 1981; Stephenson, 1988; Haring-Hidore et al., 1985; but for an opposing argument see White, 1987). According to Glenn (1989), these effects are particularly marked where children are present, and are greater for females than for males and for blacks than for whites. As a result, many people are relatively unhappy with their marriages after a dozen years; many will separate or divorce.

By the mid-1980s, fewer than one-third of Americans who first married during the 1960s were still in their first marriage and "very happy" with their marriage (Glenn, 1989).

Let's look at this phenomenon more closely. When asked about their marital satisfaction, nearly three in four newlyweds (people married less than a year) who are without children indicate the very highest level of satisfaction (Quality of Life survey, 1981), a state of mind that we shall call "enchantment." (Dorothy Tennov [1979] uses the term "limerence" to describe this state, which she says lasts for about 2 years, among people who experience it at all.) By the time people have been married for 5 years, the proportion still "enchanted" has dropped to just over one person in two. Part of the decline in marital satisfaction is due to childbearing, an effect we shall discuss at length in Chapter Six. After the fifth year, about 45 percent are reportedly still enchanted, and this continues until a marriage has gone on for 31 years or more. Then the percentage edges back up to roughly two people in three (Quality of Life survey, 1981).

After age 65, a majority of married people are extremely satisfied once again. Husbands and wives married more than 50 years are nearly as likely to be enchanted with marriage as when they were newlyweds!

How do we explain the initial drop in marital satisfaction over the course of time? Some researchers (for example, Steinberg & Silverberg, 1987) believe that it results from a growing distance between parents and their children, as the children enter adolescence. No wonder marital satisfaction increases when the children leave the family home (Lee, 1988b).

At the same time, many married people are stuck where they are—not satisfied but unable to leave. After all, the reasons people stay together are not always the same reasons they came together in the first place. The enchantment with which marriage usually begins leads to a commitment based on strong, non-rational feelings; the marriage then moves into hard-to-escape commitments: for example, children and debts. As Booth, White, and Edwards (1986) note, the accumulation of assets substantially reduces people's willingness to divorce. Thus, it is mainly among young and/or relatively new marriages that such factors as income, health, and social integration—even marital happiness—influence the divorce rate.

People who have been married for a number of years find that there are high barriers to leaving a marriage and few alternatives to remaining. That explains the apparent anomaly that both marital happiness *and* divorce risks are lower in long-duration marriages (White & Booth, 1991). As the enchantment of marriage wanes, mounting "rational" commitments take on a greater importance in keeping couples together. Later, as the debts and child-raising tasks of a marriage lighten, enchantment often starts to grow again. That makes middle age and old age a time of rediscovery for many couples. Older couples tend to stay together because they want to, not because they have to.

Though married life becomes routinized over a long period of time, a marriage, like any other social arrangement, is able to renew itself and be a source of continuing satisfaction. How do marriages achieve this renewal? How do they "stay alive" over the many difficult years between first enchantment and later enchantment? Of the many answers suggested to this question effective communication is one of the most commonly agreed on.

Communication and Marriage Satisfaction

A great many factors influence marital satisfaction, among them race, the spouse's occupational prestige, church attendance, and gender (Rao and Rao, 1986). Educated women have been found to be more satisfied as wives and parents than less-educated women (Ja-Jeong & Schumm, 1990). Women with traditional ideas about marriage are reported to be happier (with marriage and overall) than women with less traditional ideas or feminist ideas (Lueptow, Guss, & Hyden, 1989). Ziv and Gadish (1989) find spouses who think that their mate is humorous are more satisfied with marriage than other spouses; husbands who appreciate a good joke are particularly satisfied. On the other hand, couples that had experienced premarital pregnancy or remarriage, or that had stepchildren, are prone to marital dissatisfaction (Kurdek, 1991).

People who have been happily married a long time seem to think that marital satisfaction comes from being married to someone you like and enjoy being with (Lauer & Kerr, 1990); from commitment to the institution of marriage (see also Lauer & Lauer, 1986) and to a particular partner (see also Swensen & Trahaug, 1985); to a shared sense of humour; and from agreement on a wide variety of issues. On the other hand, people who remain *un*happily married for a long time tend to stay together because they see marriage as a long-term commitment, and because of the children (Lauer & Lauer, 1986).

Social class (including income and SES) affects marital satisfaction (see, for example, Ambert, 1988; and Greeley, 1991, p. 222). Generally, poor people (especially women) report the lowest levels of marital satisfaction, perhaps as a result of frequent conflicts over money that decrease satisfaction with one's spouse and, thus, with life (Berry & Williams, 1987). Economic distress has a negative effect on family satisfaction, especially in the absence of close friends (Voydanoff, Donnelly, & Fine, 1988). Perhaps this explains why financial well-being apparently has a positive effect on marital satisfaction (Thoresen & Goldsmith, 1987).

Amid the many contributing factors, however, the one that appears to stand out is how the spouses *communicate and interact* with one another. "Marital satisfaction is lower among those with frequent disagreements and infrequent shows of affection" (Rhyne, 1984, p. 21). This is not surprising. Typically, people who are happily married kiss frequently and fight relatively little—and anyone would rather kiss than fight.

There are many ways of saying this same thing. Altrocchi (1988) finds that happily married couples look on themselves as best friends and are very accepting of each other; they work harder on their marriage than other couples. They also confide in each other very often (Lee, 1988a), a habit whose frequency has a positive effect on marital satisfaction (Hansen & Schuldt, 1984). Satisfied spouses understand each other's desires for change (Tiggel et al., 1982), tend to agree with one another, and believe that they are understood by their spouse (Allen & Thompson, 1984).

The *quality* of communication matters as much as the quantity of communication. Gottman (1982) observes that happy marriages are marked by an ability to de-escalate arguments and dispel bad feelings, not simply communicate good feelings. Frequent low-intensity interactions, such as sharing the events of the day, are the key to good marital communication. Honeycutt, Wilson, and Parker (1982) find that happily married couples tend to communicate in a friendly, open, relaxed, and attentive way. Unhappily married couples communicate in less varied and satisfying ways. Some research (for example, Smith et al., 1988) suggests that couples increase their marital satisfaction by spending leisure time together. However, Holman and Jacquart (1988) find that shared leisure activity increases marital satisfaction only if the couple communicates satisfactorily in the course of that activity. High stress couples are rarely capable of this.

Other researchers argue that the relationship between good communication and marital satisfaction is spurious, in the sense that both are caused by a third factor. Barnes et al. (1984) say this factor is "positive regard." Spouses who do not like or love each other do not communicate adequately and will not be happily married; no amount of work on their communication will change the fact that they do not like each other. Still others hold that the causal relationship runs in the opposite direction to what is usually claimed. In other words, spouses who are satisfied with their marriage will communicate well with one another *because* they are satisfied (see, for example, White, 1983).

Are the effects of communication between spouses the same in all societies? Given that different cultures have different communication styles, it may not be appropriate to generalize from the American findings. So, for example, Winkler and Doherty (1983) note that Israeli couples are more verbally aggressive and less calm during conflicts than American couples, although this does not seem to decrease their marital satisfaction. Yelsma and Athappilly (1988) claim that there is little relationship between communication style and marital satisfaction in arranged marriages in India, because these marriages put less premium on emotional expressiveness than North American marriages do.

So the role of communication style in marital satisfaction is far from resolved. But at least in our culture, "kissing and fighting" are types of communication that seem to make a difference. They may sound like trivial concerns until you remember that marriage is a supercharged way of living. Domestic violence—wife abuse, elder abuse, child abuse, and even husband abuse—is a problem we read and hear about every day (see also Lupri, 1992; Ellis & Dekeseredy, 1989). People who never thought they were capable of abusive acts find themselves committing them.

Violence, common as it is, is *not* an inevitable result of family conflict. Other forms of conflict (some more benign than others) include negotiation, discussion, verbal (as opposed to physical) attack, and withdrawal; apology is an important way of dealing with conflict (Lloyd, 1990). Frequent outbreaks of verbal aggression and marital conflict are correlated with (and, perhaps, causes of) physical violence in marriage (Brinkerhoff, Grandin, & Lupri, 1992). Violence brings with it physical and emotional damage and sometimes even death. It is a serious cause of decreased marital satisfaction and deteriorating family relationships (Meredith, Abbott, & Adams, 1986). None of this is lost on the adolescent children of violent parents, who report more anger and less family satisfaction than adolescents in non-violent families (Martin et al., 1987). They have not learned appropriate ways of dealing with hurt and anger. It is not enough to say, then, that marriage increases people's well-being; what is of key importance is the *quality* of the marriage (Williams, 1988).

Domestic abuse is a problem that is likely to get worse before it gets better. Ellis and Dekeseredy note that "compared with married women, cohabiting, separated, and divorced women are more likely to be abused by the man they live or lived intimately with" (1989, p. 82).

As we have seen, cohabitation is becoming an ever more common living arrangement.

So far, we have discussed marital satisfaction in a way that suggests that the same rules apply to both husbands and wives. In fact, husbands and wives experience marriage in very different ways.

His Marriage and Her Marriage

The prevalence of violence against women in marriages points to a central fact about power relations in our society: marriage is a different relationship for men and women. Usually, it is a relationship of unequal power. This observation has led sociologist Jesse Bernard (1973) to claim that, in any marriage, there are two separate realities: *his* marriage and *her* marriage. Marriage has a different meaning for husbands and wives.

It is true that married women tend to be more satisfied with life than never-married women (who are, in turn, more satisfied with life than divorced and separated women). But generally, marriage remains a greater risk for women than for men. Women appear to gain more life satisfaction from a marriage's success, but they also lose far more if the marriage fails—especially if they are without a steady job or career. Thus, a variety of marital experiences affect wives' well-being far more than they affect husbands' well-being (McRae & Brody, 1989).

Overall, husbands tend to be more satisfied with their marriages than wives (Rhyne, 1984; Ambert, 1988; Fowers, 1991). Marital satisfaction is also more variable for women than it is for men. That is, wives are more likely than their husbands to be either very satisfied or very *dis*satisfied with marriage. Schumm et al. (1985; see also McRae & Brody, 1989) report that when there is an extremely wide difference in the marital satisfaction of husbands and wives, wives are almost always the less satisfied of the two. Patterns of marital satisfaction are slightly different among black Americans, according to Ball and Robbins (1986). For this group, married, widowed, and divorced women are more satisfied with life than separated and single women, but the differences disappear when researchers control for age, health, income, education, and social integration. When these factors are controlled for among black men, marriage is the *least satisfying* state.

Generally, the psychic costs of a failing marriage fall more heavily on wives than on husbands. Wives are more strongly affected by marital quality than husbands (Williams, 1988). This is not, apparently, because women rely more on marriage for self-validation or lack alternative sources of role gratification. Perhaps it is because unmarried women react more negatively than unmarried men to loneliness and social isolation (Cockrum & White, 1985). Or perhaps "women have higher expectations of marriage than men and thus tend to evaluate their current situations more critically" (Rhyne, 1984, p. 8).

Communication, as we have seen, has an important influence on marital satisfaction. Husbands and wives approach the expression of intimacy in quite different ways (Merves-Okin, Amidon, & Bernt, 1991). According to Schlesinger (1982), men and women do not place the same weight on recognizing their own needs, having a positive relationship with their children, sharing emotions, having similar life goals, and having a sense of humour.

Power may be even more important than communication in shaping the satisfaction of husbands and wives. Because of discrimination against women in the workplace, marriage is more *necessary* for women than for men. Yet women also experience inequality at home, in the sharing of domestic tasks and in domestic decision making. This is bound to make marriage less satisfying for women. Fowers (1991) concludes that wives enjoy fewer mental health benefits from marriage than husbands because they have less power.

When a wife is *externally oriented* (that is, feels controlled from outside) and her husband is *internally oriented* (feels that he is in control), the result is a high degree of marital dissatisfaction (Bugaighis et al., 1983). For this reason, the least satisfied wives are found in traditional marriages where the husband dominates the household. (We shall discuss this issue further in Chapter Eight.)

Husbands and wives have different ways of dealing with their marital dissatisfaction. Men tend to take a coercive approach and women a more conciliatory approach toward their partners (White, 1989). Wives who confront joint problems and enforce their own views in trying to solve them often encounter resentment (Krokoff, 1987). Nonetheless, women who display assertiveness suffer less from depression than women who maintain a passive, "typically female" role. Whisman and Jacobson (1989) report that couples receiving psychiatric treatment for depression show more-than-average inequality in decision making, and less satisfaction with the distribution of responsibilities.

The power imbalance typical of many marriages has been linked to women's inequality in society at large, and in turn, to marital breakdown. Some research has associated divorce and separation with women's "lack of job-related resources [which] may have limited [their] power within a marriage or union and, thus, may have predisposed its termination" (Pool & Moore, 1986, p. 49).

McRae and Brody (1989) conclude that women are less satisfied within marriage than men because marriage is a more negative experience for women than for men. This view is supported by evidence that marriage brings men greater physical and emotional well-being than it does women. Canadian men increase their life expectancy by five years by marrying, while women increase their (already higher) life expectancy by only one-and-a-half years (Keyfitz, 1988). The gap in mortality rates from cardiovascular diseases and neoplasms, which generally favours women over men, narrows within marriage (Trovato & Lauris, 1989).

Marriage has no significant effect on men's careers, but it has a negative effect on women's. It particularly affects women who bear children, by "depress[ing] the achievements of younger women in the full-time labour force" (Boyd, 1985, pp. 271, 273).

Whatever the criticisms that we can level at marriage, however, divorce is often even worse. People who are divorced or separated are about twice as likely as married people to feel a low level of satisfaction with their lives.

DIVORCE

How likely is divorce or separation? Rates of divorce remained fairly steady from 1952 through 1968 (Statistics Canada, 1982b, p. 4). With the 1968 law reforms that made divorces much easier to obtain, the numbers skyrocketed (see Exhibit 5.5). Divorces rose from 137 per 1000 marriages in 1969 to 331 per 1000 marriages in 1984 (Statistics Canada, 1992). Since then, the rates for some age groups have levelled off or begun to fall, while those for others have continued to rise.

For married Canadians, the risk of divorce over the course of a lifetime works out to at least 30 percent, if current rates continue (Burch & Madan, 1986; Adams & Nagnur, 1989). Some (for example, McKie, Prentice, & Reed, 1983; Eichler, 1988) even believe that the divorce risks facing young Canadians today are closer to 40 percent.

Of course, these risks may not apply to *you*. Rates of divorce vary from one part of the country, and one educational level, to another. The rates are lower than average in the East—the Atlantic provinces and Quebec—and higher than average in the West—especially, British Columbia (Burch, 1985, Table 19; Adams & Nagnur, 1989). See Exhibit 5.6. Likewise, people who complete a postsecondary education are about half as likely to divorce as people with no more than a secondary school education (Burch, 1985, Table 20). Age is another important factor: your risk of divorce is higher the younger you are when you marry. It is also higher in a second or later marriage (Ambert, 1988, Chapter 6).

If you are unlucky enough to experience it, divorce will have a significant impact on your life satisfaction. The consequences of divorce have

Exhibit 5.5
Number of Divorces, Canada, 1950–1989

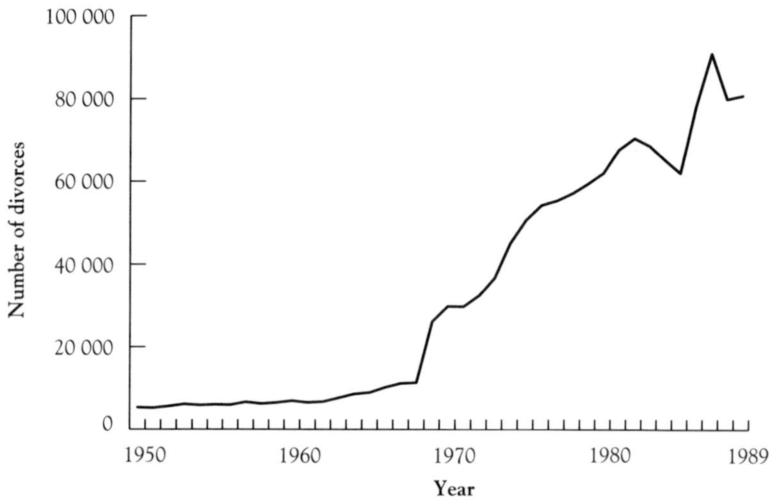

Source: Dumas, J., and Peron, Y. (1992). *Marriage and Conjugal Life in Canada.* Current Demographic Analysis, p. 47. (Catalogue No. 91-534E). Ottawa: Statistics Canada, Demography Division.

been shown to include sleeping disturbances, a deterioration in work habits, curtailment of leisure activities, and problems in relations with friends and persons of the opposite sex (Huddleston & Hawkings, 1986). Recent separation and divorce (along with poor marital quality, among those who remain married) are associated with high rates of depression and poor immune-system functioning (Kiecolt-Glaser et al., 1987).

Divorce works a hardship on everyone, but especially on women and children. Separated and divorced women report significantly lower levels of general life satisfaction, sexual satisfaction, and self-esteem than matched married women (Tcheng-Laroche & Prince, 1983), and are less likely to be highly satisfied with life than divorced and separated men, who themselves suffer an increase in emotional problems (Gove, 1970; Ambert, 1980, 1988). Women suffer especially severe financial and social hardships. According to a recent study (Finnie, 1993), one year after their divorce, the average income of women is only about 57 percent the income of men. This gap does not narrow substantially over the years: the incidence of poverty after divorce is 2.5 times higher

Exhibit 5.6
Divorce rate per 100 000 married persons aged 15 to 60, Canada and provinces, 1990

Provinces	Divorces (1)	Married population aged 15 to 60 (2)	Rate (3) = (1) ÷ (2)
Newfoundland	973	224 665	433
Prince Edward Island	268	47 947	559
Nova Scotia	2 347	345 680	679
New Brunswick	1 643	280 965	584
Quebec	19 405	2 772 325	700
Ontario	28 183	4 055 850	695
Manitoba	2 677	414 475	646
Saskatchewan	2 277	367 735	549
Alberta	9 314	1 042 295	894
British Columbia	9 649	1 295 770	745

Source: Dumas, J. (1992). *Report on the Demographic Situation in Canada, 1992:* Current Demographic Analysis, p. 45. (Catalogue No. 91–209E). Ottawa: Statistics Canada, Demography Division.

among women than it is among men. Men seem to experience a drop in their needs, while maintaining their higher earnings. Therefore, on average, divorce *increases* men's economic well-being. In contrast, women and their dependent children have the same needs as before, but no longer share the ex-spouse's income. As a result, more than one-third of women drop below the poverty line after divorce.

Children who go through divorce or separation often experience a decline in their health. In the United Kingdom, rates of reported illness are higher for children in families that have experienced separation than for other children (Blaxter, 1990). Poverty, less parental attention, and an increase in the level of stress may all have a hand in causing their poor health. These effects of divorce on children may be long-lasting. Adults whose parents divorced when they were children show lower levels of psychological, social, and marital well-being than other adults. The same holds true for adults who perceived their parents' marriage to be unhappy (Amato & Booth, 1991).

Australian research (Amato, 1988) compared adults who had been raised in intact families with adults who had gone through divorce as children. The latter group held more negative attitudes toward their family of origin. They valued marriage, but were more aware of its limitations and more tolerant of alternatives (such as divorce).

Children from divorced families have relatively little contact with their fathers (Amato & Booth, 1991). After divorce, only one father in two sees his children regularly. Only one in three makes regular child-support payments. This contributes to the fact that single-parent families headed by a woman live below the poverty line.

Single parenthood is an important topic in its own right. Some single parenthood is due to non-marital childbearing, which recent research by South and Lloyd (1992) links to a shortage of marriageable men. These single mothers are more likely than other women to have had children too soon, before acquiring sufficient education and job skills for economic independence. However, much single parenthood results from divorce or separation, which leaves many women in a situation where it is often difficult to find another mate. Men who have experienced divorce usually continue in the same line of work, meet single (typically younger) women more easily, and are free of most child-raising duties. At all ages, divorced men have higher remarriage rates than women, and remarry more quickly. Their involvement in new families lessens their commitment to previous ones. In 1985 an estimated 76 percent of divorced men could expect to remarry, while only 64 percent of divorced women could do the same (Adams & Nagnur, 1989, p. 26). Women could expect to be on their own for an average of five years before remarrying, while men would go only three years before remarrying (Adams & Nagnur, 1989, p. 26).

REMARRIAGE

The number of marriages in which at least one of the spouses was previously married has more than doubled since 1968, when divorces became easier to obtain. Given the decrease in first marriages, remarriages became more than twice as high a proportion of all marriages in 1985 as they were in 1968 (Statistics Canada, 1987a, Table 5; Ambert, 1988). Today, about three marriages in ten are remarriages for one or both partners.

However, during the 1970s and 1980s, rates of remarriage of widowed or divorced people began to decline. By 1989, rates of remarriage for divorced people were only two-thirds as high as they had been in 1955. Either fewer were remarrying, or all were taking longer to do so (see Exhibit 5.7).

The tendency of divorced people to remarry suggests that marriage retains its popularity. As Cherlin and Furstenberg (1983) write, despite high divorce rates, there is little evidence of a large-scale rejection of marriage as an institution, only of particular marriage partners. Moreover, many women need to remarry to survive economically

Exhibit 5.7

Annual remarriage rates[a] of divorced Canadians, 1955–1989

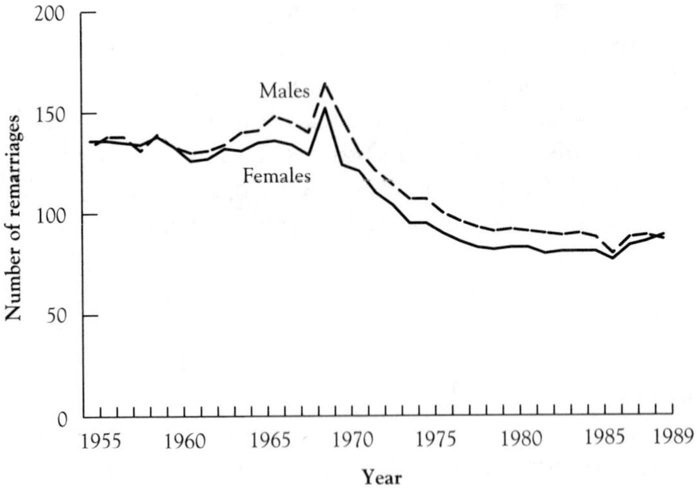

[a] Number of remarriages in a specified year per 1000 divorced people of the specified sex

Source: Dumas, J., and Peron, Y. (1992). *Marriage and Conjugal Life in Canada.* Current Demographic Analysis, p. 47. (Catalogue No. 91-534E). Ottawa: Statistics Canada, Demography Division.

(Ambert, 1988). Marriage and remarriage rates reflect economic as well as cultural and psychological forces in society. Recent declines in the rates of remarriage may reflect an easing of economic pressures or a movement into and out of cohabiting relationships.

In some respects, remarriage is very different from marriage. Rajulton and Burch (1991, p. 3) note that fewer people remarry than marry for the first time. The comparatively limited supply of eligible mates for women who want to remarry results in greater gender differences in remarriage patterns than for first marriage. However, there is a limited supply of eligible mates of either sex; therefore, candidates that men or women consider for remarriage are more varied than candidates for first marriage.

There are other differences, as well. Hobart (1991) shows that remarried couples are somewhat more likely than couples in their first marriage to disagree over child-rearing and financial issues. Children from a first marriage may also cause disagreement (see also Guisinger, Cowan, & Schuldberg, 1989; but for an opposite finding, see Kurdek, 1989).

Too-frequent contact with a former spouse is another source of conflict (Guisinger, Cowan, & Schuldberg, 1989; Weston & Macklin, 1990). However, remarried couples adjust to their new situation about as well as couples in their first marriage do. And when conflict does arise, remarried husbands are more likely to give in than husbands in their first marriage (Hobart, 1991).

For many couples, remarriage, like cohabitation, turns out to be very much like first-time marriage. The classic U-shaped relationship between marriage duration and satisfaction prevails: after the "honeymoon" period is over, about one respondent in two remains "enchanted" with his or her new spouse (Quality of Life survey, 1981). Similarities in life satisfaction are also noted, although having children and stepchildren appears to diminish satisfaction among remarried people, which is reflected in their higher rate of divorce.

This rate of divorce suggests that the remarried are no better acquainted with the satisfaction U-curve than the never-married. In fact, few people seem to know much about the natural course of marital satisfaction: its long decline and late recovery. And yet it is a pattern that anyone who wants to make an informed choice ought to take into account.

CONCLUSION

Marriage gives people the chance for both greater life satisfaction and deeper dissatisfaction than the single life normally does. If you marry, you will probably increase your standard of living and longevity, especially if you are a man. Marriage has riskier, less predictable outcomes for women, particularly when there are children involved or when the women lack skills that would allow them to earn a living. Men gain the most from a marriage that succeeds, and women—especially, mothers and poorer women—lose the most when a marriage fails.

So, especially if you are a woman, deciding about marriage means assessing your relationship realistically. If you think that there is too much fighting and not enough kissing in your relationship, marriage will not solve the problem. Remember that the "enchanted" newlywed period is normally followed by many years of declining satisfaction, particularly if children are present. The typical marriage will continue to worsen long before it starts to improve.

When you marry, avoid having children until you are fairly certain that your marriage will survive. Married women should develop the skills and habits that they will need to support themselves. A great many women have already changed their conception of marriage in significant ways, by equipping themselves for independence. Married women who continue to work put less importance on their marriage in the overall scheme of their lives than other married women (Baruch, Barnett, & Rivers, 1983, p. 294).

Most important, flee a relationship that is marked by physical violence. The violence is likely to recur. You are not to blame, and your partner is not going to change.

Do people get what they want from marriage? On the one hand, the range of possible choices is wider than ever: people are increasingly free to marry or not to marry; to have the kinds of relationships they want to; to choose the kind of mate they wish. On the other hand, what we want is patterned by our social experience. Canadians learn to want marriage as the preferred form of adult life. We mate with people who are nearby and socially like ourselves (because they are nearby), not with "ideal" mates. Some divorces occur because we have all learned to expect things out of life that marriage can scarcely provide—especially, the freedom to develop as individuals.

Do people learn to want what they get? Often, they do. We fall in love with someone who is close at hand, believing that we have discovered the "perfect" mate. On the other hand, people don't learn to like divorce. Women, who rarely choose divorce, are particularly hurt by it. Even men who divorce and remarry find the same marital satisfactions and dissatisfactions as men who had never divorced and remarried. People are slow to learn new wants; they are no happier the second time around than the first.

Chapter Six examines joys and problems of parenthood: what you want and what you get. It ties together some of the themes that we have already considered—especially, job satisfaction and marital satisfaction.

Chapter Six

◆

Childless or Parent:

What You Want and What You Get

Introduction

The decision to raise a child is an important and difficult one to make: parenthood is time-consuming and expensive. It can be frustrating, hard, and disappointing; also, thrilling, surprising, and delightful. In all of these respects, raising a child is like falling in love, running a business, learning a musical instrument, tending a farm, or mastering a sport. So even though the decision to raise a child is unique, other decisions you may have already made are similar; you can bring your past experiences to bear on the decision whether (some day) to become a parent.

Moreover, many of the decisions you have already made should influence that decision. After all, you have only so much time, money, and energy. You have to decide how to spend your scarce resources in the most satisfying way. For you, raising children may *not* be among the most satisfying ways to live.

This chapter will limit itself to two very important questions about parenthood, out of the many that we might discuss: (1) Should I have children, and if so, how many? and (2) Are people with children able to find a satisfactory balance between home and work responsibilities, and if so, how?

Answering the first question will lead us to consider what people say about parenthood, and how satisfied people are who have decided to raise children. People around the world have been rethinking parenthood for over a century. So the questions asked here, and the solutions people are considering today, are far from new. You will neither be the first nor the last person to ask them. What probably *will* be new to you are the data that bear on these questions.

Answering the second question will take us back to issues we considered in earlier chapters on education, work, and marriage: concerns about gender inequality and the problems that women face in the modern world. Again, people—especially women—throughout the world have been grappling with these issues for much of the past century. Problems of domestic and parental inequality are far from solved, but knowing that they are widely shared may help you put your own thoughts into clearer perspective.

As in previous chapters, we end by considering whether, in the domain of parenthood, people get what they want or learn to want what they get. But we must note from the outset that many people who become parents have not chosen parenthood at all. For some, parenthood results from an unwanted pregnancy and a felt obligation to bear and raise the child. For others, parenthood may result from a marriage to a person who already has children.

Likewise, many people do not choose the conditions under which they will raise their children, particularly mothers whose spouses desert them, abuse them or their children, fail to take parenthood seriously, or keep up heavy commitments to children from an earlier marriage: in short, a great many people (especially mothers).

So people do not always choose what they get, or get what they choose. The following analyses are aimed at helping people who *do* have a choice in the matter, in the hopes they will choose wisely.

Before we begin the chapter, here are a few true-false questions to see how much you know about the topic of parenting:

1. People have begun to limit the number of children they have only in the last 30 years.
   True ___ False ___
2. Women began to bear fewer children because infant and childhood mortality had declined.
   True ___ False ___
3. When children come into a marriage, a husband and wife grow closer emotionally than ever.
   True ___ False ___
4. Having teenagers in the household provides a new basis for marital conflict.
   True ___ False ___
5. More mothers are able to hold down a career today because their husbands share the housework equally.
   True ___ False ___

POPULATIONS AND BIRTHRATES

The survival of humanity has historically depended on the willingness of many—indeed, most—women to bear four or more children. When death rates were very high—say, more than three centuries ago in

Europe and North America—every family, community, and society needed many births just to stay the same size. That's because many children died in infancy; many others failed to reach adulthood, marry, and reproduce. As a result, even with four (or more) children per mother, about as many children lived to enter parenthood as had done so in the previous generation. For many centuries, the total population stayed the same size from one generation to another, and so the ratio of people to land—the source of all food—went unchanged. Since the food supply remained stable, there was little economic development or major social change.

But toward the end of the seventeenth century, death rates in Western Europe began to fall. Within a century, birth rates were also falling. Families began to change very radically.

World Trends in Childbearing

The story of modern parenthood really begins with a worldwide decline in childbearing late in the nineteenth century. Around 1871, marital childbearing in Europe and North America began a significant and never-to-be-reversed fall. Knodel and van de Walle (1979) summarize the evidence as follows:

1. Fertility declines took place under a wide variety of social, economic, and demographic conditions.
2. Family limitation was largely absent (and probably unknown) among broad segments of the population prior to the decline in fertility, even though a substantial proportion of births may have been unwanted.
3. Increases in the practice of family limitation and the decline of marital fertility were essentially irreversible processes once under way.
4. Cultural setting influenced the onset and spread of fertility decline independently of socioeconomic conditions. (p. 220)

No one knows precisely why the massive change centres on 1871, or how the onset of change in one region connected with change in another region. (For a review of the historical findings for Europe, see Coale & Watkins [Eds.], 1986.) Yet the fact remains that after 1871, European and North American childbearing decreased almost steadily.

The best explanation we have for this development is offered by "demographic transition theory" (see, for example, Petersen, 1969), which argues that nineteenth- and twentieth-century declines in the birth rate were due to eighteenth- and nineteenth-century declines in the death rate. These, in turn, were a result of better sanitation, public health, nutrition, and medical care. To assure their family's continuity, parents now only needed two children, and no longer four or more.

Large families were unnecessary, even a liability, in the urban, industrial world. Increasingly, urban middle-class parents came to decide that their children would do better in life if there were fewer of them. This would ensure that each one received more of the family's care and support (Banks, 1954).

Birth rates, however, did not fall as rapidly as death rates. For the space of a few generations, the gap that opened between them caused populations to grow very rapidly. This population growth put enormous pressure on the land and led to shortages of food. As a result, some families migrated to the New World, which offered land and opportunity. Warfare increased among European nations struggling to expand and to capture colonies for resources, markets, and room to live. In the long run, it was industrialization that provided a solution. Industrial production provided more food and consumer goods than ever in the past; prosperity led people to bear fewer children than before.

Many countries have not yet passed through the demographic transition from high death and birth rates to low ones. For example, rural Nigerian women still want (and have) about six births each. Based on a survey of 1600 Nigerian women, Ukaegbu (1977) concludes that "infant and child mortality, and the unwillingness to cease childbearing are the leading factors in the reproductive behaviour of the Nwa Igbo women" (p. 104).

Thanks to modern medicine, less developed countries are seeing a fall in their death rates that is much more rapid than the one that took place in the West. Nearly everywhere, parenthood has become a question of choice, although contraceptive use remains rare in many African countries (Sai, 1988), as in some other parts of the Third World. Given that modern technology lets people prevent all but the pregnancies they want, it is people's values and attitudes to parenthood that determine the size of their families.

As Ukaegbu (1977, p. 110) shows, Nigerians place a very high value on children. They tell researchers that (1) no amount of material wealth is superior to children; (2) the power of any household depends on its having large numbers of male members; (3) children are gifts from God; (4) large numbers of children earn a family a big income when they are grown up; (5) family responsibilities are made easier when shared by a large family; and (6) couples who have a large number of children are guaranteed a grand burial.

A cross-national study of the value of children shows that in many pre-industrial or early industrial societies, old-age security is a major concern and an important reason for having children—especially sons: "It appears that in societies with low levels of technological development without widespread social welfare institutions such as social security systems, unemployment insurance, free health care, nursing homes and the like, their functions are undertaken by families and especially by the adult-age children" (Kagitcibasi, 1982, p. 138). In rural and less-developed areas, children are a "utilitarian-economic" asset. "The more children one has, the more likely that at least one will provide old-age security, or their combined contributions will provide support" (Kagitcibasi, 1982, p. 140).

Because many societies have been slow to promote birth control and provide social security for the poor and aged, world population has continued to rise rapidly (see Exhibit 6.1). The world's 5 billionth person was added around July 11, 1987. United Nations demographers predict that the 6 billionth will be added in 1998, the 7 billionth in 2010, and the 8 billionth in 2023. This is an amazing rate of growth, given the history of the human population up to this century.

Governments in some less developed countries have come to see the advantages to be gained in limiting their citizens' childbearing. China has experienced a dramatic reduction in its fertility rate in the last 30 years. Chen (1984) reports that since 1971, the *wan, xi, shao* ("later, longer, fewer") campaign has resulted in later marriage, a longer period between births, and fewer births in total. "The total fertility rate during the decade preceding the establishment of the People's Republic in 1949 was well above five children per woman of reproductive age ... [After 1970] it fell steadily, to a low of 2.2 in 1980" (Chen, 1984, p. 52).

Chinese authorities reformed the marriage laws, vigorously promoted birth control policies (improving access to contraception, sterilization, and abortion), and, in 1979, promulgated a one-child-per-couple policy. This last coercive measure has had a significant impact on the childbearing behaviour of urban, literate populations. The change has been slower among peasants in rural villages; that is "to be expected in a society where social security allowances are almost nonexistant in rural areas, and where rural couples must depend on their children, in particular their sons, to take care of them in their old age" (Chen, 1984, p. 55).

Canadian Trends in Childbearing

Canada began its own decline in childbearing a century ago (Romaniuc, 1986). Since then, the total fertility rate has fallen from an average of 6 births per woman to 1.7 (in 1986), below the level required to replace the Canadian population (Devereaux, 1990b, p. 34; Ram, 1988).

With an average 2.1 births per woman, population size will remain stable from one generation to the next; but with 1.7 births per mother, there are 20 percent fewer children than parents (Beaujot, 1986). In the

Exhibit 6.1
World population trends

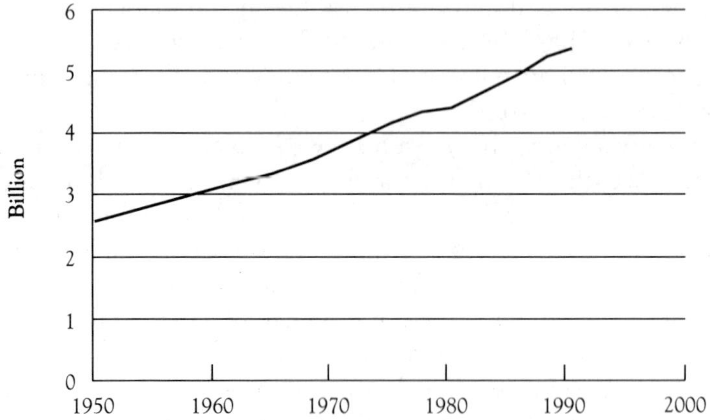

Figure a: World Population, 1950–91

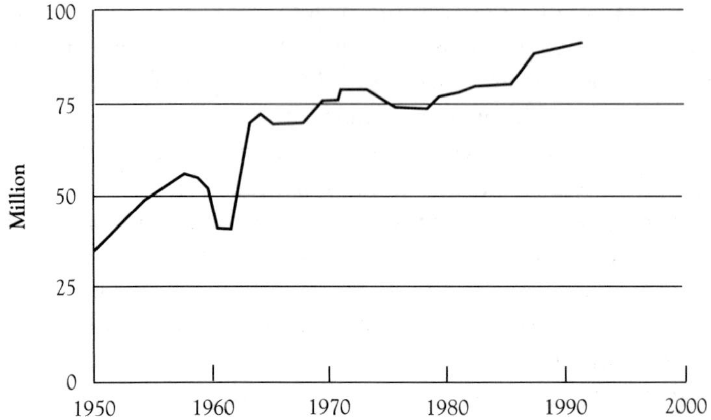

Figure b: Annual Addition to World Population, 1950–91

Source: Brown, L.R., et al. (1992). *Vital signs* (p. 77). Worldwatch Institute. New York: W.W. Norton. Reprinted with permisssion.

absence of immigration, at this rate Canada's population would shrink by 20 percent every 30 years. Canada would eventually disappear into world history, along with Babylon, Dacia, and Etruria (see Exhibit 6.2).

The most dramatic drop in fertility is to be seen in Quebec, whose total fertility rate, for a long time Canada's highest, now stands at

Exhibit 6.2
Canadas Population Future*

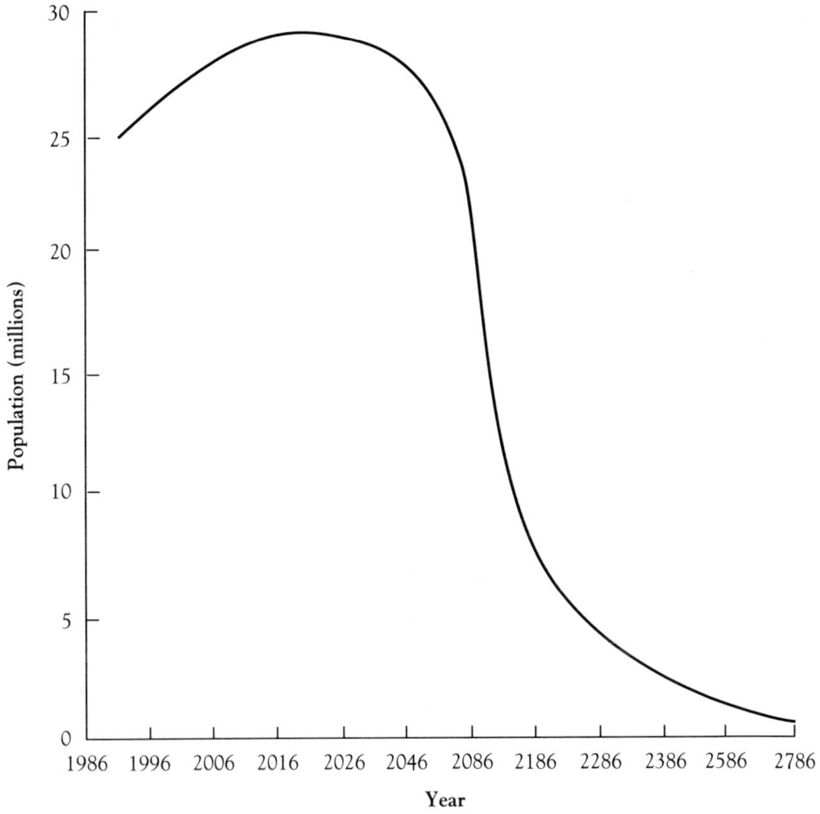

*If current vital rates continue and there is no immigration.

Source: Health and Welfare Canada (1989). *Charting Canada's Future: A Report of a Demographic Review* (Category H21-105/1). Ottawa: Health and Welfare Canada. Reproduced with the permission of the Minister of Supply and Services Canada, 1993.

1.4 births per woman, Canada's lowest (Statistics Canada, 1987a; Lachapelle, 1990, p. 154). Quebec also has the lowest rate of marriage and, with many women choosing to bear their first child after the age of 30, the most marked pattern of delayed childbearing. These demographic changes give Quebec francophones cause for concern about the disappearance of their language and culture.

Will these trends continue? It is hard to say. Demographers disagree about the likely future level of childbearing in Canada. In part, that is due to the problems of linear extrapolation we discussed in Chapter Four. Most population projections are based on the simple assumption that current behaviours, or trends, will continue in their present form. But what if they accelerate, slow down, or change completely? For example, the century-long downward slide in births may be accelerated by recent changes in marriage and divorce. One researcher writes that "greater proportions single or cohabiting, later marriage and increased marital interruption may well produce (even) more fertility decline" (Beaujot, 1987, p. 12). Indeed, most of the changes taking place in the family today work against childbearing. Poor economic prospects may have a similar effect. This could all lead to a twenty-first century Canadian population that is very much smaller than today's.

On the other hand, if Canadian governments continue to reduce social welfare benefits, in effect "privatizing" people's problems of unemployment, illness, poverty, and old age, the family may once again gain in economic and social importance and grow in size. It will again become rational for parents to have many children, who will be responsible for providing them with security. And with that, Canada's population will start to grow rapidly again.

The most likely future for Canada, however, includes a population that is growing very slowly, if at all (Foot, 1982, p. 91) and an enormous baby-boom generation moving into old age and economic dependency as you work your way through adulthood. Because the Canadian birthrate is not likely to increase by a large amount, the only realistic way to offset these developments is through much higher rates of immigration.

WHY PEOPLE CHOOSE PARENTHOOD

As you can see, the decision to have children is one of many decisions that have an impact well beyond people's own lives. The survival of the human race once depended on an almost universal "Yes" in answer to the question "Should I have children?" Today, it increasingly depends on the answers "No," "Maybe," or "Not many." People choose parenthood more carefully today, with a greater awareness of the reasons for their choice and its consequences for their lives.

Insofar as childbearing is a decision, and a purely personal one, what people think about parenthood will remain very important. So what *do* people think about parenthood? Why are they likely to choose it?

Consider what children, the next generation of parents, think about parenthood. More than 600 000 American schoolchildren participated in a "future survey" (Johnson, 1987). "The great majority, over 80%, expect to marry, although boys were slightly less likely than girls to indicate that. Most children expected to have two, one, or three children, in that order of preference; again, boys were considerably more likely to choose 'none'" (p. 37).

Yet children are often unable to say *why* they want to have children, and show little awareness of the consequences. One result is a rate of teenage pregnancy in North America—in the United States especially —that is well beyond what we find in other industrialized countries.

A team of researchers (Jones et al., 1986) tried to discover why so many American teenage girls are getting pregnant by comparing 37 countries with low and high rates of teenage pregnancy. They found three factors associated with low teenage pregnancy rates: high levels of economic development, openness about sex, and a high minimum legal age at marriage. The three factors they found to be associated with high rates of teenage fertility were a high degree of income inequality, generous maternity leaves and benefits, and overall pronatalist policies —that is, policies aimed at increasing fertility.

Six national case studies helped the researchers narrow their focus on the American problem. They concluded that, by comparison with other industrial countries (and even some less developed ones) the United States has a high degree of income inequality, leading to the existence of a large, deprived underclass, and an "ambivalent, sometimes puritanical attitude about sex." The first factor, income inequality, induces a sense of fatalism in teenagers—a lack of commitment to the idea of personal development *before* and *outside of* parenthood. The poor have less stake in the future and a weaker belief in the efficacy of their plans. They believe that they do just as well to have babies young as have them when they are older. The second factor, ambivalence about sex, influences teenagers in two ways. On the one hand, the mass media bombard Americans with messages proclaiming the ecstasy of sex, love, and marriage. This encourages impulsive sexual behaviour. On the other hand, more traditional elements in the society make it difficult for unmarried people—especially young ones—to obtain information or help in relation to sex and birth control. Paradoxically, "teenagers living in countries where contraceptive services, sex education in and out of the schools, and abortion services are widely available have lower rates of adolescent pregnancy and do not have appreciably higher levels of sexual experience than do teeangers in the United States" (Jones et al., 1986, p. 233).

The problem with poor American teenagers, then, is not so much that they place a high value on having many children. It is that they simply haven't given childbearing much thought and may not care much about preventing it. For most North Americans, though, early childbearing is rare; parenting decisions are conscious and based on certain values or goals.

For example, 73.7 percent of the "average" Canadians Beaujot surveyed in and around London, Ontario, believe that

> the ideal number of children is two or three. Asked why not more, most refer to costs, hard to afford more, hard to manage, time and emotional costs, the need to give a certain amount of time to each child each day. The world is built for smaller families: number of bedrooms in houses, seats in cars, etc. There are also population and environmental problems with larger families. Asked why not less, most say that a child should have at least one sibling or that one child does not make for a real family (1991b, p. 10).

The respondents strongly oppose the idea of having a single child. They feel that children need sibling interaction to develop as individuals, and that an only child is likely to be "lonely, selfish and spoilt, gets too much attention, does not have to share, lacks the companionship of other children." While reluctant to judge couples who had decided not to have any children, some of these respondents—especially the older ones—questioned why people would bother to marry if they did not intend to have children. Nor do these average Canadians see large families (five or more children) as a realistic choice, although they do value the idea for sentimental reasons: "Large families can mean more fun at Christmas, birthdays and family gatherings, it is a joy, and as you get older the joy of the large extended family grows."

An increasingly vocal group in North American society is characterized by a combination of traditional behaviours and beliefs. They hold a pronatalist ideology, opposing abortion and favouring large families and traditional family and gender roles. Opponents of abortion tend to be frequent churchgoers (63 percent go once or more a week) who fear that homosexuals, feminists, and the media are destroying the family. "What has galvanized them," says sociologist Lorna Erwin, "is their perception that the family is under attack, and they see [the danger] everywhere" (*The Globe and Mail*, April 2, 1987). This sense of a danger to tradition and a belief in absolute right and wrong keep attitudes static in the face of universal changes in family life and parenthood.

At the other end of the attitude spectrum is an emerging counterculture whose value system sociologist Jean Veevers (1980) calls "antinatalism." These people do not want to bear or raise children, and demand complete freedom to make this decision. Many voluntarily childless couples choose this way of life because they want the freedom to continue pursuing their own interests (Ramu & Tavuchis, 1986). Single women wanting no child or only one child desire financial and social independence in their future marriage relationships. They expect to follow their careers and interests to the fullest, and express a greater than average need to share success and intellectual stimulation with their partners. These women have relatively little interest in home ownership, budgeting, and contact with family. Single women who want to stay childless tend to be less optimistic about life, are less loving, and find life less satisfying than single women who want children (Callan, 1986).

Where do your own sentiments lie? You can choose to avoid parenthood if you so desire. Our society is increasingly able look upon marriage, sex, and childbearing as distinct parts of intimate life. Because each activity can be separated from the others, each demands a separate, rational choice. If you do not really want children, do not have them.

Exhibit 6.3 contains some questions that you might ask yourself to determine whether you are "parent material." Whether you are currently contemplating parenthood or not, you may benefit from answering these questions. Note that there are no "right" answers indicated here; the purpose of this chart is not to score your parenting potential but to provoke some hard thinking.

CONSEQUENCES OF PARENTHOOD

Every new parent will rave on about the joys of parenthood. As a parent you will have many of the following experiences: you will fall in love with your child, feel excitement at helping a new person develop, be amazed at the similarities (and differences) between your baby and other members of the family, feel pride of how kind (generous, tolerant) you are and ashamed of how selfish (short-tempered, immature) you used to be. You will find that you have learned something important about life, yourself, your own parents, and the human race.

Yet we know that marital satisfaction generally drops with the passage of time. At all ages and at every stage of marriage, wives without children are more satisfied with their marriages than wives with children (Lupri & Frideres, 1981, p. 300). Husbands without children are also more satisfied than same-aged fathers (except between the ages of 45 and 65). More generally, both partners in couples who choose to be childless tend to be more satisfied with their lives and marriages than couples with children (see, for example, Polonko, Scanzoni, & Teachman, 1982; Glenn & McLanahan, 1982).

Infertile women, who are childless against their will, may be less satisfied with their lives than women with children (De Jong et al., 1984). Infertility decreases the frequency of intercourse for married couples,

Exhibit 6.3

The NAOP (National Alliance for Optional Parenthood) "Am I Parent Material?" test

---

Raising a child? What's there to know?

1. Do I like children? When I'm around children for a while, what do I think or feel about having one around all of the time?
2. Do I enjoy teaching others?
3. Is it easy for me to tell other people what I want, or need, or what I expect of them?
4. Do I want to give a child the love (s)he needs? Is loving easy for me?
5. Am I patient enough to deal with the noise and confusion of the 24-hour-a-day responsibility? What kind of time and space do I need for myself?
6. What do I do when I get angry or upset? Would I take things out on a child if I lost my temper?
7. What does discipline mean to me? What does freedom, or setting limits, or giving space mean? What is being too strict, or not strict enough? Would I want a perfect child?
8. How do I get along with my parents? What will I do to avoid the mistakes my parents made?
9. How would I take care of my child's health and safety? How do I take care of my own?
10. What if I have a child and find out I made a wrong decision?

Have my partner and I really talked about becoming parents?

1. Does my partner want to have a child? Have we talked about our reasons?
2. Could we give a child a good home? Is our relationship a happy and strong one?
3. Are we both ready to give our time and energy to raising a child?
4. Could we share our love with a child without jealousy?
5. What would happen if we separated after having a child, or if one of us should die?
6. Do my partner and I understand each other's feelings about religion, work, family, child-raising, future goals? Do we feel pretty much the same way? Will children fit into these feelings, hopes, and plans?
7. Suppose one of us wants a child and the other doesn't. Who decides?
8. Which of the questions in this test do we need to *really* discuss before making a decision?

What's in it for me?

1. Do I like doing things with children? Do I enjoy activities that children do?
2. Would I want a child to be "like me"?

3. Would I try to pass on to my child my ideas and values? What if my child's ideas and values turn out to be different from mine?
4. Would I want my child to achieve things that I wish I had, but didn't?
5. Would I expect my child to keep me from being lonely in my old age? Do I do that for my parents? Do my parents do that for my grandparents?
6. Do I want a boy or a girl child? What if I don't get what I want?
7. Would having a child show others how mature I am?
8. Will I prove I am a man or a woman by having a child?
9. Do I expect my child to make my life happy?

Does having and raising a child fit the lifestyle I want?

1. What do I want out of life for myself? What do I think is important?
2. Could I handle a child and a job at the same time? Would I have time and energy for both?
3. Would I be ready to give up the freedom to do what I want to do, when I want to do it?
4. Would I be willing to cut back my social life and spend more time at home? Would I miss my free time and privacy?
5. Can I afford to support a child? Do I know how much it takes to raise a child?
6. Do I want to raise a child in the neighbourhood where I live now? Would I be willing and able to move?
7. How would a child interfere with my growth and development?
8. Would a child change my educational plans? Do I have the energy to go to school and raise a child at the same time?
9. Am I willing to give a great part of my life—AT LEAST 18 YEARS—to being responsible for a child? And spend a large portion of my life being concerned about my child's well-being?

Source: Veevers, J.E. (1980). *Childless by choice* (pp. 162, 164). Toronto: Butterworths Canada, Ltd. Reprinted with permission from the author.

decreases satisfaction and comfort with sex, and reduces women's self-confidence (Sabatelli, Meth, & Gavazzi, 1988). What is at issue here, then, is not only parenthood, it is the ability to *choose* parenthood. People who lack this choice are often less satisfied than average. But people who do have this choice, and choose against parenthood, tend to be more satisfied with their lives and marriages.

Adults with children at home report that they are less happy and less satisfied with their lives than other groups. They appear to worry more and experience high levels of anxiety and depression. Though the overall difference between parent and non-parents is small, it seems to have increased in the past two decades (McLanahan & Adams, 1987). Off all parents, step-parents and remarried parents report the lowest levels of satisfaction with parenthoood (Ishii-Kuntz & Ihinger-Tallman, 1991. Both husbands and wives are more likely to be very satisfied with their marriage if some or all of their children are living away from home (Rhyne, 1984, p. 19). In fact, four parents in ten would not like to see their "living-away" children more often than they already do (Quality of Life survey, 1981).

There is some research that seems to point in the opposite direction. In fact, it seems to suggest that satisfaction increases with the number of children a parent has produced (Greeley, 1991). For example, fathers of three or more children appear more satisfied with life and marriage than fathers with only one or two children (Quality of Life survey, 1981). But further analyses suggest that we have to interpret the relationship between satisfaction and number of children in another way. It is not that having children makes people satisfied, but rather that satisfied people are more likely to have children.

The Quality of Life data (1981) suggest that couples who are very satisfied with their marriage are more likely than other couples to bear children and also more likely to feel satisfied with life. Couples dissatisfied with their marriage who bear many children end up no more satisfied with their lives than dissatisfied couples who bear fewer children. And happily married couples with *many* children are only slightly more satisfied with life than happily married couples with fewer children.

So the parenting decision is largely an effect, not a cause, of marital and life satisfaction. In the long run, parenting will not make you more satisfied with your marriage or your life. Nor will the presence of children compensate for the absence of a mate: single mothers are less satisfied than mothers with live-in partners (Fine, Donnelly, & Voydanoff, 1986; Ball, 1984; for contrary findings in a study of black Americans, see Keicolt & Acock, 1990). Single mothers are less involved in the community, have less satisfying personal relationships, report higher levels of loneliness, and have lower levels of life satisfaction than married mothers (Kirkham et al., 1986). Single mothers report more child behaviour problems and feel more stress than happily and even unhappily married mothers. When interacting with their children, they make more critical statements and ask more critical questions. Their children exhibit more deviant and non-compliant behaviour than other children (Webster-Stratton, 1989).

On balance, those with the hardest parenting jobs—mothers (and especially single mothers) aged 31 to 45—report enjoying parenthood least. Those who report enjoying parenthood the most tend to have the least amount of recent experience with it: they are either under 30 or over 65 years of age. For similar reasons, younger women are more likely than older women to advise against bearing many children (Quality of Life survey, 1981).

Should you have many children? Even from the children's own standpoint, fewer may be better. In a smaller family, there is less rivalry between children for their parents' attention and love. And families with only one or two children—currently the most common number—contain no "middle children," who often feel less loved than their first-born and last-born siblings. In smaller families proportionately more children are first-borns, who share with only children the tendency to be high academic achievers, competitive, sociable, and eager to win approval (Poston & Falbo, 1990). These are all traits you may find appealing.

Family size has a small but significant negative effect on adult status attainment. The fewer brothers and sisters your child has, the more likely he or she is to attain high educational and occupational status (Pineo, 1985a). Why? Because your child receives more care and encouragement, which are associated with success in life (cf. Porter, Porter, & Blishen, 1982).

How many children should you have, then? That's like asking how many businesses should you run, how many mates should you have, how many books should you read, how many musical instruments should you learn to play. Just because one (of each) is wonderful does not mean that two will be twice as wonderful, or three, three times as wonderful. In fact, each additional child may bring less new satisfaction than the one before; the novelty wears off and you have ever fewer resources to give each one.

Why Parenthood Changes People's Lives

Why does parenthood have a negative effect on marriages and lives? And why have we failed to take note of such effects in the first place, instead romanticizing parenthood and stigmatizing people who choose to have no children? These are the questions that sociologist Anne-Marie Ambert (1992) has tried to answer. Her main purpose is to document the known facts about the consequences of having children; at the very least, her book corrects our tendency to assume that while parents influence their children, the reverse is seldom true.

Our culture teaches us that children are passive and innocent. We learn to attribute how they behave and the kind of people they become to socialization and parental influence. Though we recognize that children have certain inborn tendencies, we are far more likely to hold their parents responsible for their behaviour than the children themselves. Consequently, in our culture parents are likely to spend a good deal of time feeling worried, guilty, and ashamed on behalf of their children.

Likewise, we learn to view children as powerless. Under the law, children *are* largely powerless. Within the family, children may have difficulty in defending themselves. Parents are larger, stronger, and in control of more resources (financial and physical) than children; they start out with the advantage. And there is no denying a high incidence of child abuse in our society. Yet we have to recognize that children resemble other relatively powerless groups in their capacity to hurt and harass those who dominate them. This is just as true in relations between children and parents as it is between women and men, workers and bosses, prisoners and jailers, minorities and majorities. In each case, the weaker group has ways (whether conscious or not) of bringing the stronger to its knees. Ambert documents the distress that juvenile delinquency and children's emotional problems and chronic illnesses cause parents. Children can learn to manipulate parents with an exposed weakness—for example, guilt or anxiety about their divorce.

The transition to parenthood also involves a disruption of time schedules and a conflict over relationship rules (Worthington & Buston, 1986). With parenthood, the division of labour in the household assumes a traditional form, shared leisure activities become less frequent, interaction decreases, conflict (especially over money) increases, positive emotional exchanges decrease, and feelings of love for the spouse decline. Time constraints are also a problem, especially when the mother is doing paid work (McLanahan & Adams, 1987). On the other hand, economic constraints become a greater problem when the mother is not earning money.

These consequences of parenthood are typically modest, and merely accentuate changes that take place in most marital relationships over time (Belsky & Pensky, 1988; McHale & Huston, 1985). White, Booth, and Edwards (1986) argue that the apparent causal relationship between parenting and unhappiness may even be spurious. Parenthood may not necessarily cause unhappiness; but it does prevent many unhappily married couples from breaking up. This may be the most important reason that parenthood coincides with and *appears* to cause a decrease in marital and overall life satisfaction.

Schumm and Bugaighis (1986) believe that much of the reported decline in marital satisfaction is limited to low-income mothers with preschool children who are employed full-time and have too little opportunity to keep up a fulfilling relationship with their spouse. Thus, what appears to be moderate distress for a large group of parents may actually be severe distress for a smaller group of wives, according to these authors.

Like marriage, work, and many other life experiences, parenthood goes through better times and worse times. The onset of parenthood is particularly trying. "Young parents ... express more feeling of strain at this stage than at any other period of their married lives" (Campbell, 1980, p. 187; but for a contrary view, see Schuchts & Witkin, 1989). Campbell reports a particularly strong difference between the mothers of young children and young, married women without children. The young mothers are more likely to find life difficult, feel tied down, express concern about financial matters, and worry about having a nervous breakdown (Campbell, 1980, pp. 187–88).

The problems are especially severe when parents have failed to anticipate the effects of parenthood on their lives (Belsky, 1985)—particularly its negative effects on their marriage. Well-educated women are the most likely to foresee the consequences of parenthood; as a result, they experience less conflict and disappointment when they become parents.

Couples with small children find that disagreements become more common, believe that they get less companionship from their mate than they once did, and feel unsatisfied with marriage and parenthood. "Two out of five of these mothers of small children go so far as to admit they sometimes wish they could be free of the responsibilities of being a parent, a much larger proportion than is found among mothers of older children" (Campbell, 1980, p. 188).

In some ways, the situation improves when all the children are attending school. Once the mother resumes paid employment, the financial pressures begin to lighten. Balancing a job and child care is difficult, but the parents of a school-age child feel less tied down, less burdened by parenthood, and they are more likely to enjoy it. Once their children are in school, spouses begin to feel that they understand each other better. "But they do not regain the strong sense of companionship ... they had as young couples until they reach the next stage of life, when the children have grown up" (Campbell, 1980, p. 189).

Marital satisfaction, which tends to decline over time when children are present, reaches its lowest point ever when the children are adolescents. In part, the problem is financial: feeding, clothing, and educating adolescents becomes an increasingly heavy burden. At the same time, family income has started to level off for the middle-aged parents; this is often called the "life-cycle squeeze."

Still, parenthood is a story with a happy ending: the grown children leave home. Later married life is known for an enhanced sense of well-being, to which freedom from responsibility to children certainly contributes. The "empty nest" results in an increase in marital happiness, if not always in overall life satisfaction (White & Edwards, 1990). Yet this experience of well-being within the marriage appears to occur independently of the circumstances of parenthood. The "generally high level of satisfaction with life and with the various domains of life which we find associated with ... [later] married life is probably more strongly influenced by the simple fact of growing older than it is by the departure of the children" (Campbell, 1980, p. 191).

It takes twenty years or more to regain the loss in satisfaction that accompanies the birth of a couple's first child, so parenthood should be chosen carefully and for good reasons. Avoid having any children, or too many children, for the wrong reasons: to avoid marital breakup, or to make you satisfied with marriage or life, for example.

BALANCING PARENTHOOD AND EMPLOYMENT

Parenthood intrudes on other domains of life: marriage and career in particular. So another question students commonly ask about parenthood is how they will be able to balance the demands of raising children and succeeding in a career.

This is not a question that men often ask themselves; they rarely factor the demands of child rearing into their lifetime plan. If they think of the problem at all, they assume that their wives will take care of the children when they are busy with work. What they fail to remember is that their wives may be busy with work, too. Married women are increasingly participating in the paid labour force.

Of course, many women do not have careers, or even paid jobs, but remain homemakers for much or all of their lives. Are they content with their lives? In the past, feminists criticized traditional sex-role attitudes and the traditional division of labour that had women working as full-time housewives. Yet some research suggests that women can be happy in this traditional role (Alspach, 1982). An Australian study (Rizzo, Reynolds, & Gallagher, 1981) even finds that full-time homemakers are more satisfied with the lives they lead than women doing paid work. Women who work outside the home have more intense premenstrual syndrome (PMS) symptoms than women homemakers

(Coughlin, 1990). Stokes and Peyton (1986) report that women who hold liberal (including pro-work) views of women's roles are less satisfied with life than women with traditional or conservative views.

Not all the evidence points to the relative satisfaction of homemakers. An English study found that women who are very dissatisfied with their role of housewife have more severe symptoms of alcoholism (Farid et al., 1989). Shehan, Burg, and Rexroat (1986) found that American housewives are particularly depressed by a low total family income, limited social contacts outside the family, and low satisfaction with family life and the housewife role.

It is difficult to evaluate these two sets of findings. Women who work for pay and women who work at home are often different "kinds" of women. Employed women tend to have more education, a higher household income, fewer children, and less conservative sex-role attitudes than homemakers. They also describe themselves as more aggressive, materialistic, and rebellious (Stokes & Peyton, 1986).

It may not be possible, then, to draw conclusions about how *every* woman might regard housework. In fact, a comparison of full-time and part-time homemakers by Ivancevich and Matteson (1982) indicates that both are generally satisfied with their household role, but that each group suffers from particular stresses. Full-time homemakers feel the pressures of children and domestic work conditions, while part-time homemakers tend to be stressed by their spouse's or children's failure to share in household tasks. The failure of family members to share household tasks is felt even more acutely by women who work for pay full-time than by women who do paid work part-time. But all women in the paid work force face the problem of balancing the demands of housework and paid work. This *problem of balance* is getting more common as women increasingly find full-time employment.

Statistics from the 1986 census reveal that male and female work patterns are converging: men are spending a smaller portion of their lives in the labour force and women a greater portion (*The Globe and Mail*, March 2, 1988). Between 1971 and 1991, the percentage of Canadian women over the age of fifteen holding a paid job or looking for one rose from 39.4 percent to 58.2 percent (*The Globe and Mail*, January 15, 1993, p. A2). By contrast, men's participation in the work force dropped over the same period from 77.3 percent to 74.8 percent (see Exhibit 6.4).

Most interesting of all, the participation rate of women with children younger than six rose from 49.5 percent to 62.1 percent in a mere five years, between 1981 and 1986 (*The Globe and Mail*, March 2, 1988). These women, with paid jobs and young children to care for, are the ones who have the most difficulty balancing domestic and job demands.

Exhibit 6.4

Percentage of women and men employed, 1975–1991

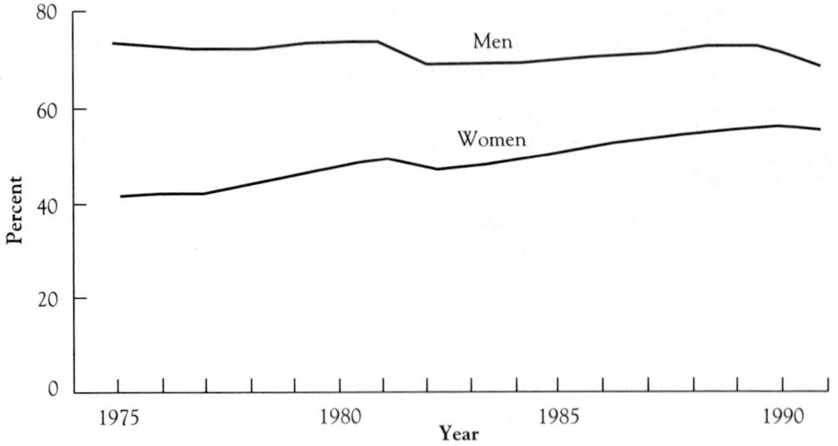

Source: Statistics Canada, Catalogue Nos. 71–001, 71–220, and 71–529. In Ghalam, N., "Women in the Workplace," *Canadian Social Trends*, Spring 1993, pp. 2–6. Ottawa: Statistics Canada.

How the Parenthood/Employment Problem Developed

The problem of balancing parenthood and paid work developed in several stages. It began with the shift from extended to nuclear families. Then, the nineteenth century saw the replacement of household-based family production by factory-based industrial production. For the first time the public, male-dominated workplace became separated from the private, female-dominated household.

This male–female division of labour had not always existed. In the Middle Ages, the extended family was a much more common type of household than it is today. Such households often included grown children, aunts and uncles, and servants, as well as fathers, mothers, and younger children. Caring for children and making a living were familial activities. Everyone took responsibility for everyone else's children, freeing the adults to work in the fields or at a trade.

Generally, husbands and wives, parents and children were near to one another throughout the day. There was little separation of family life from work life, and parents could usually carry out their normal daily work while paying attention to the children. The children they could not take care of, or afford to keep at home, were sent into service. These arrangements allowed for early marriage and unlimited childbearing.

Around the sixteenth or seventeenth century, the "European marriage pattern" arose (Hajnal, 1965), in which people married later. (Many never married at all.) The rise of this arrangement seems to have coincided with the rise of nuclear families in Western Europe. In Eastern Europe, Africa, and Asia, the traditional "non-European pattern" continued for several centuries more, but even there it began to disappear during the twentieth century.

The European pattern ensures that people are economically independent before they marry: farmers have a piece of land, and craftsmen, a trade and a shop. People simply put off marriage and childbearing until attaining economic independence. That often meant a long delay in marrying. Many women remained unmarried until they were past the age when they could bear children.

The transformation from one family pattern to the other can be outlined in a sequence of interrelated changes. First, the family gets smaller. The nuclear family contains fewer children than the extended family. Late marriage reduces the average number of children in a family, even when contraception is not practised (Henry, 1976, pp. 90–121).

With industrialization, work becomes separated from home life. The rural extended family knows little division of domestic and other duties. That is largely because there is no geographic distance between household and workplace: they are the same. The urban nuclear family lives away from the workplace. Parents take on the domestic chores for their own family, without the help of adult relatives living in the same household, and usually earn an income outside the home.

The separation of work and home life leads to the development of a gender-based division of labour within the family. Wives take on the main responsibility for home-based private life (housework and child rearing) and husbands, the main responsibility for public life (especially wage earning.) But like any division of labour, this one creates interdependence between partners and demands more communication and coordination than in the past. The nuclear family requires increased co-operation from the two spouses, who rely on each other for assistance, support, and care.

Along with a gender-based division of labour, marriage evolves in the direction of greater integration. It comes to emphasize sharing, companionship, and expressive exchange. Elizabeth Bott (1957) illustrates the nature of this change in a classic study, *Family and Social Network*, where she compares two sets of families. One lives in a stable working-class London community full of childhood friends, parents, and other relatives—essentially, an extended family setting. The other set of families, from a similar background, lives in a new community full of socially and geographically uprooted people.

Spouses in the *first*, "traditional" community maintain their childhood ties and rely heavily on parents, relatives, and old friends for support, child care, and sociability. Husbands and wives have somewhat limited communication with each other, and define their roles and duties along rigid gender lines: husbands do not change diapers or cook; wives do not repair the car or go out much with friends.

Spouses in the *second* community, cut off from old friends and family ties, form new networks of friends-in-common. They share activities and interests, and even share some domestic duties. In general, their isolation from old relationships, sharing of new friends, and greater reliance on each other for support demands better communication and co-operation within the household.

Of course, the old-style family did not disappear entirely, nor did families entirely stop providing support to their members. Recent Canadian data (see Exhibit 6.5) show that over four Canadian adults in five are still receiving some practical help from family and friends. About half of this help—especially financial support and housework—comes from family members who live in another household. In 1990, 81 percent of the 20.5 million Canadians aged 15 and over received or provided at least one unpaid service, other than child care, from or to someone living outside their household at least once during the previous twelve months. Almost one half (46 percent) both gave and received help (Paletta, 1992, p. 27). So the extended family is not completely dead, but there is no denying it plays a much smaller role in people's lives than it once did.

New Challenges for the Family

In moving from the old-style, quasi-extended family in the traditional community to the nuclear family in a new community of strangers, people gain privacy, independence, and greater opportunity for upward social mobility. The desire for these attributes spreads to nearly everyone: male and female, child and parent. But possessions of these attributes leaves a couple with no one else to rely on, so spouses must find ways of communicating and sharing. As more women enter the paid labour force, the problems of balance and co-operation become more pressing.

As the children grow older, the time pressures decrease slightly, although they never disappear completely (Robinson, 1991). With more activities to complete within 24 hours, working women are less able to

Exhibit 6.5
Type of help received from outside of household, by contributor, 1990[a]

Contributor		Type of help			
		Housework	House maintenance	Transportation	Financial support
		%			
Family		**59**	**47**	**36**	**68**
Parent		17	7	7	39
Sibling		10	10	8	9
Daughter		11	3	6	6[b]
Son		4	9	4	
Other relative		17	18	11	14
Other		**41**	**53**	**64**	**32**
Friend		37	52	62	25
Organization/Other		4	1	2	7
Total	%	**100**	**100**	**100**	**100**
	Millions	3.5	5.5	9.5	2.7

[a] Some individuals received help from more than one person so that the total number of people helping is greater than the total number of recipients. For example, 2.8 million people aged 15 or over received unpaid help with housework from a total of 3.5 million relatives, friends, or through organizations.
[b] Includes both daughters and sons.

Source: Statistics Canada, 1990 General Social Survey. In Paletta, A., "Today's extended families," *Canadian Social Trends*, Winter 1992, pp. 26–28. Ottawa: Statistics Canada.

tolerate snags and hitches. But life with children is *full* of snags and hitches. Employed mothers report having difficulty in accomplishing activities that would be easy if time were plentiful: waking the children, getting them ready for school or day care, caring for them, preparing food, cleaning the house, and getting to work on time (Michelson, 1985). Husbands, who generally feel less obligation than their wives to participate in child care and domestic duties, enjoy more leisure time as a result (Lupri, 1991a, p. 250; Robinson, 1991).

Tension levels increase when people carry out activities that they cannot control or have not chosen to do. Employed wives with children suffer from this kind of tension. Husbands typically contribute to housework when it is convenient, performing house maintenance, repairs, and gardening, which they are inclined to view as leisure or semi-leisure activities (Horna & Lupri, 1987; Harvey, Marshall, & Frederick 1991, pp. 50–51). Wives rarely enjoy this luxury.

A prime tension-producer for both spouses is daily travel. Many family responsibilites disproportionately carried out by women—such as shopping for food or taking children to and from day care—require travel, and "women often travel with less efficient resources and fewer choices" then men (Michelson, 1985). They less often have access to the family car or enough choice over where day care, shopping, and work will be located.

Effects of Employment on Satisfaction

Couples today feel the strain of a shortage of time and money, whether they have children or not. Strained husbands and wives report an increase in pessimism, a decline in marital interaction, and a rise in frequency of family conflict (Galambos & Silbereisen, 1989).

In this context, too little time for marital interaction may sometimes be a blessing. Many working couples report that their brief time together is pleasant precisely because they lack the time and energy to argue. They want to make their time together as pleasant, or at least quiet, as possible (Casale & Lerman, 1986). In fact, an absence of marital conflict may help explain why single working mothers are more satisfied with their work than married working mothers (Harrison & Minor, 1982). Conversely, family support *can* have an enormous effect on women's job satisfaction (Rudd & McHenry, 1986).

Working wives put more emphasis on job satisfaction and other nontraditional sources of satisfaction than full-time housewives do (Freudiger, 1983). Their marital satisfaction is closely related to their job satisfaction, especially when they have high career values (Faver, 1982). In single-earner families with traditional husband-wife roles, work satisfaction affects husbands' marital satisfaction but not their wives' (Terry & Scott, 1987). For dual-earner couples, however, life satisfaction demands both marital happiness and work satisfaction: both qualities are important to both spouses (Benin & Nienstedt, 1985).

Balancing work and family demands is more stressful for women than it is for men (Pittman & Orthner, 1988). It is role *conflict*—a problem of balancing the demands of work and family—not role *overload* (the total time spent on domestic and paid work activities) that may be to blame for this stress. When it arises, role conflict may lead to symptoms of ill health and decrease job satisfaction for both spouses (Coverman, 1989).

It is astonishing that working wives report as much job satisfaction as men (or even more), despite working at objectively inferior jobs (on average) and carrying more domestic responsibility. Women probably achieve this satisfaction by using different comparison groups from men (Hodson, 1989). Married women in professional jobs and clerical work evaluate their lives negatively in comparison with men, but positively in comparison with full-time housewives and unmarried working women (Shukla & Saxena, 1988). Many women, too, may be less willing than men to express dissatisfaction with their lives (Hodson, 1989). Some of their satisfaction, then, may be illusory. In turn, this may explain why women, though seemingly just as satisfied, are more likely than men to suffer stress and burnout, and why achieving success and influence in their work may bring women failure and dissatisfaction in private life (Etzion, 1987).

Parental Responsibilities and Employment

The presence of children complicates the problems faced by employed spouses, as does the presence of elder parents and relatives who need care. A Conference Board of Canada study found 80 percent of surveyed employees suffering from stress and anxiety in attempting to work out a balance between work and family life (including child care and elder care.) One-quarter report suffering "a lot" or a moderate degree of stress; absenteeism rates are about double those of people reporting no such difficulties (*The Globe and Mail*, February 6, 1990).

Part of the problem is simply too much to do and too little time in which to do it. The presence of young children in a young dual-earner family makes an enormous difference to the average number of hours wives work each weekday (counting both paid work and unpaid housework/child care). The average varies from 10.6 hours (in families with no children) to 14.3 hours (when all children are aged six and over) to 16.2 hours per day (with one or more children under six years old) (Lupri, 1991a, p. 246).

The number of children in the home has a particular effect on working wives, combining with life satisfaction and role conflict (or multiple-role stress) to influence their mental health (Sekaran, 1985). Although employed mothers have greater emotional needs than men do when there are children in the home, their job satisfaction will do relatively less to improve their mental health. With two or more preschool children at home, women employed outside the home depend more on the expressiveness and nurturance of their spouse for marital satisfaction than their husbands do (Cooper et al., 1986).

Many women find that stress and worry over leaving their children in someone else's care diminish the satisfaction they feel with their employment (Malarkey, Bootsma, & Vyn, 1990). In Brazil, a more

Exhibit 6.6

Reproductive decision making as personal solutions to structural dilemmas, showing indecision and conflict

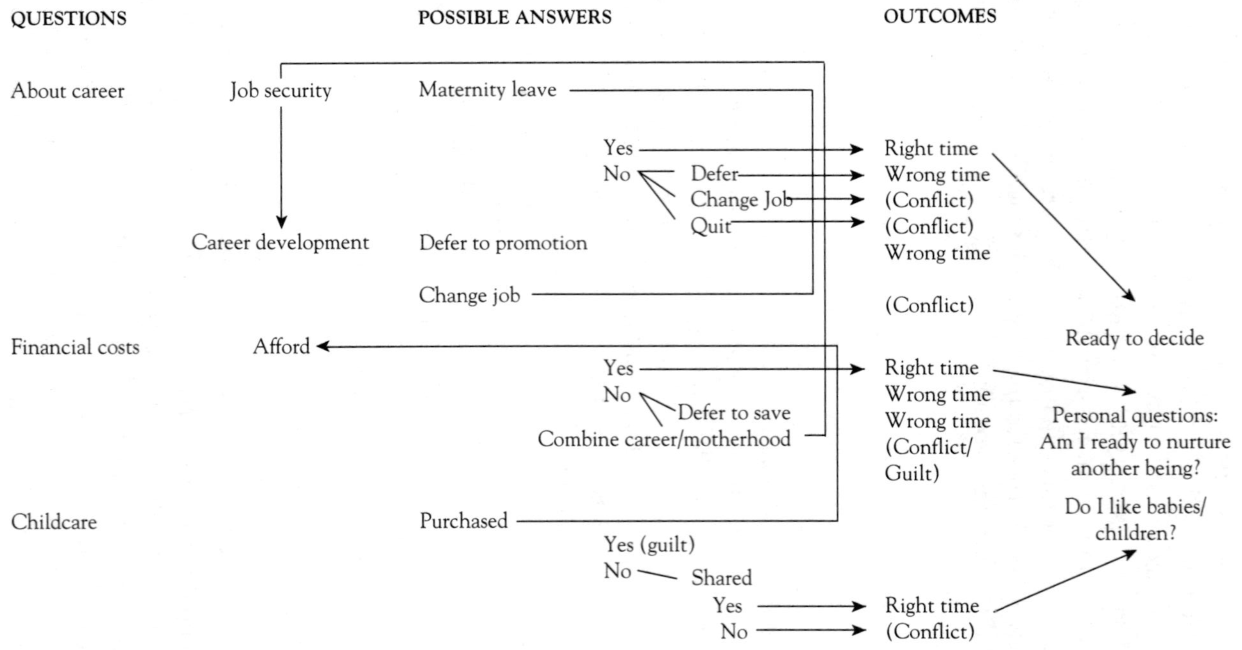

Source: Currie, D. (1988). Re-thinking what we do and how we do it: A study of reproductive decisions. *Canadian Review of Sociology and Anthropology*, *25*(2), 231–53. Reprinted with permission.

traditional society, employed women consider family duties much more important than paid work, and express concern over poor child-care resources and the difficulty of obtaining child care during illness (Meleis et al., 1990). Even in North America, young children can have a negative impact on personal and professional satisfaction. With small children in the home, satisfaction with child care plays a very important part in mediating the relationship between parenthood and wives' (but not husbands') life satisfaction (Bedeian, Burke, & Moffett, 1988). The reason for this is that wives are responsible for ensuring that the children are well cared for.

Some factors—such as education and a desire to work for pay—help to reduce the problem. Married female lawyers bear the main responsibility for the care of their children and adjust their family and work lives accordingly. Despite their demanding schedule, these women prove to be more satisfied with their careers and with the balance of their family and professional lives than other women, or even men (Chambers, 1989). In large part, this may be because they feel a strong positive motivation to work. Employed mothers who *want* to work experience less role conflict and more job satisfaction than other mothers. Such mothers also feel more favourably disposed toward their children. Mothers who are working out of financial need alone, or are experiencing role conflict, are less satisfied and stricter with their children (Alvarez, 1985).

Are children hurt by having their mother working full-time for pay? Some research (Jensen & Borges, 1986) suggests that teenage daughters of working mothers have a more distant relationship with their fathers, perceive family relationships as less happy and friendly, and experience more tension and anger within the home than other teenage daughters. This seems to disagree with other research that finds that maternal employment and job satisfaction have little impact on the family environment (Colangelo, Rosenthal, & Dettmann, 1984).

As we have already seen, a prime factor influencing the household climate is the amount of choice women have in their own lives. Career women and full-time homemakers both report having exercised a greater amount of choice in their decisions than working women without "careers." In turn, their decisions—indeed, their self-esteem and role satisfaction—were influenced by loving and accepting relationships with their own mothers, *not* by their mothers' own roles and role satisfaction (Sholomskas & Axelrod, 1986).

This suggests that balancing work and family in a way that has no ill effect on children will require that women have the freedom to choose the lives they want. They will need social supports that will allow them to give their own children the love and acceptance they need.

INDIVIDUAL AND COLLECTIVE SOLUTIONS

What is the solution to the problem of balance? In a gender-biased society there may be no real solution: every possibility is flawed. For example, when a woman with outside interests considers whether and when to have a child, there is no "right" decision (Currie, 1988). In fact, *every* parenting decision will have a negative effect on work, and every career decision a negative effect on family life. So, for women who want (or need) to work for pay, parenting decisions come with built-in conflicts, strains, and feelings of guilt. Starting out that way, mothers cannot hope to be fully satisfied.

That explains why some career women choose to marry but not bear children. Others bear one or two children in a very short time, to limit the interruption of their careers. Many of these women return to full-time employment almost immediately after bearing children. This pattern is most usual among highly educated women with careers, whose salaries are large enough to pay for high-quality child care. Less-educated women are more likely to leave the paid work force until their children begin attending school full-time.

Accordingly, labour force participation is much higher for women with children over five years old than it is for mothers of younger children. However, at no age do average mothers ever attain as high a level of labour force participation as similarly educated women without children (Statistics Canada, 1984).

Another increasingly popular solution to the problem of balancing work and children is part-time work, defined as less than 30 hours of paid work per week (Labour Canada, 1983, p. 17). In 1989, 71.6 percent of part-time workers were women (Sauvé, 1990, p. 67). In fact, part-time work accounted for about one-third of all the growth in women's work-force participation between 1975 and 1988 (Parliament, 1990, p. 102). See Exhibit 6.7.

The decision to work part-time rather than full-time is often voluntary, especially among married women. Still, much part-time work results from the unavailability of full-time work; since 1975, involuntary part-time work has more than doubled as a portion of all part-time work (Akyeampong, 1987, p. 27).

As part-time work becomes more common, the prorated payment of fringe benefits to part-time workers may become the norm; this would do

Exhibit 6.7
Percentage of employed women and men working part-time, by age, 1991

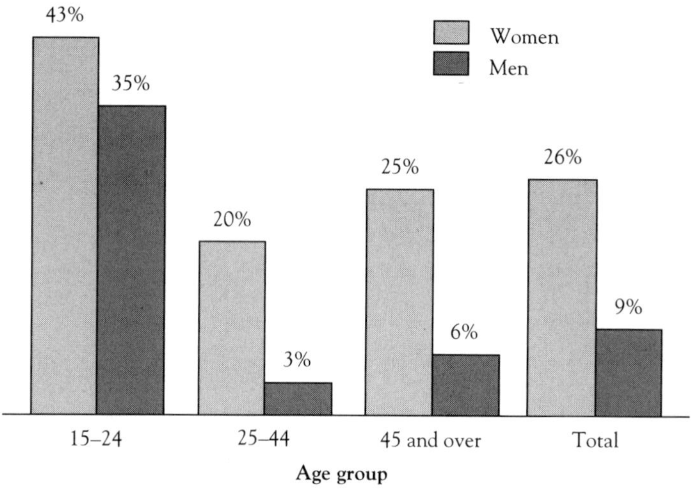

Source: Statistics Canada, Catalogue No. 71–220. In Ghalam, N., "Women in the Workplace," *Canadian Social Trends*, Spring 1993, pp. 2–6. Ottawa: Statistics Canada.

much to address the problem of balancing work and family responsibilities. At present, however, women's acceptance of the main responsibility for child care is perpetuated by the existence of part-time work as an option. Ironically, their continued subordination in these poorly paid, low-status jobs is ensured by the fact that they have accepted, and have been accepted in, the role of primary care-giver in their families.

Most female part-time workers aged 25 to 54 appear to have taken part-time work for reasons that include the need to fulfil personal and family responsibilities (Labour Canada, 1983, p. 53). Few female part-time workers want to do more hours of paid work per month than they already do (Labour Canada, 1983, p. 69; Parliament, 1990 p. 102). Part-time work offers women flexibility (Labour Canada, 1983, p. 67;) and work patterns that, under the best circumstances, can be tailored to a worker's own timetables. It helps women fulfil domestic obligations and meet income needs at a time when virtually single-handed child-rearing makes taking on full-time paid work extremely difficult. See Exhibits 6.8 and 6.9.

Exhibit 6.8

Days absent per worker and reason for absence, 1977–1990

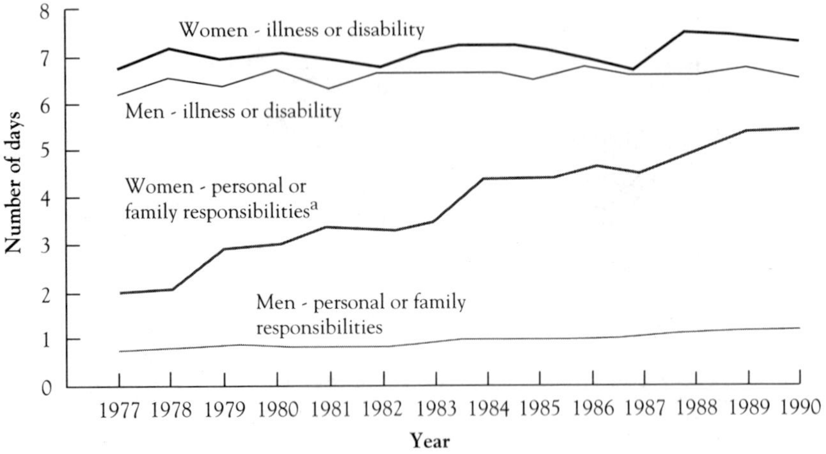

[a] Includes maternity leave.

Source: Statistics Canada, Labour Force Survey, unpublished data. In Akyeampong, E.B., "Absenteeism at Work," *Canadian Social Trends*, Summer 1992, pp. 26–28. Ottawa: Statistics Canada.

If part-time workers are successful in unionizing and winning benefits prorated to time spent on the job, working part-time will become an increasingly attractive option for both fathers and mothers. One can imagine future generations organizing their lives differently from today, moving in and out of jobs and, within jobs, between full-time and part-time status, to accommodate changing domestic demands and personal well-being (on this, see Jones, Marsden & Tepperman, 1990.) Unfortunately, at present, employers tend to use part-time workers in order to *avoid* paying fringe benefits.

Why do more people not work part-time? A great many people are as devoted to their job as they are to their family. Beyond that, employees risk hurting their chances of promotion by giving the impression that they do not take their work seriously. This means that employed mothers, who make up the main body of voluntary part-time workers, must weigh carefully whether they want to have a career and, equally important, be perceived as having a career. Consider one study of female graduate pediatricians completing their hospital residency, who were asked to estimate the amount of time they devote to professional work and

Exhibit 6.9

Average number of days absent for personal and family reasons, by presence of children, 1990

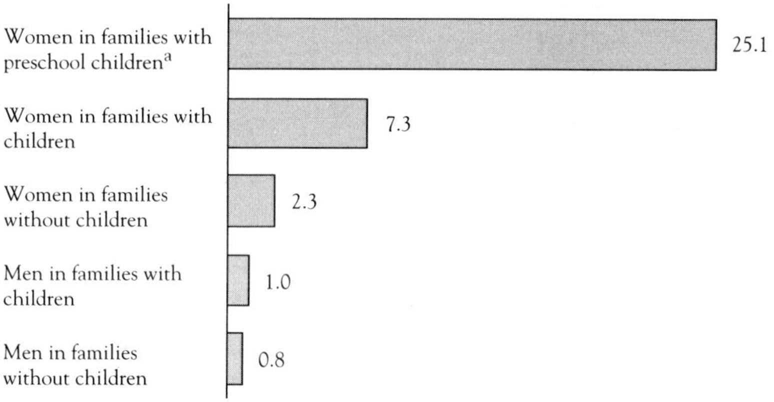

[a] Includes maternity leave.

Source: Statistics Canada, Labour Force Survey, unpublished data. In Akyeampong, E.B., "Absenteeism at Work," *Canadian Social Trends*, Summer, 1992, pp. 26–28. Ottawa: Statistics Canada.

domestic work. Residents who worked significantly more hours per week showed a lower level of work satisfaction than other residents, and a lower opinion of themselves as women and professionals (Yogev & Harris, 1983). Largely, this problem arises because highly educated women tend to be very serious about both their work and their family lives. It also shows up among married female business graduates, who feel a strong degree of job involvement and organizational commitment, and so experience conflict between job and family that reduces their satisfaction with both (Wiley, 1987).

Some women retain a full-time job but reduce their time commitment to it. Women employed full-time are much more likely than their husbands to prefer time off to an increase in pay (Young & Willmott, 1975, p. 115). Not surprisingly, working wives place a higher emphasis on convenience than their husbands do when assessing a job, though they attach a similar importance to wages, fringe benefits, and job security (Martin & Hanson, 1985). Because of the sex-based division of labour in the home, wives are less likely than husbands to take on jobs that interfere with domestic duties. In fact, women's life satisfaction decreases to the degree that they spend more of their discretionary time at work (Sekaran, 1989).

Clerical and manual work interferes in domestic life to a smaller degree than professional and managerial work (Young & Willmott, 1975, p. 117). This accounts for the finding that highly educated women in male-dominated professions are least likely of all women to marry, stay married, or bear children (Marshall, 1987). Of all women, the highly educated have the most trouble balancing parental and occupational duties.

As a result, the employers of educated women face greater demands for company-sponsored or public child care and more flexible work schedules (Sekaran, 1989). Women are no longer as willing to sacrifice their career for their family as they once were. Increasingly, dual-earner couples make joint decisions about domestic task-sharing, work time, job transfers, and relocation. Raising children demands "flextime," part-time work, sabbaticals (for both women and men), and more freedom to work at home.

In general, female home workers feel that they have more flexibility than office workers. This is less true of women with children, who are likely to work at home in order to care for their children, and not as a matter of personal choice. For the most part, home and office work provide different outcomes and satisfactions, with home clerical workers just as satisfied with their working conditions as office workers (Kraut, 1989).

Bhagat and Ford (1990) suggest three organizational strategies for preventing distress associated with work/home interactions: (1) new options for home-based workers, (2) more training in effective skills for coping with strain, and (3) changes in organizational culture to better accept and integrate work/home relations.

Employers will have to learn to accommodate family needs. Some signs suggest that they are already doing so (see, for example, Wiley & Eskilson, 1988). But in the absence of institutional and societal changes to ease the burdens of motherhood, people will continue to bear fewer children. We shall have more to say about the reduction of domestic inequality and its possible consequences in the final chapter of the book.

CONCLUSION

This chapter has presented a somewhat bleak picture of parenthood, in order to counterbalance the unrealistic picture of parenthood presented by the mass media.

When we first become parents, we experience many of the same feelings as we do when we fall in love. We become capable of superhuman feats of effort, endurance, and caring. But we soon find that we have to settle down to real life. Parents still love their children, as spouses do one another; at the same time, they are much more conscious of the *work* involved in keeping the relationship alive.

Modern parenthood is difficult, especially for mothers. Yet, on the whole, "most women seem to be in the role they prefer, and those who have chosen homemaking are as satisfied with their lives as those who have made the other choice" (Campbell, 1980, p. 139). Despite the injustices that women face in our society, women's sense of well-being comes surprisingly close to men's.

Many men and women work at jobs they hate; they would rather stay home. Others stay home because they cannot find work at all, or because they are expected to stay home. Many women who choose to do so have the opportunity to get the satisfactions that paid employment can bring, by working at jobs they like. On the other hand, many women who remain in the home are equally satisfied; and that leads to several major conclusions.

The first is that, given a choice, people look for and sometimes find the life situation that will satisfy them most. Second, people largely accommodate themselves to what their life demands, especially if they have chosen it. Finally, adulthood is becoming more complicated and stressful for women, whatever their role.

Parenthood can be extremely gratifying, exciting, and educational. Parents learn about life, other people, and themselves in raising children to adulthood. Further, parents typically fall in love with their children, just as they did with their mate, and are not willing to give them up in spite of the problems they may face. This love affair with parenting does not come about because of the child's ideal qualities, but because he or she is lovable, loving, needy, and close at hand.

Parenthood also demands time, money, and emotional energy. It may require important sacrifices. Some of the difficulties that parents confront can be remedied if spouses share the household duties more fairly. Other difficulties can be remedied if the government provides better day care facilities, guarantees paid maternity (or parental) leave, and provides other assistance.

Ultimately, the problem rests in the parents' own hands. People must choose carefully between parenthood and other demanding, fulfilling activities: romance, leisure, career, and education. No one can do everything well, or even enjoy trying. The parenting decision should be made with that simple fact in mind.

Do people get what they want out of parenthood? Though some people are undoubtedly pressured into it, more and more are freely deciding whether or not to become parents. As a result, more people are likely to be satisfied with the result: to feel they have gotten what they wanted. Moreover, a majority of people feel quite satisfied with their decision.

Yet this satisfaction varies. The people most responsible for parenting —mothers between the ages of 30 and 45—are least satisfied. Their satisfaction declines the more children they have: more is usually not better. Further, mothers with paid jobs are (often) least satisfied of all. Balancing marriage, parenthood, and paid work calls for tremendous energy and patience. Few people find such continuous demands satisfying. So working mothers are least likely to get what they wanted.

Chapter Seven will address questions having to do with residence: where people choose to live, and with what results.

Chapter Seven

◆

Locations and Lifestyles:

What You Want and What You Get

Introduction

Many students enjoy thinking about where they might live in the future: in what country or province, whether in a city or suburb, alone or with friends or family. This chapter will argue that where you live is (largely) how you live. It will discuss the reasons people live in different kinds of places and the lifestyles associated with different locations. Finally, it will consider what satisfies people about each kind of location. In particular, it will attempt to answer two main questions: (1) Why do people live where they do? Is it mainly by choice, or the result of forces beyond their control? and (2) Do people in different places, and with different lifestyles, derive different amounts of satisfaction from life? Or are there many ways of living that satisfy people more or less equally?

People are not completely free to choose where they live. For many, location is determined by the availability or cost of housing; for others, by the availability of an appropriate job; and for others still, by the location of family and friends. As in so many aspects of life, choice is also limited by social class: the rich have a wider variety of choices than the poor.

Within this context of unequal opportunity, people do exercise some choice. The locations they choose often reflect their life goals and concerns as well as their life chances. As they move through the life cycle —from the beginning of higher education to its completion, through a series of ever more responsible jobs, and into marriage, parenthood, and (eventually) an empty nest—people's life goals and concerns change.

Typically, people who move from one location to another are seeking more satisfaction as their goals and opportunities change. To answer the question "Where should I live?" we must consider what kind of life you want to live and what opportunities you have for living that life. For this reason this chapter treats questions of location and lifestyle together.

Before we begin the chapter, here are a few questions to see how much you know about the topic.

1. People in different types of housing use their time in similar ways.
   True ___ False ___
2. Once they complete their education and take a job, most Canadians stay in one location.
   True ___ False ___
3. People spend time doing very different kinds of things in different industrial countries.
   True ___ False ___
4. The objective features of neighbourhoods are what satisfy people most.
   True ___ False ___
5. It is impossible to predict how people will spend their income.
   True ___ False ___

Now we can consider a few facts about people's everday lives—starting with how people spend their time and money.

LIFESTYLES

What is *lifestyle?* A simple answer to this question is that lifestyle is the way a person, or group, spends time and money. What sociologists consider lifestyle today is a set of shared patterns of behaviour that flow from a common, underlying world view. These behaviours define the boundaries of the group.

Lifestyles consist of clusters of activities with particular characteristics. They may be person-centred (and if so, either family-centred or centred on other people) or centred on ideas or objects, passive or active, public or private, formal (organized) or informal, productive or consumptive; and in motion or at rest, at home or away from home, and indoors or out of doors (Reed, 1976).

People whose lives follow the same patterns are considered part of the group and people whose lives follow different patterns are outsiders. What is she doing? When does she do it? With whom does she do it? How much does she enjoy doing it? When we answer these and related questions, for a variety of activities—eating, sleeping, shopping, socializing, watching television—we get a picture of someone's daily life. While no one's life is exactly the same as anyone else's, a small number of dominant patterns show up; and these patterns are what we mean by the lifestyle that makes a person part of his or her group.

The first sociologist to become interested in lifestyle and its social meaning was Max Weber. We can see this interest in Weber's writings on "commensalism" and "status group." Weber shows that the ways people spend money and time together are a basis for both social integration and social exclusion. A second group of sociologists focus on the social and emotional content of *community life*. This stream of thinking begins with the German sociologists Ferdinand Tönnies and Georg Simmel; it is picked up later by the "Chicago school" of sociology, including Louis Wirth and his disciples.

Both groups depart from the thinking of Karl Marx, who had argued that economic and class relations determine all other social relations. For his part, Weber believed that social organization rests on a triad of principles: economic (or class), political (or party), and status group. People have economic and political allegiances, to be sure; but they also belong to status groups that influence their view of life and their behaviour. These status groups do not always organize people vertically—the way we now think of "social status"; they organize people horizontally as well.

A person's status group might be organized around language, ethnic, religious, or racial differences from the rest of society, or around other symbolic and non-economic principles. What defines a status group is its degree of *commensalism:* literally, the degree to which its members eat together, or more generally share daily activities and a common world view. A "status group" in Weber's terminology might today be called a "subculture." When we study the common behaviours of that group, we study a common lifestyle.

When people share a subculture, or lifestyle, they form a community. They feel emotional ties to one another of the sort that are strong in a rural society, but weaker in large, rapidly changing urban societies. These community ties anchor people emotionally. Without them, people often suffer from isolation and *anomie*, a lack of social constraints discussed by Durkheim (1951) in his famous work on suicide. Even trivial things—what you eat, where you eat and with whom you eat—can have important symbolic, social, and emotional value in modern society. These are the kinds of things that tie people together in social groups.

Lifestyles not only tie people together, they also push people apart. Thorstein Veblen's *Theory of the Leisure Class* (1934) shows how lifestyles can come to define exclusive group boundaries. The very rich invent ways of consuming their wealth that are "conspicuously wasteful" in order to define who is part of the group and who is not. By definition, lifestyles of the rich and famous are limited to a very few. Moreover, the very richest people continue to invent ever newer forms of "conspicuous consumption" to delimit the boundaries of the "leisure class." To be a member, you must have enough time and money to keep up with an endless, changing stream of fashions in conspicuous waste; you must also want to try.

Not all status groups test their "candidates" this rigorously to determine who is in the group and who is out; but lifestyle behaviours, including consumption patterns, *always* distinguish insiders from outsiders. For this reason, sociologists have long claimed that you can tell a person's social position from his or her living room. Living-room furnishings display both the "taste" (hence, status group background) and pretensions (or desired status group affiliation) of the householder. (For a humorous update of living-room assessment, see Fussell, 1983).

Since they all have a hand in creating the boundaries of their subculture, the status group members can "read" the status signals a person gives off. This fact is demonstrated in community studies conducted by Chicago sociologist Lloyd Warner and his students (see, for example, Davis, Gardner, & Gardner, 1941; Warner, Meeker, & Eells, 1960). In one community after another, researchers found that community members could easily sort local townspeople into status groups based on reputation.

When people perform this task, they regularly identify the same numbers of distinct status groups and sort people into groups in similar ways. Moreover, they characterize each grouping along similar criteria—for example, how "upper-upper-class" people differ from "lower-upper-class" people. Thus, status groups, their membership, and behaviours appropriate to members are all well known to people who live in small, stable communities.

In large, new, and transient communities the boundaries of status groups are harder to specify. As well, their membership, large and in constant flux, is harder to agree on (Jaher, 1982). That is why, people living in large, fluid communities rely more on visible behaviours to communicate their actual or intended status. Their behaviours signal not only who they think they are or want to be taken for, but also what kinds of people they want to interact with, and in what ways.

This explains why people—especially young city people—wear clothing with the designer labels prominently displayed, or clothing and hair styles that convey a point of view: for example, punk versus preppy. Increasingly, people spend their time and money to communicate who they are and who they want to be, in the effort to make themselves into a visible community within a larger society.

As we noted earlier, sociologists who study lifestyle focus on how people spend their time and their money. Each kind of spending indicates commitment to a single status group, since few people have unlimited time and money. So spending behaviour shows how important choices are made under constraints. We shall now consider the two kinds of spending behaviour in turn.

Lifestyle and Time Use

"Time budget research" asks ordinary people to keep a detailed, running record of each day's events: what they did, for how long, and in whose company. The resulting data (see Exhibits 7.1 and 7.2) offer sociologists a rich insight into the variety of everyday lifestyles.

The first thing researchers discover is that similar kinds of people lead similar lives. There are enormous similarities among people belonging to the same social class, the same age group, even the same occupational group. So, for example, mothers who work for pay outside the home lead similar lives throughout the modern world (Robinson, Converse, & Szalai, 1972). Industrialization and urbanization wipe out national differences, causing lifestyles around the world to converge. Accordingly, differences in time use around the world mainly reflect differences in the degree of "modernization": industrialization, urbanization, media availability, education, family planning, and female labour force participation, among others.

However, we also find interesting, sometimes unexplained differences among industrial nations. For example, despite the wide variety of available programming, television viewing is much less common among Germans than among North Americans (Robinson & Converse, 1972). The Germans who watch the most television have the least life satisfaction (Espe & Seiwert, 1987). It is not clear if the same holds true for North Americans. (Nor do we know whether television viewing lowers life satisfaction, or whether low life satisfaction seeks a cure in television viewing.)

Family life also varies from one industrial nation to another. People differ in the amount of time they spend at home with their spouse, and the amount spent in their spouse's company alone, without children, relatives, or friends present (Varga, 1972). In countries where married couples spend more time alone together, divorce rates are somewhat lower. This suggests that divorce is caused, at least partly, by spouses spending too little time in intimate, "courtship" behaviour.

Time budget data also show cross-national variations in the amounts of sociability at work and at home. North Americans are more likely than most people to retreat from an intensely interactive work life into solitude or relatively passive family activity—what social commentator Faith Popcorn calls "cocooning." But in many European cultures, leisure is as interactive as work.

Exhibit 7.1

Average time spent[a] on major activities for the population 15 years and over, by role groups, Canada, 1986

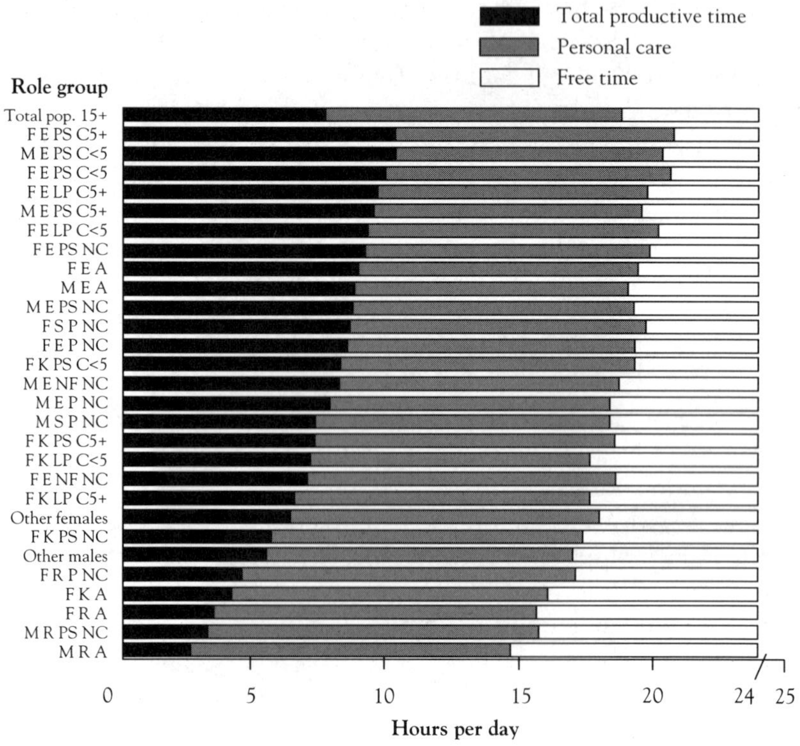

Legend for role groups

M - Male
F - Female

E - Employed
S - Student
K - Keeping house
R - Retired

PS - Living with partner or spouse
LP - Lone parent
P - Living with parent(s)
A - Living alone
NF - Living with non-family member(s)

NC - No children
C<5 - At least 1 child <5 years
C5+ - All children 5 years or over

[a] Averaged over a 7-day week.

Source: Statistics Canada (1991). Harvey, A., Marshall, K., & Frederick, J.A. *Where does time go?* General Social Analysis Series (Catalogue 11-612E, No. 4). Ottawa: Statistics Canada. Reproduced with the permission of the Minister of Industry, Science and Technology, 1993.

Exhibit 7.2

Participation rate in domestic activities for the population 15 years and over by gender, Canada, 1986

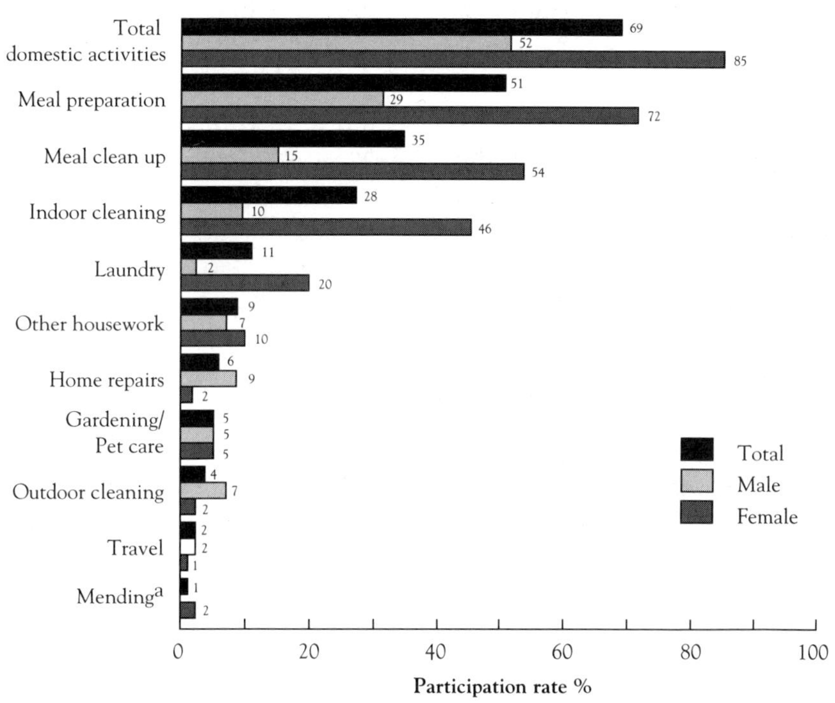

[a] The estimate for the category "Mending—males" was suppressed because sampling variability was greater than 33%.

Source: Statistics Canada (1991). Harvey, A., Marshall, K., & Frederick, J.A. *Where does time go?* General Social Analysis Series (Catalogue 11-612E, No. 4). Ottawa: Statistics Canada. Reproduced with the permission of the Minister of Industry, Science and Technology, 1993.

Mothers who work outside the home enjoy more leisure and more control over their domestic duties in countries with good public day-care, or where friends and relatives are readily available, or spouses co-operate more than in North America (Michelson, 1985; Michelson, 1990; Szalai, 1972). Generally speaking, the northern European countries (Sweden, Denmark, and Norway in particular) are far ahead in this respect (Wolfe, 1989).

A major study of time use patterns in Canada (Harvey, Marshall, & Frederick, 1991) found four main variables that affect the ways people spend their time: gender, employment status (employed, student, keeping house, or retired), living arrangement (living with partner or spouse, lone parent, living with parent(s), living alone, or living with non-family member(s)), and presence of children (no children, at least one child under five years, all children five years or older). Combining these variables yields a total of 28 (non-empty) categories of time use.

Here are a few of the study's main findings (Harvey, Marshall, & Frederick, 1991, p. 107). For further information, refer back to Exhibits 7.1 and 7.2.

- Employed parents spend the most time of all groups on productive work—an average of nine hours a day over a seven-day week. Accordingly, they have less free time than others.
- Employed women who live with a partner and no children have less free time than employed women who live alone, since they spend more time on housework.
- Female students who live at home have less free time during the week than male students who live at home.
- People do less productive work on the weekend than during the week; on the weekend, they spend almost equal amounts of time on leisure and on productive work. (They also spend more time with friends and family on the weekends than they do during the week.)
- For women with children, productive work exceeds free time even on the weekend and even with a spouse present.
- Married people spend more time with their partner on the weekend than during the week. However, this varies widely from one group to another; for example, working people spend an average of four to five hours a day with their partner during the weekend, compared to retired people, who average eight hours with theirs.
- Retired people have far more free time than other people; being female and/or married cuts into this free time.
- Retired men watch the most television (about six hours a day) while employed women with a spouse and child(ren) watch the least television (about two hours a day).
- Retired men spend the most time alone (over ten hours a day), while employed single mothers with children under five spend the least time alone (about two hours a day).

Lifestyle and Consumer Behaviour

Study after study shows that people group themselves according to how they spend their money. But even here, as with time use, we can see some convergence of patterns: over time, people are spending their money in more similar ways. This is demonstrated by how the things that used to be considered luxuries have become household necessities. Today almost everyone has a telephone, refrigerator, and television set. Yet only a minority of Canadian homes owned telephones in 1941, refrigerators in 1948, and televisions in 1952 (Devereaux, 1990a p. 259). In the last 30 years, Canadian householders have come to first value, then *need,* a second telephone, a second television, cable TV, and a VCR (Devereaux,1990a, p. 260). And since 1980, there has been a rapid surge in the ownership of smoke detectors, clothes dryers, colour TVs, and cassette recorders (Sauvé, 1990, p. 139).

High-income families possess more of all these things than lower-income families. But as they have become more common and their price has fallen these goods have also, in most cases, crossed the class line from luxury goods (available to the very few) to necessities. A majority of low-income households today have cable TV; over a third have a freezer. By this standard, VCRs, microwave ovens, and dishwashers remain luxuries absent from most low-income households and present in most high-income households (Devereaux, 1990a, p. 260). The class differences in their ownership may not continue for long, however, given present purchasing patterns.

For the time being, spending patterns remain very different for people in different income groups. The poor spend proportionately more on food and shelter and less on taxes than higher-income groups (Burke, 1990). They are far more likely to rent their home, and less likely to own it than people with a higher income (Sauvé, 1990, p. 137).

In general, the poor have less disposable income for luxury goods and leisure activities. This tells us two things. First, poor people spend a greater portion of their money on a small variety of goods and services. This leaves them with a very distinctive spending pattern whether they live in Toronto, Los Angeles, or Bangladesh (see, for example, Sadeque, 1986). Second, because they have less money and less choice, the poor hold less interest for market researchers, who are concerned with persuading people to spend their money.

In the influence they wield over consumer, market researchers are truly "captains of consciousness" (Ewen, 1976). Sociologists have played a (not always glorious) part in the market research enterprise. For example, in order to promote household products more effectively, three sociologists helped a publisher of romance magazines find out the secret fears and desires of working-class wives. They advised the publisher to play on women's fears of becoming unattractive, losing their husbands to other women, and losing the love and respect of their children (Rainwater, Coleman, & Handel, 1962).

Marketing research has become more sophisticated with the development of VALS (Values and Life Style) surveying. The foremost proponent of this type of research, Mitchell (1983), conceives of nine American lifestyle groups. Based loosely on Maslow's theory of a need hierarchy (discussed in Chapter One), Mitchell's typology relates buying behaviour to the social, economic, and demographic characteristics of each group.

Consider the group Mitchell calls "experientials." Comprising roughly 7 million Americans, or 11 percent of the adult population in 1983, the experientials are an important chunk of the baby-boom generation. A majority occupy the middle or upper class and approximately 70 percent have some postsecondary education, compared to 43 percent of the adult population.

Compared to average American adults, experientials are liberal and independent (that is, free of strong party affiliation). They are very unlikely to think that unmarried sex is wrong, or that too much money is spent protecting the environment. They derive a great deal of satisfaction from non-work activities, especially friends; but TV-watching is not their main entertainment.

Their financial status is also distinctive. Experientials' incomes are well above the national average. They are unlikely to have a credit card balance (owing) under $100, and are more likely than others to owe $1500 or more. They are less likely than others to own their home or have a home mortgage, but more likely than any other group to owe over $50 000 in loans. This highly varied group contains some very wealthy and very upwardly mobile people. Experientials are a good credit risk and they borrow regularly against their credit. Much of their income (and credit) is consumed by higher-than-average rates of leisure activity.

Experientials swim, play racquet sports, and ski. "They engage more in yoga and home meditation than any other group and are distinctly concerned with the health aspects of food. They are more likely than any other group to work at a second job or free-lance" (Mitchell, 1983, p. 132).

How do experientials spend their money? Mitchell (1983, p. 132) remarks that "key characteristics of the [e]xperientials—such as the search for direct and pleasurable experiences, their try-anything-once attitude, preference for process over product, and active outdoor orientation—are evidenced in their pattern of product ownership and use." Experiential households are much more likely than average to own compact, subcompact, and small speciality cars. More than any other group, they buy quality European cars, especially used ones. They are also above-average purchasers of motorcycles and racing bikes.

At home, experientials commonly purchase dishwashers, garbage disposals, recreational equipment, video games, and stereos and accessories. Wine and beer are their preferred alcoholic drinks, with tequila as an alternative. Experientials avoid coffee (with or without caffeine) and sugared foods and drinks; they make above-average use of frozen Chinese and Mexican foods. You can sell experientials eye makeup and shampoo, but forget about aerosol underarm deodorants, feminine-hygiene sprays, after-shave lotions, or room air-fresheners. Experientials make good use of veterinarians, but rarely buy canned dog foods. And if you invite an experiential home for dinner, hide the margarine, Jello, and Planter's peanuts (Mitchell, 1983, Table 16).

If you have not guessed yet, Mitchell's "experientials" are young urban professionals—"yuppies"—1983 style. They tend to live alone or cohabit, and they are city people, not suburbanites or rural residents. As we shall soon see, there is usually a strong connection between people's lifestyles and where they choose to live. So let us begin by examining where people *do* live today.

LOCATIONS

A majority of Canadians live in four provinces: Ontario (population 9.7 million in 1990), Quebec (6.8 million), British Columbia (3.1 million), and Alberta (2.5 million). Taken together, these four provinces make up just over 80 percent of the Canadian population.

Most Canadians live in a metropolitan area. In 1990, 8.3 million people—31 percent of Canada's population—lived in metropolitan Toronto, Montreal, or Vancouver. About 13.3 million—half of all Canadians—lived in the ten largest metropolitan areas; much of the remaining population lived in the next fifteen largest metropolitan areas. Relatively few Canadians live in rural areas or small towns at any distance from large cities. Increasing numbers live in the suburbs of large cities, and often consider a neighbourhood as distant as 80 kilometres or more from the downtown area to be still within daily commuting range.

People tend to live near other people. In fact, one person in seven lives 5 feet or less from the nearest neighbour. One in three lives 10 feet or less away, and six in ten people less than 30 feet away (Quality of Life survey, 1981). Not surprisingly, most people know at least some of their neighbours by name. One person in three knows at least ten families living close to his or her dwelling, and over half know more than five of the neighbouring families by name.

Because of this nearness and acquaintanceship, seven in ten Canadian adults consider themselves "part of the neighbourhood" (Quality of Life survey, 1981). So much for the fear that modern life spells the end of "community"! Moreover, people tend to live near others like themselves. Half say their neighbours belong to the same social and cultural group as they do; only one person in three feels out of place culturally and socially. Residential segregation by ethnic group and social class is as highly developed in Canadian cities as anywhere in North America (Balakrishnan, 1976, 1982).

Residential Segregation and Identity

Residential segregation has an enormous impact on people's social relations and their social identities. Consider the results of a study of ethnic groups in Toronto discussed earlier (Breton et al., 1990).

Ethnic groups have always segregated themselves geographically in Toronto, as in most North American cities. What is remarkable about the Toronto Jews is that they have segregated themselves to a greater degree than the other three groups—Germans, Italians, and Ukrainians—that Breton and his colleagues examined most closely.

Typically, geographic segregation diminishes with each passing generation and with a rise in an ethnic group's education level and social status. But among the Toronto Jews, residential segregation has persisted across generations and despite rises in social status.

In Toronto, as elsewhere, residential segregation affects whom you get to know. You form acquaintanceships and friendships with the people you meet: if most of those you meet are from your own ethnic group, it is they who are likely to be your closest friends. Accordingly, Jews are much more likely than people of Italian, Ukrainian, or German ancestry to name other group members as their best friends. This tendency, too, persists from one generation to another among Jews more than among the other groups.

Segregated people are also more likely to marry within their own group. As a result, Toronto Jews are extremely endogamous, compared with Ukrainian, Italian, and German Canadians, and have remained so with the passage of generations. Indeed, this is the single greatest indicator of ethnic difference among these four groups.

It is not surprising to find that people who are residentially segregated, form close friendships with one another, and marry one another also show a high degree of familiarity with their ethnic language—in this case, Yiddish or Hebrew. The Jews not only know and use these languages relatively often, they also encourage their children to learn them. (Ukrainian and Italian Canadians also show a high level of language retention across generations; by contrast, German Canadians show very little.) Likewise, we find that the Toronto Jews are more likely than other Torontonians to retain at least some of their ethnic customs across generations. These include religious rituals, styles of cooking, and the observance of ethnic holidays.

Of course, we cannot ignore the economic factors at work in maintaining ethnic identity. When the Jews first settled in Toronto, they were subjected to prejudice and discrimination equally severe as the discrimination facing West Indians and other visible minorities today.

They responded to this discrimination in several distinctive ways. First, they entered professions or created businesses that would allow them to be their own bosses; a very high percentage of Jews became self-employed, a pattern that persists even today. Second, they found customers and clients among their own ethnic group, so that they would not have to rely on acceptance by other groups. As a result, Toronto Jews are much more likely to report that their customers belong to their own ethnic group than are Canadians of Ukrainian, Italian, or German origin.

What, then, do these data tell us about the social basis for the learning and retention of an ethnic identity? Very simply, an ethnic identity flourishes when people surround themselves with others of the same ethnic group, and marry them, befriend them, sell to them, and buy from them. Under these conditions, the traditional language and customs are easily retained. This process, moreover, reproduces itself: strong ethnic identities increase the likelihood of continued voluntary ethnic segregation.

If you are a member of an ethnic community and are wondering whether your ethnic community will "survive"—whether your grandchildren will think of themselves as simply "Canadian" or something else—these data suggest that certain factors are crucial in determining the outcome. Chief among them is residential segregation—the people with whom you live—and the social and cultural relationships that flow from your location.

Living Patterns

About three Canadians in four live in family households, as someone's spouse, child, or parent. Next most common is living alone; about one household in five contains only one person. In fact, the proportion of Canadians living alone has been rising rapidly since 1940 (Thomas & Burch, 1985). Other living arrangements as well have become more common, especially in large cities.

Your age and stage in the life cycle influence the type of household you live in. Nowhere is this shown more dramatically than in the housing arrangements of people aged 15 to 29. Most 15- to 19-year-old

Canadians—in fact, 92 percent of males and 91.4 percent of females—lived in their parents' home in 1986 (Boyd & Pryor, 1990). But the vast majority could expect to become spouses and/or parents in their own household within ten years. Another 8 to 10 percent could expect to be living alone—four or five times the number that live alone at ages 18 and 19.

No change of this magnitude in household arrangements occurs again until middle age. Then, with children grown up, large numbers of widows and widowers, divorcés and divorcées, start to live alone, or with non-relatives, or with relatives who are not their spouse or their children.

This provides one more demonstration of how people's housing arrangements are outside their control, to some degree. In 1981 the bulk of Canadian live-alones—nearly half a million—were women aged 55 and over. Elderly women who are widowed or divorced are more likely to live alone if they have no adult daughters to live with (Wister & Burch, 1983; Burch & McDougall, 1991). The blind chance of having female children (or a sister) will help determine where you live in your old age.

About three in every five adult Canadians live within one hour's driving time (100 kilometres or less) of their mothers; over one-third live 10 kilometres or less away (Burch & McDougall, 1991, p. E1). Of those living within 10 kilometres, four-fifths report seeing their mother once a week or more. The frequency of visiting drops off dramatically as the distance increases, but even so, a majority of those living 100 kilometres away or less visit their mother once a month or more (Burch & McDougall, 1991, p. G1). The frequency of visits to fathers is lower, and drops off much more rapidly with distance (Burch & McDougall, 1991, p. G2).

Along similar lines, people report seeing at least one of their children (over the age of fourteen) with considerable frequency. For example, about 85 percent of people living within 10 kilometres of their child report seeing him or her once a week or more. Where the child is younger (under the age of fourteen), the frequency is somewhat less. But in both cases, the frequency of visits is determined largely by the distance to be travelled (Burch & McDougall, 1991, pp. G3, G4).

This suggests that, even when people do *not* live with their kin, they remain in close contact. When they live far apart, they may move to come into closer contact. Burch and McDougall (1991) write, "Of total moves, only 10 percent or less are described as being made for reasons of proximity to family members. For long-distance moves, the percentages are appreciably higher, reaching approximately 40 percent for those 80 and over. Clearly, for some of the 'old elderly' in Canada, long distance migration plays an important role in family reunification" (p. F2).

This brings us to the topic of migration—why people change their location.

Movement from One Location to Another

As their choices and chances change, people change their location. The migration of native-born male workers is particularly common (Pineo, 1985b, p. 486). One in three men reports having lived permanently in another province at some time or other. Two in three have lived in cities other than the one in which they were born, and one male in two is currently living in another such city.

Some relocate because family members are living in another community. "Young adults appear to migrate for family reasons more frequently than do middle-aged persons, but this may reflect primarily moves to join a spouse or partner" (Burch & McDougall, 1991, p. F2). Conversely, strong social bonds *inhibit* migration. For all but two-job families, however, employment does not (Speare, Kobrin, & Kingkade, 1982). Several key background variables—age, sex, marital status, and place of birth—all affect people's willingness to relocate, by influencing their satisfaction with a community and their social bonds within the community. Seemingly the most important influences on willingness to relocate are length of residence and the education of the household head (see Exhibit 7.3). Very highly educated people are the most mobile: Stone (1978) has called them the "hypermobile."

Demographic changes also lead people to move. Every separation or divorce brings someone a change of place: at least a change of households, and sometimes even a change of cities or regions. Likewise, every marriage means a change of place for one or both spouses. As well, increases in family size (through birth), decreases in family size (through death or children leaving home), changes in family income, and new job opportunities often lead to changes in location for many people.

With so many economic and demographic events taking place, there is considerable movement within cities. As data in Exhibit 7.4 show, nearly a fifth of Canadian adults report having lived in their present dwelling only a year or less, and half have lived there five years or less (Statistics Canada, 1990 General Social Survey).

People often change their neighbourhood when they change dwellings. Nearly 20 percent of Canadians report having lived in his or her present neighbourhood a year or less, and 45 percent have been there five years or less (Quality of Life survey, 1981). A change of dwellings is also associated, in many cases, with a change of cities or towns. So, 7 percent of survey respondents report having lived in their

Exhibit 7.3
Education levels of respondents aged 15 and over, 1990

Education level and tenure	Total population 000s	Moved in 1989 000s	%
Owners	**14 232**	**1 642**	**12**
Less than Grade 9[a]	1 213	44	4
Grades 9–13	3 605	320	9
Secondary certificate	2 043	256	13
Post-secondary non-university	4 370	558	13
Some university and university degree	2 920	449	15
Renters	**5 959**	**1 959**	**33**
Less than Grade 9[a]	485	84	17
Grades 9–13	1 517	442	29
Secondary certificate	809	249	31
Post-secondary non-university	1 853	650	35
Some university and university degree	1 267	524	41

[a] Includes no schooling.

Source: Statistics Canada, 1990 General Social Survey, special tabulation. In Che-Alford, Janet, "Canadians on the Move," *Canadian Social Trends*, Summer 1992, pp. 32–34. Ottawa: Statistics Canada.

present city or town only a year or less, and 20 percent of respondents, five years or less. More than 30 percent expect to spend the rest of their lives somewhere else.

Large cities and their surrounding suburbs gain most from intercity movement. Metropolitan Toronto, Vancouver, and Ottawa-Hull, three of Canada's four largest cities, all increased their population by 9 to 10 percent between 1986 and 1990. Some smaller cities also posted large gains, among them Saskatoon with a 10 percent gain, and Kitchener, Oshawa, and Windsor, with 8 to 9 percent gains.

But the fastest-growing census subdivisions are bedroom suburbs like Vaughan (Ontario), which more than doubled in size between 1981 and 1986, and Markham and Ajax (Ontario), which increased by 40 to 50 percent over the same period. Suburbs of Ottawa, Vancouver, and Halifax are also making large gains. As a result, many businesses have moved to these communities, significantly increasing the number and range of white-collar and service jobs available there.

The amount of movement is just as impressive if we shift our attention to larger units: provinces and even regions. Statistics Canada has

Exhibit 7.4
Mobility status of population aged 15 and over, 1990

	000s	%
Total population aged 15 and over	20 526	100
Always lived in same residence	1 050	5
Total movers	19 103	93
Moved in 1989	3 624	18
Moved since January 1985	10 253	50
Moved since January 1980	13 121	64
Not stated	373	2

Source: Statistics Canada, 1990 General Social Survey, special tabulation. In Che-Alford, J. "Canadians on the Move," *Canadian Social Trends*, Summer 1992, pp. 32–34. Ottawa: Statistics Canada.

created what it calls a "churn rate," which measures the amount of migration into and out of a given province or territory. It is a useful measure for comparing provinces.

Several variables drive the provincial churn rate up and down. One is the presence (or absence) of old communities and their degree of community organization. Another is the presence (or absence) of regional cultures and, in the case of Quebec, a distinct language. Taken together, these characteristics account for the relatively low levels of churn in the Maritimes, Quebec, and Manitoba.

A high rate of economic change—especially the rise and fall of resource-based industries—accounts for a high churn rate in Alberta and the Territories. By contrast, Ontario has had a very low churn rate for many years because of its stable economic opportunities, organized ethnic communities, and large base population.

All this migration has consequences for people's happiness. As Exhibit 7.6 shows, in 1985, happiness varied from one region of Canada to another in a way that revealed no correspondence with average regional income.

Movements between provinces reflect changing economic conditions, then. There is no evidence, however, that it increases people's happiness. The economic recession of the early 1980s was associated with a drop in overall movement between provinces, from the 16 per 1000 annual level recorded during most of the 1970s to 11 per 1000 in 1982–83 (Statistics Canada, 1987a, p. 54). But more recent figures show a return to the higher migration levels observed in the 1970s.

Exhibit 7.5

Reasons for move in 1989, by selected distance

	Movers of all distances		Movers of 50 km or less		Movers of 1000 km or more	
Reasons for move (Top five)	**% of total**	**Rank order**	**% of total**	**Rank order**	**% of total**	**Rank order**
To move to a larger home	17	1	22	1	–	–
To move to a better neighbourhood	13	2	14	3	12	4
To purchase a home	13	3	16	2	1	–
One's work	12	4	–	–	30	1
To establish one's own household	7	5	9	4	1	–
Marriage	6	–	7	5	4	–
Other family member's work	–	–	–	–	14	2
To be closer to family	–	–	–	–	14	3
To attend school	–	–	–	–	11	5

– Not one of the top five reasons.

Source: Statistics Canada, 1990 General Social Survey, special tabulation. In Che-Alford, J. "Canadians on the Move," *Canadian Social Trends*, Summer 1992, pp. 32–34. Ottawa: Statistics Canada.

"Historically, the Canadian population has always been moving westward. The trend, though uneven, has been well established" (Foot, 1982, p. 74). Many people believe that the West offers both economic opportunities and a pleasant lifestyle—a very common pair of wants that inspire a large proportion of all migration.

LOCATION AND LIFESTYLE

Where you live both affects and reflects your state of mind. It is a stage on which you play your social roles for many hours each day. Location determines what you will see, hear, smell, and touch. Where you live is a *social environment*, determining what people you will interact with regularly, what ideas you will be exposed to, and what behaviours you will see, as well as what people and things you will *not* be exposed to,

Exhibit 7.6

Percentage reporting they are "very happy," by sex and region, Canada, 1985

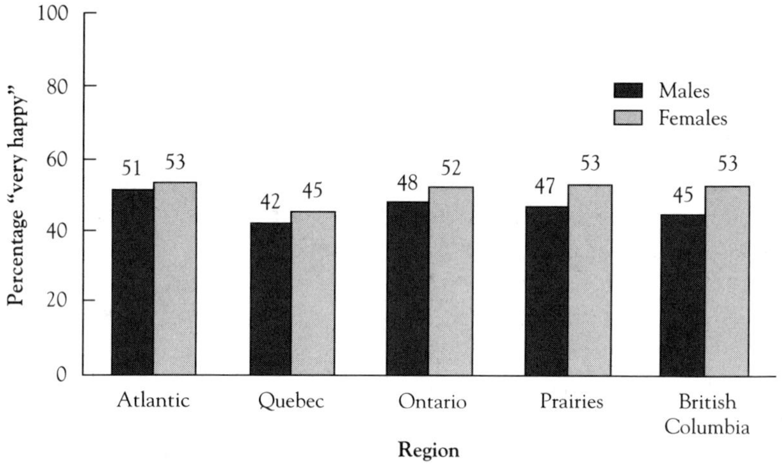

Source: Statistics Canada (1987b). *Health and Social Support, 1985*. General Social Survey Analysis Series (Catalogue 11–612E, No. 1). Ottawa: Statistics Canada. Reproduced with the permission of the Minister of Industry, Science and Technology, 1993.

see, and learn from. Such contacts and experiences will help you in some ways and may hurt you in others.

Beyond that, where you live is an *opportunity structure*. By bringing you into contact with some people and activities, your location makes some futures more likely than others. Where you live shapes your acquaintanceships, friendships, and social networks. In turn, these networks couple you to or decouple you from major institutions, as we learned in Chapter Two. Where you live will reflect your class (and ethnic) group and keep you part of it. Locked into your own community, you are also locked out of, or excluded from, other communities.

Finally, where you live is a state of mind. Where you grow up shapes your ideas about how and where you want to live as an adult. Your maturing ideas about how you want to live take material form in your choice of where to live. The choices we make about where to live—on the coast or inland, in a small or large community, alone, with family, or with friends, and so on—express the future we desire and the good life we plan to live. It is in that sense that "the upwardly mobile executive who moves from one residence into another, more elegant one is moving in psychological as well as physical space" (Campbell, 1980, p. 159).

In all these respects, where you live is like your social class: both characteristics shape and reflect choices, help or disable, close in or lock out, couple or decouple. These processes serve to sort people into different places; the resulting geographic or locational variation in lifestyles shows up clearly in modern marketing research. The claim that many lifestyles coexist in North America, and that lifestyles are interwoven with places, would find ready acceptance in the marketing community.

Increasingly, people with goods and services to sell are able to find particular locations where the demand for their products is likely to be greatest. This kind of marketing has been revolutionized by a technique called PRIZM, which, in the United States, attaches social, economic, and demographic information to each of the country's 36 000 ZIP codes. A computerized program can find the ZIP codes containing the largest fractions of people viewing "Beverly Hills 90210," eating fat-free yogurt, or buying used cars.

With this information in hand, marketers can focus their advertising, product trials, or merchandising efforts on the regions or neighbourhoods where the probable payoff is highest. Claritas Corporation, in particular, has devoted a great deal of effort to finding out how many different "kinds of neighbourhoods" exist in the United States and how they differ from one another in values and lifestyles: the "clustering of America" (Weiss, 1988).

Researchers at Claritas have identified 40 distinct neighbourhood (or lifestyle) clusters among the 36 000 ZIP code areas. Empirical research conducted for over two decades has shown Claritas that national or regional differences may not be very important. People living in one neighbourhood often have almost nothing in common in terms of values and lifestyles with people in another neighbourhood only a few miles away. Yet they might share a great deal with people living a thousand miles away, in another region, state, or city—even on the other side of the continent. As Claritas founder Jonathan Robbins puts it, "You can go to sleep in Fairfield, Connecticut, and wake up in Pasadena, California, but except for the palm trees, you're really in the same place" (quoted in Weiss, 1988, p. 14).

Consider the neighbourhood type Claritas calls "Two More Rungs."

> In the affluent cluster of Two More Rungs—consisting of communities like Skokie, Illinois; Rancho Park, California; and Flushing, New York—residents shun the extravagant trappings of success. With its high

> concentration of Jewish, Irish, Italian and Slavic stock, this cluster is filled with professionals who dedicated their lives to sending their kids to college. Today, they're comfortably settled in a paid-for condominium or split-level. Two More Rungs is filled with success stories of first-generation Americans living near the port cities to which their parents emigrated. (Weiss, 1988, p. 51)

People who live in Two More Rungs neighbourhoods—about 7 in every 1000 Americans—hold particular values and live in particular ways.

> They frequently travel to their ancestral homelands in Europe, but they tend to take discounted chartered plane trips or cruises. At home, Two More Rungs residents read *Scientific American* and *Atlantic Monthly* twice as often as the general populace, and they would rather host a family dinner than a cocktail party. In this tradition-bound neighbourhood type, status is still a son who grows up to be a doctor, lawyer or college professor—junior-high teachers don't cut it. (Weiss, 1988, p. 51)

As this example shows, neighbourhood types are partly defined by location—in this case, closeness to a port city (such as Halifax, Montreal, Toronto, or Vancouver), and partly by a combination of socio-economic status, stage in the life cycle, and racial or ethnic origin.

Why are these patterns so regular and predictable? And why do people with certain characteristics live in similar ways in the same neighbourhoods? The answer is that the inhabitants of Two More Rungs and all others who can afford to choose where they live seek neighbours who are most like themselves. People with similar educational or ethnic backgrounds, who are at similar stages in the life cycle, and have much the same amount of money to spend have similar conceptions of "the good life" and abilities to attain that kind of life. They gather together in neighbourhoods and spend their money in similar ways.

In the case of people with *less* income and *less* choice, neighbours resemble one another—whether they are rural sharecroppers or city people on public assistance—because they suffer similar disabilities of the kind we discussed in Chapter Two. Socially and economically, they are all disabled, excluded, and decoupled from power. Race and urban-versus-rural residence play a large part in shaping lifestyles among the poor. Ideas about the good life play very little part, since they cannot put these ideas into effect.

So 40 distinct, fairly stable neighbourhood types are the result. People may come and go, but neighbourhoods stay much the same over

Exhibit 7.7

The United States' forty neighbourhood types

Cluster	Thumbnail Description	Percent U.S. Households
Blue Blood Estates	America's wealthiest neighborhoods, includes suburban homes and one in ten millionaires	1.1
Money & Brains	Posh big-city enclaves of townhouses, condos, and apartments	0.9
Furs & Station Wagons	New money in metropolitan bedroom suburbs	3.2
Urban Gold Coast	Upscale urban high-rise districts	0.5
Pools & Patios	Older, upper-middle-class, suburban communities	3.4
Two More Rungs	Comfortable multi-ethnic suburbs	0.7
Young Influentials	Yuppie, fring-city condo and apartment developments	2.9
Young Suburbia	Child-rearing, outlying suburbs	5.3
God's Country	Upscale frontier boomtowns	2.7
Blue-Chip Blues	The wealthiest blue-collar suburbs	6.0
Bohemian Mix	Inner-city bohemian enclaves à la Greenwich Village	1.1
Levittown, U.S.A.	Aging, post-World War II tract subdivisions	3.1
Gray Power	Upper-middle-class retirement communities	2.9
Black Enterprise	Predominantly black, middle- and upper-middle-class neighborhoods	0.8
New Beginnings	Fringe-city areas of singles complexes, garden apartments and trim bungalows	4.3
Blue-Collar Nursery	Middle-class, child-rearing towns	2.2
New Homesteaders	Exurban boomtowns of young, midscale families	4.2
New Melting Pot	New immigrant neighborhoods, primarily in the nation's port cities	0.9
Towns & Gowns	America's college towns	1.2
Rank & File	Older, blue-collar, industrial suburbs	1.4
Middle America	Midscale, midsize towns	3.2
Old Yankee Rows	Working-class rowhouse districts	1.6
Coalburg & Corntown	Small towns based on light industry and farming	2.0
Shotguns & Pickups	Crossroads villages serving the nation's lumber and breadbasket needs	1.9

Golden Ponds	Rustic cottage communities located near the coasts, in the mountains or alongside lakes	5.2
Agri-Business	Small towns surrounded by large-scale farms and ranches	2.1
Emergent Minorities	Predominantly black, working-class, city neighborhoods	1.7
Single City Blues	Downscale, urban, singles districts	3.3
Mines & Mills	Struggling steeltowns and mining villages	2.8
Back-Country Folks	Remote, downscale, farm towns	3.4
Norma Rae-Ville	Lower-middle-class milltowns and industrial suburbs, primarily in the South	2.3
Smalltown Downtown	Inner-city districts of small industrial cities	2.5
Grain Belt	The nation's most sparsely populated rural communities	1.3
Heavy Industry	Lower-working-class districts in the nation's older industrial cities	2.8
Share Croppers	Primarily southern hamlets devoted to farming and light industry	4.0
Downtown Dixie Style	Aging, predominantly black neighborhoods, typically in southern cities	3.4
Hispanic Mix	America's Hispanic barrios	1.9
Tobacco Roads	Predominantly black farm communities throughout the South	1.2
Hard Scrabble	The nation's poorest rural settlements	1.5
Public Assistance	America's inner-city ghettos	3.1

Source: Weiss, M.J. (1988). *The clustering of America* (pp. 4,5). New York: Harper & Row, Publishers. Reprinted with permission.

the years. In some cases, that is because a particular neighbourhood is the only place where excluded, disabled, and decoupled people can live. University of Chicago sociologists were the first to discover, more than 60 years ago, that poor, isolated, deviant, and discriminated-against groups tend to concentrate in run-down inner cities.

If they gain an economic foothold, these people move to another neighbourhood—a comfortable urban or suburban district more distant from downtown. Those who are left behind, and those arriving from elsewhere with similar disabilities, ensure that the neighbourhood remains as it has always been. In some Eastern Seaboard cities such as Boston and New York, this process has been going on for generations.

In other cases, neighbourhoods retain their character because of their appeal and function. Over time, the same kinds of people find the neighbourhood appealing—and move into it—as found it appealing five, ten, or twenty years earlier, but (with changes in income or stage in the life cycle) are now moving out.

Large family homes are continuously filled with young, prosperous families; crumbling inner-city apartments blocks attract new generations of the socially and economically disabled.

In choosing a place to live, people usually reveal particular concerns that pertain to the lifestyles they hope to live. But lifestyle "appears to operate more as a latent than as a strongly explicit consideration in residential choice-making" (Reed, 1976, Abstract). The choice of location is made with specific features in mind: house price and size, convenience to work, schools, shopping, and so on. All these characteristics, as well as the lifestyle they imply, will have a major impact on people's satisfaction.

LOCATION AND SATISFACTION

People who are free to choose a location and lifestyle as they wish should be generally satisfied with where and how they live; and they are. Most people report that they are satisfied with the province in which they live. Nearly two-thirds believe that their province is better than any other—or at least better than most (Quality of Life survey, 1981).

People reveal somewhat more variation in their satisfaction with city, town, or rural life. Traditionally, quality of life research has found a negative relationship between city size and the percentage of residents who rate their neighbourhoods "excellent" (Lee & Guest, 1983). City-dwellers are more likely to report "disagreeable experiences" and less likely to report that where they live is "a good place to live" than people living in suburbs, small towns, or rural areas (Campbell, 1980, p. 150).

The difference becomes more marked the larger the city in which a respondent lives. Typically, residents have a higher level of satisfaction with urban services if they live in smaller, rather than larger, communities within a metropolitan area (Mouritzen, 1989). Perhaps that is why suburbanites are often much more satisfied with their communities than their urban counterparts (Cook, 1988). Living farther away from the city centre increases people's satisfaction and allows a family larger, better housing than it could afford downtown; in this way, it increases overall housing satisfaction (Yi, 1985).

However, recent research calls some of these findings into doubt, perhaps because of the growing similarity of rural, suburban, and urban lifestyles in North America. Rodgers (1982b) reports a weak relationship between actual urban density and *perceived* crowding. To the extent that crowding reduces satisfaction, it does so only under certain conditions—for example, among poor versus rich people, and renters versus owners—if at all (Baldassare, 1982). Moreover, there are significant cultural variations in people's responses to actual crowding (Gillis, Richards, & Hagan, 1987). So density per se may make much less difference to people's satisfaction than researchers once believed.

Perhaps this explains why data on emotional well-being show few differences between women living in a rural Pennsylvania county and women living in the city of Philadelphia (Mansfield, Preston, & Crawford, 1988). Both groups report low stress and high life satisfaction. When stresses do occur, they prove to be related to health, family and friendship matters, and, secondarily, to work. Income and the number of young children at home are more important predictors of stress for rural women than they are for urban women. But none of these result from location.

Small communities tend to grow more slowly than large ones, but when rural communities do start to grow, residents usually grow dissatisfied, epecially with health and other public services (Albrecht & Geertsen, 1982). Population growth disrupts the social and economic life of a small community. The mere anticipation of growth caused people in a town in Utah that grew rapidly during the 1980s to become less satisfied, or attached to the community (Brown, Geertsen, & Krannich, 1989). They continued to feel dissatisfied while their town was growing and after the growth had ended. In some cases, then, people's response to growth is less a result of changes in conditions and services than it is of fear of change.

Some groups may be more affected than others. For example, adults in "Boomtown," a rapidly growing Colorado community, proved to be no less satisfied than their counterparts in three nearby communities that were *not* growing. But Boomtown teenagers were much more critical of their community, held more negative attitudes toward growth, and expressed higher levels of alienation than teenagers in the comparison communities (Freudenberg, 1984). These differences cannot be explained by variations in the social or demographic composition of the four communities. Perhaps the Boomtown teenagers were there largely against their will—recent migrants without close friends and lacking familiarity with the community.

Class may also play a part in determining how people will react to population growth. Goldsmith and Jackson (1981) found that, in a growing suburban county, high-status people in high-status neighbourhoods were the most satisfied with their community and least depressed by changes.

Downtown city-dwellers in the United States are less satisfied with life overall, with the various life domains, and with their neighbourhood, than people who live in smaller communities. Moreover, city people are more likely than others to report feeling "restless, lonely, depressed, bored and upset." They are twice as likely as people in small towns and rural areas to express the willingness to settle in another country (Campbell, 1980, p. 151).

Yet "in light of these comparisons, it is rather surprising to find how little people in these communities of varying size differ in their expressions of positive affect. With regard to geographic location, there is virtually no difference in the proportions of white people who say they are very happy or who report having positive experiences in the recent past" (Campbell, 1980, p. 150). In short, people find the community that suits them and, if they have the choice, stay until it no longer suits them. They evaluate their community in terms of whether, and to what degree, it meets their needs for work, education, goods and services, leisure, and rest (Turowski, 1986; Lord & Rent, 1987).

The differences in the ways people evaluate city, suburban, and small-town life may be less marked in Canada than they are in the United States. The downtown areas of major Canadian cities are less run-down, racially segregated, and dangerous. Two Canadian respondents in three think that all or most people in their city are friendly; over half think that the shopping and services are excellent or very good; and nearly half feel that recreation and sports opportunities are excellent or very good (Quality of Life survey, 1981).

Misgivings attach to other aspects of city life. For example, Canadians are nearly as likely to say that the quality of air in their city is merely fair or poor as they are to say that it is excellent or very good. And, while four in ten think that their city's cultural and entertainment facilities are excellent or very good, over one-quarter believe that they are only fair or poor. Most seriously of all, nearly one respondent in two sees the city's job opportunities as fair or poor; only one in five considers the economic climate excellent or very good. (Bear in mind, however, that this survey was conducted in 1981, during a serious economic recession.)

Satisfaction with Neighbourhood and Community

Canadians are even more satisfied with their neighbourhood than with their city as a whole. More than half feel that their neighbourhood is better than their last one and only one in five thinks that it is worse (Quality of Life survey, 1981).

Neighbourhood or community satisfaction is the result of a mix of elements: the objective characteristics of a neighbourhood (for example, its appearance, upkeep, and access to resources and services); the social and demographic characteristics of the respondents (for example, their age, income, and length of residence); and residents' social ties and subjective definitions of the neighbourhood—how residents see it and feel about it (La Gory, Ward, & Sherman, 1985; Fried, 1984).

Some researchers focus their attention on the first of these influences: the *objective characteristics* of a neighbourhood. So, for example, Lewis and Lyon (1986) report that the local environment has a strong effect on quality of life; a list of pertinent community attributes includes general physical appearance and noise level (St. John, Austin, & Baba, 1986). Therefore, these researchers argue, it should be possible to improve people's attachment to their community by improving physical features of the community, even where the local social life is not well developed.

As if to support this view, Canadians, if they complain about their neighbourhood at all, complain mainly about the physical environment (Quality of Life survey, 1981). Nearly as many report problems with air pollution, faulty streets and roads, and noise from trains and traffic, as report no complaints with these conditions. Other frequently reported problems are insufficient good parks and playgrounds, and concern over crime.

Other researchers focus on the *demographic* and *social characteristics* of the people in a neighbourhood in their explanations of neighbourhood satisfaction. Baldassare (1986) believes that the residents of central cities, large dense urban areas, and rapidly growing communities tend to report less-than-average satisfaction with the place they live on account of the kinds of people living in these places, and not ecological factors. Such socio-economic factors as type of housing, family assistance, and marital status all influence people's residential satisfaction (Jagun et al., 1990). Fried (1982) sees neighbourhood social relations as having some importance; but they may have less importance than factors related to social class—particularly, the different kinds of housing and resources available to poor people and rich people in the community. Poor residents who lack opportunities are less satisfied with their neighbourhood than others (Lee & Guest, 1983). This is particularly unfortunate, since Fried (1984) notes that community satisfaction plays a much greater role in shaping the life satisfaction of poor people than it does for other groups.

Generally, people become more satisfied with their community (as with other domains of life) as they age. Four explanations have been proposed for this:

1. As they age, people leave a community if they do not like it.
2. People who remain in a community that they like come to like it even more with the passage of time.
3. People generally accept their surroundings more readily as they age.
4. The older generation has generally lower, and less fluid, expectations than the younger generation. (Van Es & Schneider, 1983)

Marital status affects neighbourhood satisfaction (Spain, 1988). Indeed, given the lower satisfaction of unmarried people and the increasing number of single households, we can expect a decline in overall neighbourhood satisfaction over the next few decades.

Race (ethnicity or birthplace) usually combines with income in influencing neighbourhood satisfaction (but for a contrary view, see St. John & Clark, 1984). Immigrants who are racially or culturally different from people in the local community may face prejudice and discrimination. Those who are better educated and more economically powerful than the local residents, and therefore threaten their livelihood, are at particular risk. Social class conflicts may be more important here than racial antagonisms, however (Goode, 1990).

The third category of influences on neighbourhood satisfaction is more sociological: it has to do with people's *social relations* within the community and their *perceptions* of that community. One researcher reports that "satisfaction with neighbourhood is most strongly determined by the individual's *perception* of the condition of the neighbourhood housing, of the friendliness of its residents, of its security from criminals, and of the convenience to work and shopping" (Campbell, 1980, pp. 156–57, emphasis added; see also Herting & Guest, 1985; and Austin & Baba, 1990).

How residents (excepting apartment dwellers) feel about their neighbourhood, it is claimed, is unrelated to housing type (Gruber & Shelton, 1987). Satisfaction with neighbours, home, and the aesthetic quality of the community are very important (Widgery, 1982).

People have "mental portraits" (La Gory, Ward, & Sherman, 1985) or "cognitive maps" (Ginsberg, 1985) of their neighbourhood that influence their attitudes. White (1985) reports that people's perceptions of community fall into four main categories: esthetic qualities of the neighbourhood; sense of belonging; sense of social support; and sense of personal control. Ginsberg, however, claims that these cognitive maps are primarily based on perceptions of neighbourhood prestige, and that such perceptions tend to be shared by people living in the neighbourhood. Residents in higher-status neighbourhoods tend to be more satisfied with their neighbourhoods than other people (Rigby & Vreugdenhil, 1987). Whatever their precise nature, those cognitive maps seem to vary over time and place (Bardo & Bardo, 1983). As a result, the organization of people's community satisfactions—the things that make a difference, and the amount of difference they make—are different in the United States and Britain, for example (Bardo & Hughey, 1984; Hughey & Bardo, 1984), or the United States and Turkey (Bardo & Dokmeci, 1990).

We see an interesting example of this in the cross-cultural study (Zube et al., 1985) that asked American and Saudi Arabian raters to assess the quality of four residential areas in each of two desert cities, Jeddah, Saudi Arabia, and Tucson, Arizona. The Arabian raters were less critical than the American raters (perceiving and reporting less annoyance from noise, for example), and rated all eight areas more highly than the Americans. They also perceived less difference between housing sites in Jeddah and Tucson than the Americans did. So people simply don't see places in the same way!

But of all neighbourhood characteristics, the things that people feel most satisfied about—their neighbours and other homes and buildings in the neighbourhood—are the ones most highly correlated with neighbourhood satisfaction (Gruber & Shelton, 1987). Neighbourhood satisfaction reflects the quality and quantity of social interaction within the neighbourhood (Connerly & Marans, 1985). On this score, 60 percent of Canadians report that their neighbours are excellent or very good; only 20 percent report having been upset by neighbours lately (Quality of Life survey, 1981).

Neighbourliness is important to neighbourhood satisfaction (although less so for black than white residents, according to Wittberg, 1984). That may be why neighbourhood satisfaction is lower in large cities: people move in and out too quickly to become neighbourly. But neighbourhood living remains a quest for community. Though many decry residential segregation, it may be the result of a normal social process by which individuals and families try to fulfil their needs for social interaction, attachment, and meaning (Menahem & Spiro, 1989).

Neighbourhoods become cohesive and stable through the formation of friendship and acquaintanceship networks, and the consequent reduction of anonymity (Sampson, 1991). These forces tie people together regardless of objective neighbourhood characteristics (such as size, growth, and heterogeneity) and the social and demographic characteristics of residents. In the end, social—not material or demographic—factors shape neighbourhood satisfaction most.

If you want to be satisfied with your neighbourhood, you should choose a place where you are likely to be satisfied with your neighbours. Look for neighbours who are socially and culturally like you and a neighbourhood that is relatively stable, where you can get to know people. Not only are people who live near others like themselves more satisfied with their neighbourhood, they are more satisfied with life overall (Fine-Davis & Davis, 1982).

Satisfaction with Household and Dwelling

Canadians prove to be somewhat less satisfied with their house or apartment than they are with their neighbourhood as a whole. Although two in every three respondents report that their present dwelling is better than their previous dwelling, one in six reports that it is worse. Nearly half have at least one complaint with their present dwelling (Quality of Life survey, 1981).

An eight-nation study of housing satisfaction (Fine-Davis & Davis, 1982) found that its best predictors in Europe are objective aspects of the dwelling along with satisfaction with the neighbours. Another study (Galster, 1985) found dwelling quality, interior condition, and room size to be more important than public services and the exterior condition of the house. Housing quality is particularly important to the life satisfaction of older people, perhaps because they are more confined to their homes (Golant, 1985).

Homeowners are generally more satisfied with their dwelling than home-renters. Young homeowners are especially satisfied with their dwelling. Owning rather than renting a home is especially gratifying when you are young. "Whether it is pride of ownership, sense of security, feeling of status, or some other psychological need that is fulfilled by the fact of owning one's home, there is no doubt that owners are more satisfied than renters, both in [the United States] and elsewhere" (Campbell, 1980, p. 158). However, home ownership is rarely completed until people reach middle age; people pay off the mortage on their home when they are between the ages of 55 and 64 (Sauvé, 1990, p. 137).

To repeat, all of these satisfactions with place—city, neighbourhood, and dwelling—are significantly correlated with overall life satisfaction. But neighbourhood satisfaction affects life satisfaction twice as strongly as dwelling satisfaction and city satisfaction (Quality of Life survey, 1981). What advice do these data suggest? Buy a modest house in a neighbourhood that you love, rather than renting (or buying) a fancier place in a neighbourhood or city that you hate; and do it when you are young enough to enjoy it.

Why are people so satisfied with their location and the accompanying lifestyle? Few people want to live in highrise apartments, and yet even apartment-dwelling families are satisfied: they expect to move eventually. Difficulties that are only temporary can be tolerated (Michelson, 1977). Most people end up getting more or less what they expected and adjust to their (temporary) difficulties, while waiting for a future that is likely to arrive. Many life satisfactions are like that, which explains why so many people are satisfied with life.

Community satisfaction probably helps us explain the choices that people make about finding another dwelling (Sofranko & Fliegel, 1984). That is because housing is a social adaptation process: people attempt to improve the fit, or congruence, between their residential aspirations and their actual conditions. To do this, many choose to move. Others improve their dwelling, change the ways they use it, change their thinking about it, protest inadequate conditions, or simply come to accept the lack of fit between what they want and what they have (Priemus, 1986).

CONCLUSION

In choosing where to live, people probably come closer to getting what they wanted than in many other areas of life. It is easier to keep changing places over the life course than it is to change educations, careers, marriages, or parental statuses.

As we have seen, many factors influence where you choose to live. They include where your work is located, where your spouse wants to live, what you can afford, and a variety of social and cultural barriers (for example, incomplete information and exclusion by others). Campbell (1980) remarks, "We have a remarkable ability to adapt to the peculiarities of our environment and ... most of us can learn to live with the situation we find ourselves in. We not only live with it, we can be satisfied with it" (p. 159).

But many people do not have to make a permanent adjustment to where they live. They keep moving so that, gradually, they come as close as they ever can to the "good life" they dream about. Modern people use their time and money to create satisfactory lifestyles in idiosyncratic ways. As opportunity and variety increase, so does the possibility for a unique, personal combination of living conditions. Where and how you live are perhaps the most tailor-made of all your major life choices.

Do people get what they want out of location and lifestyle? To a large degree they do. People change locations and lifestyles quite often during their lives and express satisfaction with the results of their movements. Often these moves—for example, from a downtown apartment to a suburban single-family home—are motivated by a life-cycle change and the expectations people have of the kind of life they will be able to lead in a new location. But "what satisfies families in highrise apartments in the short run is not what would satisfy them in the long run, nor in the short run either if they could not move elsewhere in the long run" (Michelson, 1977, p. 365). People are pulled forward by their dreams.

Yet people's dreams and desires are also shaped by their experiences. So, for example, people who have remained in highrise apartments, or drifted back to them, expressed a desire for suburban life and yet have come to want to stay downtown (Michelson, 1977, p. 335). People's actions are strongly influenced by factors only partly within their control (for example, aging and life-cycle changes) or well beyond their control (for example, social class, the availability of work and housing, and spouse's and children's desires).

The very best predictors of residential mobility are changes in the availability of jobs and housing. This explains Canadians' continuing shift westward and toward Ontario and, more generally, the churn rate for a given region.

Most people learn to want what they get. Many who were driven or lured to a new place by economic opportunity develop a fierce loyalty to that region, province, city, or neighbourhood. People who have given up one thoroughly enjoyed lifestyle develop a strong liking for their new lifestyle. Lifestyles based in particular locations are often "subcultures" that provide people with meaning as well as enjoyment.

We now examine the problem of a gap between what you want and what you get, and draw some general conclusions from the findings presented in this book.

CHAPTER EIGHT

◆

WHAT YOU WANT AND GET:
CLOSING THE GAP

RECAPITULATION

This book has argued that desires are patterned: different people want different things out of life. Your desires, like other people's, form a coherent package. Life satisfaction is also patterned: some people are more satisfied with life than others, for a range of reasons—social, psychological, cultural, or economic. Further, satisfactions with particular domains of life are also patterned: some people get the most satisfaction from hobbies, others from family life, and so on.

This patterning suggests that social science has something to teach us about everyday life. It is patterning that allows us to take the first steps toward explaining people's values, feelings, and behaviours. And if we can explain our feelings and actions, then managing them is also possible. As a result, advice to make one choice rather than another can be useful, since choice and change lie within our grasp.

Choice and change *are* within our grasp, but only if we understand the pattern of forces that shape our lives. This book has discussed a variety of forces that shape our satisfaction with life in general and within particular life domains. Further, it has revealed two main problems that people encounter in searching for satisfaction: downward accommodation, or the willingness to settle for a Fool's Paradise; and an inability to close the gap between what they want and what they get.

Fool's Paradise

Many people live in a Fool's Paradise. They satisfy themselves by accepting the dominant cultural goals, limiting their information, keeping their expectations low, and going after exactly what the next person has.

These people find conformity satisfying in itself. The less they know about the choices open to them, the more satisfied they are. Other things being equal, their ignorance is blissful. The lower their aspirations (wants) fall, the less often a gap opens up between what they want and what they get. They know little about other possible lives, so they can be happy with their own lives.

It's easy to get into Fool's Paradise. For many, it is simply part of the "pragmatic acceptance" of inequality that we discussed in Chapter Two. True, what we want and get from life are somewhat beyond our control, a result of our position in the class structure (and our age, education, and gender, as well). In general, everyday experience makes it likely that we will know little, want little, get little. So it is easy to learn to value what we do get.

But social class has more effect in some areas of choice than others. Educational and career choices are obviously tied to class of origin. Marriage is less strongly tied to class of origin, though people usually marry within their own social class. Parenting behaviour is even more distantly related to social class of origin, but given the costs of raising children, the experience of parenthood is very different for people of different social classes. Finally, where and how you live are also related to social class.

In each of these areas, what we get and what we want from life are often well matched. Social class and location both limit what we are likely to get and prepare us for our fate by limiting what we are likely to want. As a result, most adults have limited—and realistic—goals. When life disappoints them, they make small changes and lower their aspirations. They turn their attention from what they are lacking to what they have. Substitute satisfactions are found to replace what is missing. Some people try their hand at other things, hoping to have more success in those.

Because of this fit between what people want and what they get, few are willing to fight for major social changes that might obtain for them what they originally wanted. We find a lack of political will even among the most deprived—the poor and unemployed. This is another way in which class inequality maintains itself.

However, many people *are* aware of a gap between what they want and what they get. They do *not* live in a Fool's Paradise, yet seem unable to do anything to improve their lives. They face the second of two problems that people encounter in an attempt to satisfy themselves: an inability to close the gap.

Inability to Close the Gap

Two kinds of dissatisfaction or unhappiness have been labelled "Real Hell" and "Fool's Hell" (Michalos, 1987, p. 45).

Fool's Hell is a state of dissatisfaction based on poorly founded information. Othello is miserable because he believes, incorrectly, that

Desdemona has been unfaithful. Joe is miserable because he thinks that his large nose will prevent him from getting dates with beautiful women. Sally is miserable because she thinks that an off-colour story she told at work is going to hurt her chances of being promoted. Rashid is miserable because he thinks he might have a serious medical problem and is afraid to see a doctor to find out if he is right.

Each of these people in Fool's Hell is a little bit tragic and a little bit ridiculous. Each is unhappy and could be happier, even happy, by getting accurate information about some matter of vital importance. Instead, they remain unhappy and, worse, may act in ways that end up making themselves even unhappier. The wisdom of getting out of Fool's Hell needs little further discussion.

Real Hell is a different matter altogether. Consider the well-informed political radical who has spent a lifetime fighting injustice, yet sees that much injustice remains. That person has good reason to feel dissatisfied with the state of the world. Yet there is also reason to feel satisfied with having fought to the limit of his or her abilities in a good cause. Will that fighter enjoy what has been accomplished, or remain dissatisfied with what has *not* been accomplished? And will that person fight on, in hopes of trading Real Hell for Real Paradise?

If such people fight on, many of the same factors that limit what *you* get out of life—exclusion, disability, and decoupling—will limit *their* ability to close the gap between what they want and what they get. Exclusion denies them the resources for an assault on the social order. Disability denies the poor and powerless the sense of competence that they need to sustain their campaign in the face of powerful opposition. Decoupling denies them a network of informal influence that they might use to seek major changes through more conventional channels.

Thus, the very means by which rich and powerful people get what they want—through class exclusion, a sense of political competence, and wide contacts with others having power and authority—are those least available to poor people.

Justifying this inequality is a world view, or ideology, that supports the current social and economic order. The observed fit between what people want and what they get sustains a belief that people usually get what they want out of life. This ideology also blames the victims. It holds people responsible for what they do *not* get and treats the privileged as though they deserve their rewards. By this reckoning, the deprived deserve to fail because they have not organized their lives properly: they have chosen poorly in education, job, marriage, and so on.

Of course, many people *do* organize their lives badly and suffer for it. Yet rich people who organize their lives badly are less likely to suffer, no matter what they do. Moreover, even the best personal organization is only a temporary cure for the problem of unequal opportunity, which has a much greater part in determining people's lives. And as we have seen, unequal opportunity is rooted in unequal conditions: a class system that places people at vastly different starting points in the competition.

So, in the long run, we must look for the path to satisfaction in changes to the class structure, not in better personal organization. That is why this book does not urge you either to adjust to a Fool's Paradise or to make strenuous personal efforts. In the long run, these actions cannot solve the problem confronting most of us. It argues instead for a Real Paradise.

You will remember that, in a Real Paradise, people seek the best information about what is possible, push the possible to its limit, and try to live with the result. This book supports the old maxim that "Man [*sic*] is the measure of all things," which means that people should idealize the best that is possible, and then seek that ideal.

What is possible is what *is*, what *has been*, and what shows signs of *becoming*. A systematic understanding of the past and present is key to understanding and acting upon the future. Our understanding of what is possible will undoubtedly change with time and new evidence. But the evidence that we have on hand today, though incomplete and imperfect, is still better than ignorance.

Before considering the more effective group solutions, we shall examine the best individual solutions to the gap between what people want and what people get.

INDIVIDUAL SOLUTIONS

At present, we cannot say that people generally get what they want out of life or generally do not. We must study the question domain by domain, issue by issue. Likewise, we cannot validly generalize about whether people usually learn to want what they get. Earlier chapters have shown that sometimes people learn to want what they get—to love their mate, child, or place of residence, for example. Sometimes they do not—job dissatisfaction and divorce illustrate that point. In every realm, people adjust to their lives as they get older; but even this is only a tendency, not a certainty.

Other factors also affect the ways that people adapt. Some people have less opportunity to change situations than to adjust to them. A woman with several young children and few job skills may find it easier to stay in a bad marriage than leave it, although neither remedy is highly satisfying. Further, some personalities will prove more adaptable than others. People with a strong sense of mastery and control over their environment will find it easier to adapt to a situation (or change it) than people who feel powerless and alienated. Again, we are far from knowing all the factors that influence people's ability to get what they want, or change what they get.

But on one matter the evidence is unambiguous. Most people are only moderately satisfied with their lives: they do not live in a paradise of any kind. They have gotten less than they wanted and have not learned to want what they have gotten. If we were to examine an average person's lifecycle, we would surely find periods of non-adjustment and discontent. Most people fall out of love with their own lives at one time or another. And some people—for example, people with strong, unconventional social and political views—are likely to go through their entire adult lives in a state of Real Hell. Reality simply does not live up to their expectations. What do these people do about it?

Proposal One: Merton's Contribution

American sociologist Robert Merton (1957a) redefined Durkheim's (1893/1965, 1897/1951) concept of *anomie* to analyze the consequences of a gap, or "disjuncture," between what people want and what they can get by legitimate means. Considering anomie a result of the gap between "culture goals" and "institutionalized [or accepted] means," Merton examined the variety of "modes of individual adaptation" to this problem.

Merton argued that Americans are taught to accept society's culture goals, especially the goal of material success. They are raised to value success very highly and to evaluate themselves and others in terms of the material success that they achieve in life. And for some, the accepted roads to success—a higher education and a job or career—are open for travel and lead to suitable rewards.

For others—the one in nine who descended from black slaves or the one in two who could not vote until two decades into this century—equal opportunity in the competition for material success has been slow in coming. Job discrimination and unequal access to higher education persist today in both Canada and the United States. How do people adapt to the inadequacy of accepted means?

Logically, only so many kinds of adaptation are possible. People may continue to accept both the culture goals and accepted means: to conform to social expectations even if they are not paying off. Or they may continue to believe in the culture goals while rejecting the accepted means: Merton called these people "innovators." They may reject the culture goals but continue to believe in the accepted means: if so, they are "ritualists." They may reject both the culture goals and accepted means, becoming "retreatists." Finally, they may replace both the culture goals and accepted means with substitute goals and means: doing so makes them "rebels," in Merton's terms (see Exhibit 8.1).

Merton's analysis documents each type of adaptation and many of its forms: for example, the innovator as robber baron and racketeer, the ritualist as bureaucrat, the retreatist as tramp and drug addict, the rebel as political activist.

His analysis seems to deny that multiple goals exist within a given individual, that significant subcultures exist within the society, and that many legitimate or nearly legitimate ways of "making it" are accepted in practice. Merton's theory, then, suggests a uniformity of goals and means that belies the variety of American society.

This defect showed up most dramatically when American social scientists Richard Cloward and Lloyd Ohlin (1960), building on Merton's theory, suggested dealing with crime among young people by offering poor youths more access to legitimate means of upward mobility. Put into practice by a series of social programs in the 1960s, this theory was invalidated by the evidence that poor young people did not seem to want the lives being offered them. Other goals—excitement, pleasure, risk taking—beckoned; other means of getting by were more appealing than a nine-to-five job.

This and other research on subcultures has suggested that people are motivated by a variety of goals, not merely material success and an Anglo-Saxon middle-class lifestyle. It may be fair to say that Merton's theory has been oversimplified in practice: that Merton recognizes that people have diverse goals. But to the extent that people have understood and implemented Merton's theory, it has not proven correct. Even in North America, material success is not paramount for everyone. Many people prefer family, romance, and community life. Chapter One showed that there is no single, essential, or universal set of human concerns.

Because of this flaw, Merton's theory gives us little help in understanding rebellion, conflict, and change, except as responses to limited opportunity for material advancement. Merton's theory cannot explain the civil rights movement, the women's movement, the movements for gay rights and Native peoples' rights, or environmentalism: why they arose when they did and how they did, who participated, and with what result for themselves or for society. These movements had little if anything to do with material advancement.

Exhibit 8.1
Merton's typology of adaptations to anomie

Modes of adaptation	Culture goals	Institutionalized means
Conformity	+	+
Innovation	+	–
Ritualism	–	+
Retreatism	–	–
Rebellion	±	±

Source: Social Theory and Social Structure by Robert K. Merton. Copyright © 1957 by The Free Press, copyright renewed 1985 by Robert K. Merton. Reprinted with the permission of The Free Press, a Division of Macmillan, Inc.

Likewise, Merton's single-minded focus on material goals produces a moral equivalence between robber barons and alcoholics, racketeers and civil rights marchers. Saints and mass murderers are both deviant, both adaptors to anomie. It completely misses the hidden dynamic that explains why one person becomes a saint and the other a mass murderer. It fails to explain why some women became suffragettes in the early part of this century, and others did not. It also fails to explain how Martin Luther King's "adaptation to anomie" helped change American society, while Charles Manson's did not.

So it appears that we need to go beyond Merton's theory if we are to create a framework for individual actions that might bridge the gap between desires and realities. Doing this means, first, reviewing why people get what they get, and not always what they want.

Proposal Two: Various Individual Solutions

Chapter Two introduced four concepts—exclusion, disability, decoupling, and scarcity—to explain the limits on people's opportunity. Remedies for these problems fall into two categories, individual and group, as we have seen. These remedies can be used to close any gap between wants and achievements. They do not assume a particular want, as Merton's analysis has done. Limited space does not permit a full discussion of how each remedy applies to each type of dissatisfaction. You will have to apply these remedies to your own problems yourself. What follows are merely examples.

As an individual, you may best solve the problem of exclusion by getting whatever credentials allow you to enter the group you hope to spend your life in. Chapter Three showed that higher education is the single best investment you can make if your goals are material, and perhaps even if they are creative.

However, Chapter Two also showed that racial and ethnic discrimination continue to limit people's opportunity to enter many lines of activity. For example, members of groups that suffer discrimination may not do as well in work settings controlled by other ethnic groups as they would by remaining within their own ethnic community, even with less education. The decision you have to make here, a complex one, depends on several factors: the actual extent of discrimination against your ethnic or racial group; the chance of a significant reduction in that discrimination during your lifetime; the range of attractive occupational opportunities within your own racial or ethnic community; and the chance of a significant increase in these opportunities during your lifetime.

Alone, you can do little to influence any of these factors. As an individual you can only choose between getting a higher education (and possibly cutting yourself off from your ethnic community) or getting less education (and building contacts within your ethnic community). The first choice risks discrimination outside the community; the second limits opportunities for selecting a career and advancing within the community. Your contribution to a group cure, to be discussed shortly, will be much more important.

You can solve the problem of personal disability by changing the way you think about yourself: not an easy task, but one that a great many people manage to accomplish. This is partly what the major social movements of our time—for example, feminism, Native rights, and gay rights—are all about. Learn more about the history of your disability as a member of a despised or belittled group. Discuss this problem with others, find mentors and role models in your group who have done what others want you to think you cannot do. Most important of all, reject the victim-blaming ideology that you use to whip yourself. You have enough problems without being your own worst enemy.

Again, individual remedies are less likely to succeed than group remedies. Women (for example) will be able to demonstrate that they can succeed in activities previously thought to be outside their competence only if given a chance. Opening up new opportunities often requires that an excluded group mobilize. Your personal contribution, therefore, might best be made toward a group remedy. Still, results may be a long time in coming.

You can solve the problem of decoupling by building and making use of social networks. That is how people find good jobs (Chapter Two) and, sometimes, mates (Chapter Five). Improve the size and variety of your network by getting to know people who have larger and "better" networks: people who are themselves mobile and widely acquainted, are (typically) higher in status, or operate within institutions that encourage interpersonal contact.

Social institutions that break down traditional gender, class, and ethnic barriers to interpersonal contact include colleges, universities, and government. Thus, higher education and involvement in civic affairs are doubly beneficial: they allow self-improvement and encourage contact with others. However, both activities leave less time for participation in your own community. Here, wrong choices are potentially most costly. So try to become a "cosmopolitan" member of your community, with feet in both camps (Merton, 1957b). This connects you *and* your community into the larger networks of influence and opportunity beyond.

Finally, you can cope with real scarcity as an individual by producing more of what people need; adjusting your thinking downward from the imaginary to the possible; and seeking creative alternatives to scarce goods. It is the human ability to do this that has kept our species alive for a million years.

The danger here lies in confusing scarcity with inequality, considering scarcity beyond remedy, or lowering our heads rather than raising the bridge. French demographer Alfred Sauvy (1969, p. 391) has called this approach the "Malthusian Spirit ... a state of mind characterised by the fear of excess—faced with two quantities that need adjusting, it tends to lower the highest instead of boosting the lowest. It is the opposite of courage and generosity." The "Malthusian" is the person who, facing a dinner party with too little food for the guests, tries to turn away guests rather than find more food.

When what appears to be scarcity is really a result of inequality, or a temporary shortage that could be remedied through innovation and higher productivity, group remedies are called for. But group remedies depend on the personal commitment of individuals who are willing to accept the effects that they will have on their lives, along with the solutions that they offer.

GROUP REMEDIES

Social life today—whether conformist, ritualist, retreatist, innovative, or rebellious—is increasingly group life. The chief actors in a large, modern society—even those who suffer anomie—are organized groups, not individuals, as Merton would have it. That is why we must look elsewhere for an adequate theory of adaptations to anomie.

Proposal Three: Westhues's Contribution

A theory formulated by Canadian sociologist Kenneth Westhues (1982) deals with many of the flaws in Merton's theory by standing it on its head. Unlike Merton, Westhues sees conformity, not deviance, as the problem to be solved. Merton sees people as needing better chances of reward for conformity; and for Merton, a more stable society is the goal. Westhues believes that people need more chances for nonconformity. And because he sees "vice in conformity, virtue in deviance," more social justice is Westhues's goal. Thus Westhues equates deviance with "liberation," implying that our society is enslaved and that conformity is the shape of that slavery.

At first glance, this revision of Merton's theory is just as easily dismissed. Surely deviance is no better than conformity, and change is no better than persistence. To argue otherwise is to imply that there is nothing worth preserving in our society, just as to hold Merton's position is to imply that there is nothing wrong with it. Each extreme offers a picture of society that is far too simple.

Westhues does remedy some of the problems in Merton's theory, though. First, his analysis is less focussed on material success than Merton's. Second, it is more complex. For example, Westhues's typology of "generic forms of liberation, or deviance" contains eight types of adaptation, not four as in Merton's model. It distinguishes between types of liberation that (1) retreat from expectations or attack them; (2) deviate mildly or severely from conformity; and (3) constitute individual or group remedies (see Exhibit 8.2).

According to Westhues, the basic condition leading to liberation is a gap between previous learning and present experience. People find that old ideas, expectations, and practices fail to serve them well in new situations. Ten secondary conditions evidently help to create this gap: migration, membership in a deprived class, class mobility, intermarriage, social dislocation, Jewish identity, liberal schooling, intellectual occupations, a diverse environment, and catastrophe.

The outlets choosen for expressing discontent are influenced in three main ways. According to Westhues, (1) people withdraw when they cannot attack; (2) signs of weakening invite attack; and (3) the available tools condition how people create, protest, or misbehave.

Westhues points to one central strain in our system: the value placed on creativity (a culture goal) and the limited opportunity people have to innovate (Westhues, 1982, p. 463). We urge our children to create; then capitalism denies most of them the legitimate opportunity to do so. No wonder they go to shopping malls and get into trouble, Westhues

Exhibit 8.2

Westhues's typology of forms of liberation, or deviance

Degree	Withdrawal		Attack	
	Individual	**Collective**	**Individual**	**Collective**
Mild	Sleeping on the job Daydreams, fantasies Loafing Media opiates Occasional drunkenness Marijuana smoking Many illnesses	Escapist entertainment Sectarian religion Cults	Personal twists and new wrinkles in the performance of conventional roles "I'll do it my way" Minor innovations	Fads, crazes Under capitalism, marginally new products of private companies Reformist social movements
Severe	Refusing to settle down A hermit's life Habitual drunkenness Narcotic addiction Psychosis Suicide	Countercultural movements Utopian communities	Invention in science and technology Boldly original art New philosophic work New forms of human organization Religious prophecy	Under capitalism, major new products of private companies Revolutionary social movements Mass migrations

Source: Westhues, K. (1982). *First Sociology* (p. 433). New York: McGraw-Hill Publishing. Reprinted with permission.

laments. Evidently, Westhues has taken Merton's framework and exchanged "creativity" for "material success" as the goal that everyone wants to maximize. (Class structure remains the central factor limiting access to legitimate means of attaining the culture goal.)

In making this translation, Westhues's work perpetuates two of the problems with Merton's theory: the assumed uniformity of goals, and the moral equivalence of wonderful innovating acts (for example, inventing a polio vaccine) and horrible innovating acts (for example, establishing death camps). Perhaps creativity really is a more elevated goal than material success. Still, as we saw in Chapter One, neither is a major life concern of adult Canadians.

But Westhues has taken us beyond Merton, nonetheless. First, he has stretched our understanding of the conditions that promote (or permit) non-conforming behaviour and specified the groups and situations that are most likely to spawn such behaviour.

More important, Westhues emphasizes the difference between individual and group acts of non-conformity. Group mobilization is not only a condition under which individuals can act with greater effect: it brings about new *kinds* of non-conforming behaviour. Social movements, cults, and experimental communities are qualitatively different from individual adaptations to anomie, and they also carry a greater potential for changing society.

However, Westhues ultimately fails because, like Merton, he focusses on the single goal that he assumes people are trying to attain. This makes his analysis less than completely helpful for people with another goal in mind.

This book has repeatedly claimed the superiority of group remedies to individual ones. But some group remedies are better than others. An *ideal* group remedy will have two main characteristics: it will operate within the realm of the truly possible, and it will tie the advancement of group well-being to the advancement of individual well-being.

As this book has stressed repeatedly, sociology is interested only in the realm of the possible. One of the earliest social scientists, Thomas Malthus, stated this view as follows: "A writer may tell me that he thinks man will ultimately become an ostrich. I cannot properly contradict him.... [But] till the probability of so wonderful a conversion can be shown, it is surely lost time and lost eloquence to expatiate on the happiness of man in such a state" (Malthus, 1798/1959). And so it is with all remedies that social science might propose: as sociologists, we must leave poetry to the poets and fantasy to the dreamers, and consider only what seems truly possible—indeed, likely.

As to the second criterion, we should emphasize remedies that serve both the individual and the group. Only remedies that serve the group interest are likely to endure, but only those that promise to increase individual well-being can be expected to motivate strong individual effort. Ideally, then, remedies that serve both the group and the individual will have the greatest success and longevity. Let us now consider how groups might solve the problems raised in this book.

Proposal Four: Marx's Contribution

We have seen that social inequality is responsible for much dissatisfaction in everyday life. Inequality excludes, disables, decouples, and even creates scarcity. Marx's remedy was to attack inequality through group action.

Marx and Engels (1848/1955) contended that a revolution that would eliminate ruling and subordinate classes forever by eliminating private property—by placing the means of production in the hands of the state—would bring better conditions for all. With the eventual "withering away" of the state, communism would end history as we have known it, for it would end social classes and class conflict.

There are two problems with this formulation. First, a reading of history shows that every society of any size has had a class structure and a ruling class. This would *not* lead sociologists to the confident conclusion that a society with no class structure and no ruling class is truly possible. Rather, it would lead in the opposite direction: in the direction most often associated with the name of Robert Michels (1962), who stated the "iron law of oligarchy."

Michels's principle, based on a socialist's study of the German socialist party—a sympathetic observer studying a radically democratic organization—holds that in every social grouping a dominant group will struggle to perpetuate its power, whatever its original ideology. That is, inequality is inevitable in human groupings, whatever their size or the members' ideology.

Michels's "iron law" has not proven completely unbreakable. For example, a sociological study of the International Typographical Union, a democratic printers' union in the United States, reports finding some of the conditions that prevent or minimize oligarchy (Lipset, Trow, & Coleman, 1963). So not every organization *must* be oligarchic. Yet oligarchic organizations in our own society and elsewhere far outnumber the democratic ones. There is no evidence of a society that has broken the hold of oligarchy. At best, there is only a slim chance that Marx was right about the possibility of a fully democratic society.

Second, the premise that history can end with a democratic, class-free society is far from supported by empirical evidence. History does not show that communist revolutions have actually succeeded in bringing about equality.

In the century and a half since Marx and Engels's *Communist Manifesto*, a number of groups have experimented with communism. Some attempts have been utopian or anarchistic, based in a small community or region (see Hobsbawm, 1959; Kanter, 1972). But, except for Cuba, the Israeli kibbutzim, and Hutterite communities, these have all failed, for a variety of reasons. Some have been forcibly overturned, others have lacked a sufficient material base, while others still have suffered from demographic pressures within and attacks from without. Even the relatively successful kibbutzim and Hutterite communities have suffered serious losses of population, as native-born members deserted. For its part, Cuba's revolution has produced neither prosperity nor democracy.

Other attempts at communism have lasted longer. But contrary to Marx's expectation, they have produced new kinds of inequality. In every instance—in Russia, China, Albania, Cuba, Vietnam, Nicaragua, and so on—rule based on ownership of the means of production has merely been replaced by political and bureaucratic control. So inequality has lived on in a new form. In many places, communism has greatly reduced material inequality and the worst effects of this inequality. But the inequality that remained—rule by a political elite, or "vanguard of the proletariat," as Lenin called it—never disappeared.

Many believe that the excesses of control under communism were not just temporary, but were due to an inherent overcentralization of planning and political power. That is why, throughout Eastern Europe and the former Soviet Union, people have rejected communism as unworkable. Communism has collapsed as a system of organization. In the end, citizens' behaviour in rejecting communism suggests that Marx's remedy does not work as he thought it would.

The communist alternative has proven more attractive in some less developed parts of the world. In fact, the benefits of capitalism and liberalism have meant little to many twentieth-century Third World peoples. They consider European nations unsuitable models to imitate, since they carry the stigma of colonialism. Further, "free enterprise" seems less likely to succeed in the Third World than large-scale economic planning. "One of the outstanding attractions of communism to Asian and African eyes [is] that it [offers] the underdeveloped peoples a blueprint for development" (Barraclough, 1967, p. 223).

On the other hand, material inequality can be significantly reduced without communism, as it has been in the democratic socialist countries of Scandinavia and, to a smaller degree, in certain other countries. Moreover, many people in the industrial capitalist countries—and not simply the very rich and powerful—do not want to give up private property in favour of communism. Values justifying acquisitiveness and free enterprise arise whenever personal acquisition becomes possible. People offered the chance to improve their wealth and status appear, almost without fail, to seize that opportunity. They do not easily give it up .

This book has devoted chapter after chapter to showing that liberal democracy does not give people an equal chance to get what they want out of life. So it would be satisfying to believe that some alternative (such as communism) could do so. However, we have been unable to demonstrate that Marx's proposed remedies lie within the realm of the possible, or that they satisfactorily link the advancement of group and individual interests.

That is not to say that more modest socialist remedies would also fail to meet our needs. Indeed, any remedies that equalize income and power will benefit the majority. So let us turn to some truly possible remedies and see whether they meet our requirements.

Proposal Five: Various Group Remedies

Wherever opportunity is limited, any wholly individual remedies are no more than "quick fixes" with temporary effects. In the long run, your chance of getting more opportunity is greater as part of a group. But if we rule out the revolutionary option, what remains? Again, what follows is merely schematic. It would be impossible to encompass all remaining scenarios within the scope of this book.

Two group remedies to *exclusion* are truly possible. One is legislation and other group action that would make discrimination against people like you more difficult. To bring this about requires banding together with others who suffer discrimination, joining forces across ethnic, class, gender, and regional boundaries where necessary. It also means electing sympathetic legislators to push for changes. If successful, the result will be a more assimilated, less discriminatory society.

A second remedy is to mobilize within your own group—whether class, ethnic, religious, or regional—to increase community organization. This has the effect of discriminating in your own favour to counter the discrimination against you. Many Canadian groups use this tactic today, notably class-based political parties, unions, lobbies, and associations.

Group mobilization carries the risks of increasing intergroup conflict without eliminating the underlying conditions that gave rise to it. By pitting one group against another—women against men, blacks against whites, or gays against heterosexuals—this tactic increases the risk of misunderstanding and injustice. A society torn by such disputes is no further ahead than a society marked by smouldering resentment. Events in the Balkans, Somalia, Israel, Northern Ireland, and the former Soviet Union show that civil war is considerably worse than smouldering resentment.

Group mobilization also narrows people's field of vision. People become less available for solving problems that cut across groups: international problems of peace and scarcity, national problems of cultural unity and political or economic independence, and problems of class and gender inequality, among others. The first solution—a frontal group assault on privilege—is the only one that will benefit everyone in the long run.

Social *disability* can be reduced by education and re-education; the schools and mass media are key vehicles for such a change. As already noted, the strengthening of individual identities is best done collectively, since nothing changes people's minds more readily than the evidence that change is possible.

The benefits of slow, incremental individual change are much more limited (Kanter, 1977). For example, a sole woman given the opportunity to "model" executive abilities in a large organization is under unusual pressures to succeed "on behalf of all women" and is judged by criteria quite unlike those applied to men. Confusion will arise between the unique characteristics of the individual and the "type" she represents. For this reason, we really do not learn what excluded groups can do until we see large numbers of group members performing in common, emotionally neutral situations. Achieving this requires legislation that ensures inclusion for as many representatives of a social "type" as may seek it. Laws against discrimination not only break down traditional patterns of exclusion, they also reduce disability and decoupling. Again, governments will not pass and enforce such laws without group mobilization.

Groups can remedy *decoupling* by building bridges to other groups: for example, to other racial, ethnic, regional, and occupational groups. Typically, increased communication among the leaders of these groups is the key to success. But everyone can play a part in this process, by participating in broadly based activities and organizations.

Finally, material *scarcity* can be reduced if more of what people want and need is produced. This requires an international commitment to economic growth and redistribution and the breaking up of monopolies that restrict productivity as well as sharing.

These solutions to dissatisfaction are group remedies, not individual remedies. All are truly possible. However, they do not systematically address the question of how people might link their own advancement with that of society as a whole. C. Wright Mills maintained that personal lives are linked with public issues; another way of putting it is that personal troubles are shared and socially structured. This implies that both personal and social problems must be solved at the same time. We now turn to an examination of remedies that attempt such a solution.

Linking Individual and Group Remedies

Both Merton and Westhues discuss why gaps arise between what people want and what they get. But each theory ultimately fails. First, each assumes that all people seek a single goal; we saw in Chapter One that no such goal exists. Second, each theory implies a specious equivalence among varieties of adaptation. Third, neither theory can show the link between individual and group remedies to societal problems.

Let us take a different approach, which assumes that satisfaction is the goal that people want to attain. As we have seen, satisfaction is attainable individually or collectively, and in many life domains. All people seek satisfaction, but people do not all seek the same satisfactions, or seek satisfaction in the same ways.

Throughout the book we have discovered gaps between what people want and what they get. These gaps cause dissatisfaction, which people attempt to reduce by lowering their expectations or increasing their achievements, or both.

In some cases accommodation is almost inevitable. No alternative is truly possible, at least at present. For example, we have no means of prolonging human life indefinitely. It would be foolish to remain perpetually dissatisfied over this state of affairs, however distressing the death of a loved one may be. Life must go on. So here, reducing dissatisfaction through accommodation is justified, sensible, and moral.

In other cases, non-accommodating solutions are truly possible. Imagine that your loved one is going to die because you cannot afford costly nursing care and medical treatment. Such care and treatment might prolong life for another 10, 20, or 30 years; moreover, other people's lives are being prolonged by such a treatment. Should you accomodate to your situation, in order to reduce your dissatisfaction? If another remedy to the problem is truly possible, you should not. Instead, you should pursue both individual and group strategies for changing the situation.

Individual and group strategies may be linked: in some circumstances, increasing your satisfaction harms no one else and may even help others. Your enjoyment of a sunny day is not diminished if I enjoy it, too. Our satisfactions are perfectly compatible. Your opportunity to find satisfaction as a composer of music is not threatened by my desire to write lyrics: in fact, we can make songs together. In this case, our satisfaction is complementary or symbiotic. In some circumstances, then, individual remedies to the gap between wants and achievements are unrelated; in others, they are interdependent. We maximize them by co-operating.

But in a great many cases, one person's satisfaction depends on another's dissatisfaction, a situation that is sometimes called a *zero-sum game*. For every winner there is at least one loser. This fact leads to what Calabresi (1976) calls "tragic choices"—situations in which no remedy is equally satisfying for everyone, whatever choice is made. Examples of this are the allocation of scarce medical technology such as kidney dialysis machines among equally needy patients and the drafting of soldiers into a wartime army. Some people will live, others will die as a result.

Since creating a winner means also creating a loser, people engaged in making tragic choices are always searching for new, more acceptable principles of allocation. No principle can succeed in appearing just for long. Yet certain principles are more obviously unjust than others. Almost everyone would agree that it is unjust to allocate scarce life-prolonging machines and medicine, or exempt young people from the military draft, on the basis of income. Doing so would amount to a market in lives: the rich live, the poor die.

Another Typology

Obviously we want to find remedies that give the most people the most satisfaction possible, even in zero-sum situations. But can it be done? Imagine the following scenario. You are faced with a dissatisfying gap between what you want and what you are getting. Closing that gap is truly possible. Many strategies for closing the gap, both individual and group, are available. Further, imagine that your actions will diminish other people's well-being. To increase your own well-being, you may have to hurt someone else. To avoid doing so requires the co-operative search for a solution.

Exhibit 8.3 displays the logically possible remedies, following Merton's format presented in Exhibit 8.1. But, unlike Merton, we are concerned with possible ways of combining individual and group well-being.

Exhibit 8.3
Adaptations to a gap between what you want and what you get

	Your strategy furthers ...	
Adaptation	**Individual well-being**	**Collective well-being**
Co-operate	+	+
Sacrifice	–	+
Self-indulge	+	–
Accommodate (or Mythologize)	–	–

As Exhibit 8.3 shows, you may decide to *accommodate*—to do nothing more about your dissatisfaction than simply lower your aspirations and become resigned to wanting what you have.

Or you may *mythologize*—lower your aspirations and urge others to lower theirs, and then invent elaborate theories to prove that the current situation is the best possible. Mythologizers deny the importance of well-being in principle, saying that "suffering is good for people." They argue against protest with the argument that "people don't know when they are really well off." And they distract people's attention from their problems, with paradoxes, telling them, "Less is really more," "Bad is really good," "The universe is inside you," or "Life is only a dream, reality lies elsewhere."

A third remedy is to pursue personal goals at the expense of others—that is, to *self-indulge*. This brings more individual satisfaction, but at the possible expense of group satisfaction. The number of winners and losers is the same as before, but now you are a winner and someone else is a loser: the original problem of unequal satisfaction—whether due to scarcity or inequality—goes unchallenged. Someone else will have to challenge this situation and change it, or others will continue to suffer from it.

In fact, we can distinguish two kinds of self-indulgence, which we might call "parasitic" and "productive." Parasitic self-indulgence merely takes what you have and gives it to me. No more of any "good" is created in this way; the range of inequality may even widen. Productive self-indulgence uses the system to produce more for me, while leaving you with what you already have; here too, the range of inequality may widen. By either means, the purpose of self-indulgence is self-advancement, possibly at the expense of others.

Another remedy, the exact opposite of self-indulgence, is *sacrifice*. Here, a person makes no effort to maximize his or her own well-being and every effort to maximize group well-being. And here too we can distinguish between "productive" and "unproductive" types of behaviour. Unproductive sacrifice gives you some of what I have, reducing the inequality between us; but again nothing more is created. Productive sacrifice uses the system to produce more than before, and to distribute the new product so as to reduce the inequality between us.

A final adaptation might be called *co-operation*. This requires people to combine individual and group strategies in pursuit of both individual and group goals. They seek greater satisfaction without hurting anyone else and, if possible, while helping someone else.

An example may illustrate how this works. Recall from Chapter Six that the parents of young children—especially mothers—are very short of free time. Imagine that in the Jones family, Mr. Jones (Gord) is dissatisfied because he has only three hours a day to relax. Mrs. Jones (Sheila) is also dissatisfied; she has only one hour a day to relax. But let's focus for a moment on Gord: he wants to close the gap between what he has (three hours of free time a day) and what he wants (more!).

He can accommodate by simply shutting his eyes to the situation: by waiting for his children to grow up and leave home. Or he can mythologize about the nobility of hard work and how, in days to come, he will be rewarded for his efforts on his children's behalf. He may include Sheila in his mythology, telling her that she is a "real woman." In both these scenarios, the inequality stands still: Gord keeps his three hours of rest and Sheila has her one hour.

On the other hand, Gord may decide to close the satisfaction gap by exploiting his wife. One easy method is to pass on a few of his chores, so that he now has four hours of rest a day and she has none. This is the "unproductive" form of exploitation. Or Gord may figure out a way of reducing the household workload through better planning so that he has two more hours of rest a day. Now he has five hours of rest and Sheila still has one. As a result, the domestic inequality ratio has widened to 5-to-1 from an original 3-to-1. This is what we mean by productive exploitation. It is "productive" in the sense that it has improved the domestic system (by increasing free time), but "exploitation" in the sense that it has increased inequality.

Gord may also reduce his own dissatisfaction by reducing the household workload through better planning, and pass on some of the benefit to Sheila. Imagine that his plan has freed up two hours a day. If he takes one free hour and Sheila takes the other, each will have gained more rest and the domestic inequality ratio will also have narrowed to 2-to-1 from an original 3-to-1. This co-operative adaptation does not produce equality, but it does increase the well-being of both spouses—that is, the group well-being.

Finally, Gord may choose to sacrifice his own immediate well-being in the interests of domestic equality and, thereby, group well-being. He may value this on principle or because he believes that it will increase harmony and marital satisfaction. Whatever the reason, he may sacrifice unproductively (giving up one free hour a day to Sheila) or productively (keeping his three hours and "finding" two more for Sheila through better planning). Both strategies equalize free time in the household.

As we can see in this example, sacrifice and co-operation are potentially system-changing adaptations, while accommodation, mythologizing, and exploitation are system-preserving ones. System-changing adaptations require attention to group well-being and, often, group action. Thus, the most effective individual strategies are linked to group strategies, and they are bound to change the system of inequality in society or in a household.

To use these strategies we must be alert to the ways in which individual problems and group problems are related. We must be aware of what is truly possible, and seek satisfaction in that realm; on the other hand, we can allow ourselves to feel satisfied with accommodation when faced with the truly impossible. If given the opportunity to make truly possible changes, we are right to be satisfied if we have actively tried to make them through co-operation or sacrifice—"fought the good fight." By this scheme of thinking, exploitation never justifies our feelings of satisfaction, since it preserves and even worsens the problem that other people are facing.

If you have "fought the good fight" and failed, you are not to blame for failing to achieve the truly possible, nor for giving in to existing circumstances. More likely than not, you have enjoyed the fight; you may want to fight on.

Leaving aside ethical considerations, why should people follow this course of action? Is there any evidence that behaving in a co-operative, fair, and egalitarian way will improve your own life, as well as other people's? This is a large and complicated question. We can go part of the way toward answering it by focussing on domestic relations, and asking "Does research show that egalitarian marriages are more satisfying than inegalitarian marriages?" There is no reason to think that what applies in domestic relations may also not apply in a wide variety of other social groups and relationships.

Is Equality Satisfying?

The evidence that was examined in Chapter Six showed that, if women are to achieve a balance between paid work and family life, families will need to find better, fairer ways of integrating their members' interests and schedules. But "democracy, individualism and meritocracy, the values most closely identified with two centuries of Western history, are conspicuous by their absence from the family" (Degler, 1980, p. 471). No less than most workplaces and schools, most families are a long way from equality.

At all stages of the life cycle, husbands spend more time, on average, doing paid work than their wives. Within the home, wives do more hours of housework and child care than their husbands, even when they have a heavy commitment to paid work outside the home. The husbands of women who are employed full-time and have small children still do little housework (Harvey, Marshall, & Frederick, 1991). In fact, husbands *decrease* their average domestic work from ten to nine hours per week with the arrival of the first child. Their contribution to domestic work may increase with the passage of time, but never to the original ten hours (Lupri, 1991a, p. 246). And although the difference in the amount of time husbands and wives spend on domestic work decreases with the amount of paid employment done by the wife, (Leslie & Anderson, 1988), mothers employed full-time still work longer hours than husbands or any other kinds of wives.

Generally, husbands do as much of the domestic work as they believe they should do. This congruence between their beliefs and their behaviours seems to satisfy husbands, and some wives, with their marriages (Perry-Jenkins & Crouter, 1990). But women are almost twice as likely as men to feel overworked by household chores. Indeed, employed people of either sex who do most of the household work generally feel dissatisfied with their family life (Broman, 1988a). In the rare cases where husbands perform most of the household chores, they too are less satisfied than average with their family lives.

It does not come as a surprise, then, that about one in two married people report household conflicts over job demand, the disciplining of children, and the demands of the other spouse's job (Casale & Lerman, 1986, p. 97).

Some solutions to this problem of inequality and overwork are purely economic. One is to provide more goods and services directly to the families of women who work outside the home: for example, more, better, and cheaper day care. Another is to pay women higher wages, enabling them to purchase the services they need. Another proposal involves paying for housework. Most unpaid family work is done by married women aged 25 and over; in 1987, these women made up 36 percent of the unpaid family work force (Duchesne, 1990). It is difficult to understand why people who care for dependants at home—whether children, the physically infirm, or the very old—should not be paid for their trouble, when no one questions the right of people who work in institutions, tending other people's family members, to be paid.

Reducing the amount of housework that women do by lowering housekeeping standards might ease the pressure of daily family life. When this strategy is attempted, the results do not cause much unhappiness among the families surveyed (Malarkey, Bootsma, & Vyn, 1990). Still, many couples regret neglecting housework to meet the demands of paid work.

Other proposals include improving public transportation to make working women's travel easier and faster; loosening zoning restrictions so that shopping and child care are closer to people's homes; and allowing round-the-clock shopping for goods and services, to give working women more opportunity to perform their household chores when they find it most convenient (Michelson, 1985).

Employers have a contribution to make, too. They will have to increase flextime and permit more work to be done in the home to allow paid work and work-related travel to mesh more easily with domestic duties. It is up to them to ease the burdens of relocation by providing child-care and real-estate arrangements, relocation counselling, job-search assistance for accompanying spouses, and orientation to the new community. Otherwise, partners in two-career families will resist job transfers that require relocation—the kind of transfers long regarded as central to career development.

In most cases, however, the easiest and cheapest solution will be for spouses to redistribute their duties within the household. In particular, fathers will have to increase their involvement in child care and housework, and spend less of their mental energy on paid work and leisure. But none of this will happen without a change in the ideology that parenting is a woman's responsibility. Child raising must be seen as a collective responsibility, not a woman's problem. Changing this view may even improve the quality of the care that children receive from their families.

Assuming that equality between spouses is desirable, is it possible? Is it a true solution to the problem, in the sense that it provides everyone with long-term individual, as well as collective, rewards? Does domestic equality pay off for husbands as well as wives?

The evidence on this question is mixed. Some research suggests that equality contributes little to the satisfaction of married people. For example, Martin (1985) argues that reward level, not equality or equity (fairness, even if not strict equality), affects marital satisfaction most—for couples with both modern and traditional orientations to marriage. Both kinds of couple want to avoid the "bookkeeping" involved in making equity and equality comparisons. They pay more attention to what they are getting out of the relationship in absolute terms. Apparently, "modern" couples are even more demanding than "traditional" ones in their emphasis on such rewards.

Where both partners are closely matched in education, pay, and a high degree of career commitment, marital satisfaction may even suffer from an equal sharing of tasks (Nicola & Hawkes, 1986). This makes good sense if the basis for satisfaction is reward level, not equality, as Martin (1985) has argued. Both spouses are going to want someone else to do the housework: they're too busy! So, at least in these kinds of families, a differentiation of duties (and perhaps inequality) may be needed.

On the other hand, Ray (1990) finds that dual-career couples with non-traditional sex-role attitudes are *more* satisfied with their marriages than other couples, and that equality and reciprocity in the relationship increase marital satisfaction. The most satisfied couples tend to give and take support, become involved in each other's careers, are equally committed to the relationship, and share decision making.

Vanyperen and Buunk (1990) report that equity increases satisfaction with intimate relations and reflects a general sharing of commitment to the relationship, sociability, and attentiveness. Perceived equity in the distribution of rewards appears to make the single largest contribution to a couple's commitment to a relationship (Sabatelli, & Cecil-Pigo, 1985). Two studies conducted in Holland find that people who feel deprived of rewards in comparison to their spouses become dissatisfied with the relationship. Equality is more satisfying than disadvantage or even advantage (although husbands are more comfortable feeling advantaged than wives) (Buunk & Vanyperen, 1989).

Companionship and role sharing improve the marriages of Australian couples (Kotler, 1985). Egalitarian spousal roles increase the marital satisfaction of Puerto Rican wives (Rogler & Procidano, 1989). Both wives and husbands in Israel are more satisfied in marriages where the wife has an equal say in the family decision making (Katz & Briger, 1988). Wives in these families tend to have more than average education, lower fertility, and paid employment.

In Austria, Kirchler, de Longis, and Lehman (1989) asked couples to make entries in a diary six times a day for four weeks, recording what they were doing and with whom, and how they felt. Happy couples spent more time together at home and during recreation times. The spouse's presence was particularly satisfying to men. More often than other couples, happy couples achieved a balance of power between spouses and were able to accurately perceive the other spouse's state of mind.

Research conducted in a long list of countries agrees that spousal equality seems to produce satisfaction. The same is true among American lesbian couples. Peplau, Padesky, and Hamilton (1982) report that equality in power and involvement increases satisfaction with a relationship—and that satisfaction is more strongly related to the equality of the relationship than to individual attitudes or background characteristics of the partners.

Other research shows that when there is a power balance in a relationship, the partners are not only more satisfied, but they also use fewer strategies to increase their power and have their own way (Aida & Falbo, 1991).

In her major work *The Second Shift*, Hochschild (1989) explains the relationship between equality and satisfaction at home thoroughly and eloquently. She concludes her book with the following statement:

> The happiest two-job marriages I saw were between men and women who did not load the former role of the housewife-mother onto the woman, and did not devalue it as one would a bygone "peasant" way of life. They shared that role between them. What couples called "good communication" often meant that they were good at saying thanks for one tiny form or another of taking care of the family.... Up until now, the woman married to the "new man" has been one of the lucky few. But as government and society shape a new gender strategy, as the young learn from example, many more women and men will be able to enjoy the leisurely bodily rhythms and freer laughter that arise when family life is family life and not a second shift. (p. 270)

Equality and equity pay off for *both* spouses, in satisfaction and commitment. Inequality and unfairness produce conflict, stress, and depression.

It may be possible to generalize these findings to other kinds of groups. For example, a study of undergraduates in small work groups (Wall & Nolan, 1987) finds less conflict and more satisfaction when tasks are shared equitably. Another study (Smith, Diener, & Garonzik, 1990), finds that undergraduates are particularly likely to envy an advantaged person when they are dissatisfied or have experienced failure in another domain. If this pattern applies to marriages as well, it suggests that the less powerful partner will likely grow more envious and resentful as the other spouse becomes more successful outside marriage —for example, at work.

Here again, the individual solution achieves a symbiosis with the group solution. Behaving in a fair and co-operative way promises to improve your own satisfaction as well as others'. All people—husbands as well as wives, bosses as well as workers—ought to seek equality in their relationships, *in their own best interests*.

CONCLUSION

As you may have noticed, this book has been about one of social science's classic concerns: the relationship between consciousness and social structure. I have tried to discuss this complicated issue in relatively simple terms. Accordingly, I have translated issues of consciousness—values, perceptions, aspirations, and expectations, among others —into questions of "what you want," and translated issues of social structure—limits on your opportunity to choose among desired alternatives—into questions of "what you get."

On the surface, therefore, the book has been about the relationship between what you want and what you get. We have noted that most people at most ages get what they want and want what they get. Two alternative explanations of this fit between consciousness and social structure have been examined. One is the explanation offered by liberal ideology, which argues that people generally get what they want if they approach the matter correctly. The other, a product of the "sociological imagination," argues that people are more likely to bring their desires into conformity with what is possible, while preserving the *illusion* of choice. And we have noted that, in fact, most people do both. As well, they consider and often carry through strategies for closing the gap, when a gap exists.

In a modern society, people want choice and the knowledge that they have choices to make. Life without choice is deadening. People who think that they have no choices fail to make choices when they are truly available, or they make bad choices. In fact, we all have some choices to make in life, and so we must practise choosing them well. This book has urged you to choose wisely, carefully, and with awareness.

This is not to argue that your choice is unlimited; in fact, it argues the opposite. If choice were unlimited, wrong choices would have no important consequences: you could always make a right choice that remedied the previous wrong one. But in fact, your present choices are limited by past choices as well as by the choices that other people are making, and by factors such as the class structure which are not, in any real sense, chosen by most of us at all.

Without the possibility of choice, however limited, morality has no meaning. Morality means taking responsibility for your actions. People are not always responsible for the direction that their life has taken, for they are not always in control. When they *are* in control, they may not be aware of choosing, or their range of choices may be so small as to offer no real choice at all. Still, if we want to preserve the framework of a moral society we must increase people's opportunity to choose as freely and wisely as they possibly can, and hold them responsible for their choices.

All choice is limited: we typically act to satisfy, not optimize, our desires. No other kind of action makes sense. Yet even well-informed people differ in what they believe to be possible. This book has not tried to make you set your sights lower, to get you to make the easiest or most popular choices. Rather, it has aimed at making you aware of your choosing and of the limits placed on your choosing, and to make you ask whether our society could be better—freer, fairer, or more moral—than it is today.

In Chapter One, we learned that a Real Paradise has two elements: moral sensibility and a knowledge of the possible. Moral sensibility demands an awareness of what a "worthwhile life" and a "good society" might look like. Few people besides philosophers are encouraged to think about these questions; many believe that they are non-scientific and therefore merely speculative concerns. Yet building a good society and a worthwhile life means planning, by both individuals and groups. It means conceiving a goal—a reason for our lives. Whether our desired goal should be "the greatest satisfaction for the greatest number" or something else is beyond the scope of this book. But the question should not be dismissed from consideration simply because it challenges our usual tools of analysis.

"Good information" is another thing that we can do something about. We are well aquainted with the forces that limit the information that people have at their disposal. And we know that limited information exacts a price. According to the multiple discrepancies theory (discussed in Chapter One), people with limited information set low goals for themselves because they make modest comparisons—meaning, comparisons with others like themselves. They judge what is possible from their own history and the life histories of others just like them.

More and better information about the possibility of other lives leads to behavioural change that can make people's desires a reality. Though people often adjust their desires downwards, they do so ever less often as they are exposed to a wider variety of alternatives. As we have seen, people—especially, well-educated people—want more equality in their marriages and more say in their jobs: when they don't get these changes, they become dissatisfied. This dissatisfaction can lead to covert strategies of rebellion, overt actions such as divorce, and psychiatric symptoms such as burnout and depression. The results are harmful to every person, every relationship, and every organization.

Economic recessions and periods of high unemployment force people to accept limits on their choice that are unecessary in better economic times, such as the 1950s and 1960s. Yet there are limits to how far people can adjust their desires downward, even today. We can no longer suppose that people will remain in ignorance of the extremes of inequality, much less accept them willingly. So we owe it to ourselves to understand our lives—the choices that we are making and the chances we have for improving our situation. We also need to understand the lives of people around us. We *all* need to seek better information about what is truly possible.

In short, we need to (1) stay aware of problems and their possible solution; (2) make other people—especially those close to us— more aware; and (3) join other people in seeking solutions to the problems that confront many of us. Grass-roots social movements have played an ever greater part in changing our society; they promise to be even more important in Canada's future. But we must not lose sight of the critical role that schools and the mass media could play, if only they would.

In this context, sociology has an important job to do. Sociology is the study of the possible, since it is the study of what already is: the lives that people are already living. We are less easily tricked into downward accommodation or wrong decisions when we know that alternatives are possible, even if they are difficult and require long-term thinking and group co-operation.

In closing, then, this book carries no simple message. It encourages you to question your life more systematically, with information and awareness. Above all, recognize that as human beings we all make choices, and that all our choices are constrained. This play of choices and chances will determine your future and the future of us all.

References

ACKERMAN, N., & PAOLUCCI, B. (1983). Objective and subjective income adequacy: Their relationships to perceived life quality measures. *Social Indicators Research, 12*(1), 25–48.

ADAMS, O., & NAGNUR, D. (1989, Summer) Marrying and divorcing: A status report for Canada. *Canadian Social Trends*, pp. 24–27.

ADORNO, T.W., FRENKEL-BRUNSWIK, E., LEVINSON, D.J., & SANFORD, R.N. (1969). *The authoritarian personality*. New York: W.W. Norton.

AGOCS, C., & BOYD, M. (1993). The Canadian ethnic mosaic recast: Theory, research and policy for the 1990s. In J. Curtis, E. Grabb, & N. Guppy (Eds.), *Social inequality in Canada* (2nd ed.). Scarborough, ON: Prentice-Hall.

AIDA, Y., & FALBO, T. (1991). Relationships between marital satisfaction, resources, and power strategies. *Sex Roles, 24*(1–2), 43–56.

AKYEAMPONG, E.B. (1987, Autumn). Involuntary part-time employment in Canada, 1975–1986. *Canadian Social Trends*, pp. 26–29.

ALBRECHT, D.E., & GEERTSEN, H.R. (1982). Population growth in rural communities: Residents' perceptions of its consequences. *Journal of the Community Development Society, 13*(2), 75–90.

ALEXANDER, J. (1984). The organizational foundations of nursing roles: An empirical assessment. *Social Science and Medicine, 18*(12), 1045–52.

ALLEN, A., & THOMPSON, T. (1984). Agreement, understanding, realization, and feeling understood as predictors of communicative satisfaction in marital dynamics. *Journal of Marriage and the Family, 46*(4), 915–21.

ALLEN, L.R. (1990). Benefits of leisure attributes to community satisfaction. *Journal of Leisure Research, 22*(2), 183–96.

ALSPACH, S. (1982). Women's sex role attitudes and life satisfaction. *Sociological Focus, 15*(3), 279–87.

ALTROCCHI, J. (1988). Happy traditional and companionate marriages. *Social Casework, 69*(7), 434–42.

ALVAREZ, W.F. (1985). The meaning of maternal employment for mothers and their perceptions of their three-year-old children. *Child Development, 56*(2), 350–60.

AMARO, H., RUSSO, N.F., & JOHNSON, J. (1987). Family and work predictors of psychological well-being among Hispanic women professionals. *Psychology of Women Quarterly, 11*(4), 505–21.

AMATO, P.R. (1988). Parental divorce and attitudes toward marriage and family life. *Journal of Marriage and the Family*, 50(2), 453–61.

AMATO, P.R., & BOOTH, A. (1991). Consequences of parental divorce and marital unhappiness for adult well-being. *Social Forces*, 69(3), 895–914.

AMBERT, A.-M. (1980). *Divorce in Canada*. Toronto: Academic Press.

———. (1988). *Ex-spouses and new spouses*. Greenwich, CT: JAI Press.

———. (1992). *The effect of children on parents*. New York: Haworth Press.

AMOS, O.M., Jr., HITT, M.A., & WARNER, L. (1982). Life satisfaction and regional development: A case study of Oklahoma. *Social Indicators Research*, *11*(3), 319–31.

ANAND, U., & SOHAL, T.S. (1983). Measuring job satisfaction of scientists in an ICAR Institute. *Journal of Social and Economic Studies*, *11*(1-2), 157–64.

ANDERSON, A.B., & FRIDERES, J.S. (1981). *Ethnicity in Canada: Theoretical perspectives*. Toronto: Butterworths.

ANISEF, P. (1985). *Accessibility to postsecondary education in Canada: A review of the literature*. Ottawa: Department of the Secretary of State.

ANISEF, P., ASHBURY, F., & TURRITTIN, A. (1992). Differential effects of university and community college education on occupational status attainment in Ontario. *Canadian Journal of Sociology*, *17*(1), 69–84.

ANISEF, P., PAASCHE, J.G., & TURRITTIN, A.H. (1980). *Is the die cast? Educational achievements and work destinations of Ontario youth*. Toronto: Ontario Ministry of Colleges and Universities.

ARGYLE, M. (1992). *The social psychology of everyday life*. London: Routledge.

ARIÈS, P. (1962). *Centuries of childhood: A social history of family life*. New York: Vintage.

ARNOTI, B. (1987). Low educational attainment in Canada, 1975–1985. *Canadian Social Trends*, Spring, pp. 28–32.

ASPA (AMERICAN SOCIETY FOR PERSONNEL ADMINISTRATION). (1984). *Work in the 21st century: An anthology of writings on the changing world of work*. Alexandria, VA: ASPA.

ATCHLEY, R.C. (1982, November). Retirement: Leaving the world of work. *Annals of the American Academy of Political and Social Science*, *464*, 120–31.

ATKINSON, T.H. (1979). *Trends in life satisfaction among Canadians, 1968–1977* (Occasional Paper No. 7). Montreal: Institute for Research on Public Policy.

———. (1980). Public perceptions on the quality of life. In Statistics Canada, *Perspectives Canada III* (Catalogue No. 11-511E, pp. 275–92). Ottawa: Supply & Services.

ATKINSON, T.H., & MURRAY, M.A. (1982). *Values, domains and the perceived quality of life: Canada and the United States*. Toronto: York University, Institute for Behavioural Research.

ATKINSON, T. (1983a). Changing attitudes toward work in Canada. *Canadian Business Review, 10*(1), 39–44.

———. (1983b). Differences between male and female attitudes toward work. *Canadian Business Review, 10*(2), 47–51.

AUSTIN, D.M., & BABA, Y. (1990). Social determinants of neighbourhood attachment. *Sociological Spectrum, 10*(1), 59–78.

BAER, D.E., & CURTIS, J.E. (1984). French Canadian/English Canadian value differences: National survey findings. *Canadian Journal of Sociology*, 9(4), 405–28.

BAGAROZZI, D.A. (1990). Marital power discrepancies and symptom development in spouses: An empirical investigation. *American Journal of Family Therapy, 18*(1), 51–64.

BAKER, M. (1985). *What will tomorrow bring? A study of the aspirations of adolescent women*. Ottawa: Canadian Advisory Council on the Status of Women.

BALAKRISHNAN, T.R. (1976). Ethnic residential segregation in the metropolitan areas of Canada. *Canadian Journal of Sociology, 1*(4), 481–98.

———. (1982). Changing patterns in ethnic residential segregation in the metropolitan areas of Canada. *Canadian Review of Sociology and Anthropology, 19*(1), 92–110.

BALAKRISHNAN, T.R., RAO, V., LA PIERRE-ADAMCYK, E., & KROTKI, K. (1987). A hazard model analysis of covariates of marriage dissolution in Canada. *Demography, 4*, 395–406.

BALDASSARE, M. (1982). The effects of neighbourhood density and social control on resident satisfaction. *Sociological Quarterly, 23*(1), 95–105.

———. (1986). Residential satisfaction and the community question. *Sociology and Social Research, 70*(2), 139–42.

BALDUS, B., & TRIBE, V. (1978). Perceptions of social inequality among public school children. *Canadian Review of Sociology and Anthropology, 15*(1), 50–60.

BALL, R.E. (1983). Marital status, household structure, and life satisfaction of black women. *Social Problems, 30*(4), 400–409.

———. (1984). Parental role satisfaction of black mothers in the United States. *International Journal of Sociology of the Family, 14*(1), 33–46.

BALL, R.E., & ROBBINS, L. (1986). Marital status and life satisfaction among black Americans. *Journal of Marriage and the Family, 48*(2), 389–94.

BALTZELL, E.D. (1958). *Philadelphia gentlemen: The making of a national upper class*. New York: Free Press.

BANKS, J.A. (1954). *Prosperity and parenthood: A study of family planning among the Victorian middle classes*. London: Routledge & Kegan Paul.

BARDO, J.W., & BARDO, D.J. (1983). A re-examination of subjective components of community satisfaction in a British new town. *Journal of Social Psychology, 120*(1), 35–43.

BARDO, J.W., & DOKMECI, V. (1990). Community satisfaction in two Turkish sub-communities: Further data on the significance of cultural differentiation. *Genetic, Social and General Psychology Monographs, 116*(3), 325–36.

BARDO, J.W., & HUGHEY, J.B. (1984). The structure of community satisfaction in a British and an American community. *Journal of Social Psychology, 124*(2), 151–57.

BARIL, A., & MORI, G. (1991, Spring). Educational attainment of linguistic groups in Canada. *Canadian Social Trends*, pp. 17–18.

BARNES, H.L., SCHUMM, W.R., JURICH, A.P., & BOLLMAN, S.R. (1984). Marital satisfaction: Positive regard versus effective communication as explanatory variables. *Journal of Social Psychology, 123*(1), 71–78.

BARNETT, C.W., & KIMBERLIN, C.L. (1984). Job and career satisfaction in pharmacy. *Journal of Social and Administrative Pharmacy, 2*(1), 1–11.

BARNSLEY, R.H., & THOMPSON, A.H. (1985). Gifted or learning disabled? The age of entering school may make the difference. *Early Childhood Education Journal, 18*(1), 11–14.

———. (1988). Birthdate and success in minor hockey: The key to the NHL. *Canadian Journal of Behavioural Science, 20*, 167–76.

BARR, J.K., & STEINBERG, M.K. (1983). Professional participation in organization decision making: Physicians in HMOs. *Journal of Community Health*, 8(3), 160–73.

BARRACLOUGH, G. (1967). *An introduction to contemporary history*. Harmondsworth: Penguin.

BARUCH, G., BARNETT, R., & RIVERS, C. (1983). *Lifeprints: New patterns of love and work for today's women*. New York: Signet Books.

BAXTER, V. (1990). The differential effects of technology, individual attributes, and perceived job rewards on satisfaction. *Sociological Spectrum, 10*(2), 249–69.

BEAUJOT, R. (1986). Dwindling families: Making the case for policies to sustain or raise the birthrate in Canada. *Policy Options, 7*(7), 3–7.

———. (1987). *The family and demographic change: Economic and cultural interpretations*. London, ON: University of Western Ontario, Department of Sociology.

———. (1991a). The family and demographic change in Canada: Economic and cultural interpretations and solutions. *Journal of Comparative Family Studies, 21*(1), 25–35.

———. (1991b) *Rationales used in marriage and childbearing decisions*. Discussion Paper No. 91–7. Population Studies Centre, University of Western Ontario.

BEAUJOT, R., BASAVARAJAPPA, K.G., & VERMA, R. (1988). *Income of immigrants in Canada: A census data analysis*. Current Demographic Analysis. (Catalogue No. 91–527E). Ottawa: Supply & Services.

BEDEIAN, A.G., BURKE, B.G., & MOFFETT, R.G. (1988). Outcomes of work-family conflict among married male and female professionals. *Journal of Management, 14*(3), 475–91.

BEDEIAN, A.G., MOSSHOLDER, K.W., & ARMENAKIS, A.A. (1983). Role perception-outcome relationships: Moderating effects of situational variables. *Human Relations, 36*(2), 167–83.

BELL, D. (1960). Crime as an American way of life. Reprinted in *The End of Ideology*. New York: Free Press.

———. (1973). *The coming of post-industrial society*. New York: Basic Books.

BELSKY, J. (1985). Exploring individual differences in marital change across the transition to parenthood: The role of violated expectations. *Journal of Marriage and the Family, 47*(4), 1037–44.

BELSKY, J., & PENSKY, E. (1988). Marital change across the transition to parenthood. *Marriage and Family Review, 12*(3–4), 133–56.

BENIN, M.H., & AGOSTINELLI, J. (1988). Husbands' and wives' satisfaction with the division of labor. *Journal of Marriage and the Family, 50*(2), 349–61.

BENIN, M.H., & NIENSTEDT, B.C. (1985). Happiness in single- and dual-earner families: The effects of marital happiness, job satisfaction, and life cycle. *Journal of Marriage and the Family, 47*(4), 975–84.

BEN-SIRA, Z. (1986). The latent functions of welfare and need-satisfaction of the disadvantaged. *Journal of Sociology and Social Welfare, 13*(2), 418–44.

BERCUSON, D.J., BOTHWELL, R., & GRANATSTEIN, J.L. (1984). *The great brain robbery: Canada's universities on the road to ruin*. Toronto: McClelland & Stewart.

BERG, I. (1970). *Education and jobs: The great training robbery*. New York: Praeger.

BERLJAWSKY, A. (1986, Winter). Mortgage rates and the housing market. *Canadian Social Trends*, pp. 30–33.

BERNARD, J. (1973). *The future of marriage*. New York: Bantam Books.

BERRY, R.E., & WILLIAMS, F.L. (1987). Assessing the relationship between quality of life and marital and income satisfaction: A path analysis approach. *Journal of Marriage and the Family*,49(1), 107–16.

BETCHERMAN, G., & MCMULLEN, K. (1986). *Working with technology: A survey of automation in Canada* (Catalogue No. EC 22–133/1986E). Ottawa: Economic Council of Canada.

BHAGAT, R.S., & FORD, D.L., Jr. (1990). Work and non-work issues in the management of occupational careers in the 1990s. *Prevention in Human Services*, 8(1), 99–112.

BIBBY, R.W., & POSTERSKI, D.C. (1985). *The emerging generation: An inside look at Canada's teenagers*. Toronto: Irwin.

BIBBY, R.W., & POSTERSKI, D.J. (1992). *Teen trends: A nation in motion*. Toronto: Stoddart.

BLAU, P.M. (1964). *Exchange and power in social life*. New York: John Wiley.

BLAU, P.M., & DUNCAN, O.D. (1967). *The American occupational structure*. New York: Wiley.

BLAXTER, M. (1990). *Health and Lifestyles*. London: Routledge.

BLEDSTEIN, B.J. (1976). *The culture of professionalism: The middle class and the development of higher education in America*. New York: W.W. Norton.

BLEGEN, M.A., & MUELLER, C.W. (1987). Nurses' job satisfaction: A longitudinal analysis. *Research in Nursing and Health, 10*(4), 227–37.

BLISHEN, B.R., & ATKINSON, T.H. (1982). *Regional and status differences in Canadian values*. Toronto: York University, Institute for Behavioural Research.

BLISHEN, B.R., & MCROBERTS, H.A. (1976). A revised socio-economic index for occupations in Canada. *Canadian Review of Sociology and Anthropology, 13*(1), 71–79.

BLOOD, R.O., & WOLFE, D.M. (1960). *Husbands and wives: The dynamics of married living*. New York: Free Press.

BLOOM, A. (1987). *The closing of the American mind: How higher education has failed democracy and impoverished the souls of today's students*. New York: Basic Books.

BO, Z., & WENXIU, G. (1992). Sexuality in urban China. *Australian Journal of Chinese Affairs, 28*, July, 1–20.

BOCK, E.W., & RADELET, M.L. (1988). The marital integration of religious independents: A reevaluation of its significance. *Review of Religious Research, 29*(3), 228–41.

BONJEAN, C.M., BROWN, B.J., GRANDJEAN, B.D., & MACKEN, P.O. (1982). Increasing work satisfaction through organizational change: A longitudinal study of nursing educators. *Journal of Applied Behavioral Science, 18*(3), 357–69.

BOOTH, A., & JOHNSON, D. (1988) Premarital cohabitation and marital success. *Journal of Family Issues*, 9(2), 255–72.

BOOTH, A., WHITE, L., & EDWARDS, J. N. (1986). Divorce and marital instability over the life course. *Journal of Family Issues*. 7(4), 421–42.

BOTT, E. (1957). *Family and social network*. London: Tavistock Publications.

BOULDING, K.E. (1981). *Ecodynamics: A new theory of societal evolution*. Beverly Hills, CA: Sage Publications.

BOURDIEU, P. (1977). *Reproduction in education, society, and culture*. Beverly Hills, CA: Sage Publications.

BOUVIER, R. (1991). Education and change for aboriginal people in Canada. In R. Ghosh & D. Ray (Eds.), *Social change and education in Canada* (2nd ed.). Toronto: Harcourt Brace Jovanovich.

BOWEN, G.L. (1982). Social network and the maternal role satisfaction of formerly-married mothers. *Journal of Divorce*, 5(4), 77–85.

BOWEN, H.R. (1977). *Investment in learning: The individual and social value of American higher education*. San Francisco: Jossey-Bass.

BOWLES, S., & GINTIS, H. (1976). *Schooling in capitalist America*. New York: Basic Books.

BOWLING, A. (1990). Associations with life satisfaction among very elderly people living in a deprived part of inner London. *Social Science and Medicine*, *31*(9), 1003–11.

BOYD, M. (1985). Educational and occupational attainments of native-born Canadian men and women. In M. Boyd, J. Goyder, F.E. Jones, H.A. McRoberts, P.C. Pineo, & J. Porter (Eds.), *Ascription and achievement: Studies in mobility and status attainment in Canada* (pp. 229–95). Ottawa: Carleton University Press.

BOYD, M., GOYDER, J., JONES, F.E., MCROBERTS, H.A., PINEO, P.C., & PORTER, J. (Eds.). (1985). *Ascription and achievement: Studies in mobility and status attainment in Canada*. Ottawa: Carleton University Press.

BOYD, M., MULVIHILL, M.A., & MYLES, J. (1991). Gender, power and postindustrialism. *Canadian Review of Sociology and Anthropology*, *28*(4), pp. 407–29.

BOYD, M. & PRYOR, E. (1990). Young adults living in their parents' homes. In C. McKie & K. Thompson (Eds.), *Canadian social trends*. Toronto: Thomson Educational Publishing.

BRADBURN, N.M., & CAPLOVITZ, D. (1965). *Reports on happiness: A pilot study of behavior related to mental health*. National Opinion Research Center Monograph in Social Research. Chicago: Aldine.

BRETON, R. (1964). Institutional completeness of ethnic communities. *American Journal of Sociology*, *20*(2), 193–205.

BRETON, R., ISAJIW, W., KALBACH, W., & REITZ, J. (1990). *Ethnic identity and equality: Varieties of experience in a Canadian city*. Toronto: University of Toronto Press.

BRINKERHOFF, M.B., GRANDIN, E., & LUPRI, E. (1992). Religious involvement and spousal violence: The Canadian case. *Journal for the Scientific Study of Religion*, *31*(1), 15–31.

BROD, R.L., MAY, P.A., & STEWART, T.J. (1982). Recruitment and retention of federal physicians on the Navajo reservation. *Social Science Journal*, *19*(4), 47–66.

BROMAN, C.L. (1988a). Household work and family life satisfaction of blacks. *Journal of Marriage and the Family*, 50(3), 743–48.

———. (1988b). Satisfaction among blacks: The significance of marriage and parenthood. *Journal of Marriage and the Family*, 50(1), 45–51.

BROOK, J.A., & BROOK, R.J. (1989). Exploring the meaning of work and nonwork. *Journal of Organizational Behavior*, *10*(2), 169–78.

BROOKINGS, J.B., BOLTON, B., BROWN, C.E., & MCEVOY, A. (1985). Self-reported job burnout among female human service professionals. *Journal of Occupational Behaviour*, 6(2), 143–50.

BROWN, R.B., GEERTSEN, H.R., & KRANNICH, R.S. (1989). Community satisfaction and social integration in a boomtown: A longitudinal analysis. *Rural Sociology*, *54*(4), 568–86.

BROWN, W., & ORLANDO, D. (1988). Enhancing life satisfaction for older adults. *Journal of Applied Sociology*, *5*, 73–87.

BRUSH, D.H., MOCH, M.K., & POOYAN, A. (1987). Individual demographic differences and job satisfaction. *Journal of Occupational Behaviour*, 8(2), 139–55.

BRYM, R., & FOX, B. (1989). *From culture to power: The sociology of English Canada*. Toronto: Oxford University Press.

BUFFUM, W.E., & RITVO, R.A. (1984). Work autonomy and the community mental health professional: Guidelines for management. *Administration in Social Work*, 8(4), 39–54.

BUGAIGHIS, M.A., SCHUMM, W.R., BOLLMAN, S.R., & JURICH, A.P. (1983). Locus of control and marital satisfaction. *Journal of Psychology*, *114*(2), 275–79.

BURBACH, H.J., CNAAN, R.A., & BABBITT, C.E. (1986). Organizational predictors of college satisfaction and academic achievement among females. *Sociological Viewpoints*, *2*(1), 31–38.

BURCH, T.K. (1985). *Family history survey: Preliminary findings* (Statistics Canada, Catalogue No. 99-955). Ottawa: Supply & Services.

BURCH, T.K., & MADAN, A.K. (1986). *Union formation and dissolution in Canada: Results from the 1984 Family History Survey* (Statistics Canada, Catalogue No. 99-963). Ottawa: Supply & Services.

BURCH, T.K., & MCDOUGALL, J. (1991). Kinship in Canada: An overview with preliminary findings from the 1990 General Social Survey. Discussion Paper No. 91-11. Population Studies Centre, University of Western Ontario, London (Ontario).

BURKE, M.A. (1990). Average expenditure of urban Canadians. In C. McKie and K. Thompson (Eds.), *Canadian social trends*. Toronto: Thomson Educational Publishing.

BURSTEIN, M., TIENHAARA, N., HEWSON, P., & WARRENDER, B. (1975). *Canadian work values: Findings of a work ethic survey and a job satisfaction survey* (Catalogue No. MP 33-6/1975). Ottawa: Department of Manpower & Immigration.

BURT, R.S. (1987). A note on strangers, friends and happiness. *Social Networks*, 9(4), 311–32.

BUTLER, B.B. (1990). Job satisfaction: Management's continuing challenge. *Social Work*, *35*(2), 112–17.

BUUNK, B.P., & VANYPEREN, N.W. (1989). Social comparisons, equality, and relationship satisfaction: Gender differences over a ten-year period. *Social Justice Research*, *3*(2), 157–80.

CALABRESI, G. (1976). *Tragic choices*. New York: W.W. Norton.

CALLAN, V.J. (1986). Single women, voluntary childlessness and perceptions about life and marriage. *Journal of Biosocial Science*, *18*(4), 479–87.

CAMPBELL, A. (1980). *The sense of well-being in America: Recent patterns and trends*. New York: McGraw-Hill.

CAMPBELL, A., CONVERSE, P.E., & ROGERS, W.R. (1976). *The quality of American life: perceptions, evaluations and satisfactions*. New York: Russell Sage Foundation.

CANADA. (1976). Department of the Secretary of State. Some characteristics of post-secondary students in Canada. Ottawa: Supply & Services.

———. (1984). *Consultation Paper: Training* (Catalogue No. MP 43-159/1984). Ottawa: Supply & Services.

CANTRIL, H. (1965). *The pattern of human concerns*. New Brunswick, NJ: Rutgers University Press.

CARMEL, S., YAKUBOVICH, I.S., ZWANGER, L., & ZALTZMAN, T. (1988). Nurses' autonomy and job satisfaction. *Social Science and Medicine*, *26*(11), 1103–7.

CARNEGIE FOUNDATION FOR ADVANCEMENT OF TEACHING. (1985). The faculty: Deeply troubled. *Change*, *17*(5), 31–34.

———. (1986). The satisfied faculty. *Change*, *16*(2), 31–34.

CASALE, A.M., & LERMAN, P. (1986). *USA today: Tracking tomorrow's trends*. Kansas City: Andrews, McMeel & Parker.

CASTON, R.J., & BRAITO, R. (1985a). The worker-to-job "fit" hypothesis: Some further evidence. *Work and Occupations*, *12*(3), 269–83.

———. (1985b). A specification issue in job satisfaction research: What happens to job satisfaction models when workers place high value on increasing their satisfaction? *Sociological Perspectives*, *28*(2), 175–97.

CATES, R.M., LLOYD, S.A., & LONG, E. (1988). The role of rewards and fairness in developing premarital relationships. *Journal of Marriage and the Family*, *50*(2), 443–52.

CATES, R.M., LLOYD, S.A., HENTON, J.M., & LARSON, J.H. (1982). Fairness and reward level as predictors of relationship satisfaction. *Social Psychology Quarterly*, *45*(3), 177–81.

CETRON, M.J. (1984). *Jobs of the future*. New York: McGraw-Hill Ryerson.

CHAMBERLAIN, K., & ZIKA, S. (1988). Religiosity, life meaning and wellbeing: Some relationships in a sample of women. *Journal for the Scientific Study of Religion*, *27*(3), 411–20.

CHAMBERS, D.L. (1989). Accommodation and satisfaction: Women and men lawyers and the balance of work and family. *Law and Social Inquiry*, *14*(2), 251–87.

CHEN, P.-C. (1984). China's other revolution: Findings from the One in 1,000 fertility survey. *International Family Planning Perspectives*, *10*(2), 48–57.

CHERLIN, A., & FURSTENBERG, F.F., Jr. (1983). The American family in the year 2000. *Futurist*, *17*(3), 7–14.

CHERNISS, C., & KANE, J.S. (1987). Public sector professionals: Job characteristics, satisfaction, and aspirations for intrinsic fulfillment through work. *Human Relations*, *40*(3), 125–36.

CHILDS, P. (1985). Work and career expectations of insurance company employees and the effect of unionisation. *Sociology*, *19*(1), 125–35.

CHILVERS, M.R. (1987). Improving the quality of work life in the institutional pharmacy setting. *Journal of Social and Administrative Pharmacy*, *4*(2), 70–76.

CLARK, S.D. (1975). The post Second World War Canadian society. *Canadian Review of Sociology and Anthropology*, *12*(1), 25–32.

CLARK, W., & ZSIGMOND, Z. (1981). *Job market reality for postsecondary graduates: Employment outcome by 1978, two years after graduation* (Statistics Canada, Catalogue No. 81-572E). Ottawa: Supply & Services.

CLARK, W., LAING, M., & RECHNITZER, E. (1986). *The class of '82* (Statistics Canada, Catalogue No. S2-168/1986E). Ottawa: Supply & Services.

CLEMENT, W. (1975). *The Canadian corporate elite*. Toronto: McClelland & Stewart.

CLOWARD, R., & OHLIN, L. (1960). *Delinquency and opportunity*. New York: Free Press.

COALE, A.J. (1969). The decline of fertility in Europe from the French Revolution to World War II. In S.J. Behrman, L. Corsa, & R. Freedman (Eds.), *Fertility and family planning* (pp. 3–24). Ann Arbor: University of Michigan Press.

COALE, A.J., & WATKINS, S.C. (Eds.) (1986). *The decline of fertility in Europe*. Princeton, NJ: Princeton University Press.

COCKRUM, J. & WHITE, P. (1985). Influences on the life satisfaction of never-married men and women. *Family Relations*, *34*(4), 551–56.

COLANGELO, N., ROSENTHAL, D.M., & DETTMANN, D.F. (1984). Maternal employment and job satisfaction and their relationship to children's perceptions and behaviors. *Sex Roles*, *10*(9–10), 693–702.

COLE, B.S., HAMMOND, J.A., & TUCKER, K.W. (1989). Foster care practitioners and family preservation services: Service delivery and practice orientation. *Community Alternatives*, *1*(2), 41–51.

COLLINS, R. (1982). *Sociological insight: An introduction to non-obvious sociology*. New York: Oxford University Press.

CONNERLY, C.E., & MARANS, R.W. (1985). Comparing two global measures of perceived neighborhood quality. *Social Indicators Research*, *17*(1), 29–47.

CONWAY, P.G., WILLIAMS, M.S., & GREEN, J.L. (1987). A model of job facet satisfaction. *Journal of Social Work Education*, *23*(1), 48–57.

COOK, C.C. (1988). Components of neighborhood satisfaction: Responses from urban and suburban single-parent women. *Environment and Behavior*, *20*(2), 115–49.

COOPER, C.L., WATTS, J., BALIONI, A.J., Jr., & KELLY, M. (1988). Occupational stress amongst general practice dentists. *Journal of Occupational Psychology*, *61*(2), 163–74.

COOPER, K., CHASSIN, L., BRAVER, S., ZEISS, A., & KHAVARI, K.A. (1986). Correlates of mood and marital satisfaction among dual-worker and single-worker couples. *Social Psychology Quarterly*, *49*(4), 322–29.

COPUR, H. (1990). Academic professionals: A study of conflict and satisfaction in the professoriate. *Human Relations*, *43*(2), 113–27.

CORNISH, E. (1991, September–October). How Americans use their time: An interview with sociologist John P. Robinson. *The Futurist*, *25*(5), 23–27.

COUGHENOUR, C.M., & SWANSON, L.E. (1988). Rewards, values and satisfaction with farm work. *Rural Sociology*, *53*(4), 442–59.

COUGHLIN, P.C. (1990). Premenstrual syndrome: How marital satisfaction and role choice affect symptom severity. *Social Work*, *35*(4), 351–55.

COVERMAN, S. (1989). Role overload, role conflict, and stress: Addressing the consequences of multiple role demands. *Social Forces*, *67*(4), 965–82.

COX, H., & HAMMONDS, A. (1988). Religiosity, aging and life satisfaction. *Journal of Religion and Aging*, *5*(1–2), 1–21.

CREESE, G., GUPPY, N., & MEISSNER, M. (1991). *Ups and downs on the ladder of success: Social mobility in Canada*. General Social Survey Analysis Series. (Catalogue 11-612E, No. 5). Ottawa: Statistics Canada, Housing, Family and Social Statistics.

CROHAN, S.E., & VEROFF, J. (1989) Dimensions of marital well-being among white and black newlyweds. *Journal of Marriage and the Family*, *51*(2), 373–83.

CUNNINGHAM, J.B. (1989). A compressed shift schedule: Dealing with some of the problems of shift-work. *Journal of Organizational Behavior*, *10*(3), 231–45.

CURRIE, D. (1988). Re-thinking what we do and how we do it: A study of reproductive decisions. *Canadian Review of Sociology and Anthropology*, *25*(2), 231–53.

CURTIS, J. (1987). Unpublished tables from 1984 Canada Election Survey.

D'AMATO, T.J. (1987). Factors causing variation in the life satisfaction of the elderly. *National Journal of Sociology*, *1*(1), 54–72.

DARLING, C.A., KALLEN, D.J., & VANDUSEN, J.E. (1984). Sex in transition, 1900–1980. *Journal of Youth and Adolescence*, *13*(5), 385–99.

DAVIES, M. (1990). Work satisfaction in probation and social work. *British Journal of Social Work*, *20*(5), 433–43.

DAVIS, A., GARDNER, B., & GARDNER, M. (1941). *Deep South: A social anthropological study of caste and class*. Chicago: University of Chicago Press.

DAVIS, J.A. (1984). New money, an old man/lady, and 'two's company': Subjective welfare in the NORC General Social Surveys, 1972–1982. *Social Indicators Research*, *15*(4), 319–50.

DAVIS, K., & MOORE, W.E. (1945). Some principles of stratification. *American Sociological Review*, *10*(2), 242–49.

DAVIS, L.E. (1985). Black and white social work faculty: Perceptions of respect, satisfaction, and job permanence. *Journal of Sociology and Social Welfare*, *12*(1), 79–94.

DECKER, F.H. (1985). Socialization and interpersonal environment in nurses' affective reactions to work. *Social Science and Medicine*, *20*(5), 499–509.

DEFRANK, R.S., & STROUP, C.A. (1989). Teacher stress and health: Examination of a model. *Journal of Psychosomatic Research*, *33*(1), 99–109.

DEGLER, C. (1980). *At odds*. New York: Oxford University Press.

DE JONG, G.F., CORNWELL, G.T., HANSON, S.L., & STOKES, C.S. (1984). Childless and one child, but not by choice: A note on some long-term consequences for life satisfactions of rural-reared married women. *Rural Sociology*, *49*(3), 441–51.

DELLI-CARPINI, M.X., SIGEL, R.S., & SNYDER, R. (1983). Does it make any difference how you feel about your job? *Micropolitics*, *3*(2), 227–51.

DE MARIS, A., & LESLIE, G.R. (1984). Cohabitation with the future spouse: Its influence upon marital satisfaction and communication. *Journal of Marriage and the Family*, *46*(1), 77–84.

DEVEREAUX, M. (1990a). New necessities: popular household appliances. In C. McKie & K. Thompson (Eds.), *Canadian social trends* (pp. 258–61). Toronto: Thomson Educational Publishing.

———. (1990b, Autumn). Decline in the number of children. *Canadian social trends*, pp. 32–34.

DE VRIES, J., & VALLEE, F.G. (1980). *Language use in Canada* (Statistics Canada, Catalogue No. 99-762E). Census Analytical Study. Ottawa: Supply & Services.

DE VRIES, M.F., MILLER, D., TOULOUSE, J.M., FRIESEN, P.H., BOISVERT, M., & THERIAULT, R. (1984). Using the life cycle to anticipate satisfaction at work. *Journal of Forecasting*, 3(2), 161–72.

DHOOPER, S.S., & BYARS, L.F. (1989). Stress and the life satisfaction of black social workers. *Affilia*, 4(1), 70–78.

DIENER, E., HOROWITZ, J., & EMMONS, R.A. (1985). Happiness of the very wealthy. *Social Indicators Research*, 16, 263–74.

DIENER, E., SANDVIK, E., SEIDLITZ, L., & DIENER, M. (1993). The relationship between income and subjective well-being: Relative or absolute? *Social Indicators Research*, 28(3), 195–223.

DIMAGGIO, P., & MOHR, J. (1985). Cultural capital, educational attainment, and mate selection. *American Journal of Sociology*, 90(6), 1231–61.

DOMHOFF, G.W. (1967). *Who rules America?* Englewood Cliffs, NJ: Prentice-Hall.

DONOHUE, K.C., & RYDER, R.G. (1982). A methodological note on marital satisfaction and social variables. *Journal of Marriage and the Family*, 44(3), 743–47.

DOOLEY, M. (1986). The overeducated Canadian? Changes in the relationship among earnings, education, and age for Canadian men: 1971–81. *Canadian Journal of Economics*, 19(1), 142–59.

DOYLE, D., & FOREHAND, M.J. (1984). Life satisfaction and old age: A reexamination. *Research on Aging*, 6(3), 432–48.

DRESSEL, P.L. (1982). Policy sources of worker dissatisfactions: The case of human services in aging. *Social Service Review*, 56(3), 406–23.

DUBEY, S.N., & MELLER, Y. (1988). Relationships among task complexity, structure, job performance and satisfaction in social service organizations. *Indian Journal of Social Work*, 49(4), 321–35.

DUCHESNE, D. (1990). The decline of unpaid family work. In Craig McKie & Keith Thompson (Eds.), *Canadian social trends*. Toronto: Thomson Educational Publishing.

DUDLEY, M.G., & KOSINSKI, F.A., Jr. (1990). Religiosity and marital satisfaction: A research note. *Review of Religious Research*, 32(1), 78–86.

DUFF, R.W., & HONG, L.K. (1982). Quality and quantity of social interactions in the life satisfaction of older Americans. *Sociology and Social Research*, 66(4), 418–34.

DURKHEIM, E. (1951). *Suicide: A study of sociology*. (J. Spaulding & G. Simpson, Trans.). New York: Free Press. (Original work published 1897)

———. (1965). *The division of labor in society*. New York: Free Press. (Original work published 1893)

DYCHTWALD, K., & FLOWER, J. (1987). *Age wave: The challenges and opportunities of an aging America*. New York: Bantam.

EASTERLIN, R.A. (1974). Does economic growth improve the human lot? Some empirical evidence. In P.A. David, & W.R. Melvin, (Eds.), *Nations and households in economic growth* (pp. 98–125). Palo Alto, CA: Stanford University Press.

———. (1980). *Birth and fortune: The impact of numbers on personal welfare*. New York: Basic Books.

EDUCATION IN CANADA: A STATISTICAL REVIEW. (1960–1984). Statistics Canada, published annually. Ottawa: Supply & Services.

EDWARDS, R. (1979). *Contested terrain: The transformation of the workplace in the twentieth century*. New York: Basic Books.

EHRENREICH, B. (1983). *The hearts of men: American dreams and the flight from commitment*. Garden City, NJ: Anchor Books.

EICHLER, M. (1981). The inadequacy of the monolithic model of the family. *Canadian Journal of Sociology*, 6(3), 367–88.

———. (1988). *Families in Canada today* (2nd ed.). Toronto: Gage.

ELLIOTT, D.H., & ELLIOTT, J.E. (1990). Behaviour and the life cycle: A consideration of the role of longitudinal time use studies. *Social Indicators Research*, *23*(4), 395–414.

ELLIS, D., & DEKESEREDY, W.S. (1989, Autumn). Marital status and woman abuse: The DAD model. *International Journal of Sociology of the Family*, *19*, 67–87.

ELLISON, C.G., GAY, D.A., & GLASS, T.A. (1989). Does religious commitment contribute to individual life satisfaction? *Social Forces*, 68(1), 100–123.

EMMONS, R.A., & DIENER, E. (1985). Factors predicting satisfaction judgments: A comparative examination. *Social Indicators Research*, *16*(2), 157–67.

EMPLOYMENT & IMMIGRATION CANADA. (1986). *Job futures: An occupational outlook to 1992* (Catalogue No. MP 43-181/1986E). Ottawa: Supply & Services.

———. (1988). *Job futures: An occupational outlook to 1995* (Catalogue No. MP 43-181/1988E). Ottawa: Supply & Services.

———. (1990). *Job futures: An occupational outlook to 1995* (Catalogue No. MP 43-181/1990E). Ottawa: Supply and Services.

ENGELS, F. (1962). *The origins of the family, private property and the state.* Reprinted in Volume II of *Selected works in two volumes.* Moscow: Foreign Language Publishing House.

ENGLAND, G.W., & HARPAZ, I. (1990). How working is defined: National contexts and demographic and organizational role influences. *Journal of Organizational Behavior, 11*(4), 253–66.

ENVIRONICS RESEARCH GROUP. (1987, November). How do you like your job? *Report on Business Magazine*, pp. 112–25.

ERICKSON, B. (1991). What is good taste good for? *Canadian Review of Sociology and Anthropology*, 28(2), 255–78.

ESPE, H., & SEIWERT, M. (1987). Television viewing types, general life satisfaction, and viewing amount: An empirical study in West Germany. *Communications, 13*(2), 95–110.

ETZION, D. (1987). Burning out in management: A comparison of women and men in matched organizational positions. *Israel Social Science Research,* 5(1–2), 147–63.

EWEN, S. (1976). *Captains of consciousness: Advertising and the social roots of the consumer culture.* New York: McGraw-Hill.

FAGENSON, E.A. (1989). The mentor advantage: Perceived career/job experiences of proteges versus non-proteges. *Journal of Organizational Behavior, 10*(4), 309–20.

FARID, B., ELSHERBINI, M., OGDEN, M., LUCAS, G., & WILLIAMS, R. (1989). Alcoholic housewives and role satisfaction. *Alcohol and Alcoholism, 24*(4), 331–37.

FARRELL, J., & MARKIDES, K.S. (1985). Marriage health: A three-generation study of Mexican Americans. *Journal of Marriage and the Family, 47*(4), 1029–36.

FAVER, C.A. (1982). Life satisfaction and the life-cycle: The effects of values and roles on women's well-being. *Sociology and Social Research*, 66(4), 435–52.

FAZEL, M.K., & YOUNG, D.M. (1988). Life quality of Tibetans and Hindus: A function of religion. *Journal for the Scientific Study of Religion, 27*(2), 229–42.

FEATHERMAN, D.L., & HAUSER, R.M. (1978). *Opportunity and change.* New York: Academic Press.

FELDMAN, S.S., WENTZEL, K.R., WEINBERGER, D.A., & MUNSON, J.A. (1990). Marital satisfaction of parents of preadolescent boys and its relationship to family and child functioning. *Journal of Family Psychology*, 4(2), 213–34.

FENGLER, A.P., DANIGELIS, N.L., & GRAMS, A. (1982). Marital status and life satisfaction among the elderly. *International Journal of Sociology of the Family, 12*(1), 63–76.

FIELD, S., & DUBEY, S. (1987). Leadership styles and job satisfaction among human service workers. *Indian Journal of Social Work, 48*(1), 39–56.

FINE, M.A., DONNELLY, D.W., & VOYDANOFF, P. (1986). Adjustment and satisfaction of parents: A comparison of intact, single-parent, and stepparent families. *Journal of Family Issues, 7*(4), 391–404.

FINE-DAVIS, M., & DAVIS, E.E. (1982). Predictors of satisfaction with environmental quality in eight European countries. *Social Indicators Research, 11*(4), 341–46.

FINKELHOR, D., HOTALING, G.T., LEWIS, I.A., & SMITH, C. (1989). Sexual abuse and its relationship to late sexual satisfaction, marital status, religion, and attitudes. *Journal of Interpersonal Violence, 4*(4), 379–99.

FINN, J.L. (1990). Burnout in the human service: A feminist perspective. *Affilia, 5*(4), 55–71.

FINNIE, R. (1993). Women, men, and the economic consequences of divorce: Evidence from Canadian longitudinal data. *Canadian Review of Sociology and Anthropology, 30*(2), 204–41.

FOOT, D.K. (1982). *Canada's population outlook: Demographic futures and economic challenges*. The Canadian Institute for Economic Policy Series. Toronto: Lorimer.

FOWERS, B.J. (1991). His and her marriage: A multivariate study of gender and marital satisfaction. *Sex Roles, 24*(3–4), 209–21.

FRENCH, W.L., GROSS, E., & RESNICK, H. (1986). Effects of a budget-cut crisis on faculty at a large state university. *Sociology and Social Research, 70*(4), 272–75.

FREUDENBERG, W.R. (1984). Boomtown's youth: The differential impacts of rapid community growth on adolescents and adults. *American Sociological Review, 49*(5), Oct, 697–705.

FREUDENBERGER, H.J., & RICHELSON, G. (1981). *Burn-out: The high cost of achievement*. Toronto: Bantam Books.

FREUDIGER, P. (1983). Life satisfaction among three categories of married women. *Journal of Marriage and the Family, 45*(1), 213–19.

FREY, J.H., & CARNS, D.E. (1988). Job satisfaction of casino card dealers. *Sociology and Social Research, 72*(3), 159–64.

FRIED, M. (1982). Residential attachment: Sources of residential and community satisfaction. *Journal of Social Issues, 38*(3), 107–19.

———. (1984). The structure and significance of community satisfaction. *Population and Environment, 7*(2), 61–86.

FRYER, G.E. Jr., POLAND, J.E., BROSS, D.C., & KRUGMAN, R.D. (1988). The child protective service worker: A profile of needs, attitudes, and utilization of professional resources. *Child Abuse and Neglect, 12*(4), 481–90.

FULLER, B., & DORNBUSCH, S.M. (1988). Organizational construction of intrinsic motivation. *Sociological Forum, 3*(1), 1–24.

FUSILIER, M.R., GANSTER, D.C., & MAYES, B.T. (1986). The social support and health relationship: Is there a gender difference? *Journal of Occupational Psychology, 59*(2), 145–53.

FUSSELL, P. (1983). *Class*. New York: Ballantine Books.

GAERTNER, K.N. (1984). Work satisfaction and family responsibility correlates of employment among nurses. *Work and Occupations, 11*(4), 439–60.

GALAMBOS, N.L., & SILBEREISEN, R.K. (1989). Role strain in West German dual-earner households. *Journal of Marriage and the Family, 51*(2), 385–89.

GALSTER, G.C. (1985) Evaluating indicators for housing policy: Residential satisfaction versus marginal improvement priorities. *Social Indicators Research, 16*(4), 415–48.

GANDY, J.M., & TEPPERMAN, L. (1990). *False alarm: The computerization of eight social welfare organizations*. Waterloo: Wilfrid Laurier University Press.

GARLAND, T.N., OYABU, N., & GIPSON, G.A. (1989). Job satisfaction among nurse assistants employed in nursing homes: An analysis of selected job characteristics. *Journal of Aging Studies, 3*(4), 369–83.

GARREAU, J. (1981). *The nine nations of North America*. New York: Avon Books.

GASKELL, J. (1985). *Women and education: Branching out towards equity*. Ottawa: Economic Council of Canada.

GATEWOOD, J.B., & MCCAY, B.J. (1990). Comparison of job satisfaction in six New Jersey fisheries: Implications for management. *Human Organization, 49*(1), 14–25.

GEE, E. (1986). The life course of Canadian women: An historical and demographic analysis. *Social Indicators Research, 18*, 263–83.

———. (1990). Demographic change and intergenerational relations in Canadian families: Findings and social policy implications. *Canadian Public Policy, 16*(2), 191–99.

GEE, E.M., & VEEVERS, J.E. (1990). Religious involvement and life satisfaction in Canada. *Sociological Analysis, 51*(4), 387–94.

GEORGE, L.K., OKUN, M.A., & LANDERMAN, R. (1985). Age as a moderator of the determinants of life satisfaction. *Research on Aging, 7*(2), 209–33.

GEYER, P.D., BRANNON, Y.S., & SHEARON, R.W. (1987). The prediction of students' satisfaction with community college vocation training. *Journal of Psychology, 121*(6), 591–97.

GILLIS, A.R., RICHARDS, M., & HAGAN, J. (1987). Ethnic susceptibility to crowding. *Environment and Behavior, 18*(6), 683–706.

GINSBERG, Y. (1985). Dimensions of neighborhood prestige perceptions: Findings from Tel Aviv. *Social Science Quarterly*, 66(3), 724–32.

GLATZER, W., & BOS, M. (1992). Review of R. Veenhoven (Ed.) *How harmful is happiness?* and R. Veenhoven (Ed.) *Did the crisis really hurt?* In *Social Indicators Research, 27*(4), 375–79.

GLEASON, S.E., & MOSER, C. (1985). Some neglected policy implications of comparable worth. *Policy Studies Review*, *4*(4), 595–600.

GLENN, N.D. (1989) Duration of marriage, family composition, and marital happiness. *National Journal of Sociology*, *3*(1), 3–24.

GLENN, N.D. & MCLANAHAN, S.S. (1982). Children and marital happiness: A further specification of the relationship. *Journal of Marriage and the Family*, *44*(1), 63–72.

GLENN, N.D., & WEAVER, C.N. (1982). Further evidence on education and job satisfaction. *Social Forces, 61*(1), 46–55.

———. (1985). Age, cohort and reported job satisfaction in the United States. *Current Perpectives of Aging and the Life Cycle, 1*, 89–109.

———. (1988). The changing relationship of marital status to reported happiness. *Journal of Marriage and the Family*, 50(2), 317–24.

GLISSON, C., & DURICK, M. (1988). Predictors of job satisfaction and organization commitment in human service organizations. *Administrative Science Quarterly*, *33*(1), 61–81.

GMELCH, W.H., WILKE, P.K., & LOVRICH, N.P. (1986). Dimensions of stress among university faculty: Factor-analytic results from a national study. *Research in Higher Education*, *24*(3), 266–86.

GOFFMAN, E. (1963). *Stigma: Notes on the management of spoiled identity*. Englewood Cliffs, NJ: Prentice-Hall.

GOLANT, S.M. (1985). The influence of the experienced residential environment on old people's life satisfaction. *Journal of Housing for the Elderly*, 3(3–4), 23–49.

GOLDSMITH, H.F., & JACKSON, D.J. (1981). Community dissatisfaction and depressed mood in suburbia. *Evaluation and Program Planning*, *4*(1), 95–105.

GOODE, J. (1990). A wary welcome to the neighborhood: Community responses to immigrants. *Urban Anthropology*, *19*(1–2), 125–53.

GORDON, V.B., & GOBLE, L.K. (1986). Creative accommodation: Role satisfaction for psychiatric staff nurses. *Issues in Mental Health Nursing*, 8(1), 25–35.

GOTLIB, I.H., & WHIFFEN, V.E. (1989). Stress, coping, and marital satisfaction in couples with a depressed wife. *Canadian Journal of Behavioural Science*, *21*(4), 401–18.

GOTTMAN, J.M. (1982). Emotional responsiveness in marital conversations. *Journal of Communication*, *32*(3), 108–20.

GOUDY, W.J. (1990). Community attachment in a rural region. *Rural Sociology*, *55*(2), 178–98.

GOVE, W.R. (1970). Sex, marital status, and psychiatric treatment: A research note. *Social Forces*, *58*, 89–93.

GOVE, W.R., STYLE, C.B., & HUGHES, M. (1990). The effect of marriage on the well-being of adults: A theoretical analysis. *Journal of Family Issues*, *11*(1), 4–35.

GOYDER, J.C. (1980). Trends in the socioeconomic achievement of the university educated: A status attainment model interpretation. *Canadian Journal of Higher Education*, *10*(2), 21–38.

GRANOVETTER, M. (1974). *Getting a job: A study of contacts and careers*. Cambridge, MA: Harvard University Press.

GRAY, D.E. (1984). Job satisfaction among Australian nurses. *Human Relations*, *37*(12), 1063–77.

GRAYSON, J.P. (1986). Plant exclusions and political despair. *Canadian Review of Sociology and Anthropology*, *23*(3), 331–49.

GREELEY, A. (1989). The declining morale of women. *Sociology and Social Research*, *73*(2), 53–58.

GREELEY, A.M. (1991). *Faithful attraction*. New York: Tom Doherty Associates.

GRICHTING, W.L. (1983). Domain, scope and degree of happiness. *British Journal of Social Psychology*, *22*(3), 247–60.

GRINDSTAFF, C., BALAKRISHNAN, T., & MAXIM, P. (1989). Life course alternatives: Factors associated with differential timing patterns in fertility among women recently completing childbearing, Canada 1981. *Canadian Journal of Sociology*, *14*(4), 443–69.

GROVER, K.J., RUSSELL, C.S., SCHUMM, W.R., & PAFF-BERGEN, L.A. (1985). Mate selection processes and marital satisfaction. *Family Relations*, *34*(3), 383–86.

GRUBER, K.J., & SHELTON, G.J. (1987). Assessment of neighborhood satisfaction by residents of three housing types. *Social Indicators Research*, *19*(3), 303–15.

GRUENBERG, B. (1980). The happy worker: An analysis of educational and occupational differences in determinants of job satisfaction. *American Journal of Sociology*, *86*(2), 247–71.

GUBRIUM, J.F., & LYNOTT, R.J. (1983). Rethinking life satisfaction. *Human Organization*, *42*(1), 30–38.

GUINDON, H. (1978). The modernization of Quebec and the legitimacy of the Canadian state. *Canadian Review of Sociology and Anthropology, 15*(2), 227–45.

GUISINGER, S., COWAN, P.A., & SCHULDBERG, D. (1989). Changing parent and spouse relations in the first years of remarriage of divorced fathers. *Journal of Marriage and the Family, 51*(2), 445–56.

GUNDERSON, M., & PESANDO, J. (1980, Spring). Eliminating mandatory retirement: Economic and human rights. *Canadian Public Policy*, 6(2), pp. 352–60.

———. (1988). The case for allowing mandatory retirement. *Canadian Public Policy, 14*(1), pp. 32–39.

GUPPY, N. (1984). Access to higher education in Canada. *Canadian Journal of Higher Education, 14*(3), 79–93.

———. (1992). Does school matter: An invited comment on Anisef, Ashbury and Turrittin's "Differential effects of university and community college education on occupational status attainment in Ontario." *Canadian Journal of Sociology, 17*(1), 85–88.

GUPPY, N., & ARAI, A.B. (1993). Who benefits from higher education? Differences by sex, social class, and ethnic background. In J. Curtis, E. Grabb, & N. Guppy (Eds.), *Social inequality in Canada,* (2nd ed.). Scarborough, ON: Prentice-Hall.

GUPPY, N. & PENDAKUR, K. (1989). The effects of gender and parental education on participation within post-secondary education in the 1970s and 1980s. *Canadian Journal of Higher Education, 19*(1), 49–62.

HAAS, J., & SHAFFIR, W. (Eds.). (1978). *Shaping identity in Canadian society*. Scarborough, ON: Prentice-Hall.

HABERMAN, M., & RICKARDS, W.H. (1990). Urban teachers who quit: Why they leave and what they do. *Urban Education, 25*(3), 297–303.

HAGEN, J.L. (1989). Income maintenance workers: Burned-out, dissatisfied, and leaving. *Journal of Social Science Research, 13*(1), 47–63

HAJNAL, J. (1965). European marriage patterns in perspective. In D.V. Glass & D.E.C. Eversley (Eds.), *Population in history* (pp. 101–43). London: Edward Arnold.

HALABY, C.N. (1986). Worker attachment and workplace authority. *American Sociological Review, 51*(5), 634–49.

HALLI, S.S., & ZIMMER, Z. (1991). Common law union as a differentiating factor in the failure of marriages in Canada, 1984. *Social Indicators Research, 24*, 329–45.

HAMIL, R.E. (1987). The arrival of the 5-billionth human. *The Futurist, 21*(4), 36–37.

HANSEN, J.E., & SCHULDT, W.J. (1984). Marital self-disclosure and marital satisfaction. *Journal of Marriage and the Family*, *46*(4), 923–26.

HARDY, M.A. (1985). Occupational structure and retirement. *Current Perspectives on Aging and the Life Cycle*, *1*, pp. 111–46.

HARING-HIDORE, M., STOCK, W.A., OKUN, M.A., & WITTER, R.A. (1985). Marital status and subjective well-being: A research synthesis. *Journal of Marriage and the Family*, *47*(4), 947–53.

HARRISON, A.O., & MINOR, J.H. (1982). Interrole conflict, coping strategies, and role satisfaction among single and married employed mothers. *Psychology of Women Quarterly*, 6(3), 354–60.

HARVEY, A., MARSHALL, K., & FREDERICK, J.A. (1991). *Where does time go?* General Social Survey Analysis Series. Statistics Canada. (Catalogue 11-612E, No. 4). Ottawa: Supply & Services.

HARVEY, A., & SINGLETON, J. (1989). Canadian activity patterns across the life span: A time budget perspective. *Canadian Journal on Aging*, *8*(3), 269–85.

HARVEY, E.B. (1984). The changing relationship between university education and intergenerational social mobility. *Canadian Review of Sociology and Anthropology*, *21*(3), 275–86.

———. (1988). Science and technology. In J. Curtis & L. Tepperman (Eds.), *Understanding Canadian society*. Toronto: McGraw-Hill Ryerson.

HATFIELD, E., & SPRECHER, S. (1986). *Mirror, mirror: The importance of looks in everyday life*. Albany: State University of New York Press.

HAWKES, G.R., GUAGNANO, G.A., SMITH, J.W., & FOREST, M.K. (1984). The influence of work and non-work factors on job satisfaction for Mexican-American male workers. *Rural Sociology*, *49*(1), 117–26.

HEADEY, B., & WEARING, A. (1988). The sense of relative superiority—Central to well-being. *Social Indicators Research*, *20*(5), 497–516.

HEALTH AND WELFARE CANADA. (1989). *Health and Welfare in Canada*. Ottawa: Supply & Services.

HEATON, T.B. (1984). Religious homogamy and marital satisfaction reconsidered. *Journal of Marriage and the Family*, *46*(3), 729–33.

HEATON, T.B., & PRATT, E.L. (1990). The effects of religious homogamy on marital satisfaction and stability. *Journal of Family Issues*, *11*(2), 191–207.

HENRY, F. (1973). *Forgotten Canadians: The Blacks of Nova Scotia*. Don Mills, ON: Longman.

HENRY, L. (1976). *Population: Analysis and models*. London: Edward Arnold.

HERBERG, E. (1990). The ethno-racial socioeconomic hierarchy in Canada: Theory and analysis of the new vertical mosaic. *International Journal of Comparative Sociology*, *31*(3–4), 206–20.

HERRICK, J., TAKAGI, C.Y., COLEMAN, R., & MORGAN, L.J. (1983). Social workers who left the profession: An exploratory study. *Journal of Sociology and Social Welfare*, *10*(1), 78–94.

HERTING, J.R., & GUEST, A.M. (1985). Components of satisfaction with local areas in the metropolis. *Sociological Quarterly*, *26*(1), 99–116.

HESKETH, B., & SHOUKSMITH, G. (1986). Job and non-job activities, job satisfaction and mental health among veterinarians. *Journal of Occupational Behaviour*, *7*(4), 325–39.

HIMLE, D.P., JAYARATNE, S., & THYNESS, P. (1986). Predictors of job satisfaction, burnout and turnover among social workers in Norway and the USA: A cross-cultural study. *International Social Work*, *29*(4), 323–34.

HIRSCH, F. (1978). *The social limits to growth*. Cambridge, MA: Harvard University Press.

HOBART, C. (1991). Conflict in remarriages. *Journal of Divorce and Remarriage*, *15*(3–4), 69–86.

HOBART, C.W. (1984). Interest in parenthood among young Anglophone and Francophone Canadians. *Canadian Studies in Population*, *11*(2), 111–33.

HOBSBAWM, E.J. (1959). *Primitive rebels: Studies in archaic forms of social movement in the 19th and 20th centuries*. New York: W.W. Norton.

HOCHSCHILD, A. (1989). *The second shift*. New York: Avon Books.

HOCHSCHILD, A.R. (1975). Disengagement theory: a critique and proposal. *American Sociological Review*, *40*, 553–69.

HODSON, R. (1984). Corporate structure and job satisfaction: A focus on employer characteristics. *Sociology and Social Research*, *69*(1), 22–49.

———. (1989). Gender differences in job satisfaction: Why aren't women more dissatisfied? *Sociological Quarterly*, *30*(3), 385–99.

HODSON, R., & SULLIVAN, T.A. (1985). Totem or tyrant? Monopoly, regional, and local sector effects on worker commitment. *Social Forces*, *63*(3), 716–31.

HOGAN, D.P. (1981). *Transitions and social change: The early lives of American men*. Studies in Population Series. New York: Academic Press.

HOLLINGER, R.C. (1988). Working under the influence (WUI): Correlates of employees' use of alcohol and other drugs. *Journal of Applied Behavioral Science*, *24*(4), 439–54.

HOLMAN, T.B., & JACQUART, M. (1988). Leisure activity patterns and marital satisfaction: A further test. *Journal of Marriage and the Family*, *50*(1), 69–77.

HOLMAN, T.B., & WOODROFFE-PATRICK, M. (1988). Family structure, conflict, and children's self-esteem in Trinidad and Tobago. *Journal of Family Issues*, *9*(2), 214–23.

HOMANS, G.C. (1974). *Social behavior: Its elementary forms* (rev. ed.). New York: Harcourt Brace Jovanovich.

HONEYCUTT, J.M., WILSON, C., & PARKER, C. (1982). Effects of sex and degree of happiness on perceived styles of communicating in and out of the marital relationship. *Journal of Marriage and the Family*, *44*(2), 395–406.

HORNA, J., & LUPRI, E. (1987). Father's participation in work, family life and leisure: a Canadian experience. In C. Lewis & M. O'Brien (Eds.), *Reassessing fatherhood: New observations on fathers and the modern family* (pp. 54–73). London: Sage Publications.

HUDDLESTON, R.J., & HAWKINGS, L. (1986). The effects of divorce: A study of the reports of divorced Albertans. *Conciliation Courts Review*, *24*(2), 59–68.

HUGHEY, J.B., & BARDO, J.W. (1984). The structure of community satisfaction in a southeastern American city. *Journal of Social Psychology*, *123*(1), 91–99.

HULL, J. (1990). Socioeconomic status and Native education in Canada. *Canadian Journal of Native Education*, *17*(1), 1–14.

HUMPHRYS, P., & O'BRIEN, G.E. (1986). The relationship between skill utilization, professional orientation and job satisfaction for pharmacists. *Journal of Occupational Psychology*, *59*(4), 315–26.

HUNTER, A.A. (1987). *Formal education and initial employment: Unravelling the relationships between schooling and work over time*. Hamilton, ON: McMaster University, Department of Sociology.

———. (1988). Formal education and initial employment. *American Sociological Review*, *53*(5), 753–65.

INKELES, A. (1973). Making men modern. In A. Etzioni (Ed.), *Social change: Sources, patterns and consequences*. New York: Basic Books.

ISHII-KUNTZ, M., & IHINGER-TALLMAN, M. (1991). The subjective well-being of parents. *Journal of Family Issues*, *12*(1), 58–68.

IVANCEVICH, J.M., & MATTESON, M.T. (1982). Occupational stress, satisfaction, physical well-being, and coping: A study of homemakers. *Psychological Reports*, *50*, 3(1), 995–1005.

JAGUN, A., BROWN, D.R., MILBURN, N.G., & GARY, L.E. (1990). Residential satisfaction and socioeconomic and housing characteristics of urban black adults. *Journal of Black Studies*, *21*(1), 40–51.

JAHER, F.C. (1982). *The urban establishment: Upper strata in Boston, New York, Charleston, Chicago and Los Angeles*. Urbana: University of Illinois.

JA-JEONG, G., & SCHUMM, W.R. (1990). Family satisfaction in Korean/American marriages: An exploratory study of the perceptions of Korean wives. *Journal of Comparative Family Studies*, *21*(3), 325–36.

JANOWITZ, M. (1960). *The Professional Soldier*. New York: Free Press.

JANSON, P., & MARTIN, J.K. (1982). Job satisfaction and age: A test of two views. *Social Forces*, 60(4), 1089–1102.

JAYARATNE, S., & CHESS, W.A. (1984). Job satisfaction, burnout, and turnover: A national study. *Social Work*, 29(5), 448–53.

———. (1986) Job satisfaction: A comparison of caseworkers and administrators. *Social Work*, *31*(2), 144–46.

JAYARATNE, S., CHESS, W.A., & KUNKEL, D.A. (1986). Burnout: Its impact on child welfare workers and their spouses. *Social Work*, *31*(1), 53–59.

JAYARATNE, S., SIEFERT, K., & CHESS, W.A. (1988). Private and agency practitioners: Some data and observations. *Social Services Review*, *62*(2), 324–36.

JENCKS, C. (1988). Whom must we treat equally for educational opportunity to be equal? *Ethics*, 98(3), 518–33.

JENCKS, C., BARTLETT, S., CORCORAN, M., CROUSE, J., EAGLESFIELD, D., JACKSON, G., MCCLELLAND, K., MUESER, P., OLNECK, M., SCHWARTZ, J., WARD, S., & WILLIAMS, J. (1977). *Who gets ahead? The determinants of economic success in America*. New York: Basic Books.

JENSEN, L., & BORGES, M. (1986). The effects of maternal employment on adolescent daughters. *Adolescence*, *21*(83), 659–66.

JERRELL, J.M., & KNIGHT, M.A. (1985). Social work practice in rural mental health systems. *Social Work*, 30(4), 331–37.

JOBES, P.C. (1987). The reconstruction of social reality: Curriculum counseling and satisfaction in a sample of college educated women. *Free Enquiry in Creative Sociology*, *15*(2), 207–11.

JOHNSON, G.J. (1989). Family roles, underemployment, underpayment and happiness among working men. *International Journal of Sociology of the Family*, *19*(2), 137–50.

JOHNSON, L. (1987). Children's visions of the future. *The Futurist*, *21*(3), 36–40.

JOHNSON, W.G. (1987, February). Recruitment, training and promotion in the event of abolition of mandatory retirement. *HR Professional*, p. 18.

JONES, C., MARSDEN, L., & TEPPERMAN, L. (1990). *Lives of their own: The individualization of women's lives*. Toronto: Oxford University Press.

JONES, E.F., FORREST, J.D., GOLDMAN, N., HENSHAW, S., LINCOLN, R., ROSOFF, J.I., WESTOFF, C.F., & WULF, D. (1986). *Teenage pregnancy in industrialized countries*. New Haven, CT: Yale University Press.

JONES, L.Y. (1980). *Great expectations: America and the baby boom generation*. New York: Ballantine Books.

JONES, S. (1986). The elders: A new generation. *Ageing and Society, 6*(3), 313–31.

JURIK, N.C., HALEMBA, G.J., MUSHENO, M.C., & BOYLE, B.V. (1987). Educational attainment, job satisfaction and the professionalization of correctional officers. *Work and Occupations, 14*(1), 106–25.

KAGITCIBASI, C. (1982). Old age security value of children and development: Cross-national evidence. *Journal of Comparative Family Studies, 13*(2), 133–42.

KAKABADSE, A. (1986). Organization alienation and job climate: A comparative study of structural conditions and psychological adjustment. *Small Group Behavior, 17*(4), 458–71.

KALBACH, W.E., LANPHIER, M., RHYNE, D., & RICHMOND, A.H. (1984). *Ethnogenerational factors in socio-economic achievement in Toronto: The second generation during the 1970s.* Toronto: York University, Institute for Behavioural Research.

KALLEBERG, A.L., & LOSCOCCO, K.A. (1983). Aging, values and rewards: Explaining age differences in job satisfaction. *American Sociological Review, 48*(1), 78–90.

KAMMANN, R., FARRY, M., & HERBISON, P. (1984). The analysis and measurement of happiness as a sense of well-being. *Social Indicators Research, 15*(2), 91–115.

KANTER, R.M. (1972). *Commitment and community: Communes and utopias in sociological perspective.* Cambridge, MA: Harvard University Press.

———. (1977). *Men and women of the corporation.* New York: Basic Books.

KARP, D.A. (1987). Professionals beyond midlife: Some observations on work satisfaction in the fifty- to sixty-year decade. *Journal of Aging Studies, 1*(3), 209–23.

KATZ, R., & BRIGER, R. (1988). Modernity and quality of marriage in Israel: The impact of socio-cultural factors on marital satisfaction. *Journal of Comparative Family Studies, 19*(3), 371–80.

KAUFMAN, G.M. (1988). Relationship between marital power and symptoms of stress among husbands and wives. *Wisconsin Sociologist, 25*(1), 35–44.

KEICOLT, K.J., & ACOCK, A.C. (1990). Childhood family structure and adult psychological well-being of black Americans. *Sociological Spectrum, 10*(2), 169–86.

KEITH, P.M., BRAITO, R., & BRECI, M. (1990). Rethinking isolation among the married and unmarried. *American Journal of Orthopsychiatry, 60*(2), 289–97.

KEITH, V.M., & HERRING, C. (1991). Skin tone and stratification in the Black community. *American Journal of Sociology, 97*(3), 760–78.

KENNEDY, C.A., KING, J.A., & MURACO, W.A. (1983). The relative strength of health as a predictor of life satisfaction. *International Social Science Review*, 58(2), 97–102.

KEON, T.L., & MCDONALD, B. (1982). Job satisfaction and life satisfaction: An empirical evaluation of their interrelationship. *Human Relations*, 35(3), 167–80.

KETTLE, J. (1980). *The big generation*. Toronto: McClelland & Stewart.

KEYFITZ, N. (1988). On the wholesomeness of marriage. In L. Tepperman & J. Curtis (Eds.), *Readings in sociology: An introduction*. Toronto: McGraw-Hill Ryerson.

KHALEQUE, A., & RAHMAN, M.A. (1987). Perceived importance of job facets and overall job satisfaction of industrial workers. *Human Relations*, 40(7), 401–15.

KIECOLT-GLASER, J.K., FISHER, L.D., OGROCKI, P., STOUT, J.C., SPEICHER, C.E., & GLASER, R. (1987) Marital quality, marital disruption, and immune function. *Psychosomatic Medicine*, 49(1), 13–34.

KING, M., MURRAY, M.A., & ATKINSON, T. (1982). Background personality, job characteristics, and satisfaction with work in a national sample. *Human Relations*, 35(2), 119–33.

KING, W.L., & HAUTALUOMA, J.E. (1987). Comparison of job satisfaction, life satisfaction, and performance of overeducated and other workers. *Journal of Social Psychology*, 127(5), 421–33.

KINGSTON, P.W., & NOCK, S.L. (1987). Time together among dual-earner couples. *American Sociological Review*, 52(3), 391–400.

KIRCHLER, E., DE LONGIS, A., & LEHMAN, D.R. (1989). Everyday life experiences at home: An interaction diary approach to assess marital relationships. *Journal of Family Psychology*, 2(3), 311–36.

KIRKHAM, M.A., SCHINKE, S.P., SCHILLING, R.F. Jr, MELTZER, N.J., & NORELIUS, K.L. (1986). Cognitive-behavioral skills, social supports, and child abuse potential among mothers of handicapped children. *Journal of Family Violence*, 1(3), 235–45.

KNODEL, J., & VAN DE WALLE, E. (1979). Lessons from the past: Policy implications of historical fertility studies. *Population and Development Review*, 5(2), 217–45.

KOENIG, H.G., SIEGLER, I.C., & GEORGE, L.K. (1989). Religious and non-religious coping: Impact on adaptation in later life. *Journal of Religion and Aging*, 5(4), 73–94.

KOSLOWSKY, M. (1987). Career commitment as a predictor of behavioral outcomes. *Journal of Social Psychology*, 127(5), 435–44.

KOTLER, T. (1985). A balanced distance: Aspects of marital quality. *Human Relations*, 38(5), 391–407.

KRAUT, R.E. (1989). Telecommuting: The trade-offs of home work. *Journal of Communication, 39*(3), 19–47.

KRISHEF, C.H. (1981). A study of job satisfaction among M.S.W. direct service practitioners. *Journal of Humanics*, 9(1), 20–27.

KROKOFF, L.J. (1987). The correlates of negative affect in marriage: An exploratory study of gender differences. *Journal of Family Issues, 8*(1), 111–15.

KURDEK, L.A. (1989). Relationship quality for newly married husbands and wives: Marital history, stepchildren, and individual-difference predictors. *Journal of Marriage and the Family, 51*(4), 1053–64.

———. (1991). Marital stability and changes in marital quality in newly wed couples: A test of the contextual model. *Journal of Social and Personal Relationships, 8*(1), 27–48.

LABOUR CANADA. (1983). *Part-time work in Canada.* Report of the Commission of Inquiry into Part-time Work. Ottawa: Supply & Services.

LACHAPELLE, R. (1990). Changes in fertility among Canada's linguistic groups. In Craig McKie & Keith Thompson (Eds.), *Canadian social trends.* Toronto: Thomson Educational Publishing.

LA GORY, M., WARD, R., & SHERMAN, S. (1985). The ecology of aging: Neighbourhood satisfaction in an older population. *Sociological Quarterly, 26*(3), 405–18.

LAMBERT, R.D., & CURTIS, J.E. (1979). Education, economic dissatisfaction, and nonconfidence in Canadian social institutions. *Canadian Review of Sociology and Anthropology, 16*(1), 47–59.

LAMBERT, R.D., & CURTIS, J. (1985, February). The racial attitudes of Canadians. *Past and Present*, pp. 2–4.

LANCE, C.E., LAUTENSCHLAGER, G.J., SLOAN, C.E., & VARCA, P.E. (1989). A comparison between bottom-up, top-down, and bidirectional models of relationships between global and life facet satisfaction. *Journal of Personality, 57*(3), 601–24.

LANDEWEERD, J.A., & BOUMANS, N.P.G. (1988). Work satisfaction health, and stress: A study of Dutch nurses. *Work and Stress, 2*(1), 17–26.

LARSON, L., & MUNRO, B. (1990). Religious intermarriage in Canada in the 1980s. *Journal of Comparative Family Studies, 21*(2), 239–50.

LARSON, M.S. (1977). *The rise of professionalism: A sociological analysis.* Berkeley, CA: University of California Press.

LATTEN, J.J. (1989). Life-course and satisfaction, equal for everyone? *Social Indicators Research, 21*(6), 599–610.

LAUER, R.H., & KERR, S.T. (1990). The long-term marriage: Perceptions of stability and satisfaction. *International Journal of Aging and Human Development, 31*(3), 189–95.

LAUER, R.H., & LAUER, J.C. (1986). Factors in long-term marriages. *Journal of Family Issues, 7*(4), 382–90.

LAWLOR, E.F. (1986). The impact of age discrimination legislation on the labor force participation of aged men: A time-series analysis. *Evaluation Review, 10*(6), 794–805.

LAZEAR, E.P. (1979). Why is there mandatory retirement? *Journal of Political Economy, 87*(6), 1261–84.

LEE, B.A., & GUEST, A.M. (1983). Determinants of neighborhood satisfaction: A metropolitan-level analysis. *Sociological Quarterly, 24*(2), 287–303.

LEE, G.R. (1988). Marital intimacy among older persons: The spouse as confidant. *Journal of Family Issues*, 9(2), 273–84.

———. (1988b). Marital satisfaction in later life: The effects of nonmarital roles. *Journal of Marriage and the Family, 50*(3), 775–83.

LEE, R., & WILBUR, E.R. (1985). Age, education, job tenure, salary, job characteristics and job satisfaction: A multivariate analysis. *Human Relations, 38*(8), 781–91.

LEMERT, E.M. (1972). *Human deviance, social problems and social control.* (2nd ed.). Englewood Cliffs, NJ: Prentice-Hall.

LENSKI, G. (1966). *Power and privilege: A theory of social stratification*. New York: McGraw-Hill.

LESLIE, G.R., & KORMAN, S.K. (1985). *The family in social context* (6th ed.). New York: Oxford University Press.

LESLIE, L.A., & ANDERSON, E.A. (1988). Men's and women's participation in domestic roles: Impact on quality of life and marital adjustment. *Journal of Family Psychology, 2*(2), 212–26.

LEVINE, M.L. (1988), *Age discrimination and mandatory retirement policy*. Baltimore: John Hopkins University Press.

LEVITT, M.J., ANTONUCCI, T.C., CLARK, M.C., ROTTON, J., & FINLEY, G.E. (1985). Social support and well-being: Preliminary indicators based on two samples of the elderly. *International Journal of Aging and Human Development, 21*(1), 61–77.

LEWIS, O. (1966). The culture of poverty. *Scientific American, 215*(4), 19–25.

LEWIS, S., & LYON, L. (1986). The quality of community and the quality of life. *Sociological Spectrum*, 6(4), 397–410.

LI, P. (1982). Chinese immigrants on the prairie, 1910–1947, *Canadian Review of Sociology and Anthropology* 19(4), 527–40.

LIOU, K.T., SYLVIA, R.D., & BRUNK, G. (1990). Non-work factors and job satisfaction revisited. *Human Relations, 43*(1), 77–86.

LIPSET, S.M., TROW, M., & COLEMAN, J. (1963). *Union democracy: The internal politics of the international typographical union*. Garden City, NY: Anchor Books, Doubleday.

LIVINGSTON, D.W. (1987). Job skills and schooling: A class analysis of entry requirements and underemployment. *Canadian Journal of Education, 12*(1), 1–27.

LIVINGSTON, D.W., & HART, D. (1991). The people speak: Public attitudes towards schooling in Canada. In R. Ghosh and D. Ray (Eds.), *Social change and education in Canada*.Toronto: Harcourt Brace Jovanovich.

LLOYD, S.A. (1990). Conflict types and strategies in violent marriages. *Journal of Family Violence*, *5*(4), 269–84.

LOCKE, E.A. (1976). The nature and causes of job satisfaction. In M.D. Dunnette (Ed.), *Handbook of Industrial and Organization Psychology* (pp. 1297–349). Chicago: Rand McNally.

LOOKER, E., & MCNUTT, K. (1989). The effect of occupational expectations on the educational attainment of males and females. *Canadian Journal of Education*, *14*(3), 352–67.

LORD, J.D., & RENT, G.S. (1987). Residential satisfaction in scattered-site public housing projects. *Social Science Journal*, *24*(3), 287–302.

LOWRY, J.H. (1984). Life satisfaction time components among the elderly: Toward understanding the contribution of predictor variables. *Research on Aging*, 6(3), 417–31.

LUEPTOW, L.B., GUSS, M.B., & HYDEN, C. (1989). Sex role ideology, marital status, and happiness. *Journal of Family Issues*, *10*(3), 383–400.

LUPRI, E. (1991a). Fathers in transition: The case of dual earner families in Canada. In Jean E. Veevers (Ed.), *Continuity and change in marriage and family* (pp. 244–54). Toronto: Holt, Rinehart and Winston of Canada.

———. (1991b). *Hidden in the home: Wife abuse in Canada*. Selected Findings from a 1987 National Survey.

LUPRI, E. (1992). Why does family violence occur? In L. Tepperman and J. Curtis (Eds.), *Everyday life*. Toronto: McGraw-Hill Ryerson.

LUPRI, E., & FRIDERES, J. (1981). The quality of marriage and the passage of time: Marital satisfaction over the family life cycle. *Canadian Journal of Sociology*, 6(3), 283–305.

LUPRI, E., & MILLS, D. (1987). The household division of labour in young dual-earner couples: The case of Canada. *International Review of Sociology*, New Series, *2*, 33–54.

LUXTON, M. (1980). *More than a labour of love: Three generations of women's work in the home*. Toronto: Women's Educational Press.

LYONS, W.E., & LOWERY, D. (1986). The organization of political space and citizen responses to dissatisfaction in urban communities: An integrative model. *Journal of Politics*, 48(2), 321–46.

MACDONALD, N.E., EBERT, P.D., & MASON, S.E. (1987). Marital status and age as related to masculine and feminine personality dimensions and self-esteem. *Journal of Social Psychology*, *127*(3), 289–98.

MACPHERSON, C.B. (1962). *The political theory of possessive individualism: Hobbes to Locke*. Oxford: Clarendon Press.

MACPHERSON, C.B. (1965). *The real world of democracy*. The Massey Lectures (4th Series). Toronto: Canadian Broadcasting Corporation.

MALARKEY, R., BOOTSMA, M., & VYN, C. (1990). Marital relations and Canadian women in the urban work force. *International Journal of Sociology of the Family*, *20*(2), 163–79.

MALINOWSKA-TABAKA, E. (1987). Complex measures of job satisfaction/dissatisfaction among professionals. *Social Indicators Research*, *19*(4), 451–73.

MALKA, S. (1989). Managerial behavior, participation and effectiveness in social welfare organizations. *Administration in Social Work*, *13*(2), 47–65.

MALTHUS, T.R. (1959). *Population: The first essay*. Foreword by K.E. Boulding. Ann Arbor: University of Michigan Press. (Original work published 1798)

MANN, M. (1970). The social cohesion of liberal democracy. *American Sociological Review*, *35*(3), 423–39.

MANSFIELD, P.K., PRESTON, D.B., & CRAWFORD, C.O. (1988). Rural-urban differences in women's psychological well-being. *Health Care for Women International*, 9(4), 289–304.

MARCH, J.G., & SIMON, H.A. (1958). *Organizations*. New York: John Wiley.

MARCHAK, M.P. (1987). *Ideological perspectives on Canada* (3rd ed.). Toronto: McGraw-Hill Ryerson.

MARGOLIN, L., & WHITE, L. (1987). The continuing role of physical attractiveness in marriage. *Journal of Marriage and the Family*, 49(1), 21–27.

MARSDEN, L.R., & HARVEY, E.B. (1979). *Fragile federation: Social change in Canada*. Toronto: McGraw-Hill Ryerson.

MARSHALL, G. (1986) The workplace culture of a licensed restaurant. *Theory, Culture and Society*, 3(1), 33–47.

MARSHALL, K. (1987, Winter). Women in male-dominated professions. *Canadian Social Trends*, pp. 7–11.

MARTIN, J.K., & HANSON, S.L. (1985). Sex, family wage-earning status, and satisfaction with work. *Work and Occupations, 12*(1), 91–109.

MARTIN, J.K., & MILLER, G.A. (1986). Job satisfaction and absenteeism. *Work and Occupations, 13*(1), 33–46.

MARTIN, J.K., & SHEHAN, C.L. (1989). Education and job satisfaction: The influence of gender, wage-earning status, and job values. *Work and Occupations, 16*(2), 184–99.

MARTIN, M.J., SCHUMM, W.R., BUGAIGHIS, M.A., JURICH, A.P., & BOLLMAN, S.R. (1987). Family violence and adolescents' perceptions of outcomes of family conflict. *Journal of Marriage and the Family, 49*(1), 165–71.

MARTIN, M.W. (1985). Satisfaction with intimate exchange: Gender-role differences and the impact of equity, equality and rewards. *Sex Roles, 13*(11–12), 597–605.

MARTIN, W.B.W., & MACDONELL, A.J. (1982). *Canadian education: A sociological analysis*. Scarborough, ON: Prentice-Hall.

MARX, K. (1955). *The Communist manifesto*. New York: Appleton Century-Crofts. (Original work published in 1848)

———. (1963). *Selected writings in sociology and social philosophy*. (T.B. Bottomore & M. Rubel, Eds, T.B. Bottomore, Trans.) Harmondsworth: Penguin.

MCCONNATHA, J.T., & MCCONNATHA, P.D. (1988). The study of the relationship between wellness and life satisfaction of older adults. *Activities, Adaptation and Aging, 13*(1–2), 129–40.

MCCULLAGH, J.G. (1985). Satisfaction with the profession and career status among BSW social workers. *Journal of Sociology and Social Welfare, 12*(1), 151–61.

MCDOWELL, M., & FORSYTH, C.J. (1990). The job satisfaction of nurses: Clues to the nursing shortage. *Free Inquiry in Creative Sociology, 18*(2), 175–79.

MCGOLDRICK, A.E., & COOPER, C.L. (1988). *Early retirement*. Hants, England: Gower Publishing.

MCHALE, S.M., & HUSTON, T.L. (1985). The effect of the transition to parenthood on the marriage relationship: A longitudinal study. *Journal of Family Issues*, 6(4), 409–33.

MCKIE, D.C., PRENTICE, B., & REED, P. (1983). *Divorce: Law and the family in Canada* (Statistics Canada, Catalogue No. 89-502E). Ottawa: Supply & Services.

MCLANAHAN, S.S., & ADAMS, J. (1987). Parenthood and psychological well-being. *Annual Review of Sociology, 13*, 237–57.

MCNEELY, R.L. (1983). Organizational patterns and work satisfaction in a comprehensive human service agency: An empirical test. *Human Relations*, 36(10), 957–71.

———. (1988a). Recisions, organizational conditions and job satisfaction among black and white human service workers: A research note. *Journal of Sociology and Social Welfare, 15*(3), 125–34.

———. (1988b). Job satisfaction differences among three age groups of female human service workers. *Journal of Aging Studies, 2*(2), 109–20.

———. (1989a). Race and job satisfaction in human service employment. *Administration in Social Work, 13*(1), 75–94.

———. (1989b). Gender, job satisfaction, earnings and other characteristics of human service workers during and after midlife. *Administration in Social Work, 13*(2), 99–116.

———. (1989c). Job satisfaction and other characteristics among Hispanic-American human services workers. *Social Casework, 70*(4), 237–42.

MCPHERSON, B.D. (1983). *Aging as a social process*. Toronto: Butterworths.

MCRAE, J.A., & BRODY, C.J. (1989). The differential importance of marital experiences for the well-being of women and men: A research note. *Social Science Research, 18*(3), 237–48.

MEEK, R.L. (Ed.). (1954). *Marx and Engels on Malthus* (D.L. Meek & R.L. Meek, Trans.). New York: International Publishers.

MEIER, S.T. (1983). Toward a theory of burnout. *Human Relations, 36*(10), 899–910.

MELEIS, A.I., KULIG, J., ARRUDA, E.N., & BECKMAN, A. (1990). Maternal role of women in clerical jobs in southern Brazil: Stress and satisfaction. *Health Care for Women International, 11*(4), 369–82.

MELLER, Y., & MACAROV, D. (1985). Studying satisfaction in human service organizations: An exploration. *International Journal of Sociology and Social Policy, 5*(2), 1–15.

———. (1986). Social workers' satisfactions: Methodological notes and substantive findings. *Journal of Sociology and Social Welfare, 13*(4), 740–61.

MENAHEM, G., & SPIRO, S. (1989). Urban neighborhoods and the quest for community: Implications for policy and practice. *Community Development Journal, 24*(1), 29–39.

MENSCH, B.S., & KANDEL, D.B. (1988). Do job conditions influence the use of drugs? *Journal of Health and Social Behavior, 29*(2), 169–84.

MEREDITH, W.H., ABBOTT, D.A., & ADAMS, S.L. (1986). Family violence: Its relation to marital and parental satisfaction and family strengths. *Journal of Family Violence, 1*(4), 299–305.

MERTON, R.K. (1957a). Social structure and anomie. In his *Social Theory and Social Structure* (rev. ed.), pp. 131–60. New York: Free Press.

———. (1957b). Patterns of influence: Local and cosmopolitan influentials. In R.K. Merton, *Social theory and social structure* (rev. ed.)., pp. 387–420. New York: Free Press.

MERVES-OKIN, L., AMIDON, E., & BERNT, F. (1991). Perceptions of intimacy in marriage: A study of married couples. *American Journal of Family Therapy, 19*(2), 110–18.

METHOT, S (1987, Spring). Low income in Canada. *Canadian Social Trends*, pp. 2–7.

MEYHASZ, P. (1990, January). Top court upholds mandatory retirement. *Canadian Human Rights Advocate*, p. 7.

MICHAELS, J.W., EDWARDS, J.N., & ACOCK, A.C. (1984). Satisfaction in intimate relationships as a function of inequality, inequity and outcomes. *Social Psychology Quarterly, 47*(4), 347–57.

MICHALOS, A.C. (1981). *North American social report: A comparative study of the quality of life in Canada and the USA from 1964 to 1974. Vol. 3: Science, education, and recreation*. Dordrecht, Holland: D. Reidel.

———. (1985). Multiple discrepancies theory (MDT). *Social Indicators Research, 16*(4), 347–413.

———. (1986). An application of multiple discrepancies theory (MDT) to seniors. *Social Indicators Research, 18*(4), 349–73.

———. (1987). *Final progress report on Global Report on Student Well-Being: Applications of multiple discrepancies theory*. Guelph: University of Guelph.

———. (1988). Optimism in thirty countries over a decade. *Social Indicators Research, 20* (2), 177–80.

MICHELS, R. (1962). *Political Parties*. New York: Free Press.

MICHELSON, W. (1977). *Environmental choice, human behavior, and residential satisfaction*. New York: Oxford University Press.

———. (1985). *From sun to sun: Daily obligations and community structure in the lives of employed mothers and their families*. Totowa, NJ: Rowman & Allanheld.

———. (1990). Childcare and the daily routine. *Social Indicators Research, 23*(4), 353–66.

MILLAR, K.U., & MILLAR, M.G. (1988). Sex differences in perceived self- and other-disclosure: A case where inequity increases satisfaction. *Social Behaviour and Personality, 16*(1), 59–64.

MILLS, C.W. (1943). The professional ideology of social pathologists. *American Journal of Sociology, 49*(2), 165–80.

———. (1956). *The power elite*. New York: Oxford University Press.

———. (1959). *The sociological imagination*. New York: Oxford University Press.

MITCHELL, A. (1983). *The nine American lifestyles: Who we are and where we are going*. New York: Warner Books.

MITFORD, J. (1963). *The American way of death*. New York: Fawcett, Crest Books.

MOLCAR, C.C., & STUEMPFIG, D.W. (1988). Effects of world view on purpose in life. *Journal of Psychology, 122*(4), 365–71.

MONK-TURNER, E. (1990). The occupational achievements of community and four year college entrants. *American Sociological Review, 55*(5), 719–25.

MORGAN, M.G., & DEMARIS, A. (1986). Role-set diversity: Benefit or strain? *Journal of Sociology and Social Welfare, 13*(2), 287–305.

MORSE, D., & GRAY, S. (1980). *Early retirement: Boon or bane?* Boston: Allanheld, Osmun & Co.

MORTIMER, J.T. (1979). *Changing attitudes towards work.* Studies in Productivity Series. Scarsdale, NY: Work in America Institute.

MOTTAZ, C. (1984). Education and work satisfaction. *Human Relations, 37*(11), 985–1004.

MOTTAZ, C.J. (1985). The relative importance of intrinsic and extrinsic determinants of work satisfaction. *Sociological Quarterly, 26*(3), 365–85.

———. (1987) Age and work satisfaction. *Work and Occupations, 14*(3), 387–409.

MOURITZEN, P.E. (1989). City size and citizens' satisfaction: Two competing theories revisited. *European Journal of Political Research, 17*(6), 661–88.

MURPHY, R. (1982). The structure of closure: A critique and development of the theories of Weber, Collins and Parkin. *British Journal of Sociology, 35*(4) 547–67.

MYKLETUN, R.J. (1985). Work stress and satisfaction of comprehensive school teachers: An interview study. *Scandinavian Journal of Educational Research, 29*(2), June, 57–71.

NACHMAN, J. (1988). Laws, rules and regulations on early retirement in Israel. In S. Bergman, G. Naegele, & W. Tokarski (Eds.), *Early retirement: Approaches and variations, an international perspective*. n.p.

NAGNUR, D., & ADAMS, O. (1987, August). Tying the knot: An overview of marriage rates in Canada. *Canadian Social Trends*, pp. 2–6.

NEAR, J.P. (1984). Relationships between job satisfaction and life satisfaction: Test of a causal model. *Social Indicators Research, 15*(4), 351–67.

———. (1987). Work and nonwork: A cross-cultural comparison of Japanese and American workers. *Research in the Sociology of Organizations, 5*, 233–51.

NEVITTE, N, GIBBINS, R., & CODDING, P.W. (1988). The career goals of female science students in Canada. *Canadian Journal of Higher Education, 18*(1), 31–48.

———. (1979). *The Canadian establishment* (Vol. 1). Toronto: McClelland & Stewart.

NEWMAN, P.C. (1981). *The new acquisitors*, (The Canadian establishment, Vol. 2). Toronto: McClelland & Stewart.

NICOLA, J.S., & HAWKES, G.R. (1986). Marital satisfaction of dual-career couples: Does sharing increase happiness? *Journal of Social Behavior and Personality, 1*(1), 47–60.

NICOLSON, J. (1980). *Seven ages*. London: Fontana Paperbacks.

OBSTFELD, L.S., LUPFER, M.B., & LUPFER, S.L. (1985). Exploring the relationship between gender identity and sexual functioning. *Journal of Sex and Marital Therapy, 11*(4), 248–58.

OKUN, M.A., BRAVER, M.W., & WEIR, R.M. (1990). Grade level differences in school satisfaction. *Social Indicators Research, 22*(4), 419–27.

OLSON, G.I., & SCHOBER, B.I. (1993). The satisfied poor. *Social Indicators Research, 28*(2), 173–93.

ONTARIO. (1985). Task Force on Employment and New Technology. *Final Report: Employment and New Technology*. Toronto.

ORNSTEIN, M. (1981). The occupational mobility of men in Ontario. *Canadian Review of Sociology and Anthropology, 18*(2), 183–215.

———. (1988). Social class and economic inequality. In J. Curtis & L. Tepperman (Eds.), *Understanding Canadian society*. Toronto: McGraw-Hill Ryerson.

ORTEGA, S.T., WHITT, H.P., & WILLIAMS, J.A. Jr. (1988). Religious homogamy and marital happiness. *Journal of Family Issues*, 9(2), 224–39.

OSTROFF, J. (1989). An aging market. *American Demographics, 11*(5), pp. 26–33, 58.

OUTLOOK '87 AND BEYOND. (1986). Bethesda, MD: World Future Society.

PACKARD, T. (1989). Participation in decision making, performance, and job satisfaction in a social work bureaucracy. *Administration in Social Work, 13*(1), 59–73.

PAIN, B. (1986). Education students as consumers: Choice of a university education. *Canadian Journal of Higher Education, 16*(2), 51–56.

PALETTA, A. (1992, Winter). Today's extended families. *Canadian Social Trends*, pp. 26–28.

PALMORE, E.B. (1985). How to live longer and like it. *Journal of Applied Gerontology, 4*(2), 1–8.

PAMPEL, F.C., & WEISS, J.A. (1983). Economic development, pension policies and the labor force participation of aged males: A cross-national, longitudinal approach. *American Journal of Sociology*, 89(2), 350–72.

PAPADAKIS, E., & TAYLOR-GOODY, P. (1986) Positional satisfaction and state welfare. *Sociological Review, 34*(4), 812–27.

PARK, H.S., & MASON, T.D. (1986) The developmental parameters of relative deprivation theory. *Studies in Comparative International Development, 21*(3), 85–117.

PARLIAMENT, J. (1989, Winter). How Canadians spend their day. *Canadian Social Trends*, pp. 23–27.

———. (1990). Women employed outside the home. In Craig McKie and Keith Thompson (Eds.), *Canadian social trends*. Toronto: Thomson Educational Publishing.

PARRY, J.K., & SMITH, M.J. (1987). A study of social workers' job satisfaction as based on an optimal model of care for the terminally ill. *Journal of Social Service Research, 11*(1), 39–58.

PARSONS, T. (1964). A revised analytical approach to the theory of social stratification. In *Essays in Sociological Theory* (rev. ed.). pp. 386–439. New York: Free Press.

PEARCE, P.L., & MOSCARDO, G.M. (1986). The concept of authenticity in tourist experiences. *Australian and New Zealand Journal of Sociology, 22*(1), 121–32.

PEARSON, D.A., & SEILER, R.E. (1983). Environmental satisfiers in academe. *Higher Education, 12*(1), 35–47.

PENN, M., ROMANO, J.L., & FOAT, D. (1988). The relationship between job satisfaction and burnout: A study of human service professionals. *Administration in Mental Health, 15*(3), 157–65.

PEPLAU, L.A., PADESKY, C., & HAMILTON, M. (1982). Satisfaction in lesbian relationships. *Journal of Homosexuality, 8*(2), 23–35.

PERRY-JENKINS, M., & CROUTER, A.C. (1990). Men's provider-role attitudes: Implications for household work and marital satisfaction. *Journal of Family Issues, 11*(2), 136–56.

PETERSEN, W. (1969). *Population* (2nd ed.). Toronto: Collier-Macmillan.

PETRILLO, G. (1989). The distant mourner: An examination of the American grave-digger. *Omega, 20*(2), 139–48.

PFEFFER, J., & DAVIS-BLAKE, A. (1990). Unions and job satisfaction: An alternative view. *Work and Occupations, 17*(3), 259–83.

PHELAN, T.J., & PHELAN, J.C. (1983). Higher education and early life outcomes. *Higher Education, 12*(6), 665–80.

PICOT, W.G. (1987, Spring). The changing industrial mix of employment, 1951–1985. *Canadian Social Trends* (Statistics Canada, Catalogue No. 11-008E, pp. 8–11). Ottawa: Supply & Services.

———. (1989). Jobs and wages in the 1980's: The decline in wages for youth overshadows the shift to the service sector. *Perception, 13*(2), 11–15.

PIKE, R.M. (1988). Education and the schools. In L. Tepperman & J. Curtis (Eds.), *Understanding Canadian society*. Toronto: McGraw-Hill Ryerson.

PINCUS, J.D. (1986) Communication satisfaction, job satisfaction, and job performance. *Human Communication Research, 12*(3), 395–419.

PINEO, P.C. (1985a). Family size and status attainment. In M. Boyd, J. Goyder, F.E. Jones, H.A. McRoberts, P.C. Pineo, & J. Porter (Eds.), *Ascription and achievement: Studies in mobility and status attainment in Canada* (pp. 201–28). Ottawa: Carleton University Press.

———. (1985b). Internal migration and occupational attainment. In M. Boyd, J. Goyder, F.E. Jones, H.A. McRoberts, P.C. Pineo, & J. Porter (Eds.), *Ascription and achievement: Studies in mobility and status attainment in Canada* (pp. 479–512). Ottawa: Carleton University Press.

PITTMAN, J.F., & ORTHNER, D.K. (1988). Gender differences in the prediction of job commitment. *Journal of Social Behavior and Personality, 3*(4), 227–48.

POLANYI, K. (1944). *The great transformation*. New York: Farrar & Rinehart.

POLOMA, M.M., & PENDLETON, B.F. (1990). Religious domains and general well-being. *Social Indicators Research, 22*(3), 255–76.

POLONKO, K.A., SCANZONI, J., & TEACHMAN, J.D. (1982). Childlessness and marital satisfaction: A further reassessment. *Journal of Family Issues, 3*(4), 545–73.

POOL, I., & MOORE, M. (1986). *Lone parenthood: Characteristics and determinants* (Results from the 1984 Family History Survey) (Statistics Canada, Catalogue No. 99-961). Ottawa: Supply & Services.

PORTER, J. (1965). *The vertical mosaic*. Toronto: University of Toronto Press.

———. (1979). *The measure of Canadian society: Education, equality and opportunity*. Toronto: Gage.

PORTER, J., PORTER, M., & BLISHEN, B.R. (1982). *Stations and callings: Making it through the school system*. Toronto: Methuen.

POSTEN, D.L., & FALBO, T. (1990). Academic performance and personality traits of Chinese children: "Onlies" versus others. *American Journal of Sociology*, 96(2), 433–51.

POTTER, R.B. (1984). Perceived life domain satisfaction and social status. *Journal of Social Psychology, 124*(2), 259–60.

PRENTICE, A. (1977). *The school promoters: Education and social class in mid-nineteenth-century Upper Canada*. Toronto: McClelland & Stewart.

PRIEMUS, H. (1986). Housing as a social adaptation process: A conceptual scheme. *Environment and Behavior, 18*(1), 31–52.

QUALITY OF LIFE SURVEY. (1981). Unpublished raw data from large survey of life satisfaction conducted at the Institute for Behavioural Research, York University, Toronto.

QUIROGA, I. (1990). Characteristics of package tours in Europe. *Annals of Tourism Research, 17*(2), 185–207.

RAINWATER, L., COLEMAN, R.P., & HANDEL, G. (1962). *Workingman's wife: Her personality, world and life style*. New York: Macfadden-Bartell Books.

RAJULTON, F., & BURCH, T.K. (1991). *A behavioural model of remarriage: Motivation and market influences*. Discussion Paper No. 91–8, Population Studies Centre, University of Western Ontario.

RAM, B. (1988). Reproduction: The Canadian family in transition. *Journal of Biosocial Science*, *20*, 19–30.

RAMU, G.N. (1984). Family background and perceived marital happiness: A comparison of voluntary childless couples and parents. *Canadian Journal of Sociology*, 9(1), 47–67.

RAMU, G.N., & TAVUCHIS, N. (1986). The valuation of children and parenthood among the voluntarily childless and parental couples in Canada. *Journal of Comparative Family Studies*, *17*(1), 99–114.

RAO, V.V., & RAO, V.N. (1986) Correlates of marital happiness: A longitudinal analysis. *Free Enquiry in Creative Sociology*, *14*(1), 3–8.

RAY, J.A. (1988). Marital satisfaction in dual-career couples. *Journal of Independent Social Work*, *3*(1), 39–55.

RAY, J. (1990). Interactional patterns and marital satisfaction among dual-career couples. *Journal of Independent Social Work*, *4*(3), 61–73.

REDMOND, C.R. (1988) The effects of working nontraditional hours on life satisfaction. *Mid-American Review of Sociology*, *13*(1), 21–40.

REED, P. (1976). *Life style as an element of social logic: Patterns of activity, social characteristics, and residential choice*. Unpublished doctoral dissertation, University of Toronto, Department of Sociology.

REICHEL, A., NEUMANN, Y., & SAAD, I.A. (1986). Organizational climate and work satisfaction of male and female teachers in Bedouin elementary schools. *Israel Social Science Research*, 4(2), 34–48.

REITZ, J.G. (1980). *The survival of ethnic groups*. Toronto: McGraw-Hill Ryerson.

REITZ, J.G., CALZAVARA, L., & DASKO, D. (1981). *Ethnic inequality and segregation in jobs*. Research Paper No. 123. Toronto: University of Toronto, Centre for Urban and Community Studies.

REMPEL, J. (1985). Childless elderly: What are they missing? *Journal of Marriage and the Family*, *47*(2), 343–48.

RESNICK, A., & MASON, J.B. (1988). Switching careers between academia and industry. *Business*, 38(4), 30–39.

RHYNE, D. (1984). *Marital satisfaction in Canada: A descriptive overview*. Toronto: York University, Institute for Behavioural Research.

RICE, R.W., NEAR, J.P., & HUNT, R.G. (1979). Unique variance in job and life satisfaction associated with work-related and extra-workplace variables. *Human Relations*, *32*(7), 605–23.

RICE, S. (1989). Single, older childless women: Differences between never-married and widowed women in life satisfaction and social support. *Journal of Gerontological Social Work, 13*(3–4), 35–47.

RICHMOND, A.H. (1989). *Caribbean Immigrants: A Demo-economic Analysis, Current Demographic Analysis*.(Catalogue No. 91-536E) Ottawa: Statistics Canada.

RIFFER, R.L., & CHIN, J.C. (1988). Dating satisfaction among college students. *International Journal of Sociology and Social Policy*, 8(5), 29–36.

RIGBY, K., & VREUGDENHIL, A. (1987). The relationship between generalized community satisfaction and residential social status. *Journal of Social Psychology, 127*(4), 381–90.

RINEHART, J.W. (1987). *The tyranny of work: Alienation and the labour process* (2nd ed.). Toronto: Harcourt Brace Jovanovich.

RIZZO, C., REYNOLDS, I., & GALLAGHER, H. (1981). Job satisfaction: A study of Sydney adults. *Australian Journal of Social Issues, 16*(2), 138–48.

ROBINSON, J. (1991). Your money or your time. *American Demographics, 13* (11), 22–26.

ROBINSON, J.P., & CONVERSE, P.E. (1972). The impact of television on mass media usage: A cross-national comparison. In A. Szalai (Ed.), *The use of time: Daily activities of urban and suburban populations in twelve countries* (pp. 197–212). The Hague: Mouton.

ROBINSON, J.P., CONVERSE, P.E., & SZALAI, A. (1972). Everyday life in twelve countries. In A. Szalai (Ed.), *The use of time: Daily activities of urban and suburban populations in twelve countries* (pp. 113–44). The Hague: Mouton.

ROBORGH, P., & STACEY, B.G. (1987). Happiness and radical career change among New Zealanders. *Journal of Psychology, 121*(5), 501–14.

ROCHER, G. (1975). Formal education: the issue of opportunity. In D. Forcese & S. Richer (Eds.), *Issues in Canadian society: An introduction to sociology*. Scarborough, ON: Prentice-Hall.

RODGERS, W. (1982a). Trends in reported happiness within demographically defined subgroups, 1957–78. *Social Forces*, 60(3), 826–42.

———. (1982b). Density, crowding and satisfaction with the residential environment. *Social Indicators Research, 10*(1), 75–102.

RODGERS-JENKINSON, F., & CHAPMAN, D.W. (1990). Job satisfaction of Jamaican elementary school teachers. *Internation Review of Education*, 36(3), 299–313.

ROGLER, L.H., & PROCIDANO, M.E. (1989). Egalitarian spouse relations and wives' marital satisfaction in intergenerationally linked Puerto Rican families. *Journal of Marriage and the Family, 51*(1), 37–39.

ROMANIUC, A. (1986, November). *Fertility in Canada: A long view*. Paper presented at The Family in Crisis: A Population Crisis?, a colloquium organized by the Federation of Canadian Demographers, University of Ottawa.

RONEN, S., & SADAN, S. (1984). Job attitudes among different occupational status groups: An economic analysis. *Work and Occupations, 11*(1), 77–97.

ROOS, J.P. (1988). Behind the happiness barrier. *Social Indicators Research, 20*(2), 141–63.

ROSEN, L.N., ICKOVICS, J.R., & MOGHADAM, L.Z. (1990). Employment and role satisfaction: Implications for the general well-being of military wives. *Psychology of Women Quarterly, 14*(3), 371–85.

ROSENTHAL, J.A., WEDEL, K.R., & WILSON, M.V.K. (1989). The working part-time student: A study in student satisfaction. *Arete, 14*(2), 32–41.

RUBIN, H.J. (1989). Measures of work satisfaction among economic development practitioners. *Sociological Inquiry*, 59(2), 165–89.

RUDD, N.M., & MCHENRY, P.C. (1986). Family influences on the job satisfaction of employed mothers. *Psychology of Women Quarterly, 10*(4), 363–71.

RUSSELL, R.V. (1990). Recreation and quality of life in old age: A causal analysis. *Journal of Applied Gerontology*, 9(1), 77–90.

RUTTER, M. (1981). Social-emotional consequences of day care for preschool children. *American Journal of Orthopsychiatry, 51*(1), 4–28.

RYAN, W. (1976). *Blaming the victim*. (rev. ed.). New York: Vintage Books.

SABATELLI, R.M., & CECIL-PIGO, E.F. (1985). Relational interdependence and commitment in marriage. *Journal of Marriage and the Family, 47*(4), 931–37.

SABATELLI, R.M., METH, R.L., & GAVAZZI, S.M. (1988). Factors mediating the adjustment to involuntary childlessness. *Family Relations, 37*(3), 338–43.

SADEQUE, M. (1986, Spring). The survival characteristics of the poor: A case study of a village in Bangladesh. *Social Development Issues, 10*(1), 11–27.

SAENZ, R., GOODY, W.J., & LORENZ, F.O. (1989). The effects of employment and marital relations on depression among Mexican American women. *Journal of Marriage and the Family, 51*(1), 239–51.

SAI, F.T. (1988). Changing perspectives of population in Africa and international responses. *African Affairs, 87*(347), 267–76.

ST. JOHN, C., AUSTIN, D.M., & BABA, Y. (1986). The question of community attachment revisited. *Sociological Spectrum*, 6(4), 411–31.

ST. JOHN, C., & CLARK, F. (1984). Racial differences in dimensions of neighborhood satisfaction. *Social Indicators Research, 15*(1), 43–60.

SALAMON, M.J. (1985). Sociocultural role theories in the elderly: A replication and extension. *Activities, Adaptation and Aging, 7*(2), 111–22.

SAMPSON, R.J. (1991). Linking the micro- and macro-level dimensions of community social organization. *Social Forces*, *70*(1), 43–64.

SAUVÉ, R. (1990). *Canadian people patterns: What's in the cards for you?* Saskatoon, SK: Western Producer Prairie Books.

SAUVY, A. (1969). *General theory of population*. (Christopher Campos, Trans.). New York: Basic Books.

SCANZONI, J.H. (1972). *Sexual bargaining: Power politics in the American marriage*. Englewood Cliffs, NJ: Prentice-Hall.

SCHELL, B.H., & LOEB, A.S. (1986). An investigation of general happiness level, collective bargaining attitudes, job satisfaction, and university and union commitment of faculty members in Canada. *Journal of Social Behavior and Personality*, *1*(4), 537–56.

SCHLESINGER, B. (1982) Lasting marriages in the 1980s. *Conciliation Courts Review*, *20*(1), 43–49.

SCHLESINGER, B., & SCHLESINGER, R. (1989). Postponed parenthood: Trends and issues. *Journal of Comparative Family Studies*, *20*(3), 355–63.

SCHLOZMAN, K.L., & VERBA, S. (1979). *Injury to insult: Unemployment, class and political response*. Cambridge, MA: Harvard University Press.

SCHNEIDER, R. (1984). Technological development and its aftermath. In P. Ayrton, T. Engelhardt, & V. Ware (Eds.), *World View 1985*. London: Pluto Press.

SCHONFELD, I.S. (1990). Coping with job-related stress: The case of teachers. *Journal of Occupational Psychology*, *63*(2), 141–49.

SCHUCHTS, R.A., & WITKIN, S.L. (1989). Assessing marital change during the transition to parenthood. *Social Casework*, *70*(2), 67–75.

SCHUMM, W.R., & BUGAIGHIS, M.A. (1986). Marital quality over the marital career: Alternative explanations. *Journal of Marriage and the Family*, *48*(1), 165–68.

SCHUMM, W.R., JURICH, A.P., BOLLMAN, S.R., & BUGAIGHIS, M.A. (1985). His and her marriage revisited. *Journal of Family Issues*, *6*(2), 221–27.

SCHWOCHAU, S. (1987). Union effects on job attitudes. *Industrial and Labor Relations Review*, *40*(2), 209–24.

SEKARAN, U. (1985). The paths to mental health: An exploratory study of husbands and wives in dual-career families. *Journal of Occupational Psychology*, *58*(2), 129–37.

———. (1986). Self-esteem and sense of competence as moderators of the job satisfaction of professionals in dual-career families. *Journal of Occupational Behaviour*, *7*(4), 341–44.

———. (1989). Understanding the dynamics of self-concept in members of dual-career families. *Human Relations*, *42*(2), 97–116.

SELLECK, L. (1980). *The university graduate and the marketplace*. Toronto: Council of Ontario Universities.

———. (1982). *Manpower planning and higher education policy*. Toronto: Council of Ontario Universities.

SENNETT, R., & COBB, J. (1973). *The hidden injuries of social class*. New York: Vintage Books.

SHAPIRO, D.M., & STELCNER, M. (1987). The persistence of the male-female earning gap in Canada, 1970–1980: The impact of equal pay laws and language policies. *Canadian Public Policy*, *13*(4), 462–72.

SHAW, S.M. (1988). Leisure in the contemporary family: The effect of female employment on the leisure of Canadian wives and husbands. *International Review of Modern Sociology*, *18*(1), 1–15.

SHEBANI, B. L., WASS, H., & GUERTIN, W.H. (1986). Correlates of life satisfaction for old Libyans compared with the judgments of Libyan youth. *International Journal of Aging and Human Development*, *24*(1), 19–28.

SHEHAN, C.L., BURG, M.A., & REXROAT, C.A. (1986). Depression and the social dimensions of the full-time housewife role. *Sociological Quarterly*, *27*(3), 403–21.

SHICHMAN, S., & COOPER, E. (1984). Life satisfaction and sex-role concept. *Sex Roles*, *11*(3–4), 227–40.

SHIMONAKA, Y., & NAKAZATO, K. (1986). The development of personality characteristics of Japanese adults. *Journal of Genetic Psychology*, *147*(1), 37–46.

SHIN, D.C. (1989). Political democracy and the quality of citizens' lives: A cross-national study. *Journal of Developing Societies*, *5*(1), 30–41.

SHOHAM-YAKUBOVITCH, I., CARMEL, S., ZWANGER, L., & ZALTCMAN, T. (1989). Autonomy, job satisfaction and professional self-image among nurses in the context of a physicians' strike. *Social Science and Medicine*, *28*(12), 1315–20.

SHOLOMSKAS, D., & AXELROD, R. (1986). The influence of mother-daughter relationships on women's sense of self and current role choices. *Psychology of Women Quarterly*, *10*(2), 171–82.

SHORE, L.M., & MARTIN, H.J. (1989). Job satisfaction and organizational commitment in relation to work performance and turnover intentions. *Human Relations*, *42*(7), 625–38.

SHUKLA, A., & SAXENA, S. (1988). Women's satisfaction with the dual work role. *Psychologia*, *31*(4), 239–42.

SIGGNER, A.J. (1986, Winter). The socio-demographic conditions of registered Indians. *Canadian Social Trends*, pp. 2–9.

SIMON, J.M. (1990). Humor and its relationship to perceived health, life satisfaction and morale in older adults. *Issues in Mental Health Nursing*, *11*(1), 17–31.

SMITH, G.T., SNYDER, D.K., TRULL, T.J., & MONSMA, B.R. (1988). Predicting relationship satisfaction from couples' use of leisure time. *American Journal of Family Therapy*, *16*(1), 3–13.

SMITH, K.B., & STONE, L.H. (1989). Rags, riches and bootstraps: Beliefs about the causes of wealth and property. *Sociological Quarterly*, *30*(1), pp. 103–107.

SMITH, R.H., DIENER, E., & GARONZIK, R. (1990). The roles of outcome satisfaction and comparison alternatives in envy. *British Journal of Social Psychology*, *29*(3), 247–55.

SOCIETY. (1989). Social science and the citizen. *27*, 1 (183), 2–3.

SOFRANKO, A.J., & FLIEGEL, F.C. (1984). Dissatisfaction with satisfaction. *Rural Sociology*, *49*(3), 353–73.

SOLMAN, R., PETTY, M., & LAUGHLIN, A. (1986). Job sharing in teaching: Attitudes of teachers employed by the New South Wales Department of Education. *Australian Journal of Social Issues*, *21*(2), 126–42.

SOMERS, A.R. (1981, Autumn). Social, economic, and health aspects of mandatory retirement. *Journal of Health, Politics, Policy and Law*, *6*(3), 542–57.

SOROKIN, P.A. (1941). *The crisis of our age: The social and cultural outlook*. New York: E.P. Dutton.

———. (1957). *Social and cultural mobility*. New York: Free Press. (Original work published 1927)

SOUTH, S. J., & LLOYD, K.M. (1992). Marriage markets and nonmarital fertility in the United States. *Demography*, *29*(2), 247–64.

SPAIN, D. (1988). The effect of changing household composition on neighborhood satisfaction. *Urban Affairs Quarterly*, *23*(4), 581–600.

SPEARE, A., Jr, KOBRIN, F.E., & KINGKADE, W. (1982). The influence of socioeconomic bonds and satisfaction on interstate migration. *Social Forces*, *61*(2), 551–74.

SPECTOR, P.E. (1985). Measure of human service staff satisfaction: Development of the job satisfaction survey. *American Journal of Community Psychology*, *13*(6), 693–713.

SPRECHER, S. (1988). Investment model, equity, and social support determinants of relationship commitment. *Social Psychology Quarterly*, *51*(4), 318–28.

STAGER, D. (1983). Dynamic information for entrants to the highly qualified labour market. *Canadian Journal of Higher Education*, *13*(1), 65–74.

STAINES, G.L. (1979, May–June). Is worker dissatisfaction rising? *Challenge*, pp. 38–45.

STANDING SENATE COMMITTEE ON NATIONAL FINANCE. (1987). *Federal policy on post-secondary education*. Ottawa: Supply & Services.

STANLEY, S.C., HUNT, J.G., & HUNT, L.L. (1986). The relative deprivation of husbands in dual-earner households. *Journal of Family Issues*, *7*(1), 3–20.

STASSEN, M.A., & STAATS, S.R. (1988). Hope and happiness: A comparison of some discrepancies. *Social Indicators Research*, *20*(1), 45–58.

STATISTICS CANADA. (1980). *Perspectives Canada III* (Catalogue No. 11-511E). Ottawa: Supply & Services.

———. (1982a). *Census families in private households: 1981 census of Canada* (Catalogue No. 92-905). Ottawa: Supply & Services.

———. (1982b). *Vital statistics, Volume II: Marriages and divorces* (Catalogue No. 84-205). Ottawa: Supply & Services.

———. (1984). *Women in the world of work* (Catalogue No. 99-940). Ottawa: Supply & Services.

———. (1985a). *Education in Canada: A statistical review for 1984–1985*. (Catalogue No. 81-229). Ottawa: Supply & Services.

———. (1985b). *Population projections for Canada, provinces and territories, 1984–2006* (Catalogue No. 91-520). Ottawa: Supply & Services.

———. (1987a). *Current demographic analysis: Report on the demographic situation in Canada, 1986* (Catalogue No. 91-209E). Ottawa: Supply & Services.

———. (1987b) *Health and social support, 1985*. General Social Survey Analysis Series (Catalogue 11-612E, No. 1). Ottawa: Supply & Services.

———. (1990). *New trends in the family*. (Catalogue No. 91-535E). Ottawa: Supply & Services.

———. (1991). *Report on the demographic situation in Canada, 1991*. (Catalogue 91-209E). Ottawa: Supply & Services.

———. (1992). *Canada Yearbook 125th Anniversary edition, 1992*. (Catalogue 11-402E/1992). Ottawa: Supply & Services.

STAW, B.M., BELL, N.E., & CLAUSEN, J.A. (1986). The dispositional approach to job attitudes: A lifetime longitudinal test. *Administrative Science Quarterly*, *31*(1), 56–77.

STEINBERG, L., & SILVERBERG, S.B. (1987). Influences on marital satisfaction during the middle stages of the family life cycle. *Journal of Marriage and the Family*, 49(4), 751–60.

STEINKAMP, M.W. (1987). Social integration, leisure activity, and life satisfaction in older adults: Activity theory revisited. *International Journal of Aging and Human Development*, *25*(4), 293–307.

STEINKAMP, M. W., & KELLY, J.R. (1985). Relationships among motivational orientation, level of leisure activity and life satisfaction in older men and women. *Journal of Psychology*, *119*(6), 509–20.

STEPHENSON, M. (1988). Marital satisfaction: A multivariate study. *Free Enquiry in Creative Sociology*, *16*(2), 231–36

STOKES, J.P., & PEYTON, J.S. (1986). Attitudinal differences between full-time homemakers and women who work outside the home. *Sex Roles, 15*(5–6), 299–310.

STONE, L.O. (1978). *The frequency of geographic mobility in the population of Canada,* Census Analytical Study. (Catalogue No. 99-751E). Ottawa: Supply & Services.

STONES, M.J., & KOZMA, A. (1985). Structural relationships among happiness scales: A second order factorial study. *Social Indicators Research, 17*(1), 19–28.

SWENSEN, C.H., & TRAHAUG, G. (1985). Commitment and the long-term relationship. *Journal of Marriage and the Family, 47*(4), 939–45.

SZALAI, A. (Ed.). (1972). *The use of time: Daily activities of urban and suburban populations in twelve countries.* The Hague: Mouton.

TAHLIN, M. (1989). The value and costs of work: A study of the consequences of wage labour for the individual. *European Sociological Review, 5*(2), 115–31.

TASK FORCE ON PROGRAM REVIEW, STUDY TEAM REPORT. (1986a). *Indian and Native programs* (Catalogue No. CP32-50/12-1985E). Ottawa: Supply & Services.

———. (1986b). *Education and research* (Catalogue No. CP32-50/16 1985E). Ottawa: Supply & Services.

TAYLOR, P.A., GRANDJEAN, B.D., & TOS, N. (1987). Work satisfaction under Yugoslav self-management: On participation, authority, and ownership. *Social Forces, 65*(4), June, 1020–34.

TCHENG-LAROCHE, F., & PRINCE, R. (1983). Separated and divorced women compared with married controls: Selected life satisfaction, stress and health indices from a community survey. *Social Science and Medicine, 17*(2), 95–105.

TENNOV, D. (1979). *Love and Limerence.* New York: Stein and Day.

TEPPERMAN, L. (1974). Ethnic variations in marriage and fertility: Canada, 1871. *Canadian Review of Sociology and Anthropology, 11*(4), 324–43.

———. (1985). Musical chairs: the occupational experience of migrants to Alberta, 1976-80. *Social Indicators Research, 16*(51–67).

———. (1990). Population processes. In L. Tepperman & R.J. Richardson (Eds.), *The social world: An introduction to sociology* (2nd ed.). Toronto: McGraw-Hill Ryerson.

TERRY, D.J., & SCOTT, W.A. (1987). Gender differences in correlates of marital satisfaction. *Australian Journal of Psychology, 39*(2), 207–21.

TEULINGS, A.W.M. (1985). The power of corporate management: The powerlessness of the manager. *Economic and Industrial Democracy,* 6(4), 403–34.

THOMAS, K., & BURCH, T.K. (1985). Household formation in Canada and the United States, 1900–1901 to 1970–1971: Trends and regional differentials. *Canadian Studies in Population, 12*(2), 159–182.

THOMPSON, A.H., BARNSLEY, R.H., & STEBELSKY, G. (1991). Born to play ball: The relative age effect and major league baseball. *Sociology of Sport Journal*, 8, 146–51.

THORESEN, R.J., & GOLDSMITH, E.R. (1987). The relationship between army families' financial well-being and depression, general well-being, and marital satisfaction. *Journal of Social Psychology, 127*(5), 545–47.

TIGGEL, R.B., PETERS, M.D., KELLEY, H.H., & VINCENT, J. (1982). Correlational and discrepancy indices of understanding and their relation to marital satisfaction. *Journal of Marriage and the Family, 44*(1), 209–15.

TOKARSKI, W. (1988). Early retirement: trends and results. In S. Bergman, G. Naegele, & W. Tokarski (Eds.), *Early retirement: Approaches and variations, an international perspective*. n.p.

TOWNSEND, B., & RICHE, M.F. (1987). Two paychecks and seven lifestyles. *American Demographics*, 9(7), pp. 24–29.

TOWNSEND, J.M., & LEVY, G. (1990). Effects of potential partners' physical attractiveness and socioeconomic status on sexuality and partner selection. *Archives of Sexual Behaviour, 19*(2), 149–64.

TRAVERS, J., & MILGRAM, S. (1969). An experimental study of the small world problem. *Sociometry, 32*, 425–43.

TRICKETT, E.J., MCCONAHAY, J.B., PHILLIPS, D., & GINTER, M.A. (1985). Natural experiments and the education context: The environment and effects of an alternative inner-city public school on adolescents. *American Journal of Community Psychology, 13*(6), 617–43.

TROMBETTA, J.J., & ROGERS, D.P. (1988). Communication climate, job satisfaction,and organizational commitment: The effects of information adequacy, communication openness, and decision participation. *Management Communication Quarterly, 1*(4), 494–514.

TROVATO, F., & LAURIS,. G. (1989). Marital status and mortality in Canada. *Journal of Marriage and the Family, 51*(4), 907–22.

TUMIN, M. (1953, August). Some principles of stratification: A critical analysis. *American Sociological Review, 18*, 387–93.

TURCOTTE, P. (1990). Common-law unions: Nearly half a million in 1986. In Craig McKie and Keith Thompson (Eds.), *Canadian social trends*. Toronto: Thomson Educational Publishing.

TURNER, B.S. (1986). The vocabulary of complaints: Nursing, professionalism and job context. *Australian and New Zealand Journal of Sociology, 22*(3), 368–86.

TURNER, J.H. (1984). *Societal stratification: A theoretical analysis*. New York: Columbia University Press.

TUROWSKI, J. (1986). Evaluation of urban living environments. *Polish Sociological Bulletin, 1–2* (73–74), 125–36.

TWADDLE, A.C. (1986). Swedish physicians' perspectives on work and the medical care system: The case of district general practitioners. *Social Science and Medicine, 23*(8), 763–71.

TYNES, S.R. (1990). Educational homogamy and marital satisfaction between spouses. *Social Science Research, 19*(2), 153–74.

TZINER, A.E., & VARDI, Y. (1984). Work satisfaction and absenteeism among social workers: The role of altruistic values. *Work and Occupations, 11*(4), 461–70.

UKAEGBU, A.O. (1977). Socio-cultural determination of fertility: A case study of rural Eastern Nigeria. *Journal of Comparative Family Studies, 8*(1), 99–115.

UNIVERSITY OF TORONTO CAREER CENTRE (n.d.). *Report on University of Toronto 1982 graduates*. Toronto.

VAN ES, J.C., & SCHNEIDER, J.B. (1983). Age relates positively to community satisfaction: Some explanations and implications. *Journal of the Community Development Society, 14*(1), 31–38.

VANYPEREN, N.W., & BUUNK, B.P. (1990). A longitudinal study of equity and satisfaction in intimate relationships. *European Journal of Social Psychology, 20*(4), 287–309.

———. (1991). Sex-role attitudes, social comparison, and satisfaction with relationships. *Social Psychology Quarterly, 54*(2), 169–80.

VAN ROOIJEN, L. (1986). Advanced students' adaptation to college. *Higher Education, 15* (3–4), 197–209.

VAN-TRAN, T., & WRIGHT, R. Jr. (1986). Social support and subjective well-being among Vietnamese refugees. *Social Service Review, 60*(3), 449–59.

VARGA, K. (1972). Marital cohesion as reflected in time budgets. In A. Szalai (Ed.), *The use of time: Daily activities of urban and suburban populations in twelve countries* (pp. 357–76). The Hague: Mouton.

VEBLEN, T. (1934). *The theory of the leisure class*. New York: Modern Library.

VEENHOVEN, R. (1983). The growing impact of marriage. *Social Indicators Research, 12*(1), 49–63.

———. (1988). The utility of happiness. *Social Indicators Research, 20*(4), 333–54.

———. (1991). Is happiness relative? *Social Indicators Research, 24*(1), 1–34.

VEEVERS, J. (1980). *Childless by choice*. Toronto: Butterworths.

VERMUNT, R., SPAANS, E., & ZORGE, F. (1989) Satisfaction, happiness and well-being of Dutch students. *Social Indicators Research, 321*(1), 1–33.

VINOKUR-KAPLAN, D. (1991). Job satisfaction among social workers in public and voluntary child welfare agencies. *Child Welfare*, *70*(1), 81–91.

VOYDANOFF, P., DONNELLY, B.W., & FINE, M.A. (1988). Economic distress, social integration, and family satisfaction. *Journal of Family Issues*, *9*(4), 545–63.

WALKER, J., & LAZAR, H. (1978). *The end of mandatory retirement: Implications for management*. New York: John Wiley & Sons.

WALL, V.D. Jr., & NOLAN, L.L. (1987). Small group conflict: A look at equity, satisfaction, and styles of conflict management. *Small Group Behavior*, *18*(2), 188–211.

WANNER, R.A. (1993). Patterns and trends in occupational mobility In J. Curtis, E. Grabb, & N. Guppy (Eds.), *Social inequality in Canada* (2nd ed.). Scarborough, ON: Prentice-Hall.

WARNER, L.W., MEEKER, M., & EELLS, K. (1960). *Social class in America*. New York: Harper Torchbooks.

WATTENBERG, B.J. (1987). *The birth dearth*. New York: The American Enterprise Institute, Pharos Books.

WEBB, R.B., & ASHTON, P.T. (1986). Teacher motivation and the conditions of teaching: A call for ecological reform. *Journal of Thought*, *21*(2), 43–60.

WEBER, M. (1958). *From Max Weber: Essays in sociology* (H. Gerth & C.W. Mills, Eds. & Trans.). New York: Oxford University Press.

———. (1974). *The Protestant ethic and the spirit of capitalism*. London: George Allen & Unwin.

WEBSTER-STRATTON, C. (1989). The relationship of marital support, conflict, and divorce to parent perceptions, behaviors, and childhood conduct problems. *Journal of Marriage and the Family*, *51*(2), 417–30.

WEISS, M.G., & LISS, M.B. (1988). Night shift work: Job and family concerns. *Journal of Social Behavior and Personality*, *3*(4), 279–86.

WEISS, M.J. (1988). *The clustering of America*. New York: Harper & Row.

WELLER, L., & ROFE, Y. (1988). Marital happiness among mixed and homogeneous marriages in Israel. *Journal of Marriage and the Family*, *50*(1), 245–54.

WESTHUES, K. (1982). *First sociology*. New York: McGraw-Hill.

WESTON, C.A., & MACKLIN, E.D. (1990). The relationship between former-spousal contact and remarital satisfaction in stepfather families. *Journal of Divorce and Remarriage*, *14*(2), 25–47.

WHISMAN, M.A., & JACOBSON, N.S. (1989). Depression, marital satisfaction, and marital and personality measures of sex roles. *Journal of Marital and Family Therapy*, *15*(2), 177–86.

———. (1990) Power, marital satisfaction, and response to marital therapy. *Journal of Family Psychology*, *4*(2), 202–12.

WHITE, B.B. (1989). Gender differences in marital communication patterns. *Family Process*, *28*(1), 89–106.

WHITE, H. (1970). *Chains of opportunity: System models of mobility in organizations*. Cambridge, MA: Harvard University Press.

WHITE, J.M. (1987). Marital perceived agreement and actual agreement over the family life cycle. *Journal of Comparative Family Studies*, *18*(1), 47–59.

WHITE, L.K. (1983). Determinants of spousal interaction: Marital structure or marital happiness. *Journal of Marriage and the Family*, *45*(3), 511–19.

WHITE, L.K., & BOOTH, A. (1991). Divorce over the life course: The role of marital happiness. *Journal of Family Issues*, *12*(1), 5–21.

WHITE, L.K., BOOTH, A., & EDWARDS, J.N. (1986). Children and marital happiness: Why the negative correlation? *Journal of Family Issues*, *7*(2), 131–47.

WHITE, L.K., & EDWARDS, J.N. (1990). Emptying the nest and parental well-being: An analysis of national panel data. *American Sociological Review*, *55*(2), 235–42.

WHITE, M.J. (1985). Determinants of community satisfaction in Middleton. *American Journal of Community Psychology*, *13*(5), 583–97.

WHITESIDE, M.M. (1985). A new look at life and job satisfaction with Sunbelt MBAs. *Social Indicators Research*, *16*(2), 113–29.

WIDGERY, R.N. (1982). Satisfaction with the quality of urban life: A predictive model. *American Journal of Community Psychology*, *10*(1), 37–48.

WILEY, D.L. (1987). The relationship between work/nonwork role conflict and job-related outcomes: Some unanticipated findings. *Journal of Management*, *13*(3), 467–72.

WILEY, M.G., & ESKILSON, A. (1988). Gender and family/career: Reactions of bosses. *Sex Roles*, *19*(7–8), 445–66.

WILLIAMS, D.G. (1988). Gender, marriage, and psychosocial well-being. *Journal of Family Issues*, *9*(4), 452–68.

WILLITS, F.K. (1988). Adolescent behavior and adult success and well-being: A 37-year panel study. *Youth and Society*, *20*(1), 68–87.

WINKLER, I., & DOHERTY, W.J. (1983). Communication styles and marital satisfaction in Israeli and American couples. *Family Process*, *22*(2), 221–28.

WISTER, A.V., & BURCH, T.K. (1983). Fertility and household status of older women in Canada, 1981. *Canadian Studies in Population*, *10*, 1–14.

WITTBERG, P. (1984). The effects of local activity on neighborhood attitudes: A comparison of black and white urbanites. *Urban Affairs Quarterly*, *20*(2), 185–200.

WOLFE, A. (1989, Spring). The day-care dilemma: A Scandinavian perspective. *The Public Interest*, 95, pp. 24–23.

WOODS GORDON. (1986). *Tomorrow's customers* (19th ed.). Toronto.

WORDS ASSOCIATED. (1986). *Workable futures: Notes on emerging technologies* (Catalogue No. EC 22-132/1986E). Ottawa: Economic Council of Canada.

WORTHINGTON, E.L. Jr., & BUSTON, B.G. (1986). The marriage relationship during the transition to parenthood: A review and a model. *Journal of Family Issues*, *7*(4), 443–73.

WRIGHT, S.J. (1985). Health satisfaction: A detailed test of the multiple discrepancies theory model. *Social Indicators Research*, *17*(3), 299–313.

YAHYA, H.A.Q. (1988). Factors influencing the satisfaction of Muslim organization members in a university town in the United States (Lansing, Michigan). *Journal Institute of Muslim Minority Affairs*, 9(2), 280–95.

YANKELOVICH, D. (1982). *New rules: Searching for self-fulfillment in a world turned upside down*. New York: Bantam Books.

YELSMA, P. (1986). Marriage vs. cohabitation: Couples' communication practices and satisfaction. *Journal of Communication*, *36*(4), 94–107.

YELSMA, P., & ATHAPPILLY, K. (1988). Marital satisfaction and communication practices: Comparisons among Indian and American couples. *Journal of Comparative Family Studies*, *19*(1), 37–54.

YI, C.C. (1985). Urban housing satisfaction in a transitional society: A case study in Taichung, Taiwan. *Urban Studies*, *22*(1), 1–12.

YOGEV, S., & HARRIS, S. (1983). Women physicians during residency years: Workload, work satisfaction and self concept. *Social Science and Medicine*, *17*(12), 837–41.

YORK, R.O., & HENLEY, H.C. (1987). Women and social work bureaucracy. *Journal of Applied Social Sciences*, *12*(1), 46–61.

YOUNG, A. (1990). Television viewing. In C. McKie & K. Thompson (Eds.), *Canadian social trends*. Toronto: Thomson Educational Publishing.

YOUNG, M., & WILLMOTT, P. (1975). *The symmetrical family*. Harmondsworth: Penguin.

ZAMBRANA, R.E., & FRITH, S. (1988). Mexican-American professional women: Role satisfaction differences in single and multiple role lifestyles. *Journal of Social Behavior and Personality*, *3*(4), 347–61.

ZAUTRA, A.J., EBLEN, C., & REYNOLDS, K.D. (1986). Job stress and task interest: Two factors in work life quality. *American Journal of Community Psychology*, *14*(4), 377–93.

ZEDECK, S., MASLACH, C., MOSIER, K., & SKITKA, I. (1988). Affective response to work and quality of family life: Employee and spouse perspectives. *Journal of Social Behavior and Personality*, *3*(4), 135–57.

ZEITZ, G. (1990). Age and work satisfaction in a government agency: A situational perspective. *Human Relations*, *43*(5), 419–38.

ZIV, A., & GADISH, O. (1989). Humor and marital satisfaction. *Journal of Social Psychology*, *129*(6), 759–68.

ZOLLAR, A.C., & WILLIAMS, J.S. (1987). The contribution of marriage to the life satisfaction of black adults. *Journal of Marriage and the Family*, *49*(1), 87–92.

ZSIGMOND, Z., PICOT, G., CLARK, W., & DEVEREAUX, M.S. (1978). *Out of school—into the labour force* (Catalogue No. 81-570). Ottawa: Statistics Canada.

ZUBE, E.H., VINING, J., LAW, C.S., & BECHTEL, R.B. (1985). Perceived urban residential quality: A cross-cultural bimodal study. *Environment and Behavior*, *17*(3), 327–50.

ZUR-MUEHLEN, M. VON (1978). *The educational background of parents of post-secondary students in Canada*. Ottawa: Statistics Canada.

INDEX

READER REPLY CARD

We are interested in your reaction to *Choices and Chances, Second Edition*, by Lorne Tepperman. You can help us to improve this book in future editions by completing this questionnaire.

1. What was your reason for using this book?
   - ❑ university course
   - ❑ college course
   - ❑ continuing education course
   - ❑ professional development
   - ❑ personal interest
   - ❑ other ______________________________

2. If you are a student, please identify your school and the course in which you used this book.

3. Which chapters or parts of this book did you use? Which did you omit?

4. What did you like best about this book? What did you like least?

5. Please identify any topics you think should be added to future editions.

6. Please add any comments or suggestions.

7. May we contact you for further information?

   Name: ______________________________

   Address: ______________________________

   ____

   ____

   Phone: ____________________

(fold here and tape shut)

MAIL POSTE

Canada Post Corporation / Société canadienne des postes

Postage paid
If mailed in Canada

Port payé
si posté au Canada

Business Reply

Réponse d'affaires

0116870399 01

0116870399-M8Z4X6-BR01

Heather McWhinney
Publisher, College Division
HARCOURT BRACE & COMPANY, CANADA
55 HORNER AVENUE
TORONTO, ONTARIO
M8Z 9Z9